Typology and Second Language Acquisition

Empirical Approaches to Language Typology

26

Editors

Georg Bossong
Bernard Comrie
Yaron Matras

Mouton de Gruyter
Berlin · New York

Typology and Second Language Acquisition

edited by
Anna Giacalone Ramat

Mouton de Gruyter
Berlin · New York   2003

Mouton de Gruyter (formerly Mouton, The Hague)
is a Division of Walter de Gruyter GmbH & Co. KG, Berlin.

☉ Printed on acid-free paper which falls within the guidelines of the
ANSI to ensure permanence and durability.

Library of Congress — Cataloging-in-Publication-Data

> Typology and second language acquisition / edited by Anna Giacalone
> Ramat.
>   p.   cm. – (Empirical approaches to language typology ; 26)
> Includes bibliographical references and index.
> ISBN 3 11 017359 X
>   1. Second language acquisition.   2. Typology (Linguistics).   I. Giacalone
> Ramat, Anna, 1937–   II. Series.
>   P118.2 .T96   2002
>   418–dc21
>   2002015011

ISBN 3 11 017359 X

Bibliographic information published by Die Deutsche Bibliothek

Die Deutsche Bibliothek lists this publication in the Deutsche Nationalbibliografie;
detailed bibliographic data is available in the Internet at <http://dnb.ddb.de>.

© Copyright 2002 by Walter de Gruyter GmbH & Co. KG, 10785 Berlin.
All rights reserved, including those of translation into foreign languages. No part of this book may
be reproduced or transmitted in any form or by any means, electronic or mechanical, including
photocopy, recording or any information storage and retrieval system, without permission in writing
from the publisher.
Printed in Germany.

Contents

Introduction   1
Anna Giacalone Ramat

Typology and language acquisition: the case of relative
clauses   19
Bernard Comrie

Relative clauses in early bilingual development: Transfer and
universals   39
Stephen Matthews and Virginia Yip

Learner varieties and language types. The case of indefinite
pronouns in non-native Italian   83
Giuliano Bernini

Adnominal possession: combining typological and second
language perspectives   125
Björn Hammarberg and Maria Koptjevskaja-Tamm

Gerunds as optional categories in second language learning   181
Anna Giacalone Ramat

Iconicity and finiteness in the development of early grammar
in French as L2 and in French-based creoles   221
Daniel Véronique

Lexicalisation of aspectual structures in English and Japanese   267
Yasuhiro Shirai and Yumiko Nishi

Using nouns for reference maintenance: A seeming
contradiction in L2 discourse 291
Henriëtte Hendricks

Crosslinguistic comparison and second language acquisition:
an approach to Topic and Left-detachment constructions from
the perspective of spoken language 327
Rosanna Sornicola

Typology and information organisation: perspective taking
and language-specific effects in the construal of events 365
Mary Carroll and Christiane von Stutterheim

Typological comparison and interlanguage phonology: maps
or gaps between typology and language learning of sound
systems? 403
Stefania Giannini

Index of subjects 441

Index of authors 447

List of contributors 453

Introduction

Anna Giacalone Ramat

This book* brings together two apparently distant sub-fields of linguistics under the assumption that their interaction can enrich our understanding of both.

Typological comparison and Universal research ("different facets of a single research endeavour", Comrie 1989: 33) aim to establish limits within human language. Taking this aspect into consideration, we may state that a basic connotation of typology is cross-linguistic comparison: implicational universals which are crucial in order to create a typology of the languages of the world cannot be discovered or verified by observing only a single language (Croft 1990: 1).

Second language acquisition (SLA) research aims to describe organisational principles of learner varieties (or "interlanguages"), that is those dynamic systems that learners of a second language build during the acquisition process. Another aim is to account for greater or lesser difficulties encountered in acquiring second language constructions. The comparison of first language (L1) and second language (L2) structures has traditionally been considered to be a measure of learning difficulty. The need for comparison has been recognised since the times of the Contrastive Analysis Hypothesis (Lado 1954), which operated within a structuralist theory of language which is today inadequate.

Clearly both objectives of SLA need theoretical grounding from general linguistics (Huebner and Ferguson 1991) which can be provided both by the formal generative and the functional-typological framework. A number of recent studies have applied the Principles and Parameters model to SLA and have made specific predictions on how language acquisition should proceed. We will not discuss extensively here the Universal Grammar approach to SLA nor the question of access to Universal Grammar in L2 acquisition, since the approach proposed in this volume is mainly oriented toward the integration of syntactic, semantic and pragmatic levels.

The functional-typological approach, called "functional" in that it seeks to explain language structure in terms of language function, is primarily associated with linguists such as Talmy Givón, Paul Hopper, John Haiman and has profited from the debate on Universals based on Greenberg (1966). Potentially, functional typology has a large number of suggestions which may be useful for SLA and we intend to explore such possible suggestions in this book. We will show that notions which are current in functional typology, such as markedness or prototypicality, are relevant to SLA in order give a better account of L2-learner data. The notion of implicational hierarchy, which can account for the presence of a certain feature on the basis of the presence of another feature in the same learner variety, may lead to a number of predictions regarding acquisition. Developmental stages of acquisition may be documented and checked: e.g. it was found that a learner of Italian who has developed the imperfect will have developed the past participle and the present (Giacalone Ramat 1990, 1992).

It has also been claimed (Klein 1991) that second language acquisition research can contribute to linguistic theory: although there are relatively few instances in which it has been proposed that SLA facts may have a bearing on general linguistic theory (Eckman 1993: ix), there is anyway the expectation that insights on language nature and human cognition in general can be gained by investigating the process of acquisition (Comrie, this volume).

In the past decades, a few seminal papers (Comrie 1984, Hawkins 1987) have pointed out the relevance of implicational hierarchies found in typological studies for second language research. On the other hand, second language researchers have only considered a few typological universals in their studies. This is especially the case of the *Noun Phrase Accessibility Hierarchy* (Keenan and Comrie 1977, Comrie 1989), which has proved to be of particular interest for the study of relative clauses in second language acquisition (Gass 1979, etc.) both in past and present studies, as shown in this book. Another proposal which brings together typological universals and SLA was put forward by Eckman (1977, 1985) who used the notion of typological markedness to predict the areas of difficulty that a L2 learner is likely to find (*Markedness Differential Hypothesis*) and to analyse transfer phenomena in a more systematic manner with respect to Contrastive Analysis, thus obtaining a stronger predictive power (Braidi 1999: 86).

In recent years the amount of research on comparative typology has led to reveal regularities and to formulate new constraints upon variation for a broader range of phenomena. For the languages of Europe the series of volumes of EUROTYP (Mouton de Gruyter 1998-) marks the outcome of a collaborative effort to outline a general profile and the main typological features of a "European" area. A wide range of grammatical structures and categories has been examined: adverbial clauses, word order relations, tense and aspect marking, subordination. As the amount of typological research increased, a growing interest arose for the implications that findings in the typological field might have on acquisition: in this volume some of the issues mentioned above are discussed on the basis of empirical evidence from second languages.

The problem of explanations of language universals has been dealt with in several ways. Functional explanations typically refer to principles external to the linguistic system itself, which are based on pragmatic constraints or cognitive principles (Croft 1990) or on economy/iconicity conflicts (Haiman 1985). For instance, the typological patterns discovered for relative clause formation have been correlated with factors found outside the grammatical structure: Keenan and Comrie (1977) refer to psychological ease of perception as an independently testable factor. Acquisitional linguistics also tries to relate generalisations about the development of learners' grammar to external factors such as the learners' communicative needs or the principles of discourse organisation (Klein and Perdue 1992).

Investigations carried out within the functional-typological approach follow an inductive methodology. Analogously, several papers in this volume share a common methodology in treating learners' data: they first describe the phenomenon in question, for example negation, adnominal possesson or prenominal relative clauses, in a general typological perspective, taking into account markedness values, implicational hierarchies or other kinds of universal properties. Patterns of second language development are then examined on the basis of empirical evidence. Generally, the typological approach can help to clarify the problems learners face. In this perspective second language research makes use of suggestions from typological linguistics and serves as a testing ground for theoretical linguistics (as already noted by Comrie 1984, and Ferguson 1991). As I stated earlier, the opposite approach is also potentially viable: investigating second languages may help language typology to understand better how linguistic systems are organised. The prospect that learner varieties belong to the field of investigation of typological linguistics as fully-fledged languages do is formulated by Bernini, Carroll and Stutterheim, Koptjevskaia-Tamm and Hammarberg and other contributors to the volume. In this vein Klein's (1999: 284) claim that fully-fledged languages are borderline cases of learner varieties should also be mentioned. Klein maintains that the functioning of human language capacity can best be studied in those varieties where form/function relations are relatively transparent, and that the process of development from simple to more complex learner varieties can teach us more about organising principles, markedness values, implicational hierarchies. Some examples can illustrate this issue: second language research has shown that speakers start the learning process with no finite verbs: the stage Klein and Perdue (1997) refer to as the "basic variety" has no productive use of morphological distinctions on nouns and verbs. The study of how the marking of finiteness is acquired can provide information about the importance of inherent semantic properties of verbs in the organisation of tense/aspect distinctions in different languages. Learners of Italian and Spanish, for example, acquire the aspectual distinctions for past time relations using the imperfect inflections with stative and activity verbs, while telic verbs are more frequently used with past perfective inflections (Andersen 1991, Giacalone Ramat 1995). The native speakers' advantage over the learner is the ability to use imperfective and perfective inflections with all classes of verbs. However, the acquisition process provides us with a clue about the unmarked or prototypical associations which are part of the specific organisation of a given language.

Learner languages in the "basic variety" also show a very limited set of structural, semantic and pragmatic organisational principles: one of these principles states that the more agentive referent appears in initial position in the utterance (Klein and Perdue 1997). One should recall that typological research has proposed control hierarchies for assigning semantic roles based on the notion of control strength (Comrie 1989: 58ff). However, fully-fledged languages may introduce a number of grammatical processes which obscure the basic principles: in passive constructions the patient is moved to the first position, focalised objects can also be moved to the first position, and languages that have cleft sentences use them to focalise several kinds of low control referents. Again we can conclude that control hierarchies are more directly reflected in early learner languages.

Early learner varieties show a low degree of interclausal links: utterances are juxtaposed or coordinated by means of the scarcely informative element "and", hierarchical structures are absent, except for some sporadic use of the causal conjunction "because". The developing of clause combining strategies toward more complex forms then reveals both universal properties and language specific preferences for coding information. Typological research has shown that a language may select nonfinite constructions to code causal, temporal and other types of subordinate relations, as in the case of Turkish, or show a preference for finite subordination, as Romance and Germanic languages generally do. Givón (1990) has proposed that an iconic relation holds between integration of states of affairs and integration of clauses at the morphosyntactic level: such an allegedly universal principle can lead to the formulation of an implicational hierarchy of likeliness for non-finite ("deranked") forms to appear (Cristofaro 1998) that has been tested on data of learners of Italian (Giacalone Ramat 1999).

More examples of interaction of typological research and second language research are offered by the contributions included in this volume.

The volume

The idea of a book to enhance the dialogue between typological research and second language acquisition first arose during the discussions held at the Euroconference on "The structure of learner languages" in Maratea in the summer of 1998. Quite a few contributors to the present volume took part in the conference, including myself who organised the event: G.Bernini, B.Comrie, S.Giannini, H.Hendricks, R.Sornicola, D.Véronique. They felt that the topic deserved a forum for further discussion, since on the one hand it seems that the findings of second language research have a very limited influence on typological literature, and on the other hand typology may offer a rich theoretical basis within which to explore issues related to SLA.

In presenting the volume I will select results from each chapter which appear to be relevant when we consider an integrated vision of both concerns, typology and acquisition.

Relative clauses – as Comrie states in this volume – seem to be an area where the mutual interaction of typology and second language acquisition has been particularly fruitful. There were a considerable number of studies in the eighties, which uncovered that the acquisitional sequence for relative clauses mirrors the Accessibility Hierarchy, with some variability which does not question the Universal (Hyltenstam 1984, Pavesi 1986, etc.). The conclusion was that the Hierarchy encodes the degree of difficulty of relativising on a particular noun phrase and can be transposed into predictions about acquisition patterns. A renewed interest for relative clauses has arisen from cross-linguistic studies, in particular Comrie's (1998) treatment of the "Japanese type" of relatives, i.e. relatives where no extraction has taken place, as in English, but the modifying clause is simply attached to the head noun, keeping the internal structure of an independent clause. Such an adjoined clause is semantically nonspecific and holds a loose relation to the main clause, so that the translation with a relative clause in English is only one possibility. The real problem is, as Comrie admits: is the "Japanese type" relevant for the acquisition of languages not sharing such properties? Apparently similar cases do sporadically occur in learner languages, but so far these cases have been treated as cases of gapping.

Matthews and Yip in their study of two bilingual children exposed to Cantonese and English show that prenominal relative clauses are transferred from the dominant language, Cantonese in this case, to English, despite the marked status of prenominal clauses and the predicted parsing difficulties. Chinese languages are almost the only documented example of VO and prenominal relatives. This configuration incurs in remarkable difficulties in the parsing of NPs, as shown by Matthews and Yip. Despite such unfavourable circumstances, the authors show that transfer occurs in bilingual children. They suggest that the prenominal clause may be parsed by children as a main clause and incorporated into a NP as a premodifier. Such a developmental pattern would be in keeping with Comrie's suggestion of a continuum of prenominal modification structures which involve typological characteristics of Asian languages.

A further key aspect of this paper concerns the use of resumptive pronouns in postnominal relatives both for subject and object positions: this strategy cannot be attributed to transfer, since Cantonese would not use pronouns in such contexts. The authors point out that this is the effect of a universal option which is available to the language learners. The use of resumptive pronouns is indeed widespread across the languages of the world: it has also been documented in the case of colloquial varieties of languages such as Romance languages (Fiorentino 1999) which otherwise use the relative pronoun strategy to code relative clauses.

As stated above, the Accessibility Hierarchy has been applied successfully to language acquisition. Keeping in mind that subject relatives were proposed, primarily on typological evidence, to be a universal property of languages, research on acquisition has accordingly shown that learners acquire subject relatives first and use them far more frequently than other relatives. Less clear results are obtained for other positions, in particular the relativisation of indirect objects and obliques has yielded different results in typological research (Comrie 1989). Acquisitional research based on spontaneous learner data has in general pointed to the scarcity of occurrences of relatives for positions lower in the hierarchy. Interesting considerations may be suggested by specific constructions: Cristofaro and Giacalone Ramat (2002) focus on the relativisation strategies for a particular type of obliques, circumstantials of time, for which a number of languages seem to use predominantly a [–case] strategy and argue that this relativisation pattern is determined by the syntactic and semantic properties of the head noun and by the recoverability of information about the role of the relativised element. An Italian example will illustrate the point:

(1) *Il giorno che ci siamo incontrati pioveva*
    The day   that we met   it was raining

No prepositions are used for the head noun and in the relative clause; instead the invariable marker *che* is used, that is the strategy that is used for the more accessible roles of subject and object. Due to their unmarked status, one would expect circumstantials of time to be readily acquired by learners. This is not the case, at least on the basis of the information currently at our disposal: only a pair of relevant cases could be found in a corpus of learner Italian, such as:

(2) *e dopo un giorno   che hanno fatto cose insieme*
    and after a day   that (on which) they did things together
    "and after spending a day together" [ANT (L1 German)]

It might be that this type of relativisation on time circumstantials belongs to advanced levels of acquisition. The topic requires further cross-linguistic investigation.

Bernini's paper first examines the implicational organisation of the functions of indefinite pronouns as elaborated on a cross-linguistic basis by M. Haspelmath (1997). Then, in the light of typological results, the author discusses the development of indefinite pronouns in Italian L2 on the basis of a corpus of data. The fundamental concern is to show how learners construe the meaning of indefinite pronouns: they do so in accordance with the implicational maps established by Haspelmath. Bernini's data also reveal attempts by the learners to reconstruct the target system that may be related to different factors. These include communicative requirements, as in the case of the early emergence of the negative pronouns system.

These results are in keeping with those of other studies in this book in showing how typological generalisations and patterns of variation play a major role in acquisition.

Koptjevskaja-Tamm and Hammerberg's paper focuses on one specific aspect of possession which has received much attention in typological work (Haspelmath 1999). Adnominal possessive constructions are particularly complex in Swedish on the basis of criteria of syntagmatic and paradigmatic economy: e.g. the article/possesor complementarity is similar to the one of English and opposed to that of Italian: *the book/my book*: Swedish *min bil* "my car", Italian *la mia macchina.* Furthermore in Swedish there is incompatibility of possessive NPs with definite articles *Peter-s bord* "Peter's table", but not *Peter-s bord-et "Peter-GEN table-DEF-N" (Italian *il tavolo di Peter*) and also incompatibility of possessive NPs with the indefinite article and indefinite quantifiers: **en Peter's skjorta* "a Peter's shirt". Expectedly, second language learners of Swedish are faced with problems of definiteness marking. Learners' productions in Swedish are analyzed and reasons for deviating forms are given in the light of the general typological principles discussed. The most frequent errors concern the overgeneralisation of definite marking on NPs in possessive constructions. A further problem area for learners is the area of possessive prepositional constructions, in which the choice of different spatial prepositions is difficult for the learners who prefer to overgeneralise the preposition *av* "of". The typological viewpoint helps clarify the problems learners have with regard to the definiteness of NPs, as the authors state.

The role of typological markedness is also discussed in Giacalone Ramat's paper on the acquisition of gerunds. Gerunds in Italian are converbial forms which can express various kinds of (mostly) subordinate relations. The pattern of acquisition by second language learners shows a development according to which gerunds are first used as part of the grammaticalised progressive periphrasis *stare* + gerund. Subsequently, predicate gerunds mainly with modal values emerge in learner languages and finally sentence gerunds with causal, conditional, concessive values are found. In the data examined this sequence is implicational. It is argued that the sequence can be read as a markedness scale in which sentence gerunds represent the most marked construction. Generalisations about converbs, which have been developed by typological studies (Haspelmath and König 1995), have also shown that the function of predicate modifiers is preferred in languages. In particular, modal converbs appear to be the unmarked case. This is confirmed by many indications both from synchronic typology and language acquisition and from historical linguistics, since Italian gerunds derive from the ablative form of the Latin gerund, which had predominantly modal or instrumental value.

Véronique's contribution tries to assess the crucial role of iconicity and finiteness in the development of grammar. The author assumes that creolisation is SLA under specific circumstances of slavery and plantation economy and that the same organisational principles govern basic learner varieties and early pre-creole and creole grammars. Common properties can indeed be found in early grammar both of French as a second language and French-based Creoles: in both cases iconicity plays an important role in shaping the development. Parallel developments between French-based Creoles and SLA processes are investigated in the realm of existentials, negation and temporality. But as development over time goes on, different lines emerge: creoles develop into autonomous languages, as shown for example by the case of preverbal markers expressing temporal and modal relations, while second languages move towards the target language.

Shirai and Nishi's paper addresses the question of how languages differ in lexicalisation patterns. The comparison of two languages such as English and Japanese shows divergent lexicalisation patterns of the inherent aspect (or, in other terminology, actionality) categories of Achievements, Accomplishments, Activities and States according to a well-known proposal by Vendler (1967). Such categories are usually considered to be universal semantic concepts and should be expected to be consistent across languages. On the contrary, Japanese has by far less state verbs than English. However there are differences even between languages which are less typologically distant: postural *sit* and *stand* can be viewed as activities in English, as evidenced by their propensity to be used in the progressive form. On the contrary, their Italian counterparts *sedere* and *stare in piedi* favour a stative reading and cannot take the progressive form. Thus, there seem to be prototypical and less prototypical members within a semantic category and there seems to be room for recategorisation in single languages and within specific contexts. Then the question arises: what strategies do we expect Japanese learners of English and vice versa English learners of Japanese to develop in order to deal with such discrepancies? Shirai and Nishi show that learners have more difficulty when the correspondence between classes is not complete, as in the case of Achievements and States. This leads the authors to the conclusion that learners tend to transfer the encoding of semantic relations from the first language.

Hendricks examines various forms of overexplicitation, a phenomenon that has been noted in several second languages and seems to be typical of second learners' discourse. The term refers to the fact that L2 learners with increasing proficiency in the L2, irrespective of source-target language pairs, are more explicit in reference maintenance than native speakers of the target language. Given that principles governing the so-called information flow/discourse organisation are more or less universal (Givón 1983), adult learners of a second language should be familiar with these principles through the knowledge of their mother tongue. This is not the case, however: adult learners have been shown to use more explicit linguistic means than native speakers. The explanation provided by Hendricks takes linguistic and pragmatic factors into consideration. Results from the investigation of Chinese subjects learning French, German and English lead to the conclusion that differences between language pairs as to the coding of anaphoric relations exist and that explanations for the observed variation can be found at the linguistic level. In particular, the difficulty in acquiring the German pronominal system and the marking of pronouns for gender and case has been pointed out. Other factors have also been considered: learners are sensitive to correspondences of form/function in source and target languages: for example, the use of dislocations in French with the function of topic-promoting is readily taken up by Chinese learners who find this construction similar to the familiar function of topicalisation. Although the paper does not explicitly address typological issues, the comparison between language pairs has a broad typological interest. The comparative approach in which Chinese is maintained as the source language whereas the target languages are varied suggests insights as to the role of the input learners receive and as to the role of universal properties of anaphoric linkage.

Sornicola's paper reviews the varied approaches taken to syntactic phenomena such as Topicalisation and Left Dislocation, in typological studies, in research on spoken language, and in language acquisition research. The position endorsed by the author is that integration of these domains is highly desirable, although there are many problems regarding the possibility of interdisciplinary work using the various theoretical and methodological frameworks from each domain. Topicalisations and Left Dislocations occur in typologically different languages and differ in their formal properties, however they share at least one common property – that of having a constituent outside the sentence proper domain. In second language research a few studies regarding Left Dislocations have mostly analyzed such structures by comparing L2-learners and native speakers, children or adults. Sornicola highlights some crucial points in these discussions, in particular that Left Dislocations cannot be associated in a consistent way with a stable concept of function, such as the speaker's intention to establish a center of attention. These observations hold true also for spoken native varieties. The difficulty of acquiring the process of topicalisation in L2 is related to the lack of those levels of spontaneity and automatisation which are important conditions for these structures to occur.

Some of the issues raised by Shirai and Nishi's and by Hendrick's papers are also discussed by Carroll and Stutterheim, who attempt to provide a coherent framework for a number of features and constraints which determine how communicative tasks are performed by learners. Carroll and Stutterheim introduce the notion of *perspective taking*, maintaining that it is essential for typological consideration. Perspective taking is an overarching principle "that allows speakers to link information spanning different conceptual domains (time, space, events, etc.) in consistent terms, thereby guiding the selection of linguistic form". At the same time, however, specific grammatical meanings play a role in guiding the perspective chosen. In other words, organisation of information for expression is language-specific and driven by grammatical patterns, as the authors claim. The principle of perspective taking represents a challenge to SLA because the target language information organisation may involve subtle specific principles that are not easy to recognise by learners, since they involve clusters of form/function relations more than single forms. Differences in perspective taking for English and German speakers describing motion events are rooted in the aspectual system, or in the preference in English for the role of grammatical subject to code topic information, while in German the subject is less prominent. On the other hand, for German, the verb second constraint in main clauses leads to the preference for a spatial perspective in information structure in descriptive texts. The results of this study are not very encouraging: even advanced learners "remain rooted in the principles of conceptual organisation as constituted in the course of L1 acquisition". The authors maintain that the typological domain of interests should be extended in order to include information organisation. As also shown by Hendrick's paper, general requirements of information organisation common to all languages, which constitute a common ground for learning a second language, interact with the language specific perspective.

In Giannini's paper theoretical and methodological proposals derived from functional typology (in particular the notions of hierarchical relationships and implicational scales) are tested at the phonological level. The peculiarities of second language phonological acquisition have been examined in the last twenty years with particular regard to English L2. Flege's (1997) model is based on the study of mechanisms of perception and recognition of second language categories (phonemes) and assumes that many phonological errors in interlanguages are the result of an erroneous perceptive representation.

The perspective suggested by Giannini takes the typological classification of phonological categories into consideration and incorporates Bybee's (2000) recent theories on sound change transmission. The goal of this research line is to discover conditions of uniformity of realisation in phonological change. Giannini presents new results from a case study on the acquisition of consonant length in Italian L2 by adult learners, the first languages of whom do not have consonant length as a distinctive feature. Typological comparison clearly shows that consonant length is a marked feature in phonological inventories for every class of sounds. Giannini also addresses problems in the diachronic dimension by examining Latin linguistic history and shows that the high rate of long consonants produced correctly by learners of Italian in disyllabic structures [*fat-to*] is consistent with the historical process of retention of long consonants in Western Romania. Typology and universal principles prove to be relevant for the acquisition of the marked category in question: quite interestingly and very much in the line with the framework of this book, factors which are common to both fields such as the frequency factor, have a leading role in triggering the phonological process of consonant length in different conditions.

One important consideration that results from this volume is that variation in learner varieties depends on several factors, some of which have been extensively discussed in second language literature, while others are practically unaccounted for elsewhere. The following aspects are particularly relevant in this publication: typological generalisations on language variation, form/function relations, target language information organisation, frequency in input, different perspectives in conceptual organisation.

We hope that the effort to promote collaboration among subfields of linguistics and to bring together semantic, pragmatic, and phonetic considerations, will be useful in order to outline a dynamic paradigm for acquisition. Consequently, this will lead to a better understanding of human language capacity.

Notes

* I am most grateful to Andrea Sansò for the preparation of this manuscript.

References

Andersen, Roger W.
    1991   Developmental sequences: The emergence of aspect marking in second language acquisition. In: Thom Huebner and Charles A. Ferguson (eds.), 305-324.

Bybee, Joan
    2000   The phonology of the lexicon: Evidence from lexical diffusion. In: Michael Barlow and Suzanne Kemmer (eds.), *Usage-Based Models of Language*. Stanford, CA: CSLI Publications (Center for the Study of Language and Information).

Braidi, Susan M.
    1999   *The Acquisition of Second Language Syntax*. London: Arnold.

Comrie, Bernard
    1984   Why linguists need language acquirers. In: William E. Rutherford (ed.), *Language Universals and Second Language Acquisition*, 11-29. Amsterdam: John Benjamins.

Comrie, Bernard
    1989   *Language Universals and Linguistic Typology*. Second edition. Oxford: Blackwell/Chicago: University of Chicago Press.

Comrie, Bernard
    1998   Rethinking the typology of relative clauses. *Language Design* 1: 59-86.

Cristofaro, Sonia
    1998   Toward a typology of subordination strategies. *Sprachtypologie und Universalienforschung* 51: 3-42.

Cristofaro, Sonia, and Anna Giacalone Ramat
    2002   Relativization patterns in Mediterranean languages, with particular reference to the relativization of time circumstantials. In: Paolo Ramat and Thomas Stolz (eds.), *Mediterranean Languages*. Pa-

pers from the MEDTYP Workshop, 102-112. (Diversitas Linguarum 1.) Bochum: Universitätsverlag Dr. N. Brockmeyer.

Croft, William
1990 *Typology and Universals.* Cambridge: Cambridge University Press.

Eckman, Fred R.
1977 Markedness and the contrastive analysis hypothesis. *Language Learning* 27: 315-330.

Eckman, Fred R.
1985 Some theoretical and pedagogical implications of the markedness differential hypothesis. *Studies in Second Language Acquisition* 7: 289-307.

Eckman, Fred R.
1993 Introduction. In: Fred R. Eckman (ed.), *Confluence. Linguistics, L2 Acquisition and Speech Pathology.* Amsterdam: Benjamins.

Ferguson, Charles A.
1991 Currents between second language acquisition and linguistic theory. In: Thom Huebner and Charles A. Ferguson (eds.), 425-435.

Fiorentino, Giuliana
1998 *Relativa debole. Sintassi, uso, storia in italiano.* (Materiali Linguistici – Università di Pavia 24.) Milano: Franco Angeli.

Flege, James
1997 The role of phonetic category formation in second-language speech learning. *New Sounds 97. Proceedings of the Third International Symposium on the Acquisition of Second Language Speech*, 79-88. University of Klagenfurt, 8-11 September.

Gass, Susan
1979 Language transfer and universal grammatical relations. *Language Learning* 29.2: 327-344.

Giacalone Ramat, Anna
1990 Presentazione del Progetto di Pavia sull'acquisizione di lingue seconde. Lo sviluppo di strutture temporali. In: Giuliano Bernini and Anna Giacalone Ramat (eds.), *La temporalità nell'acqui-sizione di lingue seconde*, 13-38. (Materiali Linguistici – Università di Pavia 2.) Milano: Franco Angeli.

Giacalone Ramat, Anna
1992 Grammaticalization processes in the area of temporal and modal relations. *Studies in Second Language Acquisition* 14: 297-322.

Giacalone Ramat, Anna.
1995 Tense and aspect in learner Italian. In: Pier Marco Bertinetto, Valentina Bianchi, Östen Dahl, and Mario Squartini (eds.), *Temporal*

Reference, Aspect and Actionality, Vol.II: *Typological Perspectives*, 289-309. Torino: Rosenberg & Sellier.
Giacalone Ramat, Anna
   1999   Functional typology and strategies of clause connection in second-language acquisition. *Linguistics* 37-3: 519-548.
Givón, Talmy
   1983   Topic continuity in discourse: An introduction. In: Talmy Givón (ed.), *Topic Continuity in Discourse: A Quantitative Cross-Language Study*, 1-41. Amsterdam: Benjamins.
Givón, Talmy
   1990   *Syntax. A Functional-Typological Introduction.* Amsterdam: Benjamins.
Greenberg, Joseph H.
   1966   Some universals of grammar with particular reference to the order of meaningful elements. In: Joseph H. Greenberg (ed.), *Universals of Language*, 73-113. Second edition. Cambridge, Mass.: The MIT Press.
Haiman, John
   1985   *Natural Syntax. Iconicity and Erosion.* Cambridge: Cambridge University Press.
Haspelmath, Martin
   1997   *Indefinite Pronouns.* Oxford: Oxford University Press.
Haspelmath, Martin, and Ekkehard König (eds.)
   1995   *Converbs in Cross-Linguistic Perspective.* (Empirical Approaches to Language Typology 13.) Berlin/New York: Mouton de Gruyter.
Hawkins, John
   1987   Implicational universals as predictors of language acquisition. *Linguistics* 25: 453-473.
Huebner, Thom, and Charles A. Ferguson (eds.)
   1990   *Crosscurrents in Second Language Acquisition and Linguistic Theories.* Amsterdam: Benjamins.
Hyltenstam, Kenneth
   1984   The use of typological markedness conditions as predictors in second language acquisition: The case of pronominal copies in relative clauses. In: Roger W. Andersen (ed.), *Second Languages: A Cross-Linguistic Perspective*, 39-58. Rowley, MA: Newbury House.
Keenan, Edward, and Bernard Comrie
   1977   Noun phrase accessibility and universal grammar. *Linguistic Inquiry* 8: 63-99.

Klein, Wolfgang
   1991   SLA theory: Prolegomena to a theory of language acquisition and implications for theoretical linguistics. In Thom Huebner and Charles A. Ferguson (eds.), 169-194.

Klein, Wolfgang
   1999   Die Lehren des Zweitspracherwerbs. In: Norbert Dittmar and Anna Giacalone Ramat (eds.), *Grammatik und Diskurs/Grammatica e discorso. Studi sull'acquisizione dell'italiano e del tedesco/Studien zum Erwerb des Deutschen und des Italienischen*, 279-290. Tübingen: Stauffenburg Verlag.

Klein, Wolfgang, and Clive Perdue
   1992   *Utterance Structure. Developing Grammars Again*. Amsterdam: Benjamins.

Klein, Wolfgang, and Clive Perdue
   1997   The basic variety. *Second Language Research* 13: 301-347.

Lado, Robert
   1954   *Linguistics Across Cultures*. Ann Arbor, Michigan: The University of Michigan Press.

Pavesi, Maria
   1986   Markedness, discoursal modes, and relative clause formation in a formal and an informal context. *Studies in Second Language Acquisition* 8: 38-55.

Vendler, Zeno
   1967   *Linguistics in Philosophy*. Ithaca, N.Y.: Cornell University Press.

Typology and language acquisition: the case of relative clauses

Bernard Comrie

1. Introduction

I should start this paper by making some disclaimers. I am not myself a researcher in the area of second language acquisition, and I will thus be presenting neither new data nor new theories of second language acquisition. However, in work in my own area of specialisation, linguistic typology, I have in the past found fruitful interaction between the generalisations that typologists have proposed and the patterns of language acquisition shown by second language learners; see, for instance, Comrie (1984) for an earlier statement. Relative clauses seem to be an area where such interaction between typology and second language acquisition has been particularly fruitful. My aim in this paper is first to summarise some earlier work on the typology of relative clauses that has been viewed as relevant in this way (sections 2 and 3), then to turn to some recent work on the typology of relative clauses that may turn out to have relevance for second language acquisition studies. My paper should therefore be seen as a contribution, from the typology side, to the continuing interaction between typological and second language acquisition studies. While I cannot guarantee that the typological phenomena that I will discuss will turn out to be of major import for the investigation of second language acquisition, I believe that at least I will be able to present data and ideas that should point to phenomena that second language acquisition researchers should be on the look-out for in their work.

Before turning to particular typological generalisations that have proved or might prove relevant to second language acquisition research, I will briefly sketch the typology of relative clauses as presented, for instance, in Comrie (1989: 147-153). I will, for the most part, use "pseudo-English" constructions that translate the relevant aspects of syntactic structure of the language in question. This typology is concerned with the way in which the notional head noun is encoded within the relative clause. First, it is possible for the notional head noun to be encoded explicitly in the relative clause ("non-reduction type"), as in correlative constructions like (1).

(1) *With which knife the man killed the chicken, Ram saw that knife.*

Secondly, it is possible for the notional head noun to be encoded as an ordinary pronoun in the relative clause ("pronoun-retention type"), as in (2).

(2) *I saw the woman that Hasan gave the potato to her.*

Thirdly, it is possible for the notional head noun to be encoded as a special pronoun that is preposed in the relative clause but remains case-marked, including marking by means of an adposition, for its role in the relative clause ("relative-pronoun type"). This is the classical type of relative clause found in European languages, as in (3).

(3) *The fox saw the rabbit with whom the chicken danced.*

Although the relative-pronoun type is widespread in the languages of Europe, especially in their standardised, literary variants, it is cross-linguistically quite rare. Indeed, examples found outside Europe nearly always turn out to have arisen under influence from some European language (Comrie 1998b). Nonetheless, under such conditions of contact, the relative-pronoun type does seem to be borrowed easily, thus giving the impression of a type that arises rarely spontaneously but which, once it has arisen, is a favoured construction for borrowing. This might form an interesting topic for second language acquisition scholars, but it is not to be the focus of this paper. Finally, there may be no explicit encoding of the notional head noun in the relative clause ("gap strategy"), as in (4).

(4)   *The man saw the chicken the fox had killed.*

In section 4 I will return to some aspects of the typology of relative clauses.

2. The Accessibility Hierarchy

One of the earliest pieces of typological research on relative clauses that found an application in second language studies is Keenan and Comrie (1977). In this article, a hierarchy of accessibility to relative clause formation was proposed, such that it is easier to relativise on subjects than on direct objects, than in turn on indirect objects, than in turn on oblique objects, than in turn on possessors. These possibilities are illustrated in examples (5)-(9).

(5)   *the man that killed the chicken*

(6)   *the chicken that the man killed*

(7)   *the woman to whom the man gave the chicken*

(8)   *the chicken with whom the rabbit danced*

(9)   *the man whose dog ran away*

In Keenan and Comrie (1977), with its primarily typological thrust, more specific claims were formulated in terms of the cross-linguistic distribution of the constructions illustrated in (5)-(9). Thus, some languages were identified allowing only subject relativisation as in (5); other languages allowed both subject and direct object relativisation as in (5)-(6), but not on other elements. This gave rise to the following intuitive generalisation (complicated somewhat in the original article to take account of certain specific examples): If a language can relativise on a particular element in the Accessibility Hierarchy (see (10)), then it must be able to relativise on all higher positions.

(10) Subject
      Direct object
      Indirect object
      Oblique object
      Possessor

A number of subsequent works tried to show relevance of the Accessibility Hierarchy in other areas, one of them being second language acquisition. Here the hypothesis would be that acquirers of a second language would find it easier, or at least no more difficult, to acquire relativisation on elements higher in the Accessibility Hierarchy than on elements lower in the Accessibility Hierarchy. And a fair amount of second language acquisition literature seems to suggest that this prediction is indeed borne out; see, for instance, Gass (1979). In particular, the prediction is borne out even in such cases as the following: Suppose that L1 and L2 both allow relativisation of subjects and direct objects; some acquirers still show differential acquisition of relativisation of subjects and direct objects, with relativisation of subjects being easier than relativisation on direct objects; since both L1 and L2 allow both kinds of relativisation, this crucially cannot be attributed to transfer from L1. I take this work to have been overall a fruitful cooperation between work in linguistic typology and work on second language acquisition.

3. Matching strategies

It should not be thought that the direction of insight is always from typology to language acquisition, nor even that typologists see things this way, since in this section I want to discuss a set of examples where the direction is largely the inverse, namely where typologists were made aware of a phenomenon, or at least of its importance, by work in language acquisition. One of the early results that came from work on language acquisition (in this case, first language acquisition) and that seemed to fit less neatly with the predictions derived from the Accessibility Hierarchy was that some learners do better with relative clause constructions where the notional head noun plays the same role in both main clause and relative clause, and less well in relative clause constructions where the notional head has a different role in each clause (Sheldon 1974). In other words, such learners do better with examples like (11) and (12) than with examples like (13) and (14).

(11) The man who saw the rabbit caught the fox.

(12) The fox caught the rabbit that the man saw.

(13) The fox that the man saw caught the rabbit.

(14) The man saw the fox that caught the rabbit.

In (11), the notional head "man" is subject of the main clause and subject of the relative clause. In (12), the notional head "rabbit" is direct object of the main clause and direct object of the relative clause. In (13), the notional head "fox" is subject of the main clause, but direct object of the relative clause. Conversely, in (14) the notional head "fox" is direct object of the main clause but subject of the relative clause. This paradigm departs from the predictions of the Accessibility Hierarchy in two ways. First, not only the role of the notional head noun in the relative clause but also its role in the main clause is relevant. The Accessibility Hierarchy says nothing about role in the main clause (and is thus quite neutral with regard to any predictions about such data). Secondly, this means that a substantial set of examples relativising on subjects is actually more difficult than a substantial set of examples relativising on direct objects, namely: when the notional head is direct object of the main clause, relativisation on a subject is actually more difficult than relativisation on a direct object. This would be a counterexample to a strong version of the Accessibility Hierarchy (relativisation on all subjects must be easier than or at least not more difficult than relativisation on any direct object), though not to a weaker version that would allow interaction with other principles, those other principles sometimes winning out, for instance along the lines currently being developed within Optimality Theory.

But now the question arises whether the pattern found in language acquisition studies is also found in typological work, i.e. is manifested in the cross-linguistic distribution of relative clause types. The answer turns out to be positive, in the sense that there are some languages that have a "matching" strategy for relative clause formation, allowing a particular construction only when the notional head has the same role in both main and relative clauses. But the number of such instances that have been uncovered by typologists remains surprisingly small, especially given the robustness of the language acquisition data. One of the best known is Modern Hebrew, which allows relativisation of an indirect or oblique noun phrase (in language-particular structural terms: of objects of prepositions) using the gap strategy only if the preposition that would have been used in the relative clause would have been the same as that which occurs in the main clause (Cole 1976: 244). In other words, from the clauses (15) and (16) it is possible to form a relative clause as in (17), or more accurately as in (18), mirroring more closely the structure of the Hebrew.

(15)　*The boy took the flower from the teacher.*

(16)　*The girl took the apple from the teacher.*

(17)　*The boy took the flower from the teacher from whom the girl took the apple.*

(18)　*The boy took the flower from the teacher that the girl took the apple.*

I have no explanation as to why the typological data mirroring the language acquisition data should be so sparse, and simply leave this as an interesting phenomenon for further research.

4. Semantics and pragmatics

Two characteristics of nearly all the kinds of relative clause constructions discussed above, and more generally in the mainstream literature, is (i) that they are a distinct construction type that can be identified as "relative clause", (ii) that there is a clear syntactic link between the main clause and the relative clause, such that the relative clause can be analysed syntactically as a clause modifying a noun phrase in the main clause and such that there is a notional head that is shared by both clauses, that plays a syntactic role in both clauses. A fair amount of recent work, and also some typological work from the 1970s and early 1980s, however, deals with constructions which, while clearly serving in some sense as the translation equivalents of relative clauses, nonetheless lack some of these characteristics. In this section I wish to look at two such kinds of constructions: first, adjoined relative clauses, since these involve a particularly loose relation between main clause and relative clause of a type one might well expect to find in not yet fully elaborated versions of a language (though I must leave it to second language acquisition researchers to see if such examples are directly relevant to their investigations); second, general noun-modifying constructions, whose semantic range goes well beyond that covered by relative clauses alone. The last is perhaps particularly interesting since parallel examples, though not possible in standard English, have been encountered in non-standard varieties of the language.

4.1. Adjoined relative clauses

The term "adjoined relative clause" is used by Hale (1976) in his discussion of relative clauses, or at least of relative clause translation equivalents, in a number of Australian Aboriginal languages, including Warlpiri (Walbiri). In somewhat similar vein, Lehmann (1984) uses the term "appositive relative clause", indeed he makes the distinction between appositive and embedded relative clauses the first division within his typology of relative clauses, although, as we shall see below, the usages are not quite identical, nor are the conclusions drawn from the phenomenon.

Let us start with a Warlpiri example that has become reasonably famous, or rather with a pseudo-English version of the Warlpiri example, given in (19) (Hale 1976: 78).

(19)   *I-speared the emu SBDR it-was drinking water.*

In (19), the hyphenated pronouns represent agreement markers in the original Warlpiri; SBDR represents a subordination marker, i.e. the second clause is quite clearly marked as subordinate to the first clause. Sentence (19) is the Warlpiri translation equivalent of (20), and as such would be suitable as an answer to the question (21), for instance in a situation where two emus have been identified, one of which is drinking water and the other of which is not.

(20)   *I speared the emu that was drinking water.*

(21)   *Which emu did you spear?*

However, exactly the same sentence can also felicitously receive a number of other English translation equivalents, including (22), which might occur felicitously as an answer to the question (23), for instance in a situation where only one emu is in question.

(22)   *I speared the emu while it was drinking water.*

(23)   *When did you spear the emu?*

A number of analytical questions arise from this adjoined type of relative clause construction, and given the very loose nature of the link between main and subordinate clauses I would, if anything, be surprised if there were not some spill-over into second language acquisition. (If there turns out to be no interaction, this would seem in itself to merit comment and explanation.)

Perhaps the most important is: Is the Warlpiri construction in (19) a relative clause? Hale (1976)'s answer is equivocal. He notes that, in this and similar constructions in other Australian Aboriginal languages, it is sometimes possible to make changes that force a relative clause interpretation, sometimes possible to make changes that exclude a relative clause interpretation. But it seems to me that at least the possibility has to be entertained that the construction as given is simply neutral among all these interpretations: All it does syntactically is to subordinate 'it [= the emu] was drinking water' to 'I speared the emu'; semantically, this is compatible with any conceivable relation that could be expressed by means of subordination; the choice of a particular interpretation can only be obtained by inference, i.e. pragmatically, though of course taking into account all syntactic and semantic information that is present. (For instance, if the two clauses lacked a coreferential noun phrase, then a relative clause interpretation would be impossible.) Note that on this analysis, Warlpiri strictly speaking does not have relative clauses (at least on the assumption that there is no alternative construction that would be unequivocally identified as a relative clause). In Keenan and Comrie (1977), it was assumed, roughly speaking, that the translation equivalent ("functional equivalent") in language Y of at least a prototypical relative clause in language X will also be a relative clause, and this is by and large the convention adopted by Lehmann (1984). Indeed given this assumption, it is doubtful whether the claim that all languages have relative clauses is even an empirical claim, given that the functional equivalent in language Y is allowed to cover an unspecified range of other interpretations. I am now more inclined to adopt the viewpoint that, in order to say that a particular language has a relative clause construction, that construction must have certain syntactic properties that distinguish it from other constructions, at least in the most central uses of each construction.

In this light the account of the development of relative clauses in Tok Pisin by Sankoff and Brown (1976) can be given a slightly more specific interpretation. What characterises Tok Pisin as it becomes a native language, or at least as it expands its functional repertoire, is that a specific construction for expressing relative clause meaning develops; previously, second-language Tok Pisin had ways of getting across the information that would be conveyed in English by means of a relative clause, but they were not specific means of conveying this information rather than other possible links between clauses.

One characteristic of the adjoined relative clause is that the subordinate clause does not have to be adjacent to the notional head in the main clause. Indeed, since Warlpiri has basic SOV word order, the actual Warlpiri order in (19) would be rather something like "man emu speared, water was-drinking". But while the adjoined relative clause necessarily allows this discontinuous order – or more accurately, apparent discontinuous order, from the viewpoint of the English relative-clause translation – I would part company with Lehmann (1984) in considering all such instances of discontinuity to form a homogeneous type. Consider a literary English example like (24).

(24)   *Richard was destined to meet the woman there whom he would, after a series of unforeseeable tribulations, ask to be his wife.*

In (24), the relative clause *whom he would, after a series of unforeseeable tribulations, ask to be his wife* is separated by the word *there* from its head *the woman*, and thus technically qualifies as an appositional relative clause. But apart from this one word-order property (24) has necessarily all the characteristics of the usual literary English relative clause construction, including in particular all the characteristics of the relative-pronoun relative clause type, including preposing of the relative pronoun and its case marking for its syntactic role in its own clause. Thus the mere fact of non-adjacency is not in itself sufficient to identify an adjoined relative clause. The adjunction really does have to be loose, and the semantics underspecified. But given these characteristics of the adjoined relative clause construction, or more accurately of the adjoined subordinate clause construction, it would seem to be an ideal candidate as a stage towards the development of constructions that do function specifically as relative clauses.

4.2. General noun-modifying constructions

The adjoined clause construction discussed in the previous subsection had two characteristics: semantic nonspecificity and a loose relation, in the relative clause interpretation, to the head noun in the main clause. In this subsection, perhaps the most substantial, I want to consider a kind of construction that has played an important role in recent discussions of the syntax of relative clauses and similar constructions. One of the major sources for the account I will develop is the discussion of relative clauses and similar constructions in Japanese by Matsumoto (1997). Consider a standard Japanese relative clause like (25), in which clause structure is marked by means of square brackets.

(25) *[gakusei ga katta] hon*
      student NOM bought book
     'the book [that the student bought —]'

(In the English translation, I will repeat the indications of clause structure, and also indicate the "gap" in the English version by means of a dash; as will become clear below, this should not be taken to imply a corresponding gap, in any real sense, in the Japanese original.) At first sight, (25) might seem to be a straightforward instantiation of the gap strategy, for instance if we compare (25) with the corresponding main clause in (26).

(26) *Gakusei ga hon o katta.*
    student NOM book ACC bought
    'The student bought the book.'

However, a surprisingly large number of independent observations conspire to suggest that (25) should not be analysed in this way, but rather that the syntactic structure of (25) is pretty much what one sees on the surface: a head noun *hon* 'book' modified by a clause *gakusei ga katta* 'the student bought [it]'. I should, incidentally, emphasise at the outset that I am not claiming that all instances of what have hitherto been considered gap-type relative clauses should be reanalysed in the way I am suggesting, following Matsumoto, that the Japanese construction should be reanalysed. For instance, Turkish lacks most of the properties identified below as characterising the Japanese construction, and as far as I am aware there is no alternative but to say that Turkish has a distinct relative clause construction; see Comrie (1998a) for further discussion, including the possibility that some other Turkic languages might be more like Japanese in this respect.

The first thing to be noted is that in Japanese, as a null-anaphor language, the basic structure of the subordinate clause in (25) is perfectly well-formed as a main clause. Indeed, (27) is the normal Japanese translation of the English sentence given as translation of that example.

(27) *Gakusei ga katta.*
    student NOM bought
    'The student bought it.'

There is thus no initial objection to saying that the structure of (25) is simply a head noun to which a modifying clause has been attached. Such an analysis would not, of course, work for English, where *that/which the student bought* is not a well-formed main clause, while the alternative *the student bought* is only possible under very restricted pragmatic circumstances, for instance in discussing the student's dealings on the stock market, circumstances that are not required for the interpretation of (25).

The second important thing to note is that Japanese has other instances of a head noun accompanied by a modifying clause that do not and cannot receive relative clause interpretations, such as (28) and (29) below.

(28) [gakusei ga hon o katta] zizitu
 student NOM book ACC bought fact
 'the fact [that the student bought the book]'

(29) [dareka ga doa o tataku] oto
 someone NOM door ACC knock sound
 'the sound of [someone knocking at the door]'

In the English translation of (28), the subordinate clause can clearly be shown not to be a relative clause, for instance in that *that* cannot be replaced by *which*. In the English translation of (29), a finite subordinate clause is not even possible. All three of (25), (28), and (29) can perhaps be given a semi-English translation using the *such that* construction beloved of logicians, though even this, as in (30)–(32), seems at times quite artificial.

(30) the student such that he bought the book

(31) the fact such that the student bought the book

(32) the sound such that someone knocked at the door

The claim for Japanese would thus be that Japanese just has a single construction, attaching a modifying clause to a head noun. The semantics – in particular, the frames of the various predicates – would then interact with pragmatic inferencing to give an appropriate interpretation, which would sometimes be like that assigned to an English relative clause, sometimes not. A verb like *katta* 'bought', for instance, suggests a buyer, a seller, a sum of money, a place, and a time, but not anything that could plausibly be filled by 'fact', especially if, as in (28), the direct object of *katta* is already specified, so that even an interpretation of buying data is excluded.

Now, an obvious counter-attack to this analysis for Japanese would be to point to constraints on extraction – if necessary, in Logical Form – to show that Japanese relative clauses do have properties that are distinct from the other constructions illustrated in (28)-(29), where clearly no extraction is involved. Certainly, in English there are surprisingly robust constraints on relative clause formation of the type illustrated by (33)-(36).

(33)   *I said [the man was leaving].*

(34)   *the man [that I said [— was leaving]]*

(35)   *I said [that the man was leaving]*

(36)   **the man [that I said [that — was leaving]]*

In an important contribution to our understanding of so-called constraints on Japanese relative clause formation, Haig (1996) shows that what have often been taken to be clear instances of such constraints in Japanese are actually of a pragmatic rather than a syntactic nature. In particular, he looks at examples that would violate subjacency. Let us start with an example that already includes a relative clause (or rather: a noun-modifying clause that receives a relative clause interpretation), as in (37).

(37)   *[Inu   o   katte   ita] kodomo ga   sindesimatta.*
       dog ACC keeping was   child   NOM died
       'The child [that — was keeping the dog] died.'

In English, it is quite impossible to relativise on the noun 'dog', given that it is already within a relative clause, as can be seen in the English translation to (38). In Japanese, judgements on the noun phrase (38) vary, although I have encountered at least some native speakers who find it perfectly acceptable.

(38) *[[katte ita] kodomo ga sindesimatta] inu*
      keeping was child NOM died dog
      'the dog$_i$ [that the child$_j$ [that —$_j$ was keeping —$_i$] died]'

If, in Japanese, the structure of (38) is retained but the content is changed so that reference is to a readily identifiable situation, then there is no longer any doubt about the full acceptability of the result, as in (39), where reference is clearly (to anyone brought up in Japanese culture) to the loyal dog Hachiko, who continued until his own death to go to the railway station to meet his master, even after his master's death:

(39) *[[Kawaigatte ita] hito ga nakunatta inu] ga*
      keeping was person NOM died dog NOM
      maiban eki made kainusi o mukae ni kita.
      each.evening station to master ACC greet to came
      'The dog$_i$ [that the person$_j$ [who —$_j$ was keeping —$_i$] died] came to the station every evening to greet his master.'

Note that even under these circumstances the English translation does not improve significantly, indeed native speakers typically continue to get lost wondering whether it is the dog or the master that died.

A possible reaction to the foregoing discussion might be that this is, perhaps, fine as an analysis of Japanese, but what does it have to do with the second language acquisition of languages that do not share these properties? I think there are two reasons why this extended typological perspective on relative clauses might be of value more generally in second language acquisition studies. The first is an aprioristic one. The general noun-modifying construction is a way of transmitting the information of a relative clause by using a construction that is (i) of more general, indeed of relatively unspecified, semantics, and (ii) that avoids many of the complications (such as constraints on extraction).

The second relates specifically to recent work that has been done on English, some of which I have summarised in Comrie (1999). It turns out that in non-standard varieties of English, constructions are attested that appear to be relative clauses but which lack a notional head that plays a role in both clauses. Example (40) is taken from Miller (1993), and is an attested utterance by a speaker of a Scottish variety of English. Example (41) is taken from Matsumoto (1997), and is an attested example from a speaker of American English.

(40)   *I haven't been to a party yet [that I haven't got home the same night].*

(41)   *You come to a group [that you have eat certain foods].*

For reasons that I do not yet understand in detail, the possibilities expand considerably in non-standard English if *where* is substituted for *that*, as in (42), another example from a speaker of American English cited by Matsumoto (1997). Example (43) — and I can only apologise to Dickens lovers — is something I overheard myself saying.

(42)   *a cake [where you don't gain weight]*

(43)   *Dickens is one of the few authors [where I prefer to watch the video].*

(Note that all of these examples can be expressed using the logical pseudo-English *such that* construction.) Incidentally, the existence of this possibility in non-standard English suggests a possible reinterpretation of the pronoun-retention type of relative clause, also found in non-standard English, as in (44). Rather than regarding this specifically as an instance of pronoun-retention, it could be regarded rather as an instance of the noun-modifying construction which just happens to have coreferential noun phrases in the two clauses.

(44)   *This is the road [that I don't know where it leads].*

This analysis might be extendible to some other languages that have hitherto been analysed as having pronoun-retention relative clauses, though I emphasise that this would involve careful work on each language concerned. I also leave open the possibility whether work on spontaneous speech in other European languages might reveal similar constructions in these languages; Fiorentino (1999) suggests that this may indeed be the case in Italian and other Romance languages. But the crucial point is that the non-standard language has developed a construction that is largely analogous to the standard relative clause construction but which loosens the constraints between the two clauses so that the subordinate clause does not have to share a coreferential noun phrase, even notionally, with the main clause. If this loosening can be found in unconstrained native-speaker usage, might it not also be a good candidate for inter-language varieties?

5. Conclusions

In my introduction, I emphasised that I was not going to be presenting new materials on second language acquisition. Rather, I have tried to do what it is within my competence to do, namely to point out interesting developments within linguistic typology, in particular relating to the cross-linguistic study of relative clauses, that might prove of interest to investigators of second language acquisition. In the past there has been fruitful interaction between the two fields, as can be seen in earlier work on relative clauses. I hope and believe that such mutually beneficial interaction will continue.

Notes

1. The following abbreviations are used in glossing example sentences: ACC – accusative, AUX – auxiliary, COMP – complementiser, ERG – ergative, NOM – nominative, SG – singular, SUFF – suffix.

References

Cole, Peter
    1976   An apparent asymmetry in the formation of relative clauses in Modern Hebrew. In: Peter Cole (ed.), *Studies in Modern Hebrew Syntax and Semantics*, 231-247. Amsterdam: North-Holland.

Comrie, Bernard
    1984   Why linguists need language acquirers. In: William E. Rutherford (ed.), *Language Universals and Second Language Acquisition*, 11-29. Amsterdam: John Benjamins.

Comrie, Bernard
    1989   *Language Universals and Linguistic Typology*. Second edition. Oxford: Blackwell/Chicago: University of Chicago Press.

Comrie, Bernard
    1998a   Attributive clauses in Asian languages: Towards an areal typology. In: Winfried Boeder, Christoph Schroeder, Karl Heinz Wagner, and Wolfgang Wildgen (eds.), *Sprache in Raum und Zeit, In memoriam Johannes Bechert*, Band 2: *Beiträge zur empirischen Sprachwissenschaft*, 51-60. Tübingen: Gunter Narr.

Comrie, Bernard
    1998b   Rethinking the typology of relative clauses. *Language Design* 1: 59-86.

Comrie, Bernard
    1999   Relative clauses: Structure and typology on the periphery of standard English. In: Peter Collins and David Lee (eds.), *The Clause in English: In Honour of Rodney Huddleston*, 81-91. Amsterdam: John Benjamins.

Fiorentino, Giuliana
    1999   *Relativa debole. Sintassi, uso, storia in Italiano*. Milano: Franco Angeli.

Gass, Susan
    1979   Language transfer and universal grammatical relations. *Language Learning* 29: 327-344.

Haig, John H.
  1996   Subjacency and Japanese grammar: A functional account. *Studies in Language* 20: 53-92.
Hale, Kenneth
  1976   The adjoined relative clause in Australian languages. In: R.M.W. Dixon (ed.), *Grammatical Categories in Australian Languages*, 78-105. Canberra: Australian Institute of Aboriginal Studies.
Keenan, Edward L., and Bernard Comrie
  1977   Noun phrase accessibility and universal grammar. *Linguistic Inquiry* 8: 63-99.
Lehmann, Christian
  1984   *Der Relativsatz: Typologie seiner Strukturen, Theorie seiner Funktionen, Kompendium seiner Grammatik*. Tübingen: Gunter Narr.
Matsumoto, Yoshiko
  1997   *Noun-Modifying Constructions in Japanese: A Frame Semantic Approach*. Amsterdam: John Benjamins.
Miller, James
  1993   The grammar of Scottish English. In: James Milroy and Lesley Milroy (eds.), *Real English: The Grammar of English Dialects in the British Isles*, 99-138. London: Longman.
Sankoff, Gillian, and Penelope Brown
  1976   On the origin of syntax in discourse: A case study of Tok Pisin relatives. *Language* 52: 631-666.
Sheldon, Amy
  1974   *The Acquisition of Relative Clauses in English*. Bloomington: Indiana University Linguistics Club.

Relative clauses in early bilingual development: Transfer and universals*

Stephen Matthews and Virginia Yip

1. Introduction and Background

This paper investigates the development of English relative clauses in two bilingual children exposed to Cantonese and English from birth. The two subjects are siblings both of whom show dominance of Cantonese over English in their preschool years. Aspects of their English show features and structures that are quite unlike their monolingual counterparts, many of which are attributable to transfer from the dominant language, in this case Cantonese. One of the most striking Cantonese-based features observed in the first subject's English, the occurrence of prenominal relative clauses, is recapitulated in the second subject. Such prenominal relatives have not, to our knowledge, previously been documented in the acquisition of English by monolingual or bilingual children. In the initial stage of development, object relative clauses are produced with the head in final position, i.e. the relative clauses precede the head noun which they modify. In a subsequent stage, postnominal relatives occur with resumptive pronouns, before the target structures without such pronouns are eventually acquired.

From a typological perspective, the transfer of prenominal relative clauses is of particular interest for two reasons:

(i) prenominal relatives are a universally marked option, and especially rare in SVO languages, with Mandarin Chinese the only case instantiating this combination in many language samples (Hawkins 1990). Cantonese also instantiates the co-occurrence of SVO basic word order and prenominal relatives, as do other Sinitic languages.[1] The rarity of this combination of word order properties is attributable to processing considerations which disfavour it (Hawkins 1994). Nevertheless, prenominal relatives prove to be subject to transfer in early bilingual development. Our subjects each developed prenominal relatives in their English and Cantonese in parallel, indicating that transfer can play a prominent role in early bilingual development, as it does in second language acquisition. We shall suggest that the transfer of prenominal relatives is part of a more general pattern of prenominal modification.

(ii) the prenominal relatives observed in the bilingual children's English are restricted to object relativisation, counter to the Noun Phrase Accessibility Hierarchy (Keenan and Comrie 1977) which would predict that a language or interlanguage allowing object relatives will also allow subject relatives. We shall attribute this unusual phenomenon to the isomorphism between object relatives and main clause word order in Cantonese, which facilitates processing and production of this kind of relative clause.

In the subsequent stage of development, postnominal relatives are produced which are characterised initially by the occurrence of resumptive pronouns. Such resumptive pronouns are also observed in the acquisition of English as a first language by monolingual children (Pérez-Leroux 1995) and as a second language by adult learners from different L1 backgrounds, and we shall suggest that they reflect a universal strategy for relative clauses, rather than transfer (cf. Hyltenstam 1984, Gass and Ard 1984). The two stages of development suggest that both transfer and universal factors are crucial in accounting for early bilingual development.

We shall begin by reviewing background issues including syntactic transfer in children who are simultaneously exposed to two languages, the universally marked status of prenominal relatives, and the structure of relative clauses in adult Cantonese. Section 2 reviews the methodology of the study, giving information on the subjects and data collection. Section 3 describes the development of relative clauses in the two subjects' English and Cantonese. Section

4 discusses internal and external factors which may lead to transfer of prenominal relatives from Cantonese into English, followed by conclusions in section 5 highlighting the findings of the study.

1.1. Syntactic transfer in bilingual development

A major theme of research in bilingual acquisition has been the question of one unitary system versus two differentiated systems in children who are exposed simultaneously to two languages. Recent studies agree that bilingual children are able to differentiate between the two languages from early on (De Houwer 1990; Genesee 1989; Genesee, Nicoladis, and Paradis 1995; Meisel 1989) but the picture with regard to transfer remains more mixed. Some studies have suggested that separation of two grammars also implies autonomous development without interaction, hence developing grammars much like those of monolinguals (e.g. De Houwer 1990), while others have found various forms of interaction and cross-linguistic influence between the languages (Döpke 2000, Müller 1998). Thus the development of separate grammars in bilingual children does not preclude cross-linguistic influence; what is at issue is the nature of the influence and whether it constitutes transfer. Here we assume a working definition of transfer as "incorporation of a grammatical property into one language from the other" (Paradis and Genesee 1996: 3).

Concerning the conditions under which transfer takes place, it is often the case that one of the two languages develops faster, or shows greater complexity at a given age. This language is said to be dominant. A number of studies report incorporation of elements from a dominant to a less dominant language (Döpke 1997; Gawlitzek-Maiwald and Tracy 1996; Hulk and van der Linden 1996). Language dominance can be measured most objectively by computing Mean Length of Utterance (MLU) for each language at different stages: the dominant language is expected to have a higher MLU value than the less dominant one. Less direct indications of dominance come from children's language preferences (Saunders

1988). The amount of input from each language is thought to play a major role in determining language dominance (Döpke 1992).

Paradis and Genesee (1996: 3) suggest an important qualification to this view: "Transfer is most likely to occur if the child has reached a more advanced level of syntactic complexity in one language than the other. Such a discrepancy could occur either because it is typical in the monolingual acquisition of the two languages, or because the child is more dominant in one of his or her languages." The first possibility here, whereby the discrepancy between the bilingual child's two languages is in accordance with the normal acquisition schedules for monolingual children in each language, is one which has yet to be investigated extensively. We shall call this the *developmental asynchrony hypothesis*, which we define as follows:

> *Developmental asynchrony hypothesis*: given a property P_a which develops at an earlier stage in monolingual children acquiring Language A than a corresponding property P_b in monolingual children acquiring Language B, in a bilingual child acquiring Languages A and B simultaneously, property P_a is expected to develop in Language A before P_b in Language B. This creates a *developmental asynchrony* between the two languages, allowing property P_a to be transferred to Language B.

On this account, a discrepancy in syntactic complexity between the bilingual child's languages is not necessarily due to dominance. We shall return to this possibility in the case of relative clause development, and its relationship to language dominance, in section 4.1.

1.2. Prenominal relatives as a universally marked option

Prenominal relative clauses appear to represent a marked option in the languages of the world. Overall, there is a strong skewing in favour of postnominal relatives: even OV languages show a slight preference for [N Rel] over [Rel N], while in VO languages, [Rel N] is "virtually unattested" (Hawkins 1990), with Chinese languages the only extensively documented examples, based on an extensive language sample.[2] Dryer (1992) found that 98% N of VO languages and 58% of OV languages in his sample had postnominal relatives, i.e. there is an overall preference for postnominal relatives. Hawkins (1994) attributes this asymmetry to parsing considerations. The combination of VO order with prenominal relatives creates configurations like the following:

[$_{VP}$ V [$_{NP}$ [$_S$ Relative Clause] N]]

A hypothetical English-based example illustrating this configuration is shown in (1):

(1)   *I* [$_{VP}$ *ate* [$_{NP}$ [$_S$ *you bought yesterday*] *the cakes.*]]

With the relative clause [*you bought yesterday*] intervening between the verb *ate* and its object *the cakes*, this configuration incurs an indefinitely long delay in the parsing of NP, and hence also of VP, while the parser awaits the head noun. This delay can be measured using Hawkins' notion of Constituent Recognition Domain:

Constituent Recognition Domain (CRD): The CRD for a phrasal mother node M consists of the set of terminal and non-terminal nodes that must be parsed in order to recognise M and all ICs [Immediate Constituents] of M. (Hawkins 1994: 58).

In the case of (1), VP is a mother node dominating the immediate constituents V and NP. Let us assume that for NP to be recognised, its head N must be parsed. The CRD for VP then extends from V, through the relative clause to the head N:

[$_{VP}$ V [$_{NP}$ [$_S$ Relative Clause] N]
|_____|
Constituent Recognition Domain for VP

The longer and the more complex the prenominal relative clause in this VO configuration, the longer the CRD and the lower the parsing efficiency achieved by the configuration (some experimental evidence for this is provided by Matthews and Yeung, 2001). The combination of word orders exemplified by (1) is predicted to be strongly dispreferred, as is borne out by Dryer's (1992) statistics cited above, and must be regarded as a marked option in universal terms. Transfer of prenominal relatives in the acquisition of a VO language such as English would create an interlanguage with the anomalous combination of SVO basic word order and [Rel N] order, as instantiated in Chinese. We shall see that this can indeed occur, at least in early bilingual acquisition. To the extent that marked structures are not expected to undergo transfer (a common assumption in second language research, cf. Braidi 1999), the systematic transfer of prenominal relatives comes as a surprise. In section 4 we shall suggest a number of factors which might explain this finding.

1.3. Prenominal relatives in adult Cantonese

In order to establish the transfer basis of the prenominal relatives in the bilingual subjects' English, we need to consider the properties of the corresponding structures in adult Cantonese. Cantonese employs prenominal relative clauses as in (2), where the modifying clause precedes the head noun *saam1* 'clothes', whereas in English it follows the head noun *clothes* as in (3):[3]

(2) [[*Ngo5 zung1ji3* _ $_S$] *go2   di1 saam1* $_{NP}$] *hou2 gwai3*.
     I   like   those CL clothes   very expensive
     'The clothes I like are expensive."

(3) [$_{NP}$ *The clothes* [$_{CP}$ *(that) I like* _]] *are expensive*.

The type of relative clause in (2) uses a demonstrative *go2* 'that' and classifier *di1* but no overt marker of relativisation or subordination. Termed "classifier relatives" in Matthews and Yip (1994), these structures are characteristic of spoken Cantonese, as opposed to Mandarin and written Chinese, and hence represent the predominant type of relative clause in the language input addressed to young children. A notable property of object relatives of this type is that they resemble a main clause. Thus the relative clause in (2) has, at least superficially, the same form as the main clause in (4):

(4)   [$_S$ *Ngo5 zung1ji3 go2 di1 saam1.*]
         I   like   those   CL   clothes
      'I like those clothes.'

As we shall see, this resemblance has a number of implications. Methodologically, it means that Cantonese relatives with an object gap like (2) and their transfer-based counterparts in English are not easy to identify in the child data, since they will resemble main clauses in having the same linear order; theoretically, it raises the possibility that children could use such relative clauses without having to acquire any subordination strategies.[4]

From a typological perspective, the parallel between object relatives and main clauses raises the possibility that "classifier relatives" such as (2) are internally headed relative clauses: that is, constituents having internally the syntax of a clause but externally that of a Noun Phrase (cf. Keenan 1985: 161):

(5)   [$_{NP/S}$ *Ngo5 zung1ji3 go2 di1 saam1*]   *hou2 gwai3.*
          I   like   those CL clothes   very expensive
      'The clothes I like are expensive.'

When such an analysis is pursued for adult Cantonese, a number of problems arise (Matthews and Yip, 2001). While the simplest type of object relative as in (2) resembles a main clause, evidence from a number of more complex constructions shows that the main clause and relative clause structures are not in fact parallel. In the double object construction, for example, the main clause V-DO-IO order as in (6) cannot be used in a relative clause (7) where the head *syu1* 'book' would be internal to the relative clause:

(6) [s Ngo5   bei2   go2   bun2 syu1 lei5]
        I   give   that CL   book you
     'I gave you that book.'

(7) *[NP Ngo5   bei2 go2   bun2 **syu1** lei5] hou2
         I   give that CL   book   you   good
     m4   hou2   tai2   aa3?
     not   good   read   PRT
     'Is the book I gave you good?'

Instead, the relative clause based on (6) requires the head to be in final position as in (8):

(8) [NP Ngo5   bei2   lei5   go2   bun2   **syu1**] hou2
         I   give   you   that CL   book   good
     m4   hou2   tai2   aa3?
     not   good   read   PRT
     'Is the book I gave you good?'

Similarly, the head-internal analysis would predict that the object of an SOV pretransitive construction with *zoeng1* (the Cantonese counterpart to Mandarin *ba*) can be relativised to create a head-internal relative. The result is not grammatical, however:

(9) *[Ngo5   zoeng1   di1   **syu1**   bun1   zau2]
         I   displace   CL   books   move   away
     lei5   baai2   hai2   bin1dou6   aa3?
     you   put   at   where   PRT
     'Where did you put the books I moved away?'

Finally, such an analysis would also be inapplicable to subject relatives, where the word order is clearly not that of a main clause:

(10) [NP Ting1jat6   jin2-gong2   go2   go3   jan4]
         tomorrow   perform-talk   that   CL   person

ceot1-m4-ceot1meng2	*gaa3?*
famous-not-famous	PRT

'Is the person who's giving the talk tomorrow famous?'

While the analysis of classifier relatives as internally-headed relative clauses may not be tenable for adult Cantonese beyond the case of simple object relatives such as (2), these are precisely the structures which appear in the child data. The possibility therefore remains open for child language. Moreover, the identity of the typical object relative with a main clause may facilitate parsing and production of object relatives. This possibility is discussed further in section 4.3 below.

2. Methodology

The data for this study come from longitudinal case studies of two siblings. The longitudinal data form part of the Hong Kong Bilingual Child Language Corpus, and are available at the CHILDES database.[5] These transcript data are supplemented by diary data recorded by the parents.

In this section we review the background of the subjects and the methods used in data collection. The functions of relative clauses in the subjects' diary data will be addressed, followed by a discussion of measuring dominance by means of comparing MLUw in Cantonese and English.

2.1. Subjects and data collection

The subjects of the present case study are the first two children of the co-authors, the mother being a native speaker of Hong Kong Cantonese and the father of British English. Timmy is the first-born son, Sophie the daughter born 2 years and 9 months later. Both children were exposed to Cantonese and English regularly from birth. The family lives in Hong Kong and follows the one parent-one language principle when addressing the child. The language between the parents is mainly Cantonese, with frequent code-mixing, as is characteristic of the speech of Hong Kong middle class families. Despite the one parent-one language principle, the quantity of input from the two languages is by no means balanced: on the whole, the children had more Cantonese than English input in their first three years. The language of the community is Cantonese, while the children's extended family (the maternal grandmother and relatives) also speak Cantonese, and in some cases Chiu Chow.[6] Timmy attended a bilingual kindergarten from age 2;4 for three hours a day, with approximately equal amounts of input from each language; from 3;4, he attended a Cantonese-medium kindergarten in the morning and an English-medium kindergarten in the afternoon. Sophie attended a Cantonese-medium kindergarten from 2;06, and from 3;02 also attended an English kindergarten in the morning. At home, regular input in English came solely from the father and the family's Filipino domestic helper, while other English-speaking relatives visited only occasionally.[7]

The children's language development was investigated using (a) longitudinal recordings, and (b) diary data, which provide almost the entire corpus for the present study of relative clauses. The longitudinal data come from a bilingual corpus created by regular audio (and in Sophie's case, video) recording over a period of two years. The researchers sought to reproduce the one person-one language approach in the elicitation environment by having one of the two research assistants involved in each recording session responsible for speaking each language, though English was a second language for all the assistants. Spontaneous speech data were recorded at the subject's home where the routines included activities such as playing with toys and telling stories. These speech data were transcribed by the research assistants.

Following a long tradition in bilingual acquisition research, the parents kept their own record of the two children's language development in the form of diary entries. The availability of diary data enables us to address the development of phenomena such as relative clauses which appear rarely, if at all, in the longitudinal corpus data. The diary was kept from 1;03-6;00 for Timmy and 1;06-5;06 for Sophie. The diary includes several entries per week and was intended to complement the audio-recording data. Both parents were involved in recording the data in the two languages, although the coverage of English data was more extensive than for Cantonese. The contexts of these data were mostly interaction between the child and parents at home or occasionally away from home. Relevant contextual information was given as far as possible in the diary entries. We believe that the diary data are reliable to the extent that they are systematic: all the patterns described here are instantiated at least three times, and frequently more. Such recurrent patterns imply developing competence rather than performance alone. How representative the diary data are presents a more serious problem: there is inevitably selection bias, whereby unusual and non-native-like utterances are more likely to be recorded than unremarkable and well-formed ones.

2.2. Functions of relative clauses in the diary data

A striking finding is that while we have not identified any clear examples of relative clauses in the longitudinal recordings, there are some 25 clear cases in the diary data for Timmy from age 2;07 to 4;05, most of which are cited in the body of this paper. For Sophie, there are some 60 examples in the diary data between age 3;03 and 5;05. The diary data therefore provide almost the entire corpus for the present case study.

The lack of clear exemplification of relatives in the longitudinal recording, compared to their regular occurrence in the diary data, calls for explanation. It might be argued that relative clauses are merely a low frequency structure and the regular recording time is not sufficient for such structures to occur naturally. However, the corpus for Timmy contains a total 85 files, each representing approximately half an hour's speech in each language, making a total of around 40 hours of transcribed speech. A more likely explanation involves the discourse functions of relative clauses. In speaking to their parents, the children use relatives to identify objects on the basis of shared knowledge, typically involving family members and activities. A typical example is (11) where Timmy is looking for a water pistol given to him by "Santa Claus" at a Christmas family lunch:

(11)   *Where's the Santa Claus give me the gun?* (2;07;05)

In this utterance, the toy gun is identifiable to the parents, who were present at the Christmas lunch, but not to the research assistants conducting the recording who visited the children at most once per week. The research assistants have a relatively small repertoire of knowledge and experiences shared with the child, hence the opportunities for the child to use relative clauses for purposes of identification are limited. The children's spontaneous production of relative clauses is thus heavily dependent on shared knowledge.

2.3. Measuring dominance: MLUw

We take Mean Length of Utterance (MLU) to be the most objective indicator of a child's linguistic development in each language, and hence of language dominance. The calculation of MLUw (Mean Length of Utterance measured in words) depends on decisions regarding what constitutes a word – a problem which has not been resolved, either in general or with regard to Chinese in particular. Our MLUw calculations depend on the word divisions as made in the transcripts, which are in turn modelled on Matthews and Yip (1994).[8]

While useful for within-language comparisons, it is recognised that MLUw may not be directly comparable across languages, especially those of different morphological types (cf. Döpke 1998: 564). We suggest two responses to this problem. Firstly, Cantonese and child English can both be treated as predominantly isolating languages, since in young children's English (and especially that of our subjects) inflectional morphology is not yet fully in place. Secondly,

MLUw differentials between a bilingual's two languages can be used in a relative, rather than an absolute sense: to compare individual bilingual children with each other, and to show changes in dominance patterns over time. In this way, we find that the mean MLUw for Timmy is 3.46 for Cantonese (based on 34 files from 2;00;26 – 3;06;25) and 3.065 for English (based on 38 files from 2;01;22 – 3;06;25), with the discrepancy especially great in the period 2;01 to 2;08. Taken at face value, this suggests that Cantonese developed faster than English, especially in the period 2;01 to 2;08, while after age 2;09 the MLUw figures are closely matched. Given the uncertainty concerning comparability of MLU across languages, this pattern allows for a number of possible interpretations (Yip and Matthews, 2000: 198). The most plausible interpretation, however, is that the MLUw differential between the two languages indicates Cantonese to be dominant, at least in a relative sense (during the period when prenominal relatives appear, i.e. around age 2;07 in Timmy). For Sophie, the differential in mean MLUw is even greater, and more consistent over the entire period of study: 2.586 for Cantonese, compared with 1.885 for English (based on 40 files for each language from 1;06;00 – 3;00;09).

3. Development of relative clauses in the bilingual subjects

The data show two distinct stages in development of English relatives. In the first stage, prenominal object relatives emerge based on a Cantonese pattern. In the second, postnominal relatives appear, initially with resumptive pronouns. Relative clauses in the children's Cantonese data are essentially target-like throughout, showing no apparent influence from English.

3.1. Prenominal relatives in Timmy's English

As recorded in the diary data, prenominal relative clauses emerge in Timmy's English at age 2;07:

(12)   *Where's the motor-bike? You buy the motor-bike? That you buy the motor-bike. Where's you buy that one, where's you buy that one the motorbike?* (2;07;03)

In this example, the utterance *You buy the motor-bike* is not to be interpreted as a full main clause ("Did you buy the motor-bike?"), as this interpretation would be incompatible with the following linguistic context (*Where's you buy that one?*) as well as the extralinguistic context, in which the child is looking for a certain toy. Rather, the utterance is intended as a relative clause ("the motorbike that you bought") being used to specify reference to a particular toy. The structure for (12) therefore follows the Cantonese prenominal pattern described in (2) above, as shown in (13):

(13)   *Where's* [[*you buy _* $_S$] *that one* $_{NP}$],
       where's [[*you buy _* $_S$] *that one the motorbike* $_{NP}$]

Similarly in (14), where comprehension of the relative depends on the addressee's knowledge that uncle Patrick (alias Pet-Pet) bought a certain videotape for the child:

(14)   *I want to watch videotape. Butterfly. Patrick buy that one. I want Pet-Pet buy that one videotape.* (2;11;25)

Here the utterance *Patrick buy that one* is not to be interpreted as a main clause ("Patrick bought that one"), but a relative clause ("the one that Patrick bought") being used to specify a particular videotape. Similarly, *I want Pet-Pet buy that one videotape* cannot mean "I want Pet-Pet to buy that videotape", because the tape concerned has already been bought.

In examples such as (12) and (14) we can see how the child expands a headless relative with *one* into a head-final one by adding a head noun. In (15), the child replaces *that* with the lexical head noun *tape*:

(15) *This is who buy? Have butterfly? You bought that have butterfly?*
[referring to a new video tape with a butterfly on the cover]
[later] *You buy that tape is English?* (2;10)

Here the child's last question, concerning the same videotape, uses a full relative clause with *tape* as the head noun. Note that the demonstrative *that* appears regularly. As in Cantonese relatives such as (2) illustrated above, this has the force of a definite rather than a deictic determiner (i.e. the distal/proximate distinction is neutralised in this context). The corresponding adult Cantonese relative, as in (16), has the demonstrative *go2* 'that' followed by the classifier *beng2*:

(16) *Lei5   maai5 go2   beng2 daai2 hai6   Jing1man2 ge3.*
     you   buy   that   CL   tape   is   English   PRT
     'The tape you bought is English.'

In the child's English, *one* serves a generic classifier as in example (14) above. This pattern is more extensively attested in Sophie's English (see 3.3 below).

3.2. Prenominal relatives in Timmy's Cantonese

Cantonese relative clauses are recorded in Timmy's diary data during the very same week in which prenominal relatives appear in English, the first example being (17):

(17) *Jan   maai5 go2   tiu4*
     Jan   buy   that   CL
     'The one that Jan bought' (2;07;04)

This is a classifier relative of the type described in section 1.3 above, with the classifier *tiu4* denoting an elongated object (in this case a pair of pants) but the head noun is omitted, as in *Patrick buy that one* (14). Subsequent examples include a head noun, as in (18):

(18) *Po4po2   maai5 di1   tong4-tong2   ne1?*
     Grandma   buy   CL   candy-candy   PRT
     'What about the candies Grandma bought?' (2;7;12)

One Cantonese example (19) not only exhibits similar structure to those already described in Timmy's English, but refers to the very same referent as the English example (11) above:

(19) *Santa Claus   bei2   lei5   go3   coeng1   le1?*
     Santa Claus   give   you   CL   gun   PRT
     'Where's the gun Santa Claus gave me?' (2;8;25)

Here the child appears to use the default classifier *go3* (adult Cantonese would use both *go2* 'that' and a more specific classifier, either *zi1* or *baa2* for *coeng1* 'gun', while the pronoun *lei5* 'you' is a case of pronoun reversal (the child clearly intends reference to himself, so that the target is *ngo5* 'I'). By age 2;10 we see fully well-formed classifier relatives:

(20) *Go2   di1   Lego   le1,   Mannings   maai5 go2*
     that   CL   Lego   PRT,   Mannings   buy   that
     di1   Lego   le1?
     CL   Lego   PRT
     'What about the Lego, the Lego we bought at Mannings?' (2;10;14)

In structure, function and even topic (cf. the 'Santa Claus') the Cantonese relatives parallel the English examples such as (11-15) discussed in section 3.1. Given the simultaneous emergence and productive use of prenominal relatives in both languages, the role of transfer in the English examples can be established.

3.3. Prenominal relatives in Sophie's English

Prenominal relative clauses appear rather later in Sophie's English, at around age 3;03. This relative delay is expected since Sophie began to produce Cantonese at 11 months and English only at around age 2. One implication of this timing is that Sophie's production of prenominal relatives cannot readily be attributed to input from the elder sibling. At the time when Timmy was producing them (up to age 4) Sophie was between 1 month and 1;03, well before she had begun to produce English sentences. The development of prenominal relatives in her English can therefore be considered independent, and the strikingly parallel paths taken by both children can be seen as the product of interaction of English and Cantonese grammars under similar input conditions.

Between ages 3;03 and 4;03, Sophie produces only relatives headed by *one*, without a lexical head noun:[9]

(21)   Child: *Timmy take that one, I want.*
       Father: *Which one do you want?*
       Child: *She take that one. Timmy take that one.* (3;03;12)

(22)   Child: *I also want.*
       Father: *What do you want?*
       Child: *Timmy said that one.*
       [the child has been asking for a piggy-bank] (3;08;21)

(23)   *I want have ear-ear that one*
       [wanting to wear a coat that has ears] (3;10;9)

(24)   *Daddy, I want ice-cream. Carmen eat that one.* (4;01;11)

(25)   *I buy in the store that one is yummy.*
       [Talking to her brother about lemon sweets] (4;03;17)

With *one* serving as the head, these are based on the "headless" Cantonese construction with demonstrative and classifier but no head noun, as in Timmy's (16). The adult Cantonese counterpart of *Timmy said that one* in (22) is shown in (26):

(26)　　Timmy　　　　waa6　go2　go3
　　　　Timmy　　　　say　　that　CL
　　　　'The one Timmy talked about'

The structure with *one* can be expanded into a full-fledged relative clause by adding a head noun, as we saw in the case of Timmy's (11-13). Instead of this, Sophie replaces *one* with a head noun, as subsequent examples show:

(27)　　Father: *Which dress?*
　　　　Child: *The... you take for me that one.*
　　　　　　 *...Where is it, you said **it** that dress?* (4;04;20)

Here the two relative clauses used to specify the same dress are revealing: the first has *one* as the head, while the second has *that dress* as the head, as well as a resumptive pronoun *it*. Here the context confirms that *you said it that dress* means "the dress you mentioned", as the father had recommended a certain dress to go with her gloves and shoes (cf. the use of the verb *waa6* 'say' in (26) above).

Similar examples of headless relatives to those in Sophie's English are attested in Singaporean children's English (Gupta, 1994). These children are exposed to a variety of Chinese languages including Mandarin, Cantonese, Hokkien and Teochew (Chiu Chow), and in some cases also Malay, alongside English. The English of Gupta's subjects is strikingly similar to what we have observed in our Hong Kong bilingual subjects: although the sociolinguistic situations differ considerably, the influence of southern Chinese dialects through transfer and as substrate languages results in similar effects on the structure of English. In particular, we find relative clauses with *one* as a pronominal head:

(28) *My this can change one ah.*
'Mine is the sort that can change'(Child EB, 5;11, Gupta 1994: 90)

Such examples are (to say the least) not immediately recognizable as relative clauses. Alsagoff and Ho (1998: 134-135) describe similar headless relative clauses in adult Colloquial Singapore English (CSE):

(29) *They grow one very sweet.*
'The fruit that they grow is very sweet.'

(30) *Don't have car one, I don't want.*
'I don't want [a man] who does not own a car.'

Here *one* appears as a clause-final relative marker. When extended to include a lexical head, however, the relative clause is typically postnominal:

(31) [NP *The fruit they grow one*] *very sweet.*

(32) [NP *That boy pinch my mother one*] *very naughty.*

In the authors' analysis, these relative clauses in Colloquial Singapore English "show an amalgamation of both substrate (i.e. Chinese) and superstrate (i.e. English) grammatical features" (Alsagoff and Ho 1998: 127). The substratal influence manifests itself in the use of *one* as a relative marker linking the relative clause to the nominal head. This use of *one* is argued to arise through calquing of the Chinese nominaliser (Mandarin *de*, Hokkien *e*, Teochew *kai*, etc.) into English. This analysis is not directly applicable to our subjects, whose grammar is influenced specifically by the Cantonese classifier relative as illustrated in (2) above. In our subjects *that one* corresponds to the Cantonese demonstrative + classifier complex: *go2 go3* as in (33).

(33) [NP *Lei5   bei2   ngo5   go2   go3*]
         you   give   me   that   CL
      'The one you gave me'

Despite the superficially similar use of *one* as clause-final relative marker, then, the Singaporean data differ from our child data in:

(i)   the position of the relative clause (postnominal in the Singaporean case vs. prenominal in ours), and
(ii) the source structure (nominaliser in the Singaporean case vs. classifier in the Hong Kong data).

3.4. The emergence of postnominal relatives and resumptive pronouns

Between prenominal relatives and the eventual emergence of target-like postnominal relatives, we see an intermediate stage in which relatives are produced in postnominal position, with the target word order but with resumptive pronouns. At the beginning of this stage there is overlapping of the pronominal and postnominal types. The last prenominal relatives produced by Timmy are recorded around age 4:

(34) *Daddy, I want the water gun, the Santa Claus give me that water gun.* (3;11;12)

(35) *Actually I like the best game is Tetris.* (4;00;15)

(36) *Daddy, which that you record tape?* (4;02;25)
      [asking which tape is the one Daddy recorded]

When postnominal relative clauses begin to appear in Timmy's English, no relative pronoun or complementiser is used, but resumptive pronouns are employed. The first example of this type in Timmy's data is recorded at 3;04:

(37) *It's like the one you bought **it**.* [seeing picture of toy car]
      *It's not like the one you bought **it**.* [seeing difference]
      (3;04;07)

There is the possibility of transfer here, since Cantonese allows resumptive pronouns in positions below subject on the NP Accessibility Hierarchy of Keenan and Comrie (1977). In the case of object relatives the pronoun is not used in simple clauses (38), but optional in more complex ones such as (39) where there is a complementation structure in the relative clause (cf. Yip and Matthews 2001: 123):

(38) Ngo5 ceng2 (*keoi5dei6) go2   di1 pang4jau5
      I   invite (*them)   those CL   friend
      'Friends that I invite'

(39) Ngo5 ceng2 (keoi5dei6) sik6-faan6 go2   di1
      I   invite (them)   eat-rice   those CL
      pang4jau5
      friend
      'Friends that I invite to have dinner'

However, there are several reasons to believe that the appearance of resumptive pronouns in the child's English is *not* due to transfer:

(a) while in adult Cantonese the resumptive pronouns are restricted to animate nouns as in (39), in the child data they are used to refer to inanimate nouns as in (40):

(40) *I want the sweet, the sweet that you put **it** there yesterday.*
      (4;00;03);

(b) unlike in Cantonese, resumptive pronouns are occasionally used by Timmy even in the subject position of relative clauses:

(41) *Daddy where's the thing?*
      *Where is the thing **it** hangs? The one **it** says one for me, one*
      for Sophie? (3;10;23)
      [looking for coat-hangers with the children's names painted on them];

(c) the children's Cantonese does not show resumptive pronouns in either subject or object position of relative clauses (cf. the examples in 3.2 above);

(d) the children's English does not show resumptive pronouns when the relative clauses occur in prenominal position (with the single exception of (27)), as would be expected if this property were subject to transfer from Cantonese.

These considerations lead us to conclude that the resumptive pronouns observed in our subjects instantiate a universal developmental strategy rather than transfer. Such resumptive pronouns are known to be widely used in second language acquisition by learners regardless of L1 language backgrounds (Hyltenstam 1984, Gass and Ard 1984).

In Sophie's English, resumptive pronouns are again observed in object position when postnominal relatives first appear:

(42) *I got that red flower dress that Jan give **it** to me.* (4;10;28)

(43) *This is the homework that I do **it**. But, I done already at school.* (4;11;04)

No cases are recorded of resumptive pronouns with subject relatives in Sophie. This may be because she uses the complementiser *that* regularly. In English, subject relatives require *that* in order to distinguish the subordinate structure from a main clause. Compare example (41) from Timmy, repeated as (44), with the subject pronoun *it* but without *that*:

(44) *Where is the thing it hangs? The one **it** says one for me, one for Sophie?* (3;10;23)

In the absence of the complementiser *that*, the resumptive subject pronoun *it* serves to mark the relative clause status, since without it the string [*the one says*...] would be indistinguishable from a main clause.

More generally, the rarity of resumptive pronouns in subject relatives is consistent with the status of subject relatives at the top of the Noun Phrase Accessibility Hierarchy, and hence universally less likely to exhibit resumptive pronouns (Keenan and Comrie 1977, Hawkins 1999). In a picture description task eliciting relative clauses from 11 children from 3;05 to 5;05, Pérez-Leroux (1995) did not find any resumptive pronouns in more than one hundred subject relative clauses, while resumptive pronouns did appear in relative clauses with relativised object and object of preposition.

3.5. *The transition from prenominal to postnominal relatives*

Both children exhibit transitional structures during the shift from the prenominal to postnominal stage. In Timmy, such a transitional case is (45):

(45) *But some children buy the boat **it** stands.* (4;1;2)

At least two possible analyses present themselves for this utterance:

(a) a prenominal relative with *the boat* as its head, followed by a coreferential subject pronoun as in left-dislocation:

(45a) *But* [$_{NP}$ *some children buy* [$_{NP}$ *the boat*]] [$_{S}$ *it stands*]
       'But the boats that some children buy, they stand up.'

(b) a postnominal relative with resumptive pronoun in subject position:

(45b) *But some children buy* [NP *the boat* [S *it stands*]]
'But some children buy boats which stand up.'

At this age, when Timmy uses both prenominal relatives (34-36) and postnominal ones (37, 40-41), example (45) is genuinely ambiguous.

In Sophie, different transitional structures are observed in the period of transition from prenominal to postnominal relatives. One is the introduction of the complementiser *that* in the prenominal relative:

(46) *Where is that 'mou tiu', that Mummy wrote that paper?*
(4;09;08)

(47) *Daddy, I haven't got that Mickey Mouse, that Chloe gave me that one.* (5;04;24)

In these examples we seem to have three distinct occurrences of *that*:

(a) demonstrative *that* (*that mou tiu, that Mickey Mouse*)
(b) complementiser *that* (*that Mummy wrote, that Chloe gave me*)
(c) a restrictive use of *that* (*that paper, that one*) corresponding to the demonstrative *go2* in Cantonese classifier relatives such as (2) above.

While in adult speech the complementiser usage would be distinguished by reduction of the vowel to schwa, in Sophie's speech these uses of *that* are pronounced alike, suggesting that she has yet to distinguish the complementiser from the demonstrative usage.

Another transitional example is (48):

(48) *Where's just now that one I give you?*
[looking for a puzzle done by her father] (5;04;22)

Here the adverbial *just now* belongs semantically in the relative clause, but comes before the head, as if the child begins to construct a prenominal relative [*Where's just now I give you that one*] but then thinks better of it and postposes the remainder of the relative clause.

A second transition can be observed from the resumptive pronoun strategy to the target gap strategy. Relative clauses using a gap strategy appear shortly before Timmy's fourth birthday; these are ill-formed in the case of subject relatives (49) but target-like in the case of object (50) and prepositional relatives (51-52):

(49) *Daddy, do you know where is the thing goes here?* (3;10;25)

(50) *I want to build the car we saw in Mannings.*
I want to build the one we saw in Mannings. (3;10;30)

(51) *Daddy, where's the gun you put water in?* (3;11;01)

(52) *Daddy, we go to the shop we haven't been to, the mall inside the shop*
[i.e. the shop inside the mall] (4;00;04)

Following the well-formed gap relative [$_{NP}$ *the shop we haven't been to*] in (52), we note the resurgence of the prenominal modification construction: *the mall inside the shop* meaning 'the shop inside the mall' (see 4.2 below).

When the complementiser *that* appears at age four, resumptive pronouns are used sporadically, for example in sentences with the verb *put*:

(53) *I want the sweet, the sweet that you put **it** there yesterday.* (4;00;03)

(54) *Where is the thing that I just put here?* (4;01;29)

(55) *Where is the thing that put inside? Where is the thing that go inside?* (4;1;30)

A similar shift away from resumptive pronouns is seen in Sophie, though at a slightly later stage than in Timmy (who made the shift around age 4). As we have seen, Sophie began to produce postnominal relatives shortly before age 5, initially with pronouns in object position as seen in (42) and (43). One month later similar object relatives appear without the pronouns:

(56) *Thank you for the dress that you give to me, for the dolly.* (5;00;04)

(57) *Hey, this is the clips that Belma buy.* (5;00;05)

Pronouns reappear in more complex structures, such as an object of an embedded clause within a relative clause:

(58) *Daddy, where's the fox hole, that you said you find **it** yesterday?* (5;04;15)

The use of the pronoun here does recall our Cantonese example (39). Such examples are also explainable on universal grounds, however. Compare a similarly complex example from Timmy, in which the pronoun occurs twice in a coordinate construction:

(59) *I need the train that you push **it** and **it** goes.*
      'I need the train that goes when you push it.' (4;03;09)

In this case the pronouns might be used even in adult English: "English gaps in complex NP environments can some times be rescued by pronoun retention" (Hawkins 1999: 265).

Perhaps appropriately, one of Sophie's first fully well-formed relatives was produced during a visit to Oxford (60), followed by a number of well-formed examples:

(60) *Then we buy that lipstick that you want*
      [shopping in Oxford, England] (5;04;19)

(61)   Father: *You want to choose something?*
       Child: *Choose something that I want to eat.* (5;04;20)

Sophie has thus reached the target English relative clauses at age five, as Timmy did at age four. Both children have, however, reached it by a very different route from a monolingual child. In Mckee, McDaniel and Snedeker's (1998) experimental study of 28 monolingual English subjects between 2;02 and 3;10, 80% target relative clauses were produced by the subjects, while occasional errors involved resumptive pronouns (62) and non-target relative pronouns such as *what* (62) and *why* (63) (Mckee et al. 1998: 586-587, emphasis added):[10]

(62)   Strawberries – *pick those two up **what** the dinosaur is eating **them**.* (CT, 2;10)

(63)   Bicycle – *pick this one up **why** Dorothy's riding.* (CT, 2;10)

Mckee et al. (1998: 589) suggest a performance account of the resumptive pronouns on the grounds of their sporadic appearance and processing demands, just as in the case of resumptive pronouns in adult English. However, the productive use of resumptive pronouns in our bilingual subjects' production data argues for a grammar that systematically generates resumptive pronouns in relative clauses at this transitional stage.

3.6. The absence of wh-relatives

One final observation to note is the absence of *wh*-relatives in the English data in the period concerned. While monolingual children acquiring English use *wh*-relatives extensively (and indeed misuse them, as in 62-63), the postnominal relative clauses produced by Timmy are overwhelmingly *that*-relatives or zero-relatives, with wh-relative pronouns essentially absent from both the longitudinal recordings and diary data. This again matches findings for Singaporean children who are observed to produce only *that*-relatives (Gupta 1994: 90) and more generally the finding that *that*-relatives predominate over *wh*-relatives in English interlanguages and emerging Asian varieties of English (Newbrook, 1999; Gisborne, 2000). This is attributable in part to the lack of *wh*-relatives in the Asian languages which act as substrates in these new Englishes. Moreover, the invariant form of *that* makes it a straightforward relative marker for a learner to use, whereas in *wh*-relatives the form of the relative pronoun varies with animacy, etc. Register may also be an important factor here: the colloquial spoken English addressed to our children contains largely *that*-relatives.

One example of an apparent *wh*-relative does appear in Timmy's data:

(64) *The one who breaks is the not-winner.*
 [playing with toy trains] (4;10;16)

Although (64) looks superficially like a *wh*-relative, it is in all probability a quite distinct construction, based on a Cantonese one as in (65) which does use a *wh*-word, *bin1go3* 'who':

(65) *Bin1go3   zing2 laan6 zau6   syu1.*
 who   makes broken then   loses
 'Whoever breaks [it], loses.'

The structure in (65) is treated as a free relative in Matthews and Yip (1994: 113). To the extent that the only apparent examples of wh-words in relatives are such free relatives, the child's example (64) may owe more to this Cantonese construction than it does to English *wh*-relatives. A series of utterances produced by Sophie conclusively demonstrates transfer of such free relatives with *wh*-words:

(66) [entering apartment] *I bath! I always come back I bath.*
 Who bath tomorrow can go in...
 [makes bed]

Who want to sleep over here, then you can sleep.
If who want to sit on this, you can.
Daddy, you can sit on this thing, if you like. (5;01;03)

As Sophie's paraphrases with *if* show, the construction has an implicitly conditional function, which is characteristic of the Cantonese construction as in (65).

4. Discussion

We now discuss factors involved in the transfer of prenominal relatives. One set of factors is external – the dominance of Cantonese over English in our subjects, which in turn derives from the less-than-balanced input conditions described in section 2.1 above. Another set of factors involve typological characteristics of Cantonese – the relationship of relative clauses to other prenominal modification structures, and the resemblance between object relatives and main clauses.

4.1. Language dominance and developmental asynchrony

The period of transfer of prenominal modification structures in Timmy begins at age 2;07, during a period (2;00 – 2;10) in which the MLUw for Cantonese utterances is markedly ahead of that for English. Moreover, there is relatively little evidence of transfer from English to Cantonese in either child. Together, these findings implicate dominance of Cantonese as a causal factor. Yip and Matthews (2000) discuss other aspects of syntactic transfer in Timmy, including *wh*-in-situ (67) and null objects, as in (68):

(67)   *It is for what?* (2;05)

(68)   Adult: *Where shall we stick it?*
         Child: *Put here.* (2;05;05)

The occurrence of these structures is shown to be qualitatively and quantitatively distinct from that found in monolingual development. The occurrence of *wh*-in-situ and null objects peaks during the period when Timmy's MLUw for Cantonese is most clearly ahead of that for English, suggesting a close relationship between direction of transfer and language dominance.[11] In the case of Sophie, dominance of Cantonese is clearer still, based on indicators such as MLUw differential (see 2.3 above) and first use of Cantonese and English (cf. 3.3 above).[12] Language dominance must therefore be considered a major factor favouring transfer from Cantonese to English.

In section 1.1, however, we entertained another possibility raised by Paradis and Genesee (1996), which we formulated as the developmental asynchrony hypothesis. In the case of transfer at issue here, it is possible that Cantonese monolingual children's prenominal relatives in general develop earlier than English monolingual children's postnominal ones. If so, it would also be expected that Cantonese relative clauses would develop before English ones in bilingual children, thus fulfilling Paradis and Genesee's condition for transfer. This would constitute a "developmental asynchrony" in the bilingual child, who would then have reason to transfer the Cantonese structure to English (perhaps as a stop-gap measure or "relief strategy") without dominance necessarily playing a role. Unfortunately we are not able to distinguish between dominance and developmental asynchrony in this case, for two reasons:

(a) the monolingual Cantonese data needed to establish such a baseline for the acquisition of relative clauses are lacking. While corpora for monolingual Cantonese children exist, the rarity of relative clauses in spontaneous production (as noted in 2.2) means that diary and/or experimentally elicited data would be required.

(b) our subjects show clear signs of dominance, so that the effects of dominance and language-specific acquisition schedules could not be distinguished. That is, even if it were established that Cantonese object relatives typically develop earlier than their English counterparts, we would be unable to tell whether such a developmental asynchrony is responsible for transfer, as opposed to the general dominance of Cantonese, since the predictions of the two factors coincide in our case study. Studies of relatively balanced and English-dominant children, in whom dominance of Cantonese could be excluded, would be needed to test the hypothesis. If transfer of prenominal relatives were indeed observed in such children, the developmental asynchrony hypothesis would be supported.

Finally, we should note that the dominance and asynchrony accounts of transfer are not fundamentally at variance with each other. Dominance essentially means that at a given stage of development Language A is ahead of Language B in overall complexity, while developmental asynchrony refers to the phenomenon whereby specific aspects of Language A are ahead of Language B, for language-specific reasons. The actual mechanisms of transfer could well be the same in each case, i.e. the child has competence in Language A which she lacks in Language B, and some property of Language A is transferred to Language B as an interim strategy.

4.2. Relative clauses and other prenominal modifiers

As we noted in section 1.2 above, Sinitic languages are almost unique in the co-occurrence of SVO basic order with prenominal relatives. Part of the explanation for the exceptional status of Sinitic in this regard lies in the fact that relative clauses follow a consistent pattern of prenominal modification. Indeed, it can be argued that there is a continuum from adjectival modification to relative clauses, with some structures being of indeterminate or intermediate status as between adjectival modifiers and relative clauses. This unity of noun-modifying structures is a typological feature widespread in Asian languages (Comrie 1996). This proves to be a fruitful way of looking at our subjects' relative clauses. Alongside the prenominal relatives, we find PP and other phrasal modifiers in Timmy's data:

(69)   *Where is the tank of the part?* [i.e. the part of the tank] (3;02)

(70)　*Some whales is small. The school in the whale is small.*
　　　[i.e. the whale in the school] (3;09;19)

There are also examples which might be seen as intermediate between adjectival modifiers and full relative clauses:

(71)　*I like to eat no seeds inside the grapes.* [i.e. seedless grapes]
　　　(3;09;24)

(72)　*This is a nobody can find me place.* (4;00;19)

The modifying "clause" *no seeds inside* in (71) lacks a verb, while (72) lacks a preposition or other indicator of the spatial relationship between the head noun and the modifying clause *nobody can find me*.

The developmental parallel between relative clauses and other modifiers also finds support in English monolingual development, albeit this time in postnominal position. Tager-Flusberg (1989) describes an experiment in which younger children tended to produce PP modifiers, as in (73), rather than relative clauses (74):

(73)　*The boy gave the dog to* [$_{NP}$ *the bear* [$_{PP}$ *with the wagon.*]]

(74)　*The boy gave the dog to* [$_{NP}$ *the bear* [$_{CP}$ *who is holding the wagon.*]]

Tager-Flusberg concludes:

> Children may be using their knowledge of simpler constructions to guide the acquisition of more complex constructions. In this [elicitation] task both forms, prepositional phrases and relative clauses, fulfil the function adequately, but younger children used primarily simpler prepositional phrases, while older children used primarily relative clauses. Perhaps the developmental roots of relative clauses lie in simpler constructions. This study, using production data, suggests that prepositional phrases are one such possible origin… (Tager-Flusberg 1989: 157)

A particular case of the continuum scenario outlined by Comrie (1996) with regard to Japanese involves prenominal modifying phrases which are clearly clausal (rather than adjectival) and yet not prototypical relative clauses in the sense that there is no grammatical relation between the head noun and the clause; rather, there is a looser relation of association between them, analogous to that which obtains in topic-comment constructions. Such structures are equally possible in adult Cantonese.[13] In (75), for example, the instrumental relationship between *bat1* 'pen' and the predicate *waak6-waa2* 'draw pictures' is unexpressed, while in (76) there is no grammatical relation at all between *soeng2* 'pictures' and *waat6-syut3* 'ski':

(75)   Ngo5   waak6-waa2   go2   zi1   bat1
       I   draw-picture that CL   pen
       'The pen that I draw pictures [with]'

(76)   Lei5   waat6-syut3   go2   di1   soeng2
       you   slide-snow   those CL   pictures
       'The pictures of you skiing; your skiing pictures'

There is good evidence that the children's developing grammar allows modifying clause of this type, which involve no grammatical relationship between the head and the relative clause. A rare example of a clausal modifier in the longitudinal corpus data for Timmy is (77):

(77)   Co5   fei1gei1   go2   di1   ze4ze1   bei2
       sit   plane   those   CL   elder-sister   give
       ngo5   gaa3.
       me   PRT
       '(These are) given to me by those ladies on the plane.'
       (3;02;26)

Referring to a toy given to the child by the flight attendants ("big sisters"), this example could in principle be analyzed as a subject relative ("the ladies who take the plane"), with a gap in subject position as shown in (78):

(78) [[_ co5 feilgeil$_S$] go2 di1 ze4ze1 $_{NP}$] bei2 ngo5 gaa3.

More plausibly, however, the child means "the ladies associated with taking the plane", in which case the head noun *ze4ze1* 'sisters' would bear no grammatical relation to the predicate *co5 feilgeil* 'sit plane' (meaning to take a plane). Rather, it would be a relationship by way of association, of the kind often found in Chinese topic-comment structures: there would be no gap, and the structure would be intermediate between a relative clause and other premodifying phrases. A similar example is recorded in Sophie's English:

(79) *The go to Australia things!*
      [pointing to things packed for trip to Australia] (4;03;24)

This example could either be a subject relative ('the things which are going to Australia') or an associative clause ('the things involved in (our) going to Australia'). On the latter analysis, the children would be extending Comrie's "Asian" type of noun-modifying clause to their English. Some later examples from Sophie clearly call for such an "associative" analysis:

(80) *Where's my medicine? That here painful that one.*
      [pointing to gums] (4;09;11)

(81) *I want that blue thing, I go to Chinese school that.* (4;11;17)

The relative clause in (80) is intended to mean "the medicine that I use when it hurts here", in which there is no grammatical relation between the modifying phrase *here painful* and *that one* (the medicine). Similarly:

(82) *How 'bout... I wear the go P.E. shoes, that one.* (4;10;18)

Here *the go P.E. shoes* are clearly not shoes which go to P.E. (Physical Education) lessons themselves, but those which the child wears when going to P.E. lessons. This is not a subject relative, but an associative one of the kind we identified in Timmy's Cantonese (77) and Sophie's English (79).

4.3. Object relatives and parsing

A notable characteristic of the data is that the earliest prenominal relatives recorded, in both English and Cantonese, are object relatives – those in which the head noun functions as the object of the relative clause. As we showed in connection with adult Cantonese (see 1.3), it is precisely in the case of object relatives that the relative clause matches the main clause order. This resemblance has consequences for production and processing:

(i) prenominal object relatives are easily constructed using the canonical word order of a main clause (and possibly the actual structure of a main clause, if the internally-headed analysis as sketched in section 1.3 above is applicable);

(ii) if the child should parse or analyse the relative clause as a main clause, the resulting interpretation will still be similar. Our example (2) above would allow such a conjoined clause interpretation, as shown in (83):

(83) [s *Ngo5*   *zung1ji3*   *go2*   *di1*   *saam1*]
          I   like   those   CL   clothes
      [s *hou2*   *gwai3.*]
          very   expensive
      'I like the clothes (and/but) they are expensive.'

The finding that prenominal object relatives are first to emerge in our bilingual subjects may be compared with English monolingual development in which postnominal subject relatives are acquired earliest, and also most readily processed under experimental conditions (Tavakolian 1981). Given the combination of SVO and postnominal relatives, the situation in English is the reverse of that in Cantonese, and it is in subject relatives that the word order matches that of a main clause. As argued by Tavakolian (1981), a relative clause such as (84) can be given a conjoined clause interpretation as in (85):

(84)   *The rabbit [that kissed the duck] is happy.*

(85)   *The rabbit kissed the duck, (and) is happy.*

The account we have given for Cantonese makes a prediction which might be tested experimentally in future work: object relatives in Cantonese should be processed and produced by children more easily than subject relatives.

5. Conclusions

The simultaneous acquisition of Cantonese and English in bilingual children raises possible forms of transfer not seen in other language pairs. The combination of SVO word order with prenominal relative clauses, virtually unique to Sinitic languages, is a case in point. In this study of the development of relative clauses in two Cantonese-dominant bilingual subjects who have been regularly exposed to English and Cantonese from birth, two main findings have emerged. Firstly, prenominal relative clauses in Cantonese prove to be transferable to English. Despite the cross-linguistically marked status of prenominal relative clauses in SVO languages, they readily lend themselves to transfer from Cantonese to English. These prenominal relatives are invariably object relatives, in which the word order resembles that in main clauses, facilitating processing and production of this structure. Secondly, the development of postnominal relatives shows the use of resumptive pronouns in object and occasionally also in subject position. While the prenominal relatives represent a clear case of transfer, the resumptive pronoun strategy cannot plausibly be attributed to transfer as resumptive pronouns are not attested in the children's Cantonese. To the extent that different groups of learners including simultaneous bilingual children, monolingual English children and adult second learners of English all make use of resumptive pronouns in their production of relative clauses at a certain developmental stage, the resumptive pronoun strategy appears to represent an option universally available to the language learner.

A number of developmental and typological factors conspire together to favour transfer of prenominal relatives in the bilingual subjects' English. The dominance of Cantonese over English, as indicated by the MLUw differential, largely determines the directionality of transfer in the acquisition of relative clauses. The prenominal relatives share important properties with other types of prenominal modification, which surface as interlanguage structures with adjectives and prepositional phrases modifying the head noun. Comrie's (1996) suggestion of a continuum of prenominal modification structures finds developmental confirmation in the parallel development of relative clauses and other prenominal modifiers. In particular, a type of modifying clause instantiated in Timmy's Cantonese and in both children's English involves a kind of association rather than strict grammatical relationship between the head and the predicate in the prenominal modifying clause.

In addition, the prenominal object relatives, though typologically dispreferred in languages with SVO basic order, share the canonical word order of the main clause, which offsets the parsing difficulty of prenominal relatives predicted by Hawkins (1990, 1994). This also explains why only prenominal object relatives are attested in the bilingual subjects' English: prenominal relatives with other relativised positions would not preserve the canonical word order of main clause. The canonical word order proves to be a powerful strategy that overrides the potential difficulty presented by prenominal relatives in a SVO language.

Notes

* An earlier version of the paper was presented at the Annual Meeting of the American Association for Applied Linguistics in Vancouver, March 2000. We are grateful for comments from participants at this presentation including Annick De Houwer, Fred Genesee, Hiro Oshita and Johanne Paradis. We are also indebted to William O'Grady for comments on an earlier version of this paper. The research reported here was supported by two grants from the Hong Kong Research Grants Council (HKU336/94H and CUHK4002/97H). We thank each member of the research team for their help in the course of the project, especially Huang Yue Yuan, Peng Ling-Ling, Bella Leung, Simon Huang Pai-Yuan, Gene Chu, Uta Lam and Angel Chan.
1. We use the term "Sinitic languages" for what have traditionally been called "Chinese dialects" in order to reflect the magnitude of structural differences between varieties of Chinese (cf. Chappell 2001).
2. The Tibeto-Burman language Karen, which has switched from SOV to SVO order under the influence of surrounding Tai languages, apparently has prenominal as well as postnominal relatives (Solnit 1997).
3. Cantonese examples are transcribed orthographically in the JyutPing romanisation system developed by the Linguistic Society of Hong Kong. Tones are marked numerically (1: high level, 2: high rising, 3: mid level, 4: low falling, 5: low rising, and 6: low level). Abbreviations used in the glosses are CL for classifier, PFV for perfective aspect and PRT for particle.
4. In theoretical terms, while English relatives have been assumed to be formed by *wh*-movement (in the case of *wh*-relatives) or by null operator movement (for *that*-relatives), Cantonese relatives clearly do not involve such movement. Structures resulting from transfer will thus be qualitatively different from a target relative clause derived by *wh*-movement. In the case of Cantonese adult second language learners of English, Hawkins and Chan (1997) argue that their representation of English relatives involves pronominal binding by a base-generated null topic, rather than operator movement.
5. We are grateful to Brian MacWhinney for making the bilingual corpus available for world-wide access at Carnegie Mellon University. The corpus data are deposited at the CHILDES archive at http://childes.psy.cmu.edu under the heading "bilingual corpora" and include sample transcripts linked to audio and video recordings.
6. Chiu Chow (or Chaozhou), the ancestral language of a sizeable minority in Hong Kong, is spoken in eastern Guangdong province and belongs to the southern Min dialect group. Although diverging from Cantonese in many respects, it shares the broad typological characteristics at issue here, including prenominal relatives. The children have some passive knowledge of Chiu Chow but seldom produce it.

7. The question of what role the Filipino English spoken by the domestic helpers has in the children's language development is a pertinent one. As far as the features discussed in this paper are concerned, we observe that the English of the helpers conforms to standard English: they do not, for example, use prenominal relatives.
8. We use MLUw (mean length of utterance in words) rather than MLUm (mean length of utterance in morphemes). Huang (1999) compared the MLUm and MLUw of Timmy's English data and showed that the two methods of calculation yielded essentially the same pattern of development.
9. There is also one example of what appears to be a headless free relative in Sophie's data:
   You already eat is what? (3;11;12) [What is it that you already ate?]
10. In the examples elicited by Mckee et al. (1998), the nouns *strawberries* in (62) and *bicycle* in (63) indicate the target head nouns of the relative clauses.
11. Peng (1998) investigated the development of *wh*-interrogatives in Timmy and found a stage where Cantonese-based in-situ structures were produced in English during a period when Cantonese dominance prevailed. Huang (1999) found that null objects in Timmy's English showed both quantitative and qualitative differences from the monolingual counterparts: the higher percentage of null objects and transfer-based null object structures were also found in the period of Cantonese dominance.
12. The MLUw differential for Sophie applies to age 1;06-3;00;09, as discussed in section 2.3. At the time of writing, transcripts of the recordings, and hence MLU values, are not yet available for the subsequent period 3;00-4;00 in which relative clauses appear. Our observations suggest, however, that the pattern of Cantonese dominance persists into this period and beyond.
13. We are grateful to Professor Rudolf de Rijk of Leiden University for drawing our attention to the possibility of relative clauses which lack strict grammatical relations and their potential significance for Cantonese grammar.

References

Alsagoff, Lubna, and Ho Chee Lick
    1998   Relative clauses in Singapore English. *World Englishes* 17: 127-138.
Braidi, Susan.
    1999   *The Acquisition of Second-Language Syntax*. London: Arnold.
Chappell, Hilary (ed.)
    2001   *Sinitic Grammar: Synchronic and Diachronic Perspectives*. Oxford: Oxford University Press.

Comrie, Bernard
    1996   The unity of noun-modifying clauses in Asian languages. *Proceedings of the 4th International Symposium on Pan-Asiatic Linguistics*, 1077-1088.

De Houwer, Annick.
    1990   *The Acquisition of Two Languages from Birth: A Case Study.* Cambridge: Cambridge University Press.

Döpke, Susanne.
    1992   *One Parent, One Language: An Interactional Approach.* Amsterdam: John Benjamins.

Döpke, Susanne
    1997   Is the simultaneous acquisition of two languages in early childhood equal to acquiring each of two languages individually? In: Eve Clark (ed.), *Proceedings of the 28th Annual Child Language Research Forum.* Stanford: Center for the Study of Language and Information.

Döpke, Susanne
    1998   Competing language structures: The acquisition of verb placement by bilingual German-English children. *Journal of Child Language* 25: 555-584.

Döpke, Susanne (ed.)
    2000   *Cross-Linguistic Structures in Simultaneous Bilingualism.* Amsterdam: John Benjamins.

Dryer, Matthew
    1992   The Greenbergian word order correlations. *Language* 68: 81-138.

Gawlitzek-Maiwald, Irene, and Rosemary Tracy
    1996   Bilingual bootstrapping. *Linguistics* 34: 901-926.

Genesee, Fred
    1989   Early bilingual development: One language or two? *Journal of Child Language* 6: 161-179.

Genesee, Fred, Elena Nicoladis, and Johanne Paradis
    1995   Language differentiation in early bilingual development. *Journal of Child Language* 22: 611-631.

Gass, Susan, and Josh Ard
    1984   Second language acquisition and the ontology of language universals. In: William Rutherford (ed.), *Language Universals and Second Language Acquisition*, 33-68. Amsterdam: John Benjamins.

Gisborne, Nikolas.
    2000   Relative clauses in Hong Kong English. *World Englishes* 19: 357-371.

Gupta, Anthea Fraser
 1994 *The Step-Tongue: Children's English in Singapore*. Clevedon, UK: Multilingual Matters.
Hawkins, John A.
 1990 A parsing theory of word order universals. *Linguistic Inquiry* 21: 223-262.
Hawkins, John A.
 1994 *A Performance Theory of Order and Constituency*. Cambridge: Cambridge University Press.
Hawkins, John A.
 1999 Processing complexity and filler-gap dependencies across grammars. *Language* 75: 244-285.
Hawkins, Roger, and Cecilia Yuet-Hung Chan
 1997 The partial availability of Universal Grammar in second language acquisition: The 'failed functional features hypothesis'. *Second Language Research* 13: 187-226.
Huang, Pai-Yuan
 1999 The development of null arguments in a Cantonese-English bilingual child. Unpublished M.Phil. Thesis, Chinese University of Hong Kong.
Hulk, Aafke, and Elizabeth van der Linden
 1996 Language mixing in a French-Dutch bilingual child. *EUROSLA 6: A Selection of Papers*, 89-101. Amsterdam: VU Uitgeverij.
Hyltenstam, Kenneth
 1984 The use of typological markedness conditions as predictors in second language acquisition: The case of pronominal copies in relative clauses. In: Roger Andersen (ed.), S*econd Languages: A Cross-Linguistic Perspective*, 39-58. Rowley, Mass.: Newbury House.
Keenan, Edward
 1985 Relative clauses. In: Timothy Shopen (ed.), *Language Typology and Syntactic Description*, Vol. II: *Complex Constructions*, 141-170. Cambridge: Cambridge University Press.
Keenan, Edward, and Bernard Comrie
 1977 Noun phrase accessibility and universal grammar. *Linguistic Inquiry* 8: 63-99.
Matthews, Stephen, and Louisa Yeung
 2001 Processing motivations for topicalization in Cantonese. In: Kaoru Horie and Shigeru Sato (eds.), *Cognitive-Functional Linguistics in an East Asian Context*, 81-102. Tokyo: Kurosio Publishers.
Matthews, Stephen, and Virginia Yip
 1994 *Cantonese: A Comprehensive Grammar*. London: Routledge.

Matthews, Stephen, and Virginia Yip
    2001   The structure and stratification of relative clauses in contemporary Cantonese. In: Hilary Chappell (ed.).

McKee, Cecile, Dana McDaniel, and Jesse Snedeker
    1998   Relative clauses children say. *Journal of Psycholinguistic Research* 27: 573-596.

Meisel, Jürgen, M.
    1989   Early differentiation of languages in bilingual children. In: Kenneth Hyltenstam and Lorraine Obler (eds.), *Bilingualism Across the Lifespan: Aspects of Acquisition, Maturity, and Loss*, 13-40. Cambridge: Cambridge University Press.

Müller, Natascha
    1998   Transfer in bilingual first language acquisition. *Bilingualism: Language and Cognition* 1.3: 151-171.

Newbrook, Mark
    1999   Which way? *That* way – relative clauses in Asian Englishes. *World Englishes* 17: 43-59.

Paradis, Johanne
    2000   Beyond 'one system or two': Degrees of separation between the languages of French-English bilingual children. In Susanne Döpke (ed.), *Cross-Linguistic Structures in Simultaneous Bilingualism*, 175-200. Amsterdam: John Benjamins.

Paradis, Johanne, and Fred Genesee
    1996   Syntactic acquisition in bilingual children: Autonomous or interdependent? *Studies in Second Language Acquisition* 18: 1-25.

Peng, Ling-Ling
    1998   The development of wh-questions in a Cantonese/English bilingual child. Unpublished M.Phil. Thesis, Chinese University of Hong Kong.

Pérez-Leroux, Ana
    1995   Resumptives in the acquisition of relative clauses. *Language Acquisition* 4: 105-138.

Saunders, George
    1988   *Bilingual Children: From Birth to Teens*. Clevedon: Multilingual Matters.

Solnit, David
    1997   *Eastern Kayah Li*. Honolulu: University of Hawaii Press.

Tager-Flusberg, Helen
    1989   Putting words together: Later developments in the pre-school years. In: Jean Berko-Gleason (ed.), *The Development of Language*, 135-65. Second Edition. Columbus, Ohio: Merrill Publishing Company.

Tavakolian, Susan
   1981   The conjoined clause analysis of relative clauses. In: Susan Tavakolian (ed.), *Language Acquisition and Linguistic Theory*, 167-87. Cambridge: MIT Press.

Yip, Virginia, and Stephen Matthews
   2000   Syntactic transfer in a Cantonese-English bilingual child. *Bilingualism: Language and Cognition* 3: 193-207.

Yip, Virginia, and Stephen Matthews
   2001   *Intermediate Cantonese: A Grammar and Workbook*. London: Routledge.

Learner varieties and language types. The case of indefinite pronouns in non-native Italian[*]

Giuliano Bernini

1. Introduction

This paper investigates in a functional framework the particular case of the development of lexical repertoire and semantics of indefinite pronouns in second language acquisition of Italian. The investigation pursues two major aims of general relevance for both second language acquisition research and typology.

The first aim is the assessment of the empirical relevance of second language acquisition research for the validation of principles proposed in typological studies in order to account for the structural regularities found in fully-fledged languages, as originally advocated by Comrie (1984). This perspective has a fairly long tradition of studies, which may be illustrated by Hawkins's (1987) employment of implicational universals as predictors of the route of development of second languages, relative timing of acquisition of different structures, and expected types of error; this perspective may be further illustrated by the more recent investigation of the learners' (re)-construction of the means for clause connection available in Italian as the target language, carried out by Giacalone Ramat (1999a). The implicational hierarchy proposed on the basis of cross-linguistic evidence, governing the use of different verb forms in subordinate clauses in accordance with the higher or lesser degree of integration of the states of affairs described in the clauses to be conjoined is validated by the acquisitional path followed by the learners.[1]

The second aim is the tentative definition of the position learner varieties may be assigned among language types as identified on the basis of regularities found in fully-fledged languages. This implies that learner varieties are not considered here as imperfect realisations of the respective target language, but as systems in their own right, as advocated in Klein and Perdue (1997) in the functional perspective known as the "Basic Variety" approach, the framework in which the present investigation was carried out. The major points characterising this approach are the following.

(a) Organisation of the utterance and expression of complex semantic relations such as temporal, spatial and scope relations show a remarkable degree of systematicity in learners at different stages of acquisition, both initial and advanced ones, despite the different amount of lexical items and of syntactic rules available to the learners at each stage (cf. Dietrich et al. 1995, Becker and Carroll 1997, Dimroth and Klein 1995). The systematic behaviour appears to result from the interplay of a small set of phrasal, semantic, and pragmatic organisational principles (Klein and Perdue 1992).

(b) Salient in the acquisition process is the stage observed in most learners of different European languages and called the "Basic Variety". This appears to be a stable system "... largely (though not totally) independent of the specifics of source and target language organisation, ... simple, versatile and highly efficient for most communicative purposes" (Klein and Perdue 1997: 303). Stability is mainly effected in the Basic Variety by the interplay of the semantic principle called "Controller first" and by the pragmatic principle called "Focus last", which constrain the phrasal organisation of the utterance and govern the position of NPs with respect to the verb in the absence of inflectional morphology.[2] The verb appears in an invariable form, in Italian mostly the third person singular of the present indicative.

(c) The development beyond the Basic Variety towards more complex forms of organisation of the utterance is the result of the solutions elaborated by the learners to cope with problems of expression derived, e.g., by the application of conflicting principles, as in the case of the position of a focal NP whose referent happens to have a high degree of control over the state of affairs described in the utterance. The new morphosyntactic means introduced into the learner varieties –such as focalisation devices solving the conflict between the semantic principle "Controller first" and the pragmatic principle "Focus last" alluded to above – define post-basic stages where a growing role is played by inflectional morphology and syntactic rules as the learner variety develops toward the target language.[3]

Functional motivations of the shaping of linguistic expressions are shared by the Basic Variety approach as summarised in points (a) to (c) above within second language acquisition research and by the typological approach, constituting the common ground for a fruitful interaction in the consideration of the regularities found at cross-linguistic level. In fact, as neatly summarised by Cristofaro and Ramat (1999: 32) in their introduction to a collection of seminal papers in the development of typological studies, the typological approach hypothesises that:

(i)   different language types obey different functional motivations, and satisfaction of different motivations effects in each case the alternation of different types;
(ii) language structures are employed by the speakers in order to cope with particular communicative requirements;
(iii) grammar is a temporary compromise solution satisfying in each case one or the other of the communicative requirements.[4]

On this common methodological and theoretical background of the Basic Variety approach within second language acquisition research and of typology within theoretical linguistics, the case of the acquisition of indefinite pronouns by second language learners of Italian is considered with reference to the implicational organisation of the functions of indefinite pronouns as elaborated on a cross-linguistic basis by Haspelmath (1997). After a short presentation of Martin Haspelmath's framework, the development of indefinite pronouns in Italian L2 is described on the basis of the data drawn from eight mostly untutored learners of Italian with different social and first language backgrounds, comprised in the data base of the Pavia Project on second language acquisition of Italian. The paths of acquisition found in the eight learners considered are then discussed with respect to the universals of indefinite pronouns found in Haspelmath's investigation and to the definition of the language type(s) instantiated by learner varieties with respect to fully-fledged languages as effected by the interplay of different functional motivations.

It is noteworthy that indefinite pronouns can be expressed by alternative lexical means and do not belong to the functions learners cannot do without, such as negation. This may be illustrated by the case of indefinite negative pronouns, whose meaning can be construed by the use of generic nouns which receive a non-referential interpretation under the scope of negation, as in examples (1) and (2).[5]

(1)   Peter, 2 months, 28 days
      perchè sì   perchè in   fotografia   ci   sono
      because yes   because in   picture   there   are
      cinque persone   tutte persone   ragazza
      five   persons   all   persons   girl
      **not   fair* @   no   persone   ragazzo   in*
      not   fair   no   persons   boy   in
      fotografia
      picture

      'Because in the picture there are five people and all people are girls. This is not fair. Nobody is a boy in the picture/there are no boys in the picture'

(2)   Ababa, 1 year, 28 days (I = Interviewer; A = Ababa)
   I. *ma   la   carne:-così,   ?c'   era?*
      but   the   meat   so   there   was
      'But was there any meat [to buy]?'

A. *car/   anche carne **non** c'   era-   **tutto***
   mea/   also   meat   not   there was   all
   'There was not even meat – nothing'

Example (1) illustrates the case of the alternative expression of the missing item for 'nobody' (Italian *nessuno*) by means of the generic noun for 'persons' preceded by the negative particle resorted to by a multilingual initial learner (Cantonese, Malay and English); (2) is a case of alternative expression of the item for 'nothing' (Italian *niente*) by means of the universal quantifier in a negative context, found in an advanced Eritrean Tigrinya speaker as a rhetoric device for increasing the dramatic force of her narrative.

2. A typological framework for the description of indefinite pronouns

As anticipated above, the typological framework adopted for the investigation of indefinite pronouns in L2 Italian is the one elaborated by Martin Haspelmath (1997) on the basis of two samples comprising 40 and respectively 100 languages, construed according to different criteria. As a widespread, although apparently not universal feature of language (Haspelmath 1997: 57), repertoires of indefinite pronouns appear to be organised across languages in series of items sharing the same functional domain, as will be explained below (Haspelmath 1997: 21-31). Italian, as the case in point, has three series of indefinite pronouns, listed in (3), the number of series comprised in Haspelmath's 40 languages sample ranging from two – as e.g. in Ancash Quechua – to seven – as in Russian (cf. pp. 68-75).

(3) a. *qualcuno* 'somebody', *qualcosa* 'something', *qualche* 'some'.
    b. *nessuno* 'nobody', *niente* 'nothing', *mai* 'never', *nessuno* 'no'.
    c. *chiunque* 'whoever', *dovunque* 'wherever', *comunque* 'however', *qualsiasi* 'any'.

Individual indefinite pronouns may combine the expression of indefiniteness and of one of a series of ontological categories such as person, thing, time, place, manner. These two components may be coded in a transparent way, as in Italian *qual*[*c*]+*cosa* 'INDEF+thing', or fused in the indefinite pronoun, as in the case of Italian *mai* 'NEG.INDEF.time'.[6]

Indefinite pronouns are used across languages for nine functions, which are shown to be organised on the basis of implicational relationships and which may be represented as in the implicational map reported here as figure 1 and drawn from Haspelmath (1997: 64).[7]

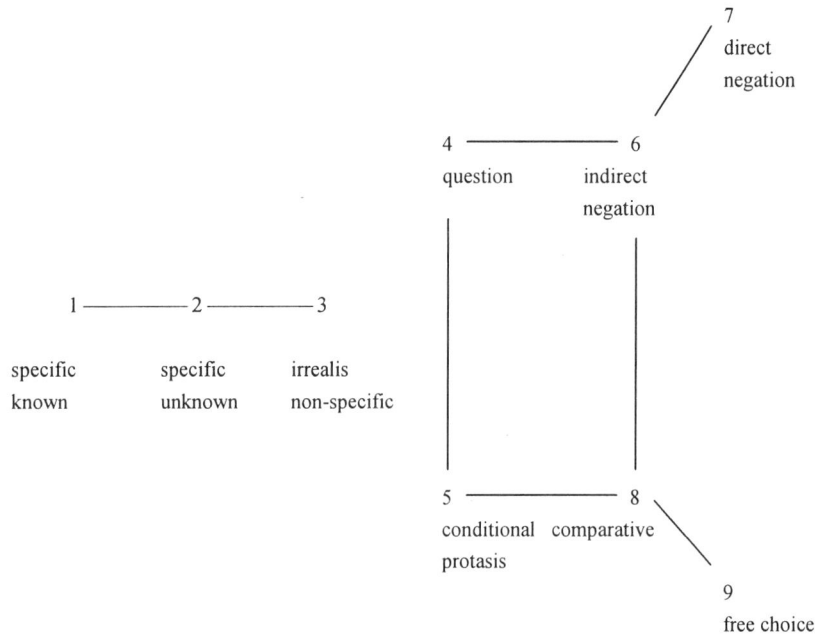

Figure 1. The two-dimensional implicational map for indefinite pronoun functions (Haspelmath 1997: 64)

The implicational map defines the semantic space which indefinite pronouns appear to cover across languages and at the same time constrains the possible range of polysemy of indefinite pronouns in individual languages (Haspelmath 1997: 62). Three major regularities characterise the distribution of indefinite pronouns among the nine functions of the implicational map and the lexicalisation patterns of indefinite pronouns inventories. As to the functional distribution, indefinite pronouns must cover adjacent functions as reported on the map. The three series of Italian indefinite pronouns listed in (3), e.g., distribute over the functional space as in figure 2.

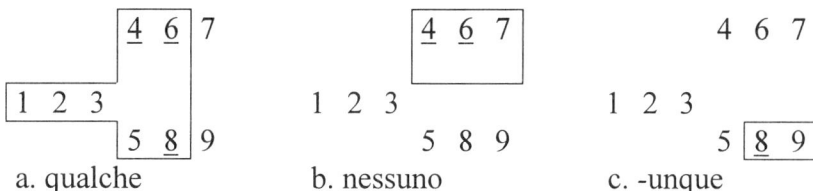

a. qualche   b. nessuno   c. -unque

Figure 2. Italian indefinite pronouns (number of functions where different series overlap are underlined)

As apparent in figure 2, series may overlap in some functions, as in the case of functions 4 and 6 for the *qualche* and the *nessuno* series and in the case of function 8 for the *qualche* and the *-unque* series. However, no gap is allowed in the area of distribution of individual series, and no gap is actually comprised in the area of distribution of the three series of Italian.

As to lexicalisation patterns of indefinite pronouns inventories, cross-linguistic regularities point to a polarisation of the semantic space represented in the implicational map toward the functions on the left and the functions on the lower right side: in fact no language combines both functions 9 and 8 with function 1 (Haspelmath 1997: 77). In other words, languages may lexicalise by means of different series function 1 on the one hand and functions 8 and 9 on the other hand, or else may combine functions 1 and 8 on the one hand and 9 and 8 on the other hand; however no language is attested where an indefinite pronouns series combine all three functions 1, 8 and 9. The former case may be illustrated by Ancash Quechua, where functions 1 and 2 are covered by a series represented by bare interrogative pronouns, which are in opposition to a second series, formed with the suffix *-pis*, which covers all remaining functions 3456789 (Haspelmath 1997: 310). The latter of the two attested combinations mentioned above is illustrated by the two major indefinites of Swedish, i.e. *någon*, which distributes among functions 12345678, and *som helst*, whose range comprises both functions 8 and 9 (Haspelmath 1997: 249). Italian shows, as Swedish does, the case of a language which combines functions 1 and 8 on the one hand, as in the *qualche* series, which distributes over functions 1234568, and functions 8 and 9 on the other hand, as in the *-unque* series – cf. figure 2.

Function 7 on the implicational map may be considered as a subordinate pole of lexicalisation with respect to the two main poles represented by functions 1 and both 8 and 9, and may give rise to negative indefinite pronouns. These may be defined, although not in a straightforward way, on the basis of their ability to occur in elliptical contexts with intrinsically negative meaning, as in (4).

(4)   a.   Chi hai visto? — *Nessuno*.
        b.   Who did you see? — *Nobody*.

The ability for an indefinite pronoun with the direct negation function to occur in elliptical contexts with intrinsically negative meaning appears to be in inverse proportion to the extent of its polysemy, or, in other terms, to the range of adjacent functions it may cover besides direct negation (Haspelmath 1997: 198). In Italian, the negative indefinite pronouns of the *nessuno* series distribute over two functions beside direct negation, as shown in figure 2 above; in English, the negative indefinites of the *no* series are only found in the direct negation function, contrary to the non-negative indefinites of the *any* series, covering functions 45689 besides direct negation (cf. Haspelmath 1997: 68).

The functional and cognitive relevance of Haspelmath's implicational map of indefinite pronouns functions and the lexicalisation patterns found in the organisation of indefinite pronouns inventories across languages which may derived from it, makes the implicational map a useful frame of reference also for the assessment of the ways in which second language learners with different source languages reconstruct the target system, as will be discussed in the next sections.

3. Indefinite pronouns in L2 Italian
3.1. The learners

Acquisition of indefinite pronouns in L2 Italian is considered on the basis of longitudinal recordings of eight mainly untutored learners of Italian[8] comprised in the data base of the Pavia Project, as anticipated in the introductory section, and mainly consisting of narratives and free conversations between an interviewer and the learner(s).[9] The features of the learners considered here are displayed in table 1.[10] The eight learners, four women and four men aged between 12 and 48, allow the observation of different acquisition stages, assessed on the basis of the features differentiating them from the ones defining the Basic Variety, as explained in the introductory section. In particular, the poor lexical stock of content words found in pre-basic varieties (cf. Hagos and Peter) does not show a consistent differentiation of nouns and verbs and only allows the learners to construe the utterance according to a topic-focus pattern. On the other hand, initial post-basic varieties (cf. Chu, Tughiascin, Frieda) are characterised by a consistent tense/aspect opposition in the verb between a semantically unmarked base form corresponding to the third or to the second person singular of the present indicative of the target (e.g. *lavora/lavori* 'to work') and a form corresponding to the past participle of the target (e.g. *lavorato* 'worked'), semantically marked for the perfective past. Advanced post-basic varieties (cf. Xiao, Ababa) show some complexification in verbal morphology with addition of imperfective past and of future forms, and in clause structure with development of subordination.

Table 1. The learners

Learner, age, sex	Length of stay in Italy at 1st recording	First language	Input	Learning speed	Learner variety
Xiao, 12, f	1y. 6m.	Wú Chinese	frequent, varied	slow	advanced post-basic
Hagos, 15, m	21 days	Tigrinya	infrequent reduced	slow	pre-basic
Chu, 17, m	11 months	Wú Chinese	frequent varied	slow	initial post-basic
Markos, 20, m	1 month	Tigrinya	frequent varied	fast	basic > post-basic
Ababa, 21, f	1 year	Tigrinya	frequent varied	fast	post-basic
Peter, 25, m	25 days	Cantonese, Malay, English	infrequent reduced	slow	pre-basic > basic
Tughiascin, 45, f	4 years	Wú Chinese	infrequent reduced	fossilised	initial post-basic
Frieda, 48, f	6 months	German	infrequent reduced	fossilised	initial post-basic

Besides the fossilised learners Tughiascin and Frieda, the remaining six learners are either fast or slow learners – cf. Markos, Ababa vs. Xiao, Hagos, Chu, Peter. Slow rate of learning is not directly dependent on reduced input, as shown by Xiao and Chu, who are enrolled in public schools and are therefore exposed to the wide range of registers provided by teachers during classes and by school mates during play time. Other factors are at work in such cases, individual as well as social ones, to which typological distance of first and second language might be tentatively added.[11] In the case of the Chinese learners, some degree of enclosure of the ethnic group they belong too must be considered too, as is the case for Tughiascin, who had been living for 4 years in Italy at the time of her first recording but was in actual contact with Italian since only one year.

As displayed in table 1, the learners' first languages are German (cf. Frieda), Tigrinya – the Semitic language of Eritrea – (cf. Hagos, Markos, Ababa), Wú Chinese – spoken in the Shanghai area – (cf. Xiao, Chu, Tughiascin). These three learners have some knowledge of Mandarin Chinese too as the official language (*Pǔ Tóng Huà*) of the People's Republic of China. The learner called Peter is a multilingual subject with Cantonese and Malay as first languages and English as the actual primary language, i.e. the major language used for communication in the factory where Peter works as an engineer and the language of the university education Peter received in the United Kingdom.

The learners' first languages are representatives of language types partly quite different from Italian in either morphology or syntax or both. Wú Chinese and Cantonese are isolating and SVO, Malay has some agglutinative, mainly derivational morphology and SVO syntax, Tigrinya is inflectional and SOV, finally German, as is well known, is inflectional and V2/SOV and English is partly inflectional and SVO. As to indefinite pronouns, two major characteristics may be pointed to here, disregarding Wú Chinese and Malay, for which no reliable data on indefinite pronouns are available, and comprising Mandarin Chinese as one of the languages known by the three Chinese learners.[12]

The first point pertains the lexical type of the indefinite pronouns found in the languages at issue. English and German, as Italian, possess separate sets of indefinite pronouns distributing over a larger or over a restricted number of adjacent functions, cf. Eng. *somebody, anybody, nobody*; Ger. *etwas, irgend, je, jeder, niemand*.[13] In Mandarin Chinese and Cantonese the functions of indefinite pronouns are mainly formed by means of question words, e.g. Mandarin Chinese *shénme* 'what', Cantonese *bīngo dōu* (lit. 'which all') 'any', or generic nouns in existential constructions, e.g. Mandarin Chinese *yǒu rén* (lit. 'exist man') 'someone', Cantonese *móuh yàhn* (lit. 'not-exist man') 'nobody'.[14] Tigrinya shares with Chinese and Cantonese the use of generic nouns accompanied by indefiniteness markers, e.g. *gälä säb* (lit. 'some person') 'somebody', *ḥadä säb* (lit. 'one person') 'anybody', which can appear in existential constructions too. Tigrinya free choice indefinites are derived from relative clauses, as *zətäräxbä* 'what you find' (*zə-* 'REL').[15]

The second point to be touched with respect to the indefinite pronouns of the learners' first languages pertains the presence of free standing negative indefinites, i.e. of negative indefinites able to occur in elliptical contexts such as the reply exemplified in (4). English and German share with Italian free standing negative pronouns (cf. (4) and Ger. *Wen hast du gesehen? – Niemanden*). Mandarin Chinese and Cantonese, on the contrary, lack free standing indefinite pronouns. In fact the items used for the 'direct negation' function in Haspelmath's implicational map reported in figure 1 cover a wider area of adjoining functions.[16] Finally, according to grammatical descriptions, Tigrinya also lacks true negative indefinites. However, in colloquial varieties, the compound form *wala ḥadä* used in elliptical contexts and reported in (5), can be used in the direct negation function as well.[17]

(5)
a. *(ḥadä)säb   rə'a-ka-do?   —   Wala ḥadä*
   one person   see:PERF-2SG.M-INT   nobody
   'Did you see anyone? – Nobody'

b. | ***Wala ḥadä*** | *melsi* | *zə-fällit̤* |
| --- | --- | --- |
| nobody | answer | REL:3SG.M-know:IMPF |

yällo-n
NEG:be:3SG.M-NEG

'(There is) nobody (who) knows the answer'

On the basis of the general picture of indefinites in Chinese dialects, a set of negative indefinites may be supposed to be absent in the language background of the three Chinese learners. The remaining five learners can be said to possess negative indefinites in their language background, either as a major category, as in the cases of Frieda and of Peter, whose primary language is English, or as an available choice, as in the case of the Tigrinya speakers. Moreover, it should be also noticed that the two older Tigrinya speakers Ababa and Markos had had some contact with English prior to Italian, English being used as a means of instruction in Eritrean secondary schools.

3.2. The data

The construction of the system of Italian indefinite pronouns is presented in this section, starting with the order of emergence of the three series of indefinite pronouns – the *qualche* series, the *nessuno* series, and the *-unque* series as reported in (3) and with the constitution of their functional domains on Haspelmath's implicational map as reported in figure 1. As will be explained below, the lexicalisation pattern in L2 Italian starts with the *nessuno*-series of negative indefinite pronouns, whose acquisition will be examined in detail with respect to the lexical items involved and to their interaction with sentence negation.

3.2.1. Order of emergence of the series of indefinite pronouns: forms and functions.

The three series of Italian indefinite pronouns emerge in the order shown in table 2. Negative indefinites, i.e. the *nessuno* series, precedes the two series of 'positive' indefinites and, of these two series, the *qualche* series precedes the *-unque* series. The order of emergence of the three series is also mirrored in the growing lexical repertoire of each series across the learners as shown in table 2.

Table 2. Order of emergence of indefinite pronouns series

	nessuno series >			*qualche* series			*-unque* series
	niente 'nothing'	*nessuno* 'nobody'	*mai* 'never'	*qualche* 'some'	*qualcosa* 'something'	*qualcuno* 'somebody'	*qualsiasi* 'any'
Hagos	(+)*	–	–	–	–	–	–
Peter	+	+	–	–	–	–	–
Chu	+	+	+	–	–	–	–
Tughiascin	+	+	+	+	–	–	–
Markos	+	+	+	+	+	+	–
Frieda	+	+	+	+	+	+	–
Ababa	+	+	+	+	+	+	–
Xiao	+	+	+	+	+	+	+

**niente* is used by Hagos as a general negator, see below.

The first item to enter a learner variety is *niente*, first used as a general negator as in example (6), and only later as an indefinite – as will be explained in detail below – followed by the other two negative indefinites of the *nessuno* series and by the items of the *qualche* series.

(6) Hagos, 6 months, 22 days
  I. ma   ?non vai   neanche   a   giocare
      but not   you-go neither   to   play-INF
      a   pallone?
      to   ball
      'Aren't you going to play soccer?'
  H. %   **nente- pallone**%
          nothing ball
      'I don't (play) soccer'

On the other hand, in the last series to emerge, the *-unque* series in the function of "free choice", the only item found in the learner varieties is *qualsiasi* 'any' in adjectival form, as illustrated in Xiao's example reported in (7).

(7)   Xiao, 2 years, 9 months, 17 days
 I: e   la   tua   mamma   ?meglio   o
      and   the   your   mother   better   or
      peggio   *del*   *tuo*   *papà?*
      worse   of-the your   father
      'And is your mother better or worse than your father?'
 X: @   *peggio*
                worse
      'Worse'
      mia   *madre* *non*   *sa*   *niente*
      my   mother not   knows   nothing
      'My mother knows nothing'
      [...]
      mio   *padre* +   **qualsiasi**   **cosa**   *lo*   *sa*
      my   father   any   thing   it   knows
      'My father knows anything'
 I: *qualsiasi*   *cosa?*
      any   thing
      'Anything?'
 X: *!non!*   *tutto* *ma:*   *mh* + *non*   *so*   *cosa*
      not   all   but   mh   not   I-know   what
      'Not everything, but, I don't know what'

The order of emergence of negative indefinites and of the *qualche* series can be detected in a longitudinal perspective in Markos's corpus; on the other hand the order of emergence of the *qualche* series and the *-unque* series can be observed in a longitudinal perspective in Xiao's corpus. *Niente* as a negative indefinite is found in Markos after 2 months and 22 days since arrival in Italy, whereas *qualcosa* 'something' is first used after 5 months of stay in Italy. *Qualcosa* appears in Xiao's recordings after 1 year, 9 months and 22 days of stay in Italy, whereas *qualsiasi cosa*, as reported in (7), emerges almost one year later.

As to the functional domain of the learners' indefinite pronouns, negative indefinites first appear as free standing negative pronouns or in the "direct negation" function; items belonging to the *qualche* series appear in the "specific unknown" function and the only item of the *-unque* series in the "free choice" function already exemplified above, as illustrated in figure 3.

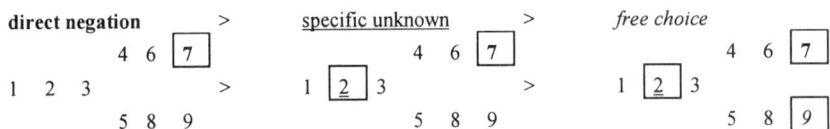

Figure 3. Functional domains of emerging indefinites

"Direct negation" and "specific unknown" as the functions *nessuno* and *qualche* indefinites are used in when they first occur in the learner varieties are illustrated in examples (8) and (9).

(8) Chu, 1 year, 6 months, 5 days (first occurrence of *nessuno*)

qua	lui	eh eh +		vedere eh		++	dietro
here	he	eh eh		see-INF eh			behind
di	lui	eh ++	mh+++		**nessuno** p/		eh +++
of	him	eh	mh		no		eh
nessuno	mh	pampino					
no	mh	child					

'Here he can see no child behind himself'

(9) Markos, 5 months, 8 days (Retelling of an illustrated story)

M. *secondo   me*
   according   me
   'In my opinion'
I. *eh*
   eh
M. *l'   uomo- ha   trovato-   sì*
   the   man   has   found   yes
   ha   trovato-   quel   gatto
   has   found   that   cat

'The man has found that cat'
I. *mh*
mh
M. *quando   lui   ha   mangiato   **qualcosa***
   when   he   has   eaten   something
   sull'   albero   ?no?
   on-the   tree   no
   'when the cat (= he) had eaten something which was on the tree'

On the basis of the available data it is not possible to reach definitive results on the ways in which learners organise the semantic space reproduced in figure 1 in their second language beyond the basic functions with which single indefinites enter into interlanguage as illustrated above. However, it is possible to recognise general trends of development in the widening of the original functional range of the single series of indefinite pronouns. Some clues seem to point to a certain relevance of the principle of adjacency also in acquisition: as a matter of fact, early uses of the *qualche* series in Markos show a development toward the area of the non-specific, irrealis functions 3 and 5, as illustrated in (10), line 12, with respect to line 6.

(10) Markos, 6 months, 27 days
      (Discussing the chances of being allowed to return to his home country and the potential danger of being observed in Italy by the Ethiopian intelligence service)
   I. *ho   capi/   le   spie,   ci   sono*
      have:1SG   underst   the   spies   there   are
      'I understand. Spies are there'

   M. *sì*
      yes
6   **siaiei*,   *siaiei*   o   così   **qualcuno***
      CIA   CIA   or   so   somebody
      'Yes, somebody such as CIA'
      allora   se   loro   non   bugiàno   così   posso,

	then	if	they	not	they-report[?]	so	I-can
	andare						
	go-INF						
	'If they don't spy/report[?] I can go back'[18]						
12	*se*	*ho*	*trovato*	***qualcosa***	*non-*	*non*	
	if	I-have	found	something	not	not	
	posso	*tornare*					
	I-can	return-INF					
	'but if they (should) find something/anything (about me), I cannot go back'						

Furthermore, the variable use of *qualcosa* 'something' in direct negation function with the meaning of 'nothing', found in advanced learners as Xiao, Frieda, Ababa, and the absence of uses of negative indefinites in positive contexts shows that the widening of the functional domain of single series of indefinite pronouns involve the positive series and not the negative one. *Qualcosa* in direct negation function is illustrated in (11), drawn from Ababa's corpus.

(11) Ababa, 1 year, 6 months, 28 days
(talking about camels)

I. | *ah,* | *perchè non* | | *fa* | *rumore* |
|---|---|---|---|---|
| ah | because not | | makes | noise |

'Ah it isn't noisy'

A. | *eh,* | *anche* | *non-* / | ***non*** | *ha* | *bisogno* | *di* |
|---|---|---|---|---|---|---|
| eh | also | not | not | has | need | of |

qualcosa
something

'Moreover it doesn't need anything'

quando	*beve_*	*acqua* =
when	drinks	water

I. | | = | *è* | *a* | *posto* |
|---|---|---|---|---|
| | | is | at | place |

'When it drinks water... – it is ok'

3.2.2. Negative indefinites and sentence negation

In the preceding section it has been shown that the *nessuno* series of Italian negative indefinites is the first series to emerge in interlanguage. It is therefore interesting and appropriate to look in some detail at potential regularities in the establishment of this indefinite pronouns series across learners.

Emergence of negative indefinites is quite early: they are already found in the stage called the Basic Variety, as shown in table 3.

Table 3. Development of the repertoire of negative indefinites

Learner	Learner variety (> 'develops to')	Presence of single negative indefinites (> indicates order of emergence in the recordings)
Hagos	Pre-basic	niente as a general negator
Peter	Pre-basic > Basic	nessuno (1occurrence only at 6m.) > niente (6m 13d)
Chu	Initial post-basic	niente (1y 2m 15d [?]) > nessuno, mai (1y 6m 5d)
Markos	Basic > Post-basic	mai (2m 6d) > niente > nessuno (3m 12d)
Tughiascin	Post-basic	all items
Frieda	Post-basic	all items
Ababa	Post-basic	all items
Xiao	Advanced post-basic	all items

In the overall development from pre-basic to basic to post-basic varieties, negative indefinites represent a stage of complexification of the learners' negative utterances and their introduction presupposes the establishment of some means for expressing utterance negation. In particular, the development of a repertoire of negative indefinites goes along with the establishment of target-like preverbal negation in the Basic Variety by means of the target negator *non* or of the non-target negator *no*, actually used for holophrastic negation in responses in native Italian.[19]

As displayed in table 3, a full inventory of negative indefinites is found since the first recording in the four learners whose interlanguage had developed beyond the Basic Variety and who all show a firmly established expression of sentence negation in preverbal position – Ababa and Xiao, who have had the richest exposure to the target language, as well as Tughiascin and Frieda, whose exposure to the target language is qualitatively and quantitatively reduced (cf. table 1). On the other hand no negative indefinite is found in Hagos, the learner who didn't develop beyond the pre-basic stage during the period of his observation. The item *niente*, one of the negative indefinites of the target occurring twice in Hagos's last recording and already exemplified in (6), is actually a lexical variant of the basic negator *no* characteristic of pre-basic varieties. As *no*, *niente* occurs in front of the item to be negated – cf. (6) again – as well as in negative replies, as in (12).

(12) Hagos, 6 months, 22 days
I. ?*che   è   un   tuo   amico o   un   tuo*
   who   is   a   your   friend or   a   your
   parente?
   relative
   '(and) is this a friend or a relative of yours?'
A. [piece of discourse in Tigrinya]
H. *no* +   **nente**
   no   nothing
   'No'

The relevance of the establishment of preverbal negation for the development of negative indefinites in the continuum of acquisition of Italian sentence negation is shown by the three remaining learners Peter, Chu and Markos. Markos develops the three negative indefinites in a short span of time starting two months after his first exposure to the target language, as soon as preverbal sentence negation is established. Contrary to Markos, first attestations of negative indefinites in Chu's corpus are dispersed over a much longer span of almost four months, during which preverbal negation doesn't appear to be firmly established, being challenged by the alternative, and earlier, strategy of putting the negator in front of the item to be negated, usually the focus of the utterance.[20] The late attestation of *nessuno* 'nobody' in Chu's corpus is not due to vagaries of the recorded conversations, as evidenced in (13), where the meaning of 'nobody' is expressed by resorting to the generic noun *gente* 'people' under the scope of negation.

(13)   Chu, 1 year, 1 month, 27 days
       (description of some pictures representing an untidy house)

eh	*cucina* +	*ah* ++ *ah*	s/ +	*ah* +	**non:**
eh	kitchen	ah ah	s	ah	not
eh	*eh*	**gente** ++	*la(v)ora*+	*lavore*	
eh	eh	people	works	wash(?)	

'Nobody is working/washing in the kitchen'

The most reduced inventory of negative indefinites is found in Peter after six months of exposure to Italian, a period during which preposing of the negator to the element to be negated irrespective of the presence or of the absence of a verb form in the utterance, is the predominant, although not the exclusive strategy employed for negation. As a matter of fact, the potential occurrence of the negator in front of any word or phrase makes the presence of negative indefinites unnecessary, as already pointed out with respect to example (1); on the contrary, the fixing of the negative particle in preverbal position results in a reduction of syntactic flexibility and calls for specific means of expression such as negative indefinites.

As to the sequence of emergence of single negative indefinites in the acquisition process, available data – as resumed in table 3 – allow to point to a leading role of *niente* 'nothing' in the constitution of the repertoire of negative indefinites. First of all, as already shown for Hagos, *niente* very early enters interlanguage as an independent lexical item with a general negative meaning. This use is derived from native input, as illustrated in (14) and in (15).[21]

(14)   Native interviewer's example from Hagos's corpus
  I. | *domenica* | *non* | *si* | *viene* | *a* | *scuola,* |
      |---|---|---|---|---|---|
      | Sunday | not | IMPERS | comes | to | school |

       ?no?
       no
       'On Sundays one doesn't go to school, does one?'
  H. *sì*
       yes
       'Yes'
  I. *?no?*
       no
       niente scuola
       nothing school
       'No? [There is] no school'

(15) Native interviewer's example from Tughiascin's corpus
  I. *certo senti,? tu   leggi   giornali   italiani?*
      sure   listen   you   you-read   newspapers Italian
      'Sure. Listen. Do you read Italian newspapers?'
  T. *no   +   no   capace*
      no   no   able
      'No, I am not able'
  I. *no*
      no
      niente
      nothing
      'No, nothing'

This kind of use is not only attested in initial learners, but in advanced ones too, as Xiao.

(16) Xiao, 1 year, 11 months, 4 days
      io   invece due   fratelli ++   mh
      I   instead two   brothers   mh
      niente *sorella*
      nothing sister
      'I have two brothers. No sister'

A second clue is the overextension of *niente* to contexts where other negative indefinites are expected, found in early learners as Markos – examples (17a) and (17b) – and occasionally in advanced learners too, as is the case for Xiao – example (18).

(17) Markos, 2 months, 2 days[22]
a. **non** c'è **niente** uomo
   not there is nothing man
   'There was no man/nobody'
b. *adesso in Kassalà* **non** *c'è* **niente**
   now in Kassala not there is nothing
   ufficio, ?sì?
   office yes
   'At that time there was no office in Kassala'

(18) Xiao, 1 year, 10 months, 21 days[23]
I. *ah qui* **non** *sei* **mai** *stata in*
   ah here not you-are never been in
   Italia allo zoo?
   Italy to-the zoo
   'Here in Italy, have you ever gone to the zoo?'
X. *eh sì qua/ eh l'anno sco(r)so sì*
   eh yes here eh the year past sì yes
   'Yes, last year'
I. *ma ?con la scuola o con la tua*
   but with the school or with the your
   famiglia?
   family
   'With the school or with your family?'
X. *famija* ++ *scuola* **non** *è andato* **niente**
   family school not is gone nothing
   'With my family. I have never been there with the school'

Whatever the order in which negative indefinites emerge in interlanguage, they appear with an intrinsically negative meaning, attested by their early uses in elliptical contexts and in utterances with no negation particles. The first attestation of *mai* in an elliptical context is attested in Chu's recordings, as illustrated in (19).

(19) Chu, 1 year, 6 months, 5 days
(talking about snakes)
I. | *mh +* | *ma* | *?non* | *ti* | *ha* | **mai** | *morsicato?* |
    |--------|------|--------|------|------|---------|--------------|
    | mh | but | non | you | has | never | bitten |

'Did any ever bite you?'

C. *no*
    no

I. | *?**mai**?* | *+ e* | *?a* | *dei* | *tuoi* | *amici* | *è* |
    |-------------|-------|------|-------|--------|---------|-----|
    | never | and | to | of-the| your | friends | is |

    capitato? +
    happened
    'Never? And did it happen to any of your friends?'

?che	*qualcuno*	*li*	*ha*	*morsicati?*
that	someone	them	has	bitten

    'That some snake bit them?

C. **mai** @
    never
    'Never'

Niente with no negation particles within an utterance occurs for the first time in Peter, as reported in (20).[24]

(20) Peter, 6 months
I. | *[...]* | *e* | *poi* | *?la* | *vita* | *è* | *molto* | *cara* |
    |---------|------|-------|-------|--------|-----|---------|-----------|
    | | and | then | the | life | is | very | expensive |

    giù?
    down
    'Is life expensive down there [in Singapore]?'

P. *no*
    no

I. | *no* | *come* | *in* | *Italia* |
    |------|--------|------|----------|
    | no | as | in | Italy |

    'Not as in Italy'

P.	*no*	*ma*	*abità*	*in*	*mio*	*mio*	*casa*	*è*
	no	but	live	in	my	my	house	is

niente @
nothing

'No, but living in my home costs nothing'

The only exception in this respect is found in Frieda for the item *mai* 'never', which seems to be unable to occur alone in elliptical contexts such as the one reported in (21), where it is preceded by the negative particle until the tenth month of exposure to Italian. This rather peculiar behavior might be the result of an attempt of restoring a sort of regular paradigm of negative items on the basis of German *niemand, nichts, nie(mals)*, transfer being actually a learning strategy characterising this learner. In the last line of example (21) the learner's *non mai* corresponds to *mai* in the target.[25]

(21) Frieda, 7 months, 19 days

adulti	*sono*	*andati +*		*con*	*amici*	*äh*	*fare*
adults	are	gone		with	friends	eh	do-INF
qualcosa	*però*	*io*	***non***	***mai***			
something	but	I	not	never			

'Adults used to go out to do something, I never did'

With the eventual establishment of preverbal negation, negative indefinites appear as a rule in postverbal position, cooccurring with the preverbal negative particle, as in the multiple negation pattern of the target, as in the following example drawn from Markos's corpus.[26]

(22) Markos, 2 months, 22 days
(talking about the mopping up operations of the Ethiopian governmental forces in Eritrea in the 1980's)

anche:-	*il*	*bambini*	*non*	*c'è*	*la*
also	the	children	not	there is	the

forsa +?mh?
strength mh

'The children are not strong'

loro-	**non**:-	fanno	nents/ **niente**
they	not	they-do	nothing

'[Therefore] they [= the Ethiopian soldiers] do not do anything to them'

4. Discussion

The trends and the regularities found in the development of indefinite pronouns in second language acquisition of Italian described in detail in the preceding section may be now commented upon in the perspective of typology in the framework of Martin Haspelmath's implicational map introduced above – cf. figure 1.

The overall pattern of development of indefinite pronouns evidenced on the basis of the longitudinal data of the eight learners examined is first resumed and evaluated with respect to the lexicalisation patterns instantiated by the single stages as identified in the preceding section and to the factors, communicative or others, which may be of relevance in their establishing. The organisation of indefinite pronouns functions is then evaluated with particular regard to the position of free standing negative indefinites and of the principle of adjacency.

Four major stages can be recognised in the development of indefinite pronouns in Italian L2.

(a) Pre-basic learner varieties lack indefinite pronouns. Their meaning may be expressed, in case, by lexical items, as shown in (1) for the particular case of negative indefinites. However pre-basic varieties comprise in their lexical stock the target item *niente*: this is used in the target both as a general negator and as a negative indefinite pronoun ('nothing'), whereas in learner language only the first of these two functions is attested and *niente* appears to be a lexical variant of the main negator *no*.[27]

(b) Quite early in the development of the second language, in basic varieties, the *nessuno* series of negative indefinites is established as the first pole of lexicalisation. Negative indefinites seem to enter interlanguage as individual lexical items with intrinsically negative meaning, i.e. as free standing pronouns in Haspelmath's terminology.[28] In fact their first occurrences are found in elliptical contexts and in utterances which are not elsewhere marked as negative utterances, as shown above – cf. examples (19) and (20) respectively. On the basis of the evidence found in various learners it may be hypothesised that the eventual attraction of these items into the implicational map in the direct negation function starts with *niente*. In fact, the general negative function of *niente* as attested in pre-basic varieties appears to be distinguished from the function of utterance negation once the target-like marking of negation by the preverbal particle *no(n)* is established. The early examples drawn from Markos's corpus and reported in (17) may show this route of development: in these examples, *niente* seems to be re-employed by the learner with the peculiar function of tagging the NPs under the scope of negation in connection with indefiniteness. On the other hand, *niente* seems also to be able to function as a general negative indefinite in negative utterances, as in Xiao's non-early example reported in (18), where it can be interpreted as carrying the meaning of 'never'. These uses of *niente* appear to found the pattern of the multiple negation pattern of the target language and to trigger the extension of the direct negation function to the other two free standing negative indefinites *nessuno* and *mai*. Multiple negation patterns with cooccurrence of preverbal negative particle and postverbal negative indefinite – cf. *loro* **non** *fanno* **niente**, liter. 'they not do nothing' as in Markos's example (22) – and direct negation function are stable properties of the negative indefinites in the period of observation of the eight learners examined.

(c) The *qualche* series of indefinite pronouns emerges as the second set in post-basic varieties with the original 'specific unknown' function in the left area of Haspelmath's implicational map (see. figure 1). Contrary to the *nessuno* series, members of the *qualche* series appear to enlarge their functional domains towards the non-factual conditional protasis and irrealis non-specific functions in the central area of the map as well as towards the direct negation function, overlapping in this latter case with the *nessuno* series – cf. examples (10) and (11). Whereas pronouns of the *qualche* series acquire the direct negation function under the scope of negation, members of the *nessuno* series are not found outside non-negative contexts, as is the case in the target language, where the *nessuno* series can appear in questions without an accompanying negation – cf. *Hai visto nessuno?* [lit. have you seen nobody] 'Have you seen anybody?'.[29]

(d) The last, and apparently late item to emerge is *qualsiasi*, the determiner of the series used in the free choice function, found in only one learner among the eight considered here.

In the perspective of the typological patterns of lexicalisation and organisation of the functions within the implicational map as in figure 1, second language acquisition of Italian shows a different relative weight of the major poles of lexicalisation detected across (fully fledged) languages. Unlike native Italian, the major pole of lexicalisation appears to be the direct negation function (number 7 in the implicational map in figure 1) whereas the two major poles of lexicalisation across languages – the known specific function (number 1 in the implicational map in figure 1) and the comparative and free choice functions (numbers 8 and 9 in the implicational map in figure 1) – have only a subordinate role, apparent in their late emergence and acquisition.

This fact might be tentatively related to the central role negation has in discourse. It is indeed crucially important to be able to negate utterances and to negate the existence of persons, things, and spans of time, whereas stating that somebody has done something is not as a central function in actual discourse. In this respect, the language type instantiated by the learner varieties of Italian possessing only free standing negative indefinites used in the direct negation function may be interpreted as the result of a compromise solution functionally motivated by communicative requirements, in terms of Cristofaro and Ramat (1999: 32). The different weight of negative indefinites in grammar and use and the prominence of negative indefinites in spoken language was claimed by Bernini and Ramat (1996: 147-150) to be evidenced in fully fledged languages in the diachronic development of new negative indefinites from older non-negative indefinites, as in Maltese, and in some instances of analogical levelling of non-negative indefinites on the basis of negative ones, as in some Gallo-Italic dialects.

An asymmetry in functional weight is evidenced in learner Italian for the other two series of indefinite pronouns too, which act across languages as the main series of indefinite pronouns and which are actually the only series available in most languages outside Europe.[30] The *qualche* series is, in this respect, much earlier in emergence in interlanguage than the *-unque* series, represented by only one lexical item in only one learner of the eight considered here. It may be hypothesised that the availability of the universal quantifier *tutto* 'all' in the learner varieties makes the presence of a specific item for the expression of free choice unnecessary.

The very beginning of the developmental path of indefinite pronouns appears to be dependent on second language input – as shown by the early introduction of *niente* into prebasic varieties with the value of a general negator as a result of the widespread uses of *niente* in native Italian and in foreigner talk – rather than by transfer. Indeed, the presence of a set of negative indefinites in the first language appears to play a marginal role, as shown by the differring rates of acquisition of learners with the same language background as Hagos and Markos, and by the comparable rates of development of learners with different language backgrounds as Chu and Peter – cf. the early uses of negative indefinites with no cooccurring negative particles in both learners reported in examples (8) and (20) respectively, transfer from English being plausible only for the latter learner.

As to the organisation of indefinite pronoun functions in the implicational map it is important to notice that the functions comprised in the implicational map are defined on the basis of different criteria.

On the one hand function 2 (specific unknown) and function 9 (free choice) involve the lexical meaning of the single indefinite pronouns in declarative clauses – cf. *I heard **something*** and ***Anybody** can solve this problem*. On the other hand the definition of the other functions is dependent on syntactic contexts or constructions, as shown e.g. respectively by function 1 (specific known)[31] and by function 6 (indirect negation, found in a subordinate clause whose matrix clause is negative as in *I **don't** think that **anybody** knows the answer*).

In the overall developmental path of indefinite pronouns as described in the preceding section and as resumed above functions defined on the basis of the lexical meaning of the indefinites involved are learned earlier than functions defined on the basis of the syntactic context. This sequence may be schematised as follows:

lexical functions > syntactic functions

This sequence is confirmed for the *qualche* series, for the determiner *qualsiasi*, the only item of the *-unque* series to emerge in learner Italian, as well as for the *nessuno* series of negative indefinite pronouns. In fact, as explained in detail under point (b) above, members of the *nessuno* series enter interlanguage as independent lexical items with intrinsically negative meaning – able to occur alone, i.e. free standing and in utterances not otherwise marked for negation – and appear in function 7 (direct negation) once utterance negation is established.

Data available in the learners' corpora, although scanty, point to the fact that negative indefinites seem to remain stable in the early acquired direct negation function, in accordance with the crosslinguistic generalisation as to the behaviour of free standing negative indefinites suggested by Haspelmath (1997: 198). According to this generalisation indefinites in the direct negation function are more likely to occur as free standing negative indefinites the narrower is their functional range in the implicational map. On the other hand, widening of the functional range, attested in Markos, Ababa and Xiao, seems to involve only the items of the *qualche* series, which are used in the direct negation function by Ababa (example 11) and perhaps by Xiao.³² Only cautious conclusions are in order in this respect, because transfer of the functional range of the corresponding items of the first language may be at work. Indeed, it should be reminded that Tigrinya, Ababa's and Markos's first language, has in colloquial varieties a marginal set of negative indefinites and that Chinese dialects – Wú Chinese is Xiao's first language – seem to lack any negative indefinites. Finally, lack of evidence for the widening of the functional range of *qualsiasi* beyond the original free choice function may be related to its late emergence in the period of observation of the learners considered here.

The last point to be mentioned with regard to the organisation of indefinite pronouns functions in the implicational map concerns the principle of adjacency, the major principle governing the distribution of individual indefinites in the implicational map. In this regard, it is to be noticed that the potential widening of the functional range of an indefinite pronouns series in learner language involves the syntactic functions and is therefore subject to the development of the corresponding syntactic constructions. Of the syntactic functions comprised in the map, direct negation (function 7) is very early established as repeatedly mentioned above, questions (function 4) emerge quite early, but conditionals (function 5), indirect negation (function 6: cf. *I don't think that **anybody** knows the answer*) and comparative (function 8: *In Freiburg the weather is nicer than **anywhere** in Germany*) involve the development of subordination and of comparative constructions and therefore may appear, if they do appear at all, in later more advanced learner varieties.³³

It may then be hypothesised that the adjacency principle apply at each stage to the functions which the syntactic development of the learner variety allows in a gradual and finer differentiation of the semantic space delimited by the three major functions 7 (direct negation), 2 (specific unknown) and 9 (free choice), which are located at the periphery of the semantic space represented in the map. The widening of the functional range of the *qualche* series towards function 5 (conditional protasis) and function 7 (direct negation), where it overlaps with the negative indefinites attested e.g. in Markos and in Ababa, may be interpreted as the application of the principle of adjacency in stages where more complex and later syntactic functions such as indirect negation aren't yet available.

5. Concluding remarks

Consideration of the development of indefinite pronouns in learner Italian in the light of typological research has shown how the reconstruction of the target system in the process of acquisition may be related to different factors. On the one hand, the salience of free standing indefinite pronouns in the direct negation function was motivated by the central role negation has in discourse. On the other hand the further development of the system was shown to involve typological regularities. Negative indefinites remain stable in the direct negation function – as they generally appear to be across languages. Furthermore, the principle of adjacency applies at each stage at the functions available to the learner in dependence on the syntactic development of interlanguage.

The evidence discussed in this paper has shown that the principles governing the organisation of indefinite pronouns systems across languages is mirrored in the way learners construe their target system. However, the organisation of the available linguistic means in learner varieties was also shown to obey specific functional motivations and to be employed in order to cope with particular communicative requirements, as in the case of the early emergence and stabilisation of the negative pronouns series in the direct negation function. In this regard it is plausible to apply to learner varieties too the notion of language type as discussed in the introductory section on the basis of the definition suggested by Cristofaro and Ramat (1999: 32), and to try to detect potential features characterising types of language arising in (second) language acquisition on the basis of the comparison of learner varieties of different second languages.[34]

In this perspective, second language learner varieties, as well as non-standard dialect data and sign language data as instantiations, though in different respects and in different conditions, of the same human language capacity,[35] should belong to the field of investigation of typological research as fully-fledged languages are. The methodological and theoretical framework of the functional-typological approach allows the interpretation and explanation of the variation patterns resulting from the interaction of the same organising principles – as asserted by Cristofaro and Ramat (1999: 32)[36] – beyond synchrony and diachrony of fully-fledged languages as the traditional field of observation of typology.

Notes

* Research on indefinite pronouns in L2 Italian was carried out within the European project "The Structure of Learner Varieties" and profited by financial support of the Italian Ministero dell'Università e della Ricerca Scientifica e Tecnologica for the joint project "Linguistica acquisizionale: sintassi, discorso e percorsi di formazione dell'italiano lingua seconda" (grant 40%/1998 assigned to the University of Pavia) and of the University of Bergamo ("Fondo d'Ateneo di Ricerca", grant 1998 assigned to the Dipartimento di Linguistica e letterature comparate). The empirical results of the present investigation were at first presented at the Euroconference on "The Structure of Learner Language. From Pragmatics to Syntax: Organizational Principles of Second Language Acquisition" in Acquafredda di Maratea, Italy (26 September - 1 October 1998). I am particularly grateful for their helpful comments and valuable remarks to Camilla Bardel, Monica Berretta, Anna Giacalone Ramat, Peter Jordens, Clive Perdue, Daniel Véronique, Suzanne Schlyter. The author is obviously responsible for any error or shortcoming of the paper.

1. In a slightly different perspective, other studies on second language acquisition have profited by the results obtained in typology, such as implicational universals or tendencies and markedness relations, in the search for language internal explanations of the regularities found in interlanguages as to order of acquisition of grammatical features, learning difficulties and permeability to L1 transfer. The results of these studies are surveyed, albeit in a quite critical perspective, by Ellis (1994: 417-429).

2. An example of the interplay of these principles drawn from the corpus of the learners of Italian considered here is the following: *il governo de Tiopia-vuole io + militari* (Markos, 1 month), liter. 'the government of Ethiopia wants I military (man)' for 'I must serve in the Ethiopian army'. The first NP's referent is the source of the obligation imposed on the speaker to serve in the Ethiopian army, i.e. the controller of the forced recruitment.

3. In fact fully-fledged languages are consistently considered within the Basic Variety approach as stable "borderline cases of learner varieties" (Klein and Perdue 1997: 308) reached in the acquisition process at the point when the learner's linguistic behaviour matches the one found in the surrounding linguistic environment. In this perspective, learner varieties do not belong any longer to the area of applied linguistics, but must be considered as important pieces of the phenomenology relevant for theoretical linguistics just as fully fledged languages are (cf. Klein 1999).
4. In the original wording: "... l'approccio tipologico ipotizza che diversi tipi linguistici obbediscano a diverse motivazioni funzionali, e che la soddisfazione di motivazioni di volta in volta diverse determini l'alternanza tra i vari tipi. ... le strutture linguistiche sono utilizzate dai parlanti per risolvere particolari esigenze della comunicazione ... e la grammatica rappresenta una soluzione di compromesso provvisoria – e di volta in volta rinegoziabile – che soddisfa ora l'una ora l'altra esigenza" (Cristofaro and Ramat 1999: 32).
5. The learners' utterances are transcribed according to the following notational conventions: New paragraph with no preceding point and no indentation: *end of declarative utterance and beginning of a new utterance*; indentation: *continuing utterance*; ?...? : *interrogative utterance*; - at the end of a word: *suspensive intonation (often with lengthening of final vowel)*; comma: *intonation break with no pause*; ↑ : *rising intonation*; ↓ : *falling intonation*; !...!: *emphasis*; CAPITAL: *high volume*; % % : *low volume*; + ++ +++ : *pauses of growing length (ca. 1/2" to 3"; duration in seconds of longer pauses is indicated)*; / : *self-correction by speaker*; * *: *non Italian items*; & : *border of overlapping (parts of) utterances*; = : *border of utterances of different speakers in immediate succession*; @: *laughter*; () : *contains less audible items*; (x) : *incomprehensible syllable*; [] : *contains remarks of the transcriptor*; [...] : *expunctions*; NVC : *non-verbal comunication.* I: : *Interviewer.*
6. Among the derivational bases of indefinite pronouns found across languages, question words and generic nouns, alone or accompanied by an indefiniteness marker as in Chinese are also widespread, cf. Haspelmath (1997: 21-29).
7. The functions of the indefinite pronouns comprised in the map may be illustrated by means of following examples, all drawn from Haspelmath (1997: 2-3): 1: **Somebody** *called while you were away: guess who!*; 2: *I heard* **something**, *but I couldn't tell what kind of sound it was*; 3: *Please, try* **somewhere** *else*; 4: *Did* **anybody** *tell you anything about it?*: 5: *If you see* **anything**, *tell me immediately*; 6: *I don't think that* **anybody** *knows the answer*; 7: **Nobody** *knows the answer*; 8: *In Freiburg the weather is nicer than* **anywhere** *in Germany*; 9: **Anybody** *can solve this problem*.
8. All learners but one – Frieda, see below – had some kind of formal instruction during the period of the recordings. However their linguistic behaviour does

not show the features of the standard variety of Italian as taught in schools (as in the case of Xiao and Chu, enwolled in a public school) or in courses of Italian for foreigners (as in the case of Hagos, Markos, Ababa, Peter, Tughiascin). Influence of formal instruction can therefore be considered as marginal or irrelevant for these learners.

9. The Pavia Project on second language acquisition of Italian joins research groups on L2 acquisition active at the universities of Pavia, Bergamo, Milan, Siena, Trento, Turin, Vercelli and Verona. For a general outline of the project and for details of methodology of data collection and interpretation, the reader may refer to Giacalone Ramat (1995).

10. Short biographical notes for each of the eight learners investigated are reported here. All learners were living in the metropolitan area of Milan in the period of observation but Chu and Xiao, who were living in Turin.
    Ababa: Eritrean. Secondary school in the home country. Works as a housemaid. Longitudinal recordings: October 1986-June 1987.
    Chu: Chinese. Enrolled in the first grade of secondary school ('scuola media'). After school C. helps the parents, who work as tailors. Longitudinal recordings: December 1988-December 1989; supplementary recording: April 1990.
    Frieda: German. Fr. moved to Italy in order to marry. Housewife, works as a tailor in a local factory. Only Italian spoken at home and with acquaintances; passive exposure to the local Gallo-Italic dialect. Longitudinal recordings: October 1985-December 1986.
    Hagos: Eritrean. Emigrated in order to join the family. Parents work with a cleaning contractor. H. goes to work with his father early in the morning and late at night. Longitudinal recordings: November 1986-May 1987.
    Markos: Eritrean. Secondary school in the home country. His mother works since more than ten years in Italy as housemaid. At first unemployed, then electrical contractor. Longitudinal recordings: October 1986-June 1987.
    Peter: Malaysian. Secondary education partly in the home country and partly in the United Kingdom; graduation in the United Kingdom. Engineer in a factory. Longitudinal recordings: December 1986-July 1987.
    Tughiascin: Chinese. In Italy since 4 years when first recorded, but exposure to Italian only since one year. Milan. Waitress in a restaurant and embroideress. Longitudinal recordings: October 1986-June 1987.
    Xiao: Chinese. Enrolled in primary school, where she also attends a special course of Italian for foreigners. Longitudinal recordings: December 1988-December 1989, supplementary final control recording in April 1990.

11. Typological distance as one of the potential factors slowing down the acquisition process was discussed for these two learners by Bernini (2000) in the investigation of the development of negation. For a general assessment of the

role of typological distance in second language acquisition cf. Giacalone Ramat (1994).
12. A sketch of Wú Chinese is comprised in Ramsey (1987: 88-95).
13. The pronouns listed here are representatives of the series they belong to. For the details of their distribution, not relevant for the purpose of the present paper, cf. Haspelmath (1997: 248-249, 243-246 respectively).
14. For Mandarin Chinese cf. Haspelmath (1997: 307-310); for Cantonese reference should be made to Matthews and Yip (1994: 257-259, 261-272). In the Cantonese examples, -*h* inserted after a vowel or a diphthong is the notation for low-register tones (Matthews and Yip 1994: 7). Cantonese examples are transcribed according to Matthews and Yip (1994).
15. Data drawn from Kogan (1993) and Agosṭinos-Tädlā (1994: 64).
16. Mandarin Chinese actually has a series formed with question words and the indefiniteness markers *yě/dōu*, which appear to be restricted to the "direct negation" function and are therefore liable to occur as free standing. However, as Haspelmath (1997: 309) reports, it is doubtful whether the two particles may be considered real indefinitness markers, since the *dōu* formations are also used as universal quantifiers and the negative indefinite meaning may result from the combination of negation with their (wide) scope.
17. This example was kindly supplied by Tesfamikael Mehretab (Bergamo) and shows the opposition between positive *hadä* and negative *wala ḥadä* in actual native colloquial use. No mention of this pattern is found in grammar descriptions, as e.g. in Kogan (1997: 442 in particular).
18. *bugiáno* is a learner's, non-target derivation from the noun *bugía* 'lie'. In this context, the word may be interpreted as referring to the disguised control of Eritrean expatriates by the Ethiopian intelligence service.
19. The development of utterance negation in the framework of the Basic Variety approach is discussed in Bernini (2000).
20. Competition of the two strategies results in some instances of double marking of negation within the same utterance, as in: *eh tembo u/ una settimana ++ io no ab/ + io no a/ abito no qua* [1 year, 22 days], lit. 'time one week I not live not here', i.e. 'Since one week I do not live here (any longer)'.
21. *Niente* is also reported by Berruto (1993) as a substitute of *non* in elicited foreigner talk, cf. *Qui niente fumare* (liter. here nothing smoke) against *In questo scompartimento non si può fumare* 'In this compartment smoking is not allowed' as in the native sentence used to elicit foreigner talk.
22. In both examples the target language requires *nessuno* in adjectival function, preposed to the noun, with which it agrees in gender (i.e. *nessun uomo* and, respectively, *nessun ufficio*).
23. The target version of the utterance reported in the last line requires the negative adverb *mai* 'never' instead of *niente*, e.g. *Con la scuola **non** ci sono an-*

    *data **mai***, lit. 'with the school not there am gone never'. Cf. also the interviewer's question reported in the first line of this example.
24. First occurrence of *nessuno* in an utterance with no negative particle was reported in (8) above.
25. In fact *non mai* is also used in preverbal position as a kind of fixed expression, as in: *no mai siamo noi due @ siamo sempre insieme* 'We are never by ourselves, we are always together (with other people)'. Transfer interacts with input in this learner in a rather peculiar way discussed by Berretta (1990).
26. Negative indefinites can also appear in preverbal position in the target language, as in *Nessuno parli!* 'Let nobody talk!'. In this case, preverbal *non* must be dropped. This pattern seems to be acquired quite late and only by some advanced learner. Since the development of this aspect of the syntax of negative indefinites is not relevant for the aim of this paper, it will not be further discussed.
27. *No* is both more frequent and apparently earlier than *niente*.
28. Acquisition of negative indefinites as independent items was also found in first language acquisition of both Hebrew (cf. Berman 1985: 323) and Polish (Smoczyńska 1985: 633), where negative indefinites are at first used without the sentence negation particle on the verb obligatorily cooccurring with them in adult speech. The opposite development was found in first language acquisition of English, as evidenced by sentences such as *Nobody don't like me*, originally reported by McNeill in four year old children and related by Bickerton (1981: 195) to the order of acquisition of indefinites, which are claimed to develop independently of sentence negation.
29. In other words, the learners' *nessuno* resembles more English *nobody* than English *anybody* or, as a case in point, regional usage of Italian *nessuno* as may be heard in Tuscany, cf. *Se nessuno venisse, ditegli* [lit. if nobody came, say-to-him] 'If anybody came, tell him' (Rohlfs 1949/1968: 216).
30. Cf. the data reported in the Appendixes in Haspelmath (1997: 244-329) and in Kahrel (1996).
31. In English and Italian the same *some* and *qualche* series cover both functions 1 and 2. Function 1 can only be distinguished from function 2 on the basis of contextual clues, cf. Haspelmath's (1997: 2-3) examples: ***Somebody*** *called while you were away: guess who!* (specific known) vs. *I heard **something**, but I couldn't tell what kind of sound it was* (specific unknown). In other languages functions 1 and 2 may be expressed by separate lexical series, as the *koe-* series and the *-to* series respectively in Russian (e.g. *koe-kto* and *kto-to* 'somebody').
32. Cf. *sei qualcuno eh se hai telefonato non n/ non le dico mai dopo se **non** ha dato **qualcosa** vero?* 'If anybody calls, I never say [that I am going to meet him] afterwards if he did not give me anything/something' (1 year, 10 months).

33. For the development of subordination, both functional types – adverbial, completive, relative – and syntactic types – finite and non-finite – in Italian L2 cf. Giacalone Ramat (1999a, 1999b).
34. Recall the case of creole languages. Although allegedly showing shared peculiar features in different areas of grammar such as the organisation of the verb system and complementation, and therefore treated as a particular "type" of language resulted from non-targeted first language acquisition in similar social conditions, they are hardly considered as a language type in standard typological terms.
35. For the importance of non-standard dialect data in the typological programme see Kortmann (1998), who warns that "especially in languages with a long literary tradition (like most European languages) the setting of norms plays and played a great role, so that certain features of the standard variety may not be the result of natural language change, of natural solutions of linguistic problems, but rather of more or less arbitrary changes forced on the language by prescriptivists [...]" (§ 1). The challenge represented by sign languages for the investigation of typology and universals is pointed at by Dotter (1999) with respect to the different role played by the very same gestural 'paralinguistic' features in spoken and sign languages, which makes it plausible that there might be only gradual differences between the two types of languages, thus requiring "to partially revise language universals and typology because the hitherto existing theory was developed merely on the basis of research in spoken languages [...]" (Dotter 1999: 19).
36. In the original wording "[...] tutti i tipi di variazione linguistica, tanto quella che si riscontra sincronicamente a livello interlinguistico, quanto quella che si riscontra diacronicamente, vengono in questo modo unificati e ricondotti ai medesimi principi esplicativi" (Cristofaro/Ramat 1999: 32).

References

Agostinos-Tädlä (Abbā [father], ofmcap.)
    1994   *La lingua abissina. Q^walnəq^{w}ā ḥabäšā*. Asmara: Edizioni "Adveniat Regnum Tuum".
Becker, Angelika, and Mary Carroll
    1997   *The Acquisition of Spatial Relations in a Second Language*. Amsterdam: Benjamins.
Berretta, Monica
    1990   Apprendimento di lingue seconde con input substandard: l'analisi di un caso. In: Gaetano Berruto and Alberto A. Sobrero (eds.), *Studi di sociolinguistica e dialettologia italiana offerti a Corrado Grassi*, 151-177. Galatina: Congedo.

Berman, Ruth
1985   The acquisition of Hebrew. In: Slobin (ed.), 255-371.
Bernini, Giuliano
2000   Negative items and negation strategies in nonnative Italian. *Studies in Second Language Acquisition* 22/3: 399-440.
Bernini, Giuliano, and Paolo Ramat
1996   *Negative Sentences in the Languages of Europe. A Typological Approach.* Berlin: Mouton de Gruyter.
Berruto, Gaetano
1993   Italiano in Europa oggi: "*foreigner talk*" nella Svizzera tedesca. In: *Omaggio a Gianfranco Folena*, 2275-2290. Padova: Editoriale Programma.
Bickerton, Derek
1981   *Roots of Language.* Ann Arbor: Karoma.
Comrie, Bernard
1984   Why linguists need language acquirers. In: William R. Rutherford, (ed.), *Universals and Second Language Acquisition*, 11-29. Amsterdam: Benjamins.
Cristofaro, Sonia, and Paolo Ramat
1999   Introduzione. In: Sonia Cristofaro and Paolo Ramat (eds.), *Introduzione alla tipologia linguistica*, 15-32. Roma: Carocci.
Dietrich, Rainer, Wolfgang Klein, and Colette Noyau
1995   *The Acquisition of Temporality in a Second Language.* Amsterdam: Benjamins.
Dimroth, Christine, and Wolfgang Klein
1995   Fokuspartikeln in Lernervarietäten. *Zeitschrift für Literaturwissenschaft und Linguistik* 104: 73-114.
Dittmar, Norbert, and Anna Giacalone Ramat (eds.)
1999   *Grammatik und Diskurs. Grammatica e discorso. Studi sull'acquisizione dell'italiano e del tedesco. Studien zum Erwerb des Deutschen und des Italienischen.* Tübingen: Stauffenburg.
Dotter, Franz
1999   Sign language "between" gestures (non-verbal behavior) and spoken language? *Sprachtypologie und Universalienforschung* 52: 3-21.
Ellis, Rod
1994   *The Study of Second Language Acquisition.* Oxford: Oxford University Press.
Giacalone Ramat, Anna
1994   Il ruolo della tipologia linguistica nell'acquisizione di lingue seconde. In: Anna Giacalone Ramat and Massimo Vedovelli (eds.), *Italiano lingua seconda/lingua straniera*, 27-43. Roma: Bulzoni.

Giacalone Ramat, Anna
    1995   Présentation. *Acquisition et Interaction en Langue Étrangère* [Aix-en-Provence] 5: 3-13 [Monographic issue: L'acquisition de l'italien langue étrangère].

Giacalone Ramat, Anna
    1999a   Functional typology and strategies of clause connection in second-language acquisition. *Linguistics* 37: 519-548.

Giacalone Ramat, Anna
    1999b   Le strategie di collegamento tra proposizioni nell'italiano di germanofoni. Una prospettiva tipologica. In: Dittmar and Giacalone Ramat (eds.), 13-54.

Haspelmath, Martin
    1997   *Indefinite Pronouns*. Oxford: Oxford University Press.

Hawkins, John A.
    1987   Implicational universals as predictors of language acquisition. *Linguistics* 25: 453-473.

Kahrel, Peter
    1996   Aspects of negation. PhD dissertation, Universiteit van Amsterdam. Meppel: Krips repro.

Klein, Wolfgang
    1999   Die Lehren des Zweitspracherwerbs. In: Norbert Dittmar and Anna Giacalone Ramat (eds.), 279-290.

Klein, Wolfgang, and Clive Perdue
    1992   *Utterance Structure. Developing Grammars Again*, Amsterdam: Benjamins.

Klein Wolfgang, and Clive Perdue
    1997   The Basic Variety (or: Couldn't natural languages be much simpler?). *Second Language Research* 13: 301-347.

Kogan, Leonid E.
    1997   Tigrinya. In: Robert Hetzron (ed.), *The Semitic Languages*, 424-445. London: Routledge.

Kortmann, Bernd
    1998   Typology and dialectology. In: *Proceedings of the 16th International Congress of Linguists*, Paper 0060. Oxford: Pergamon.

Matthews, Stephen, and Virginia Yip
    1994   *Cantonese. A Comprehensive Grammar*. London: Routledge.

Ramsey, S. Robert
    1987   *The Languages of China*. Princeton (NJ): Princeton University Press.

Rohlfs, Gerhard
    1948   *Historische Grammatik der Italienischen Sprache und ihrer Mundarten*, Bd. II: *Fomenlehre und Syntax*. Bern: Francke. Italian

translation, 1968: *Grammatica storica della lingua italiana e dei suoi dialetti*, Vol. 2: *Morfologia*. Torino: Einaudi.

Slobin, Dan I. (ed.)
1985   *The Crosslinguistic Study of Language Acquisition*, Vol. 1: *The Data*. Hillsdale: Lawrence Erlbaum.

Smoczyńska, Magdalena
1985   The acquisition of Polish. In: Slobin (ed.), 595-686.

Watorek, Marzena (ed.)
1998   Structure des lectes des apprenants. *Acquisition et Interaction en Langue Étrangère* [Aix-en-Provence] 11.

Adnominal possession: combining typological and second language perspectives

Björn Hammarberg and Maria Koptjevskaja-Tamm

1. Introduction

The notion of possession and its linguistic manifestations have been a popular topic in linguistic literature for a long time. What we will attempt here is to explore the domain of adnominal possession – possessive relations and their manifestations within the noun phrase – in one particular language from two combined points of view: the typological characteristics of the system, and the picture that emerges from second language learners' attempts to handle adnominal possession in production. We are focusing on Swedish, a language with a distinctive and rather elaborate system of adnominal possession. Our aim is twofold: to present an overview of how the Swedish system of adnominal possessive constructions works, and to show how acquisitional aspects connect with typological aspects in this domain.

The English phrases *Peter's hat, my son* and *a boy's leg* all exemplify prototypical cases of adnominal possession whereby one entity, the possessee, referred to by the head of the possessive noun phrase, is represented as possessed in one way or another by another entity, the possessor, referred to by the attribute. It has become a commonplace in linguistics that possession is a difficult, if not impossible, notion to grasp (for a survey of adnominal possession in a cross-linguistic perspective cf. Koptjevskaja-Tamm 2001). However, even though it seems impossible to give a reasonable general definition for all the meanings covered by possessive constructions across languages and even in one language, we can still provide criteria for identifying a possessive construction, or possessive constructions in a language. Our first *semantic criterion* for a possessive construction departs from the prototypical cases of adnominal possession – i.e., whether it can be used at all for referring to legal ownership (*Peter's hat*), or to kinship relations (*my son*) or to body-part relations *(a boy's leg)*. Note that reference to just one of these relations to the exclusion of the other two will be fine – as is well known, a number of languages regularly employ different possessive constructions for reference to alienable possession (e.g. legal ownership) and to inalienable possession (e.g., kinship relations and/or body-part relations). According to our second, *formal criterion*, the possessor and the possessee in adnominal possession together form one NP, a possessive NP, or at least belong to one NP. Adnominal possession is, thus, opposed to at least two other related phenomena: predicative possession, such as *Peter has a hat* or *The hat belongs to Peter* (for a definition cf Heine 1997: 29–33), and external-possession constructions, in which a possessor "does not occur as a dependent constituent of the modified NP, but NP-externally as a constituent of the clause" (Haspelmath 1999a: 109), e.g. in Swedish *Jag tittade honom i ögonen* 'I looked in his eyes', lit. 'I looked him in the eyes'. Finally, we will only be interested in the most common, unmarked, 'standard' means of building possessive constructions. For English, this means that we will exclude examples like *the house which is in Peter's possession*. On the other hand, *Peter's school/dreams/wife* or *cat's plate*, which hardly refer to possession stricto sensu, will all count as possessive NPs since they have the same structure as the typically possessive noun phrases such as *Peter's hat/brother/leg*.

By combining the two criteria we can identify the possessive adnominal constructions in a language, which together will constitute its domain of adnominal possession. Languages differ considerably in how many and what structural types of adnominal possessive constructions they have, and also how, according to what parameters the whole domain is stratified among these constructions. The first type of question has been particularly popular in cross-linguistic studies – Ultan (1978); Seiler (1983); Croft (1990: 28–39); Plank (1995), Koptjevskaja-Tamm (forthc. a) all present structural classifications of adnominal possessive constructions. The second type of questions has also been approached cross-linguistically, particularly in the work by Seiler and linguists connected with the tradition of the Cologne typological school (Serzisko 1984; Lehmann 1998, to mention a few). Further, there are numerous publications (too many to be listed) dealing with possessive constructions in a single language, without relating it to other languages.

The connection between second language research and linguistic typology is not a new one. Early studies combining a multilingual description in a functional-typological framework with L2 error analysis made it clear that the typological properties of especially the target language can shed light on the nature of the acquisitional task, and, conversely, the L2 acquisitional aspect will highlight inherent properties of the languages involved, notably the target language (cf. e.g. Hammarberg and Viberg 1977). Studies applying the Greenbergian notion of markedness (cf. Greenberg 1966; Croft 1990) to second language acquisition have demonstrated learners' preference for adhering to unmarked linguistic structures (cf. Eckman 1977, 1996; Hyltenstam 1984, 1986, among others). There is a wide literature on linguistic universals and second language acquisition, both in functionalist and formal-generative frameworks.

Grammaticalisation is a further aspect which connects second language studies to typology. We should be careful here to keep apart two related, but different senses in which this term is used. It has been taken over into (first and second) language acquisition research from diachronic typology, where it is well established in the sense of a process which gradually develops grammatical elements and constructions in a language out of lexical material. In the second language acquisition literature, grammaticalisation has mostly come to refer to the emergence and development of learners' grammars (cf. Dittmar 1992; Perdue and Klein 1992; Pfaff 1992; Giacalone Ramat 1992; Skiba and Dittmar 1992). The connections between phylogenetic and ontogenetic domains of application and the similarities and differences in nature between *diachronic-typological grammaticalisation* and *acquisitional grammaticalisation* can be debated (for a discussion of the two notions, cf. Giacalone Ramat 1992: 297–300). But it is clear that the two perspectives have rather different implications for the understanding of what the second language learner is acquiring. In the present study we will refer to grammaticalisation in the diachronic-typological sense, unless we state otherwise.

In the following, we will first outline the system of adnominal possessive constructions in Swedish in section 2, then in section 3 analyse the main problems with adnominal possession encountered in L2 Swedish production, and finally in section 4 discuss the combined picture that emerges from these two approaches.

2. Adnominal possessive constructions in Swedish
2.1. General

In Modern Swedish, adnominal possession, as defined in section 1, is mainly expressed by three constructions:

- the "standard possessive noun phrase", in which the possessor precedes the possessee;
- noun-noun compounds, in which the first part modifies the second one; and
- constructions in which the head nominal is modified by a postposed prepositional phrase.

According to the semantic criterion, all these constructions are possessive: thus, both "standard possessive noun phrases" and noun-noun compounds can refer to both legal ownership, kinship relations and body-part relations, whereas constructions with postposed prepositional phrases can refer to kinship relations and to body-part-relations (although not to legal ownership). According to the formal criterion, the three constructions represent adnominal possession, since the possessor and the possessee belong to one and the same NP.

In the following subsections we will go through the main properties of these three construction types and the factors behind the choice among them. In the last subsection, we will present the typological profile of Swedish adnominal possession.

2.2. Standard possessive noun phrases

In the "standard possessive noun phrase", abbreviated as PNP in the rest of this paper, the possessor adnominal precedes the possessee. The possessor is

- either a special possessive pronoun (for the first and second persons and reflexives) agreeing with the possessee in gender and number, cf. *min bil* 'my:COM car' vs. *mitt bord* 'my:N table' vs. *mina bilar* 'my:PL cars',
- or marked with the element -*s* (these are normally referred to as "genitives"), cf. *Peters bil/Peters bilar* 'Peter's car/Peter's cars', *hans bil/hans bilar* 'his car/his cars'.

Morphosyntactically, the Swedish (and, generally, Standard Continental Scandinavian) possessive -*s* behaves similarly to its English counterpart -*'s*. Thus, it always appears at the very end of a noun, after all suffixes, cf. *en pojke-s* 'a boy-GEN', *pojke-n-s* 'boy-DEF.COM-GEN', *pojk-ar-s* 'boy-PL-GEN', *pojk-ar-na-s* 'boy-PL-DEF.PL-GEN'. It also shows the tendency to attach to the final word of a NP resulting in what is traditionally called "group genitives", as in *mannen på gatans åsikter* – lit.'the man in the street's opinions' (i.e., an ordinary person's opinion). Its form is even more consistent than the form of -*'s* in English in that is is always pronounced in one and the same way. The structure of PNPs with genitives is, thus, very simple and uniform: attach -*s* at the end of the possessor NP and put the whole expression in front of a possessee. This behaviour of the marker -*s* justifies its analysis as a clitic (cf. Delsing 1993; Börjars 1994). In the 3rd person pronouns *hennes* 'her', *deras* 'their' and *dess* 'its', however, -*s* is clearly a bound morpheme since it combines with a special form of the pronominal stems.

Remarkably, in both English and in Continental Scandinavian the possessive clitic has replaced the earlier constructions with the morphological genitive case (for the history cf. Norde 1997).

Thus, the notion of PNP actually includes two different subtypes – one with the invariable -*s*- form and one with agreeing possessors.

The property of agreement will not be considered in this paper, nor will the distinction of reflexive versus non-reflexive possessive pronouns.

2.2.1. The meanings of PNPs

PNPs cover a wide range of meaning relations. In some instances, the meaning relation is more or less determined by the semantics of the head nominal, as the case is with KIN relations ('Peter's brother') or BODY-PART vs. person/animal relations ('Peter's leg'), where the head noun is a typical relational noun. Non-relational nouns may enter into multiple relations with their possessors, the most prominent being that of LEGAL OWNERSHIP ('Peter's hat') and DISPOSAL ('Peter's office'); also mention should be made of TEMPORAL and LOCATIVE relations ('Monday's performance', 'Stockholm's banks'). However, one and the same noun phrase with preposed possessors can in principle be interpreted in various way; thus, *Peter's bag*, in addition to its "normal" interpretation 'a bag which belongs to Peter' may receive a number of other interpretations, even though some of these have a very little chance of occurring in real discourse – 'a bag which Peter is carrying for the moment but which not necessarily belongs to him', 'a bag which Peter has designed', 'a bag which Peter dreams of and therefore constantly talks of', etc.

The common semantic (or pragmatic) denominator in the majority of PNPs is the function of the possessors as *anchors* (Hawkins 1978, 1991; Fraurud 1990), or *reference point entities* (Langacker, e.g. 1991: 170, 1995; Taylor 1996: 17) for identification of the head's referents. In other words, in many instances we can identify the referent of a nominal via its relation to the referent of the genitive. Thus, knowing who Peter is we can identify Peter's bag, arm, brother: in Taylor's (ibid.) words, "in opting to use a possessive expression, the speaker is instructing the hearer on how best to identify the referent that he, the speaker, intends".

Clearly, however, not all entities are equally good in providing clues for identification of other entities. First of all, anchors themselves have to be sufficiently salient in the context. Thus, accordingly, the best and most frequent possessors are humans. Also, most standard possessive NPs involve either definite (in the majority of cases[1]) or indefinite specific possessors, with pronominal possessors representing the absolutely clearest and most frequent instances of definite human (or, occasionally, animate) possessors. More than that, indefinite inanimate possessors may be dispreferred in PNPs, which results in the alternation between PNPs and prepositional constructions. Thus, whereas *kyrkans väggar* 'the walls of the church' is perfectly all right, the PNP *en kyrkas väggar* 'the walls of a church' requires a very special context, with the more frequent alternative being *väggarna på en kyrka* 'the walls "on" a church'. There are also certain restrictions on what kinds of relations between what kinds of entities can be evoked in a standard possessive NP – both the category of the possessor and the possessee interact here in intricate ways. Thus, e.g. PNPs are dispreferred or even forbidden for reference to OBJECTS of deverbal nouns, where prepositional phrases have to be used. Cf. **Clintons val* vs. *valet av Clinton* 'the election of Clinton' (cf. section 2.4, the discussion of the relation between PNPs and constructions with prepositional possessors).

2.2.2. PNPs as definite NPs

PNPs in Swedish have normally a definite interpretation, i.e., their referent is often unique within the pragmatic set of entities shared by the speaker and the listener (Hawkins 1978, 1991, also quoted in Haspelmath 1999b: 231; Teleman, Hellberg and Andersson 2000: 27-28). Thus, a sentence such as (1)

(1) *Var   är   Peter-s   skjorta?*
    where is   Peter-GEN   shirt
    'Where is Peter's shirt?'

normally presupposes that there is one particular shirt of interest in the current situation, which both the speaker and the listener can identify, even though Peter might have others as well. An appropriate reply to (1) would be *Här är den* 'Here it is', whereas by uttering *Här är en* 'Here is one' the speaker is not particularly cooperative. Unique reference, though usual is, however, not always necessary for using a PNP: sentence (2) does not presuppose that the speaker either has only one friend, or that (s)he and the listener can identify the one referred to by the PNP:

(2)   *Det   här   har   jag   hört   av   min   polare*
      DET   here have   I   heard   of my:COM friend
'I've heard this from a friend of mine.'

In various morphosyntactic respects, PNPs are also treated as definite NPs. Before going into this issue, we have to say a few words about definiteness marking in Swedish NPs[2].

Swedish has both indefinite and definite articles, which have different morphosyntactic status in that the indefinite article is a clitic introducing a NP (cf. *en stol* 'a:COM chair', *ett bord* 'a:N table'), whereas the definite article is a nominal suffix (*stol-en* 'the:COM chair', *bord-et* 'the:N table', *stolar-na* 'the:PL chairs') – more about its shape will be said in section 3.2. There is also a morphologically unbound preposed definite article (determinant) *den/det/de* used only under special conditions (see below). Adjectives distinguish between indefinite (strong) and definite (weak) forms, but the choice between those is always dependent on the presence of other (in)definiteness markers in the NP and can therefore be considered an agreement marker (Börjars 1994: 219), or secondary (in)definiteness indicator (cf. *ett grön-t bord* 'a:N green-N table' vs. *detta grön-a bord* 'this:N green-DEF table').

It is possible to formulate the following GENERAL PRINCIPLE OF DEFINITENESS MARKING IN THE SWEDISH NP:

> Definiteness in Swedish NPs is marked as early as possible (i.e., on the first word in a NP): either by means of preposed definite determiners, or, in the absence of such words, by means of the definite suffix on the first noun.

The primary definiteness indicators in Swedish NPs show, thus, the following patterns:

1. Definiteness is marked by means of preposed definite determiners, such as demonstratives *denna/detta/dessa* 'this/these'; the words *samma* '(the) same', *nästa* '(the) next', *följande* '(the) following', *föregående* '(the) preceding'; and possessors – cf. ex. (3) below.
2. In the absence of a definite preposed determiner, if a NP consists of a single noun or a noun followed by dependents (such as relative clauses, prepositional phrases, infinitives and subordinate clauses), definiteness is marked by means of the definite suffix on the head noun – cf. ex. (4) below.
3. With the preposed demonstratives *den/det/de*, often combined with the deictic adverb *här/där* 'here/there' for specifying deixis ('this'/'that'), head nouns have to attach the definite suffix. In this case, definiteness is marked twice, by elements which both can function independently as semantic determiners – cf. ex. (5a) below. This is termed DOUBLE DETERMINATION – a phenomenon specific to Swedish and Norwegian (cf. Börjars 1994 for a thorough analysis of this phenomenon). The same pattern is required whenever definite NPs involve adjectival modifiers or numerals. All the accompanying modifying adjectives appear in the definite form, which thus functions as an agreement marker. For some modifiers, the preposed determiner is optional , e.g. , for the ordinal numbers *första* '(the) first', *andra* '(the second)' etc., *sista* '(the) last', *förra* '(the) previous'. Cf. ex. (5b) below.

(3) Definiteness marked by means of preposed definite determiners
a. *detta hus*   'this:N house'
b. *samma hus*   '(the) same house'
c. *Peters hus*   'Peter's house'

(4) Definiteness marked by means of definite suffixes on the head noun

a. *Titta på hus-et!*
Look at house-DEF.N
'Look at the house!'

b. *Hämta klänning-en med rosor på.*
fetch dress-DEF.COM with roses on
'Fetch the dress with roses on it.'

(5) DOUBLE DETERMINATION – a NP combines two determiners (a preposed independent determiner and a definite suffix on the head noun)

a. *det här hus-et*
DET:N here house-DEF.N
'this house'

b. *det grön-a bord-et*
DET:N green-DEF table-DEF.N
'the green table'

Now, back to PNPs. PNPs are treated as definite NPs in various morphosyntactic respects:

- PNPs, as other definite NPs, are normally not allowed in existential constructions, cf. *Det ligger en hatt på stol-en* 'There is a hat lying on the chair' vs. **Det ligger Peter-s hatt på stol-en* ?'There is Peter's hat lying on the chair'.
- PNPs are incompatible with indefinite articles and cannot be directly quantified by indefinite and negative quantifiers, such as *någon* 'some', *ingen* 'none', as well as by numerals.

(6) a. **en   Peters skjorta*
         a:COM/one:COM   Peter's shirt
    b.   *några/inga/två   skjort-or*
         some:PL/none:PL/two   shirt-PL
         'some/no/two shirts'

c.	*några/*inga/*två
some:PL/none:PL/two	skjort-or-na
shirt-PL-DEF.PL
d.	*några/*inga/*två
some:PL/none:PL/two	Peter-s skjort-or
Peter-GEN   shirt-PL

- Adjectives following possessors and pertaining to the possessee appear in the definite form, cf. *Peter-s grön-a bord* 'Peter-GEN green-DEF table', i.e. 'Peter's green table' with the example in (5b).
- Finally, and most important for our purposes, preposed possessors (both pronominal and lexical) in Swedish NPs are incompatible with definite articles pertaining to the host nominal – either the definite suffix or the unbound preposed determiner, cf. *Peter-s bord* 'Peter's table', but not **Peter-s bord-et* 'Peter-GEN table-DEF.N' or **det Peter-s bord* 'DET:N Peter-GEN table-DEF.N'.

To summarise, PNPs are definite NPs, and, from the point of view of definiteness marking, preposed possessors in a NP align themselves with preposed definite determiners listed in 1. above.

Whenever a possessee has to be explicitly indefinite, PNPs have to give place to other constructions – either to partitive constructions, (ex. (7a)), to compounds (ex. (7b)), or to prepositional constructions (ex. (7c)).

(7) a. *en/ några/inga/två   av   Peter-s   skjort-or*
one/some:PL/none:PL/two of   Peter-GEN   shirt-PL
'one/some/none/two of Peter' shirts'

b. *en   kung-a-son*
COM/one:COM   king-LINKER-son
'a king's son'

c. *en   vän   till mig*
a:COM/one:COM   friend   to me
'a friend of mine'

2.3. Compounds

In noun-noun compounds the first part modifies the second. Compounds are also notorious for their multiple potential interpretations, or rather, for the vagueness of the semantic relation between their two parts, cf. *änke-stuga* 'widow-hut' (i.e., 'widow's hut', LEGAL OWNERSHIP or PREDESTINATION), *hund-ben* 'dog-bone' (i.e., 'dog's bone', BODY-PART), *präst-dotter* 'priest-daughter' (i.e., 'priest's daughter', KINSHIP), *guld-ring* 'gold-ring' (i.e., 'golden ring', MATERIAL), *bröd-kniv* 'bread-knife' (i.e., 'bread knife', PURPOSE) and *höst-blommor* 'autumn-flowers' (i.e., 'autumn flowers', TIME). (The hyphens are added here in order to show the components of the compound words.) Possible interpretations of a compound depend on the semantics of its parts and on the context.

As mentioned above, PNPs normally involve either definite possessors (in the overwhelming majority of cases) or indefinite specific ones. In compounds, on the contrary, the first part is normally non-referential and its primary function consists in qualifying or classifying the second nominal, the whole compound functioning more or less as a classificational label. This has consequences for how the relation between the parts of a compound tends to be interpreted. Thus, classifications often imply a more or less stable situation, and an object previously classified as owned by a person of a certain type can all of a sudden come into possession by a completely different person. As a result, in compounds LEGAL OWNERSHIP or DISPOSAL par excellence often gives way to an interpretation of PREDESTINATION – i.e., an object is supposed to be owned or used by a certain category, but does not have to. (8a) and (8b) illustrate the basic difference in use between PNPs and compounds:

(8) a. *Jag bor i en students lägenhet.*
'I live in a student's apartment.' (= an apartment belonging to a student)
b. *Jag bor i en studentlägenhet.*
'I live in a student apartment.' (= an apartment for students)

Many compounds are lexicalised, but the process of compounding is on the whole very productive. Compounds are distinguished from word combinations and from simplex words by a special compounding prosody. For all morphological and syntactic purposes, nominal compounds behave like nouns, more particularly, like their last part. Thus, e.g., compounds show the usual nominal inflectional oppositions: *en änke-stuga* 'a:COM widow-hut', *änke-stuga-n* 'widow-hut-DEF.COM', *änke-stug-or* 'widow-hut-PL', *änke-stug-or-na-s* 'widow-hut-PL-DEF-GEN' etc.

The border between PNPs and compounds is, however, far from clear-cut.

1. Semantically, PNPs and compounds are sometimes quite close to each other. In certain cases noun-noun compounding and a genitive construction are both possible, sometimes with only a minimal semantic difference between the two. Thus, PNPs with a non-specific or generic possessor are very close to compounds, e.g. an *elephant's trunk* in the sentence *An elephant's trunk can be two meters long* might be translated into Swedish either as a PNP with a non-specific possessor, *en elefants snabel*, or as a compound *en elefantsnabel*.

Similarly, possible semantic differences are neutralised in the case of the PNP *husets tak* 'the roof of the house' vs. the compound *hustaket* 'the house roof' in the context *There was a stork nest on the roof of the house*. Since houses normally have one roof, one and the same entity is identified in both cases, either directly, by the compound, or by being related to the already identified entity.

Finally, some situations can be conceptualised in different ways, so that both PNPs and compounds, although semantically different, may be pragmatically equivalent. We will discuss this point in section 3.3.

2. Formally many Swedish noun-noun compounds are close to PNPs in that they are formed with a compound marker *-s-,* which, thus, looks like the genitive marker, e.g. *värld-s-marknad-en* 'world-LINKER-market-DEF.COM' (i.e., 'the world's market'). This marker has developed historically from a genitive inflection into a

mere marker of the compound juncture – a situation familiar from quite a few other languages. In a few rare cases there are some other linkers, e.g. *gat-u-korsning-en* 'street-LINKER-crossing-DEF.COM' (i.e., 'the street crossing'). More often, the two parts of a compound appear as juxtaposed to each other, e.g. *pojk-skjorta* 'boy-shirt' (i.e., 'a boy's shirt').

3. Finally, in Modern Swedish there is an ever growing tendency to write the parts of compound words as separate words – a usage condemned by Swedish normative linguists, but attested in writing even with those (usually young) Swedes who otherwise follow the standard spelling rules (for some discussion cf. Mobärg 1998).

To conclude, even though the standard possessive NPs and compounds in prototypical cases are quite different entities, they sometimes converge on such important parameters as semantics, morphosyntactic makeup and spelling.

2.4. Constructions with postposed prepositional modifiers

In Swedish, as in related Germanic languages, constructions with genitives or possessive pronouns can alternate with prepositional constructions to express various types of possessive relations. Curiously, the relations of LEGAL POSSESSION (*Jennys bok* 'Jenny's book'; *min bok* 'my book') and DISPOSAL (*sekreterarens rum* 'the secretary's office') cannot be expressed by a prepositional construction in Swedish, but have to be rendered with a genitive or a possessive pronoun.

Some languages have a common preposition expressing a possessive. Thus, e.g., English *of*, German *von*, Spanish *de*, Hebrew *šel*, and Bulgarian *na* are used as "general possessive preposition". The Scandinavian languages, however, use different spatial prepositions in many types of possessor-possessee relations where related languages will use a standard possessive preposition. The rationale for this is of course the relatedness of spatial inclusion and possession.

This merging of spatial and possessive conceptualisations results in what we may call *locative-possessive constructions*, i.e. constructions with various types of spatial prepositions which correspond in meaning to constructions with genitives or possessive pronouns. The two constructions can alternate under favourable conditions, even though the prepositional constructions can sometimes express additional meaning nuances as compared to the corresponding PNPs (e.g., the difference between *ingredienserna i/till soppan* 'the ingredients "in"/"to" the soup' in the list below). This applies in Swedish particularly in certain types of possessor-possessee relations, such as

LOCATION WITHIN DOMAIN:
huvudstaden i Ghana   'the capital "in" Ghana'
invånarna i Stockholm   'the inhabitants "in" Stockholm'
PART–WHOLE:
benet på stolen   'the leg "on" the chair'
ingredienserna i soppan   'the ingredients "in" the soup'
BODY-PART:
kinden på Lisa   'the cheek "on" Lisa'
i magen på fågeln   'in the stomach "on" the bird'
SUBSET:
några bland barnen   'some "among" the children'
POSSESSED QUALITY:
färgen på blomman   'the colour "on" the flower'
namnet på gatan   'the name "on" the street'
kompetensen hos personalen   'the competence "at/with" the staff'
fördelen med förslaget   'the advantage "with" the proposition'
REPRESENTATION:
teori om film   'theory "about" film'
historia över måleriet   'history "over" painting'
CONNECTION:
locket till burken   'the lid "to" the jar'
ingredienserna till soppan   'the ingredients "to" the soup'
INTERPERSONAL RELATIONS:
en granne till oss   'a neighbour "to" us'

KINSHIP:
pappan till bröderna   'the dad "to" the brothers'
CAUSE:
orsaken till olyckan   'the cause "to" the accident'

In cases like the ones cited, the underlying spatial sense is that of 'location at/on/in/with etc' or 'direction to'. Here the preposition *av* 'of' is ruled out. But where the underlying spatial sense is that of 'direction from', source prepositions such as *av* 'of', *från* 'from', *efter* 'after' are used:

TRACE:
spår av/efter tjuvarna   'traces of the thieves'
resterna av/från/efter måltiden   'the remains of the meal'
RESULT/EFFECT:
konsekvenserna av misstaget   'the consequences of the mistake'
ORIGINATOR:
symfonier av Mozart   'symphonies by Mozart'

In some cases of PART–WHOLE or SUBSET relations it is possible to use either *av* or a locative-possessive variant, as e.g. *en avdelning av/i bolaget* 'a division "of/in" the company', *i början av/på april* 'in the beginning "of/on" April', *några av/bland dem som var med* 'some "of/among" those who were present', thus giving more prominence either to the partiality or to the location. In Standard Swedish there is a (somewhat fuzzy) border zone in this area. *Av* tends to be preferred when the head noun (the possessee) presupposes a relation of partiality and, to a certain degree, quantification. While *en vägg på huset* 'a wall of the house' is preferred to *en vägg av huset*, *en del av huset* 'a part of the house' could not be rendered as *en del på huset – an important difference between 'a wall' and 'a part' is that the first word denotes an entity which in principle can be recognised without the whole (the house), while the latter can only be understood in relation to the whole. And in general, PARTITIVE constructions consisting of a nominal measure word quantifying definite entities, involve *av*, e.g. *en kopp av det goda kaffet* 'a cup of the good coffee'. By contrast, NPs with nominal measure words quantifying indefinite entities simply involve juxtaposition of the two, e.g. *en kopp kaffe* 'a cup (of) coffee'.

A special case of variation occurs with pictures, where *på* competes with *av* in the DEPICTING relation, whereas *av* prevails in the ORIGINATOR relation; for details of this competitive situation cf. Lyly's (1996) discussion of examples like *en bild på/av Picasso* 'a picture of P.' as compared to *en bild av Picasso* 'a picture by P.'.

Av is also used to mark OBJECTS of deverbal nouns, as in *Alexanders erövring av Egypten* 'Alexander's conquest of Egypt', and not **Alexanders Egyptens erövring* or **Egyptens erövring av Alexander*.

Thus, the choice of a preposition introducing a postposed attribute is most often intimately connected with the semantics of the head noun. This is obvious for typically relational nouns, such as body-parts nouns and nouns referring to other parts, kin terms and nouns referring to other interpersonal relations, or words like *consequence* or *result* – not only do these words invoke a special relation to another entity, but cannot simply be understood without this entity. Thus, a person cannot be a neighbour or a son without being someone's neighbour or son. It seems, however, that many more nouns are relational in a weak sense, in that their meaning itself presupposes or invokes specific relations. Thus, although a book can perfectly well be conceptualised without any reference to other entities and there are no problems at all with sentences like *Here's a book*, as opposed to **Here's a wife*, books are strongly associated with their authors and with their content. In other words, the semantic structure of the word *book* readily invokes relations of ORIGINATOR (*en bok av Strindberg* 'a book by Strindberg') and of REPRESENTATION (*en bok om Japan* 'a book about Japan')[3]. In this perspective, the absence of a preposition for coding the relations of LEGAL POSSESSION and DISPOSAL might perhaps be interpreted as a symptom of the essential difference between these and all the other relations listed above: the former are much more general and much more loosely connected to the semantics of particular nouns than the latter. After all, all artefacts and certainly many more concrete entities are potentially possessible and/or at someone's disposal.

A prepositional construction is particularly useful when the possessee is indefinite. Thus, for example, while *husets väggar* and *väggarna på huset* 'the walls of the house' are both possible, *en vägg på huset* 'a wall of the house' cannot be rendered with a genitive. Also, as mentioned in section 2.2.1, whereas PNPs are frequent with animate and definite possessors, inanimate indefinite possessors very often call for other constructions, primarily prepositional constructions, such as *väggarna på ett hus* 'the walls of a house'. In many contexts, a prepositional construction is perceived stylistically as less formal than a genitive.

However, when a possessee in the relation of LEGAL POSSESSION is indefinite, the corresponding expression will be a partitive construction of the type illustrated in ex. (7a) in section 2.2.2.

2.5. The Swedish system of adnominal possession: summarising

Table 1 summarises the various formal and semantic properties of the three constructions described in sections 2.1 – 2.4.

As mentioned in section 1, linguistic possession is hard or even impossible to define. However, most people would agree that the core of this category is made up of cases where there is an exclusive asymmetric long-term relation between two entities – for each possessee there is only one possessor, who has the right to make use of the possessee – and the possessor is an individuated human being (cf. Taylor 1996: 340). In accordance with this, PNPs in Swedish constitute the best expression format for adnominal possession since it covers all the more prototypical cases of this category. Both other construction types provide worse matches here: in compounds, the possessor is not individuated, and constructions with postposed prepositional modifiers cannot express LEGAL POSSESSION and DISPOSAL.

Table 1. Summary of the formal and semantic properties of the major adnominal possessive constructions in Swedish. D = Possessor; H = Possessee.

Properties	PNPs	Compounds	NPs with prepositional modifiers
Morphosyntactic status	Definite NP	Noun	NP
Order of Possessor (D) and Possessee (H)	D-H	D-H	H-D
Reduction of inflection and/ or combinability	For H: no articles are permitted. Normally only definite interpretation for H.	For D: no inflectional categories. Normally only non-specific interpretation for D.	———
Markers of relation between H and D	The clitic -s in the majority of cases; Agreeing possessive pronouns for 1 and 2 person, and reflexives.	No marker, or the linking elements – -s- and, sporadically, a few others. The choice determined by several factors, often in an unpredictable fashion.	Different prepositions for different relations. The choice often determined by semantics of the D in a fairly complicated fashion.
Disfavouring factors	Indefiniteness of H. Other semantic factors (types of relations) to a certain degree.	Specificity of D.	Primarily semantic: some relations, such as LEGAL POSSESSION and DISPOSAL.
Other alternatives under disfavouring conditions.	For LEGAL POSSESSION and DISPOSAL: partitive constructions. For other relations: constructions with prepositional modifiers. With non-specific D: compounds.	PNPs or constructions with prepositional modifiers.	PNPs or, for non-specific D, compounds.

With regard to the simplicity of their form, PNPs, and particularly those with *s*-genitives, are also clearly superior to the other two constructions. The choice between the two formal subtypes (the one with a possessive pronoun that shows agreement and an *s*-genitive) is completely transparent, and *s*-genitives are formed in an absolutely uniform way. In compounds, the choice of the technique for combining the two parts (no marker, the -*s*-linker or other linkers) is often difficult to determine, and the same concerns the choice of the preposition for postposed modifiers to nouns.

In short, PNPs, in particular those with *s*-genitives, are an unmarked, or default construction for adnominal possession in Swedish.

2.6. The typological profile of the Swedish system of adnominal possession

In what follows we will provide a general typological background for the two aspects of the Swedish system of adnominal possession which in one way or another are typologically interesting and can present problems in L2-acquisition:

- the definiteness of PNPs, and
- the existence of several adnominal possessive constructions

2.6.1. Possessor-article complementarity and definiteness of PNPs

Swedish, or rather Mainland Scandinavian, is of course not unique in showing possessor-article complementarity – such languages are attested in several families and areas, e.g English, Welsh and Irish, Romani, Vai, Amharic, Hebrew and Maltese. They are opposed to others, such as Portuguese and Italian, in which possessors co-occur with (and, normally, even require the presence of) articles, cf. Ital. *un mio vestito* 'one of my dresses' vs. *il mio vestito* 'my dress', as well as *un/il bel vestito di Anna* 'a beautiful dress of Anna's/Anna's beautiful dress'. Finally, in still other languages, such as most of the Slavic languages or Chinese, the question of possessor-article complementarity simply does not arise due to the lack of grammaticalised articles.

There are also concomitant cross-linguistic differences in the interpretation of possessive NPs: while PNPs in Swedish are normally definite, their counterparts in Italian, Russian and Chinese may be both definite and indefinite, depending on the article (in the Italian case) and/or on the context.

A fairly well-spread structural account suggests that article-possessor incompatibility follows from a requirement for a unique determiner position in a NP (a claim which itself can be debated). In languages of the Swedish type, possessors occupy the determiner slot in a possessive NP. In languages like Italian, possessors have a different structural status, comparable to those of modifying adjectives, cf. examples above with *un bel vestito* 'a beautiful dress' and *il bel vestito* (Lyons 1986: 138; Giorgi and Longobardi 1991). The fact that possessors and definite articles in Swedish are structurally and positionally different – possessors introduce the NP, while articles are suffixes on the head noun – is a complication for this analysis.

Haspelmath (1999b) and Koptjevskaja-Tamm (forthc. b) suggest instead that article-possessor complementarity in certain languages has a functional rationale stemming from the frequent function of the possessors as anchors or reference point entities for identifying other entities. Thus, Haspelmath (1999b: 227) states that

> such patterns of article-possessor complementarity are ECONOMICALLY MOTIVATED (in the sense of Haiman 1985): the definite article can be omitted because possessed NPs have a very high chance of being definite, for semantic and pragmatic reasons ... By conventionalising an articleless possessive construction languages obtain a syntactic pattern that allows for more economical (i.e., shorter) utterances.

Languages like Italian, on the other hand, show preference for EXPLICITNESS at the cost of economy. Haspelmath argues also that the functional account has a better explanatory value, in particular for those languages where the article and the possessor appear in different positions with Swedish as an example par excellence.

2.6.2. Splits in the system of adnominal possession

Co-occurrence of several different possessive constructions in one and the same language is a fairly frequent phenomenon; there are various recurring types of split possession systems in the world's languages. The alternating possessive constructions are thus opposed to each other according to various parameters. In the case of Swedish, as in many other languages, these parameters include properties of possessors, properties of possessees and the type of relation between a possessor and a possessee.

1. *PNPs vs compounding: anchoring vs non-anchoring relations.* The choice between *PNPs* and *compounds* is mainly determined by specificity vs. non-specificity of possessors: only the former can normally function as anchors in anchoring relations. Quite a few languages have different constructions for expressing anchoring and non-anchoring relations, even though the details may differ. Thus, non-anchoring relations can be expressed by compounds, by constructions with denominal adjectives ("relational adjectives") or by structures which share certain, but not all morphosyntactic properties with standard possessive NPs (e.g., English, in which examples like *a women's magazine* have been analysed differently by different linguists, as involving descriptive or classifying genitives, or as possessive compounds). A common formal denominator across these strategies is a reduction of typical nominal inflectional and combinatorial properties by a non-specific modifier.

It is, however, even more usual to have one and the same construction for both anchoring and non-anchoring relations.

2. *PNPs vs locative-possessive prepositional constructions.* The choice between *PNPs* and *locative-possessive prepositional constructions* is mainly determined by the (in)definiteness of possessees,

by the type of relation between the possessee and the possessor, as well as by stylistic factors (cf. the end of section 2.4). All these factors are known to be instrumental in split possession systems across languages, but the details differ considerably, and rarely do the factors interact in such an intricate way as they do in Swedish. PNPs are by far more frequent than any one of the prepositional constructions and even all of them together.

3. *Choice of preposition in locative-possessive constructions.* Finally, the choice among the different prepositions in locative-possessive prepositional constructions is determined by the semantics of a possessee and its relation to a possessor. As we saw in section 2.4, the most prominent prepositions in the locative-possessive system are *på* 'on', *till* 'to' and *av* 'of/from'. Spatial markers with more or less comparable semantics (AT/ON, TO and FROM) are generally known to give rise to possessive markers across languages. One reason for this is the abstractedness of linguistic possession as a cognitive domain. Thus, e.g., how do we actually know that a hat is Peter's or that Mary is John's wife? Figuring this out or understanding what this would mean would demand quite complicated perceptual and cognitive strategies and a huge cultural background. A basic and generally applied cognitive strategy for dealing with relatively abstract, less easily accessible or understandable domains is by understanding and describing them in terms of more concrete domains (cf., e.g., Lakoff and Johnson 1980; Heine 1997: 45). Spatial experiences are fairly easily accessible – under normal circumstances no great efforts are required for seeing whether a hat is on Peter's head, or is in his hand or is not in his vicinity at all. Moreover, an experience (in particular, if it is repeated) of seeing a hat on Peter's head gives rise to a natural inference that it is his. Likewise seeing Mary and John together, in the spatial proximity to each other in various places can, under certain circumstances, be a ground for suspecting that they are a couple. Thus, spatial experiences can be used for understanding possession and spatial expressions, and therefore provide an important grammaticalisation source for possessive expressions (Heine 1997: 45-186; Koptjevskaja-Tamm forthc. a).

Grammaticalisation leads to expansion and generalisation of one spatial marker to the whole cognitive domain of possession and the gradual loss of the others. There are signs in the locative-possessive prepositional system that witness to such ongoing grammaticalisation processes. Thus, e.g., as mentioned above, some of the prepositions are the clear "leaders" in the sense that they take care of the main bulk of the relations expressed in the system, with the result that there is a certain degree of apparent arbitrariness in the choice of prepositions in Swedish. Historical changes in the distribution of the prepositions are described for the older periods of Swedish by Norde (1997) and for the latest 300 years by Pitkänen (1979). Pitkänen's data point to the conclusion that the least marked and the more expanding preposition during that period has been *på* 'on'. However, both *till* 'to' and *av* 'from' show a high degree of grammaticalisation; this is particularly obvious in the case of *av* which in Modern Swedish is used very restrictedly for referring to spatial relations, compared to its more abstract uses. The present Swedish system might perhaps be seen as transitional from the stage when more prepositions were actively involved and the choice between them was sufficiently transparent, to a stage when one spatial preposition is generalised to a large portion of the possession domain. Among the Scandinavian languages the latter case is found in Norwegian with its preposition *til* 'to' as the general possessive marker and some of the Norwegian and Northern Swedish dialects (curiously, the general possessive preposition in these varieties comes either from TO or from FROM). In standard Swedish and Danish, and also Faroese (cf. Stolz with Gorsemann forthc.) the grammaticalisation processes have not yet been carried through. Transitional systems are generally characterised by a high degree of complexity, and this is also true of the Swedish locative-possessive system.

3. Problems facing learners of Swedish as L2
3.1. The data source

In order to obtain evidence for how Swedish possessive constructions are handled by young adult L2 learners, we have used the *ASU Corpus*, a text database which has been compiled in the nineties at the Department of Linguistics, Stockholm University. This is a body of Swedish recorded conversational speech and written essays collected from foreign and native university students in Stockholm. For the present purpose, the *written learner part* of the corpus has been used. Cf. Hammarberg (1999) for a full account of the design and contents of the ASU Corpus.

The learner part of the corpus is longitudinally designed, tracing the developing interlanguage from the beginner stage when the subjects had just arrived in Sweden and began their university language preparatory course, to a stage where they were participating in university studies in Swedish. Ten subjects, 3 women and 7 men aged 19-28, were followed, representing various L1s. They will be referred to below with a letter-and-digit identification: German and English, represented by a bilingual L1 speaker (subject E2), Portuguese (Q1, Q2), Spanish (S1), Greek (G2, G3), Polish (P1) and Chinese (C1, C2, C4). (Concise typological information on adnominal possession in these languages is given in the Appendix.) The subjects each produced two short essays on each of 11 occasions, which yielded a total of 220 texts, or 50 000 word tokens. The texts comprise narratives, descriptions and discussions on given general and current topics.

The subjects can be broadly characterised as *"semi-formal learners"*, since they lived in the Stockholm area at the time and received their Swedish language input partly from the course and partly from the outside environment. All corpus material was collected in separate sessions outside class and was not evaluated in the course. They can be categorised as *"qualified learners"* in the sense that they all had secondary education, previous experience with foreign languages, and strong instrumental motivation to learn the language of the host country in order to proceed with the studies in their fields.

All were acquainted with English and most of them with one or two other L2s prior to Swedish. Relatively speaking, they were *"fast learners"* since they proceeded from the beginner stage through or close to the Swedish proficiency level required for university studies in Sweden within one to two years. Their overall L2 development did not show a noticeable plateau, but progressed continuously. They certainly did not reach perfection in L2 during the period of observation; rather, the corpus spans stages when complex grammar and discourse structure was gradually taking shape in their free production.

Generally speaking, the interlanguage of these learners differs considerably from the type that has been described in major European L2 research projects, such as the Heidelberg Project (Klein and Dittmar 1979), ZISA (Clahsen, Meisel and Pienemann 1983) and the "ESF Project" (Perdue 1993). It is clearly more target-oriented. Thus the present corpus does not display an extended period dominated by a "basic variety" (cf. Klein and Perdue 1997), but the learners are inclined from early stages to develop a grammaticalised interlanguage (here in the sense of acquisitional grammaticalisation). Although this can be observed also in the learners' oral production (as evidenced in Hammarberg 1996, 2000), it is particularly obvious in the written part of the corpus which we have chosen to investigate here.

The 11 sessions of data collection were distributed with five sessions (Time 1–5) from September to December 1990, four sessions (Time 6–9) from January to May 1991, one (Time 10) in March 1992, and one (Time 11) in April 1993.

We have excerpted and analysed the instances of adnominal possessive constructions occurring in the written learner corpus and will concentrate here on the various types of target-deviant solutions that occur, and the acquisitional problems that they evidence.

Productive use of possessive constructions emerges already in the early sessions with some of the subjects, but the bulk of instances appear in the second semester and thereafter (Time 6–11). No clear time sequence of developmental solutions for possessive constructions can be observed in the data we have inspected (which does not rule out the possibility that other comparable learner language data might be more conclusive in this respect). Yet it is clear enough that there are some tendencies for the learners to use certain specific patterns of target-deviant solutions or to favour particular constructions. We will discuss and exemplify such cases in the following sections.

3.2. PNPs and definiteness

In sections 2.2.2 and 2.6.1, we described the the following typologically interesting properties of Swedish PNPs:

- PNPs are inherently definite; and
- possessors in PNPs function as preposed definiteness markers in being incompatible with definite articles and requiring definite forms for the following adjectives.

As should be clear from the discussion, the two properties are actually two sides of one and the same phenomenon, particularly seen "from the inside" of the Swedish nominal system with its highly grammaticalised definiteness category. Our corpus shows that learners can have problems with both of them (in what follows, for considerations of space, we will not consider the form of adjectives in PNPs).

In the example (9) the PNP is treated as an indefinite NP in two respects: by occurring in the existential context and by containing an indefinite quantifier *många* 'many' (cf. the end of section 2.2 and ex. (6)). Here, as in subsequent learner's examples, we first give the learner's version with an English word-by-word gloss, then a reconstructed Swedish target version followed by an English translation of the target version. It should also be noted that, to save space, we omit the glossing of gender in learner utterances, since the choice of gender has no bearing on the present topic. A source reference is given by stating the subject and the session of data collection; thus "C1-3" refers to subject C1, session 3.

(9)   *Det*   *fanns*   *många Mings*   *vänner*   *i hans*
       there   were   many   Ming-GEN   friend-PL   in his

rummet.
room-DEF.SG
'*Det fanns många vänner till Ming i hans rum.*'
'There were many friends of Ming's in his room.' (C1-3)

Interestingly, a sentence later the same learner tries to use a periphrastic construction of the partitive type for the same purpose.

(10) Det   fanns   olika   personer   av Mings   vänner
     there were   various persons   of Ming-GEN   friend-PL
     som   komde från   Kina   förstårs
     who   came from   China   of course
     '*Det fanns olika vänner till Ming, som kom från Kina förstås.*'
     'There were various friends of Ming's, who came from China of course.' (C1-3)

There are several instances in which PNPs contain indefinite articles, showing thus other signs of being treated as indefinite NPs:

(11) en   stor   landets   stad
     IND.ART   big   country-DEF.SG-GEN   town
     '*en stor stad på landet*', '*en stor landsortsstad*'
     'a big town in the country', 'a big countryside town' (G2-8)

Much more frequent in our corpus are examples in which the head noun in a PNP erroneously attaches a definite suffix, cf. (12):

(12) a. hennes   huvudet
         her   head-DEF.SG
         '*hennes huvud*'
         'her head' (P6-3)
     b. ... *men jag tycker om läsar tidningarnas familjesidan*
         '... *men jag tycker om att läsa tidningarnas familjesida.*'
         '... but I like reading the papers' family page.' (C4-7)

In what follows we suggest two different interpretations for such errors which we will refer to as DEF-in-PNP1 and DEF-in-PNP2. To show our grounds for these interpretations we have chosen two texts by one and the same learner, C4. Since her native language, Chinese, lacks a grammatical category of definiteness in nouns, in acquiring Swedish she is confronted with the task of understanding both the semantics of this category in Swedish and its complicated system of (in)definiteness marking.

The learner C4 during session 4 shows that she is coming to grips with the simplest definiteness alternations in Swedish. This is shown in Table 2. The learner is clearly following the rule that new referents in a discourse are often introduced in an indefinite form, but starting from the second mention are treated as definite NPs. This is seen in the introduction of and the subsequent reference to the main protagonists in the story – a ticket seller and three men, where definite suffixes are used in the second mention, combined with the preposed determiner in the case of numeral expressions. The same pattern, however, is applied to the word *handväska* 'hand bag', which is introduced with an indefinite article, but on the second mention is used as the head of a PNP with the preposed possessor *hennes* 'her' and the definite suffix. In learning the Swedish definiteness marking system, learners of Swedish have to acquire both the different patterns for expressing definiteness (by a preposed definite determiner, by a definite suffix on the head noun and by combination of the two), and also keep in memory their distribution, which is far from obvious. Thus, why should the demonstrative *denna* require the absence of the definite suffix on the head noun, whereas the demonstratives *den* and *den här* require its presence? Similarly, why should the same difference be triggered by the words *samma* '(the) same', *nästa* '(the) next', *följande* '(the) following', *föregående* '(the) preceding', as opposed to *andra* '(the) second)' and *förra* '(the) previous'? In a corpus of spoken data from 60 learners of Swedish, Axelsson (1994) observes that single nouns with definite suffixes are the second most frequent type of definite lexical NPs (following proper names), even though the learners make mistakes with the pattern for a longer time than with PNPs. In language instruction, the definiteness category itself is also normally introduced and exemplified by the simplest definiteness alternation of the type *en kassörska* → *kassörskan*.

Table 2. Referent chaining in C4-4.

Referent	First mention	Indefiniteness marking	Second mention	Definiteness marking
Ticket seller	en kassörska	Indef. article with nouns in SG	kassörskan	Def. suffix on single nouns (pattern 2 in section 2.2.2.)
Three men	Tre män	No indef. art. with nouns in PL	de tre mänen (for 'de tre männen')	Preposed determiner and def. suffix on the head noun 'overdetermination', pattern 3 in section 2.2.2.)
A hand bag	En handväska	Indef. article with nouns in SG	Hennes handväskan	Error: preposed possessors are incompatible with def. suffix on the head noun (pattern 1 in section 2.2.2.)

Thus, it seems reasonable to us that the sheer frequency of the patterns involving definite articles combined with the attention it gets in language instruction can lead to one possible reason for the errors of the type "head noun + DEF in PNPs":

DEF-in-PNP1: The most frequent type of definite marking in NPs involves single nouns marked with the definite suffix. In L2 acquisition this pattern is overgeneralised to other definite NPs, including PNPs.

DEF-in-PNP1 can be seen as an example of what Andersen (1984: 79) has called the "One-to-One Principle" in L2 acquisition, "An interlanguage system should be constructed in such a way that an intended underlying meaning is expressed with one clear invariant surface form (or construction)". The corpus shows similar generalisations of the simplest definiteness patterns for other cases. Thus, e.g., the learner E2 on session 5 writes *samma tiden* instead of *samma tid* 'the same time' (since on an earlier occasion he used the word form *tid* it is reasonable to suggest that *tiden* is used here as the definite and not an unalysed basic form). And in general, the definiteness marking of NPs with the word *samma* 'same' causes problems for several learners.

The data above point to the conclusion that the learner C4 erroneously generalises the simple definiteness marking pattern by means of definite suffixes to PNPs. However, sometimes the same learner makes errors of the same type, but, most probably, motivated by a different reason – the definite form of a word is wrongly analysed as its basic form. Thus, during session 7, the learners were asked to write a text with the title *"Familjesidan i en daglig tidning"* – 'The family page in a daily newspaper'. The word *familjesidan* 'the family page' was thus introduced in the definite form already in the title of the task itself. In the essay produced by C4, this word occurs only in this form, all in all five times. In three of these contexts the definite suffix is used wrongly, because either the context requires an indefinite form (cf. ex. 13) or the noun functions as the head of a PNP (ex. 12b):

(13)   *Det finns inte familjesidan i kinesiska tidningarna.*
        '*Det finns ingen familjesida i kinesiska tidningar.*'
        'There is no family page in Chinese newspapers.' (C4-7)

Similar use of *familjesidan* and other comparable nouns as unanalysed basic forms is also found with other learners in the corpus.

On the basis of such cases we suggest the second possible reason for errors of the type "head noun + DEF in PNPs":

DEF-in-PNP2: The definite form of a noun is sometimes perceived as its basic form.

The main reason for this are the various morphosyntactic properties of the Swedish nominal suffixes which may lead to considerable difficulties in finding out the basic form for a certain noun. And in fact, the corpus contains a number of nouns with definite suffixes used in typical contexts for basic forms – e.g., *en fabriken* 'a factory-DEF.COM' (C4-7), *en sidan* 'a page-DEF.COM' (C1-11), *en stor skoggen* 'a big forest-DEF.COM' (E2-2). Earlier studies on L2 acquisition of Swedish (cf. Axelsson 1994; Wijk-Andersson 1993) show that the relative degree of correctness in the use of definite suffixes in Swedish is often higher at the earliest stage of L2 acquisition than during some of the subsequent stages. The explanation suggested is in the line with ours – a number of very frequent nouns are acquired in the definite form, while the productive and correct use of the definite suffix starts later.

Axelsson (1994: 49) also notes several cases of nouns taking definite suffixes in the presence of possessors and some other preposed determiners which in Standard Swedish are not compatible with this pattern. She suggests basically the same two explanations as we have done in this section.

The two explanations do not, of course, exclude each other, and in many cases it is difficult to find sufficient evidence for which of the two is at work. Both, however, provide a good account for why errors of the type "head noun + DEF in PNPs" occur at the early stages in the acquisition of the definiteness category. However, while the DEF-in-PNP1 is a phenomenon intrinsically connected to the properties of PNPs in Swedish, the DEF-in-PNP2 stems from the Swedish nominal morphology in general.

3.3. Genitive constructions and compounds

All the learners spontaneously form both PNPs and noun-noun compounds. Often, however, a PNP, or more precisely, a nominal genitive construction is used in contexts where a compound would be more appropriate. The general tendency is to overuse the genitive at the expense of the compound, not the reverse. Typical instances of this are cases where the first noun is not intended to be referential and should hence not normally be constructed as a possessor in a PNP. Thus, sentence (8a) in section 2.3 above is actually cited from a learner's text (G2-4), but known facts reveal that the intended meaning is that of (8b).

The issue is complicated by the fact that the formal distinction between a genitive construction and a compound is often not very clearly expressed in the learners' production.

Several factors combine to yield this effect. First, as we noted in section 2.3 above, many Swedish noun-noun compounds are formed with a linker, or compound marker -s-, which is similar to the genitive clitic. Learners use – and overuse – the linking -s- productively in many compound formations, as e.g. in *oljaspris* for 'oljepris' 'oil price' (C2-6).

Secondly, learners occasionally also form compounds with the first noun inflected for plural or definiteness as well, e.g. *tidningars-läsning* 'newspaper-PL-s-reading' for 'tidningsläsning' (C1-6), *högskolansprov* 'university-DEF.SG-s-test' for 'högskoleprov' (C2-10). This results in target-deviant word structures. But considering the fact that learners do produce such formations where the first noun of the compound is obviously inflected, it may well be the case that they similarly perceive the -s- in compounds as a true genitive marker.

Thirdly, the learners often tend to write compounds as separate words. Although this can also be observed with many young Swedes today, the phenomenon is even more frequent with the learners.

Separated compounds in combination with the two other factors just mentioned results in a variety of structures in the learners' production. Focusing on the form of the first noun, we may distinguish the following structure types:

1. The two nouns are merely juxtaposed as two graphic words, e.g. *tunnelbana station* for 'tunnelbanestation' 'tube station' (Q1-8), *introduktion kurs* for 'introduktionskurs' 'introduction (introductory) course' (S1-9). Examples of this type are quite common in our data, and are attested with all the ten learners. The instances occurring in

the corpus generally represent cases where compounding is an appropriate strategy.

2. The first noun is marked for plural or definiteness: *bilar fabriker* 'car-PL factory-PL' for 'bilfabriker', 'car factories' (S1-4), *samhället politik* 'society-DEF.SG politics' for 'samhällets politik' or samhällspolitiken' 'the politics of society' (C1-8), *framtiden melodi* 'future-DEF.SG melody' for 'framtidens melodi' 'the melody of the future' (G3-8). Such cases are target-deviant. They are rare in the corpus, only stray examples occur.

3. The first noun is marked with -*s* and may also carry a plural and/or definiteness marking. This type regularly produces target-like, appropriately used genitive constructions, either with an indefinite possessor, as in *människors liv* 'people's lives' (E2-7), *andra länders konkurrens* 'other countries' competition' (G3-9), or with a definite possessor such as *mannens skor* 'the man's shoes' (S1-5), *nästa generations ungdomar* 'the next generation's young people' (E2-10). But there also occur genitive constructions which are inappropriately used, i.e. cases which by formal criteria have the structure of a PNP but contain a non-specific first noun, e.g. *i sin fisks tallrik* for 'på sin fisktallrik' 'on his plate of fish (fish plate)' (G2-2), *en vanlig tidnings sida* for 'en vanlig tidningssida' 'an ordinary page from a newspaper (newspaper page)' (Q1-7). An additional determiner or adjective may in such cases seem to form a constituent with the genitive-inflected noun. Thus e.g. *sin fisks tallrik* will appear to mean 'the plate of his fish' (rather than 'his plate of fish'), and *en vanlig tidnings sida* 'the page of an *ordinary newspaper*' (rather than 'an ordinary page from a newspaper').

Summing up, it is obvious from these examples that the quoted learners, at their current stage, do not consistently separate genitive and compound constructions. Nor have they fully acquired the ±specific possessor criterion for making functional use of the distinction between the two constructions. From the point of view of the target language, formal and semantic-contextual criteria for interpreting the learner's utterances may come into conflict. When the two nouns occur in separate words, especially the -s marking will function as a strong indicator of a genitive reading, whereas the equivalence of a compound formation in the target language will be the preferred reading if an -s is lacking and/or the context suggests that the first noun should be understood as non-referential.

As shown in section 2.3 above, there are also cases in Swedish where noun-noun compounding and a PNP are both possible. In many such cases the learners in our study tend to favour genitive-like forms. One type is illustrated in (14), where (14a) is the occurring learner's version and (14b) and (14c) are alternative target versions. The compound version in (14b) can here be replaced by a PNP as in (14c) where the possessor noun is conceived as generic and put in the definite form. From the point of view of the target language, the learner's version is a hybrid form, most likely to be interpreted as a PNP.

(14) a. *... den viktigaste frågan som måste lösas först är diskriminerings   problem.*
discrimination-GEN   problem
'... the most important issue which must be solved first is the problem of discrimination' (G3-8)
b. *... diskrimineringsproblemet.*
discrimination-LINKER-problem-DEF.SG
c. *... diskrimineringens   problem.*
discrimination-DEF.SG-GEN   problem

In other cases, it is possible to conceptualise a message variably, either with a specific possessor expressed with a genitive, or as a non-referential classifying element as the first noun in a compound. (15a) is an example of such a case where the learner does not observe the distinction. (The writer is describing the page of a newspaper.)

(15) a. *Uppe i sidan står
ett   sidans   nummer,*
IND.ART   page-   number-DEF.SG-GEN

	ett	tidningens	namn	och	ett
	IND.ART	newspaper-	name	and	IND.ART

datum.
date DEF.SG-GEN
Lit.: 'at the top of the page stands a the page's number, a the newspaper's name and a date' (S1-7)

b. *Upptill på sidan står ett sidnummer, ett tidningsnamn och ett datum.*
'... a page number, a newspaper name and a date'

c. *Upptill på sidan står sidans nummer, tidningens namn och datum.*
'... the number of the page, the name of the newspaper and [the] date'

Assuming that the indefinite articles in (15a) are purposefully used by the learner, the intended message should be as in (15b), where the target language uses the compounding strategy. But it is also possible to express the 'page', 'newspaper' and 'date' as referring to specific entities, by using the genitive for the first two items and dropping the indefinite articles, as in (15c). The learner apparently conceptualises the utterance as in (15b) but uses a genitive strategy, more like (15c), for the construction.

In summary, the learners show clear tendencies to favour genitive-type constructions at the expense of compounding, both in cases where the non-referentiality of the first noun would motivate a compound and in cases where the choice between compound and PNP is optional. This is accompanied by tendencies to blur the formal distinction between a noun-noun compound and a nominal genitive construction.

3.4. Genitives and prepositional constructions

In connection with possessive prepositional constructions, there are two main problem areas in which the learner data show characteristic solutions, viz., (i) the relation between PNPs and prepositional constructions and (ii) the choice of preposition in prepositional constructions.

In most of the cases where a possessive prepositional construction is used in Standard Swedish, it can be replaced in a more or less natural way by a PNP (as long as the possessee is thought of as definite). But there are contexts where a genitive would appear unnatural to native users of Swedish, who will prefer a locative-possessive construction instead. The learners' inclination to favour the PNP becomes apparent in such cases. Examples of this are (16) and (17), illustrating cases of LOCATION and PART–WHOLE, respectively.

(16) *Det är en stor ansvar för de, som bestämmer om*
världens   situation ...
world-DEF.SG-GEN   situation
'*Det är ett stort ansvar för dem som bestämmer om situationen i världen*'
'It is a great responsibility for those who decide about the situation in the world' (P1-6)

(17) *Det är inte lätt när lever*
dagens   största   i mörket.
day-DEF.SG-GEN   great-SUP-DEF
'*Det är inte lätt när man lever största delen av dagen i mörker.*'
'It is not easy when you live the greatest part of the day in darkness.' (Q1-9)

As we pointed out earlier, learners show a tendency to use PNPs even with indefinite possessees. This is a further cause of underrepresentation of prepositional constructions in learners' utterances, since prepositional constructions would usually be the natural way of expressing adnominal possession in the target language in such cases. In (18) the genitive is used in a DEPICTING relation where the indefinite possessee (normal in an existential sentence) would call for a prepositional construction.

(18) *Det finns även många människors*   *bildar.*
           many   human-PL-GEN   picture-PL
      '*Det finns även bilder på/av många människor.*'
      'There are also pictures of many persons.' (C2-7)

In section 3.2 we quoted several cases where a genitive is combined with an indefinite article or quantifier, and the possessee is obviously intended as indefinite. Again, a locative-possessive construction is a way of getting around this problem. This phenomenon occurs with various possessor-possessee relations, e.g. LOCATION as in example (11) *en stor landets stad* 'en stor stad på landet' 'a big city in the country' and INTERPERSONAL RELATION as in (9) *många Mings vänner* 'många vänner till Ming', lit.: 'many friends to Ming'.

The other main tendency in the learner data is to overgeneralise the preposition *av* when using a prepositional construction, thus underusing the various locative-possessive constructions. There is ample evidence of this in the corpus. It also cuts across various types of possessor-possessee relations, as the following examples show:

(19)   LOCATION
         Då kan det contraler prise   *av*   *hela*
                            price   of   whole-DEF
         världen.
         world-DEF.SG
         '*Då kan det kontrollera priset i hela världen.*'
         'Then it can control the price in the whole world.' (C4-6)

(20)   PART–WHOLE
         en   *ben*   *av*   *stolen*
         IND.ART   leg   of   chair-DEF.SG
         '*ett ben på stolen*'
         'a leg of the chair'   (E2-5)

(21) REPRESENTATION
en   ganska   lång   historia   av
IND.ART   rather   long   history   of
deras   liv
their   life(-PL)
'*en ganska lång historia om/över deras liv*'
'a rather long history of their lives' (S1-7)

(22) INTERPERSONAL
en   vän   av   de
IND.ART   friend   of   they
'*en vän till dem*'
'a friend of theirs' (C1-9)

(23) CONNECTION
Hon öppenar handväska och tar
nyckelen   av   dörren.
key-DEF.SG   of   door-DEF.SG
'*Hon öppnar handväskan och tar fram nyckeln till dörren.*'
'She opens her handbag and takes out the key to the door.' (C1-3)

In the cases illustrated above, the underlying spatial sense for the target language user is one of 'location at/in/on etc.' (ex. 19 - 21) or 'direction to' (ex. 22-23). Such cases are frequent in the corpus and indicate that the learners are using *av* in the function of a general possessive preposition. The use of one general possessive preposition instead of a range of different spatial prepositions for different locative-possessive relations can be interpreted as a case of reductive simplification: in this way the learner avoids a variation in form which is quite subtle and bound to be difficult to master at a pre-advanced stage.

However, the question arises why precisely *av* is chosen as such a general marker. To start with, the learners also use *av* regularly in such cases where it is normal usage even in the target language. These include cases for which 'direction from' is the underlying spatial sense, e.g. TRACE relations as in (24a), or ORIGINATOR relations as in (24b), as well as OBJECTS of deverbal nouns, as in (24c).

(24) a. *lukten av en afrikansk dag*
'the smell of an African day' (E2-9)
b. *klassik film av p.ex. Bresson*
'*klassisk film av t.ex. Bresson*'
'classical film by e.g. Bresson' (G2-1)
c. *Iraks annektering av Kuwait*
'the annexation of Kuwait by Iraq' (G3-6)

Other important cases in this connection are PART–WHOLE relations where the nominal head is a relational noun, as in (25a-b), and SUBSET relations as in (26a-b):

(25) a. *i mitten av sidan*
'in the middle of the page' (G3-7)
b. *resten av dagen*
'the rest of the day' (P1-5)

(26) a. *en av hans fickor*
'one of his pockets' (C2-10)
b. *somliga av dessa myter*
'some of these myths' (G2-10)

In some such cases the choice between *av* and a specific locative-possessive preposition is optional in the target language, depending on whether one wants to give prominence to the partiality or the locative element. This variation is possible e.g. in *i mitten av/på sidan* 'in the middle "of/on" the page' (cf. 25a) and *somliga av/bland dessa myter* 'some "of/among" these myths' (cf. 26b). The fact that the choice is freer in some cases than others is likely to be a difficult point for learners. Thus, e.g. *resten av dagen* (ex. 25b) could not be replaced by *resten på dagen; with 'rest' the perspective of partiality prevails. In cases like these, both when variability is and is not permitted in the target language, the learners tend to use *av*.

The fact that there is a certain range of cases where learners can use *av* successfully in various possessor–possessee relations is likely to support *av* as an attractive candidate for use in a general possessive function in the learner language.

This is further supported by the complications involved in choosing a locative preposition. With some types of locative-possessive constructions it is far from self-evident, which spatial relation is applicable. Should, for example, 'the key that belongs to the door' (cf. ex. 23) be conceptualised as 'the key to the door' or 'the key from the door'? The former applies in Swedish, but other languages may differ; cf. e.g. Russian *ključ ot dveri* 'key from door:GEN'. Likewise, is it 'a leg on the chair' or 'a leg from the chair'? 'A friend to them' or 'a friend from them'? These choices are hard to foresee for a learner.

It seems then that the learners, in the need for a simple-choice solution, tend to rely on *av*, which appears widely applicable and is found to cover various basic conceptual relations such as 'FROM' relations, origin, partiality and the like.

The use of *av* is also overgeneralised to NPs with nouns being used as units of measurement, which are constructed without a preposition in the target language, e.g. *ett paket av cigaretter* for 'ett paket cigaretter' 'a pack of cigarettes' (P1-5); *ett oändligt antal av sjöar* for 'ett oändligt antal sjöar' 'an infinite number of lakes' (E2-9).

We should of course also note the possible role of several of the learners' background languages in supporting a simple choice of *av* in the place of other prepositions (cf. Appendix). German *von* and Spanish and Portuguese *de* provide L1 models; and in particular, since all the learners in our study were acquainted with English which has great over-all similarity with Swedish, the wide use of English *of* in analogous cases is a possible source of influence for all our subjects.

Summarising briefly the findings in connection with prepositional constructions, we have noted two main phenomena in the learners' production:

1. Since learners tend to favour the PNP, which becomes apparent in cases where it is either less natural or impossible in the target language, they underexploit the available prepositional constructions.

2. Learners tend to overgeneralise the preposition *av* when using a prepositional construction, applying it as a general possessive preposition. This strategy appears to be supported by various cases in Swedish where a construction with *av* is appropriate, by the complexities in the conceptualisations governing the choice of locative-possessive prepositions in Swedish, and by models in the learners' background languages.

4. Concluding discussion

In the preceding sections, we presented an overview of the Swedish system of adnominal possession and explored its main characteristics partly in a typological context and partly from the point of view of second language learners of Swedish who try to acquire and handle this grammatical system.

Although the grammatical domain of adnominal possession is an open-ended domain which cannot be sharply delimited, it is still possible to identify a core area of adnominal possessive constructions in a language. Among the three main types of constructions which are used to express adnominal possession in Swedish, viz. the standard possessive noun phrase (PNP), noun-noun compounds, and prepositional constructions, we identified the first one, particularly PNPs with *s*-genitives, as the unmarked, or default type, due to its simple and invariant form, its transparency, and its applicability to prototypical cases of possessive relations. Typologically, the Swedish system is characterised by the inherent definiteness of PNPs with article-possessor complementarity, and by the complex pattern of distribution between PNPs, compounding and various locative-possessive prepositional constructions.

The learners who served as subjects generally acquired the major types of Swedish possessive constructions and used them productively. To a great extent their use of the basic types of constructions is accurate and functionally adequate from the point of view of the target language. But when it deviates from the Swedish standard norm, we can observe certain systematic patterns.

In particular, all the basic constraints that shape and differentiate the Swedish system in a language-specific way show a tendency of not being observed by the learners: PNPs are used with indefinite possessees, possessive pronouns and nominal genitives are combined with articles or other determiners, PNPs are used where the first noun is non-referential, and PNPs or prepositional constructions with *av* are used in cases where various locative-possessive constructions would be preferred by Swedes. These various tendencies are of course tendencies toward simplification; if they had been carried through consistently, this would have simplified the L2 system radically.

We believe that a typological viewpoint can help clarify the problems learners have with the definiteness of PNPs and article-possessor complementarity in Swedish. A PNP is superficially a morphologically simple structure – a possessor overtly marked for the relation combines with the basic form of the head. For an outsider, since a PNP does not contain any articles, which are the grammaticalised markers for indefiniteness or definiteness par excellence, the form of a PNP simply does not signal whether it is definite or indefinite. As we suggested in section 2.6.1, the pattern of article-possessor complementarity in possessive NPs which is found in languages like Swedish and English is opposed to the pattern found e.g. in Italian according to the parameters of ECONOMY VS. EXPLICITNESS in the expression of definiteness. It is thus difficult to say a priori which of the cross-linguistically attested structures for possessive NPs is more marked than the other one, or which one will be most difficult to acquire – the "economic" one, à la Swedish or English, or the "explicit" one à la Italian. Both have advantages and disadvantages. For instance, explicit structures seem to be generally favoured at early stages in L2 acquisition. Also, economy can be understood in various ways. Thus, structures showing article-possessor incompatibility are, of course, shorter – here economy refers to

SYNTAGMATIC ECONOMY, which primarily has to do with production of utterances in real time.

Somewhat paradoxically, however, the more explicit structures can also be considered as more economic in other respects, namely, from the point of view of PARADIGMATIC ECONOMY. Thus, whereas possessive NPs allowing articles can express the definiteness opposition basically by means of one and the same construction, possessive NPs showing article-possessor complementarity have to alternate with constructions of a different type in those relatively rare cases where the whole NP is not definite. Cf. *il/un bel vestito di Anna* and *Anna's beautiful dress* vs. *a beautiful dress of Anna's*.

It is also important to consider the PNP constructions in relation to the whole system of definiteness marking in the language. The Swedish system shows a high degree of complexity with its different patterns of marking definiteness, a system which can be termed PARADIGMATICALLY NON-ECONOMIC. Against this background, a PNP showing article-possessor complementarity implies a higher number of the different construction patterns to memorise.

Here it is instructive to compare Swedish and English. Even though article-possessor complementarity has arisen due to the same historical process (with a new definite article going through the grammaticalisation process, spreading to new contexts, but not all the way, cf. Haspelmath 1999b: 237–239), the concrete manifestations of this pattern and its place in the system are quite different in the two languages. Thus, English has a fairly uniform and PARADIGMATICALLY ECONOMIC system of marking (in)definiteness by means of the first element in a NP – an article, a demonstrative, an indefinite or negative quantifier, a possessor etc. The articles have a fairly standard form, and there are normally no problems in identifying the basic form of a noun. It would be instructive to study whether L2 learners of English show deviations from the article-possessor complementarity pattern in English comparable to those reported in our study.

The tendency for the learners to disregard the various characteristic properties of the target system, such as PNP definiteness, ±specific possessor, and the Swedish preference for locative-possessive constructions, have the combined effect that the use of some types of constructions gets extended and other types get underused in the learners' production, as compared to the target usage. Thus the learners are seen to favour PNPs and especially the *s*-genitive of nouns at the cost of noun-noun compounds and prepositional constructions. With prepositional constructions they extend the use of a common possessive *av* and avoid the more specific locative-possessive conceptualisations.

This means that the learners not only tend to simplify the L2 system by ignoring distinctions and reducing the use of alternants for something which they perceive as the same meaning (Andersen's "One-to-One Principle", 1984, 1990). What is important, they simplify in particular directions.

By extending the *s*-genitive, the learners are seen to favour precisely the type of construction that we have identified as unmarked on formal and semantic grounds. It is invariant in form, transparent, and more salient than compounding. This makes it easy to handle from a formal point of view. Furthermore, it is a construction that is regularly used in Swedish in all the prototypical cases of possession that we identified above. If learners are inclined to orient themselves to what they can perceive as the "proper", or prototypical way of expressing possessive relations, then it appears natural that they will tend to opt for the genitive construction in Swedish, given the uses that the genitive is bound to have in the learners' target language input.

As for the constructions with agreeing possessive pronouns, they may be said to be both problematic and unproblematic for the learners. The restriction of these constructions to definite NPs and the incompatibility of the possessive pronouns with articles and other determiners is indeed a problem for learners, as we have seen. But on the other hand, pronominal constructions do not seem to be underused. One obvious reason for this is that they have few natural substitutes. Compounding is not a realistic option; PNPs generally are not found to be replaced by compounds – and if compounding were to replace pronominal constructions, what would the first part of the compound be? The contexts where prepositional constructions could replace pronominal ones are few in practice. A further circumstance is that, like genitives of nouns, the pronominal constructions usually apply in highly prototypical cases of possession: with definite, human possessors, with legal possession, body-parts, kinship etc. Hence the same orientation towards the prototypical as we argumented for above should apply to pronominal as well as to genitive constructions.

The learners' handling of prepositional possessive constructions appears to be governed by at least in part the same principles. The underexploitation of prepositional variants applies to locative-possessive constructions, and not so much to constructions with *av*. *Av* is adequately used in numerous cases where native Swedes would use it, but also extended to cases where other prepositions would be used. In general, we could expect adnominal prepositional constructions to be relatively easy for learners to manage since they represent an analytic and salient type of construction. To master the differentiated and subtle nature of the Swedish system of locative-possessive variants is on the other hand a complex task. Making extended use of *av* as a general, or default possessive preposition means widening the domain of invariance in this area. The choice of *av* is supported by the fact that it already has a rather wide applicability in the target language (which can be assumed to be reflected in the learners' Swedish input). Although *av* does not qualify as a prototypical possessive marker according to our criteria (it is not used with LEGAL POSSESSION, and not typically with BODY-PART or KINSHIP relations), it still applies to a range of rather kindred types of relations in the area of partiality-subset-origin etc.

It is interesting to view the learner's acquisitional task in the context of (diachronic-typological) grammaticalisation. First of all, the fact that possessive *av* in Swedish represents a case of grammaticalisation from the underlying spatial 'FROM' sense, and that this spatial sense is still more or less transparent, constitutes a parallel to the nearest counterparts in English and some of the other background languages (Engl. *of*, Ger. *von*, Sp. and Por. *de*). (Note that all our subjects were acquainted with the use of *of* in English.) This is a case in point for the set of L2 operating principles that Andersen (1983,

1990) has brought together as the "Transfer to Somewhere Principle":

> A grammatical form or structure will occur consistently and to a significant extent in the interlanguage as a result of transfer *if and only if* (1) natural acquisitional principles are consistent with the L1 structure or (2) there already exists within the L2 input the potential for (mis-)generalisation from the input to produce the same form or structure. Furthermore, in such transfer preference is given in the resulting interlanguage to *free, invariant*, functionally *simple* morphemes which are congruent with the L1 and L2 (or there is conguence between the L1 and natural acquisition processes) and [to] morphemes [which] occur frequently in the L1 and/or the L2. (Andersen 1983: 182, italics in original.)

We might add that, as has become clear in modern L3 acquisition research, prior L2s may also, besides L1, have a substantial influence on learners' interlanguages. (For some discussion of this point and further references, cf. Hammarberg 2001.) This has relevance for English *of* constructions in the present connection.

The fact that the grammaticalisation of a 'FROM' preposition has gone much further in the background languages and taken over a wider domain than in the case of Swedish *av*, has at least two further implications in the present context. One is that the wider applicability of *of, von, de* supports widened use of *av* by the learners. Andersen's conditions (1) and (2) are both fulfilled. The other implication has to do with the extent to which grammaticalisation has taken place in the language. Languages like English, German, Spanish and Portuguese have undergone a development where one spatial preposition has been generalised in an abstract role and taken over a very wide domain of adnominal relations including those of prototypical possession. Swedish appears to be midway in such a process, showing a state with several locative-possessive constructions, numerous cases of variation and fine distinctions, and on the whole a relatively strong role still for the locative element. Particularly, the process has not fully involved the prototypical cases of possessive relations. As we touched upon earlier, such transitional systems often tend to be complex. This points to a type of positive connection between grammaticalisation and acquisition. On the one hand, there is the learner's need for a simple and dependable way of expressing an abstract notion such as possession. The task in this case is obviously complicated by the fact that the domain of possession is so complex and fuzzy-edged. On the other hand, the existence of highly grammaticalised forms of encoding in the learner's input and background languages provides a model for what turns out to be an attractive interim solution for the learner.

Appendix – Concise information on the encoding of adnominal possession in the first languages of the learners in the ASU Corpus

English expresses possession by (i) preposed non-agreeing possessive pronouns, (ii) preposed nouns with *'s*-genitives, (iii) noun-noun compounds, and (iv) postposed prepositional modifiers mostly with *of*, but also (v) to a lesser extent than Swedish, with locative-possessive constructions. The distribution of genitives and compounds depends on ±specificity of the modifying noun; genitives and *of* constructions are partly interchangeable and partly complementary, depending on a complicated system of factors. Possessive NPs type (i) and (ii) are inherently definite, with article-possessor complementarity. Similarities and differences compared to the Swedish system will be apparent in the examples throughout this article.

German expresses possession by (i) preposed agreeing possessive pronouns, (ii) possessor nouns in the genitive, usually postposed but preferably preposed in the case of personal proper names, (iii) noun-noun compounds, (iv) postposed prepositional modifiers mostly with *von*, but also (v) to some extent with locative-possessive constructions. The distribution of genitives and compounds depends on ±specificity of the modifying noun, much as in Swedish; genitives and *von* constructions are partly interchangeable, subject to stylistic factors, genitive being used more in Standard German than in Standard Swedish. Possessive NPs with preposed genitives or pronominal possessors are inherently definite with article-possessor complementarity, but those with postposed genitives are not.

Spanish expresses possession by (i) agreeing possessive pronouns, pre- or postposed, and (ii) postposed prepositional modifiers with *de*, which are used for a wide variety of relations. No genitive inflection of nouns. Only very limited use of noun-noun compounding. NPs with preposed possessive pronouns are inherently definite and do not combine with definite articles or determiners; NPs with postposed possessive pronouns may be definite or indefinite and do combine with articles or determiners.

Portuguese expresses possession by (i) preposed and postposed agreeing possessive pronouns, and (ii) postposed prepositional modifiers with *de*, which are used for a wide variety of relations. No genitive inflection of nouns. Only limited use of noun-noun compounding. Possessive NPs type (i) are not necessarily definite. Possessive pronouns combine with definite and indefinite articles or determiners.

Modern Greek expresses possession by (i) postposed enclitic non-agreeing genitives of pronouns, (ii) pre- or postposed possessor nouns in the genitive, (iii) noun-noun compounds, and (iv) postposed prepositional modifiers with *apó* 'from' for a range of non-prototypical relations of possession, to some extent alternating with genitives. Possessive NPs type (i) and (ii) are most often but not always definite; possessors are combined with definite or indefinite articles.

Polish expresses possession by (i) preposed (partly agreeing) possessive pronouns, (ii) preposed agreeing possessive adjectives, (iii) preposed agreeing relational adjectives, and (iv) postposed nouns in the genitive. No significant use of noun-noun compounds or possessive prepositional constructions. Adjectives of type (ii) are derived from proper names or some other personal referents such as kin terms. Types (ii) and (iv) are used with specific possessors, whereas type (iii) is not. Since definiteness is not grammaticalised and articles are not used, article-possessor combinability is not an issue.

Chinese marks possessors by the general relational postposition *de* which can govern both pronouns and full NPs. The possessor then precedes the possessee. Chinese has a rich system of various types of compounding, one of which is noun-noun compounding with the first noun qualifying the second. Chinese is on the whole an isolating language, so there is no genitive inflection or pronominal agreement, nor is there any grammaticalised definiteness category.

Notes

1. Definite possessors constitute 65% NPs with preposed genitive attributes in Pitkänen's (1979: 70) corpus covering Swedish texts from the 17th-20th centuries. For modern texts this figure might be even higher (Kari Fraurud p.c.).
2. The structure of Swedish NPs, in particular their definiteness marking has received much attention, among other things, within various syntactic theories.

See e.g. Börjars 1994, Cooper 1984, Delsing 1993, Holmberg (ed.) 1992, Perridon 1989.
3. A useful notion for describing the choice of prepositional attributes is valency, accepted and elaborated in various theories (and also incorporated into Langacker's Cognitive Grammar, cf. Taylor 1996: 93-96 for the usefulness of this notion in the interpretation of English -'s-genitives). For an attempt to apply this notion to the system of prepositional attributes in Swedish cf. Pitkänen (1979). A related notion is Pustejovsky's (1991) notion of qualia structure.

References

Andersen, Roger W.
1983   Transfer to somewhere. In: Susan Gass and Larry Selinker (eds.), *Language Transfer in Language Learning*, 177–201. Rowley MA: Newbury House.
Andersen, Roger W.
1984   The one to one principle in interlanguage construction. *Language Learning* 34: 77-95.
Andersen, Roger W.
1990   Models, processes, principles and strategies: Second language acquisition inside and outside the classroom. In: Bill VanPatten and James F. Lee (eds.), *Second Language Acquisition/Foreign Language Teaching*, 45–68. Clevedon/Philadelphia: Multilingual Matters.
Axelsson, Monica
1994   Noun phrase development in Swedish as a second language. Ph.D. dissertation. Stockholm: Stockholm University, Centre for Research on Bilingualism.
Börjars, Kersti
1994   Swedish double determination in a European typological perspective. *Nordic Journal of Linguistics* 17: 219–252.
Clahsen, Harald, Jürgen M. Meisel, and Manfred Pienemann
1983   *Deutsch als Zweitsprache: der Spracherwerb ausländischer Arbeiter*. Tübingen: Gunter Narr.
Cooper, Robin
1984   Svenska nominalfraser och kontext-fri grammatik. [Swedish noun phrases and context-free grammar.] *Nordic Journal of Linguistics* 7: 115–144.
Croft, William
1990   *Typology and Universals*. Cambridge: Cambridge University Press.

Delsing, Lars-Olof
1993   The internal structure of noun phrases in the Scandinavian Languages. Ph.D. dissertation. Lund University, Dept. of Scandinavian Languages.
Dittmar, Norbert
1992   Grammaticalization in second language acquisition: introduction. *Studies in Second Language Acquisition* 14: 249-257.
Eckman, Fred R.
1977   Markedness and the contrastive analysis hypothesis. *Language Learning* 27: 315–330.
Eckman, Fred R.
1996   A functional-typological approach to second language acquisition theory. In: William C. Ritchie and Tej K. Bhatia (eds.), *Handbook of Second Language Acquisition*, 195–211. San Diego: Academic Press.
Fraurud, Kari
1990   Definiteness and the processing of noun phrases in natural discourse. *Journal of Semantics* 7: 395–433.
Giacalone Ramat, Anna
1992   Grammaticalization processes in the area of temporal and modal relations. *Studies in Second Language Acquisition* 14: 297–322.
Giorgi, Alessandra, and Giuseppe Longobardi
1991   *The Syntax of Noun Phrases: Configuration, Parameters and Empty Categories*. Cambridge: Cambridge University Press.
Greenberg, Joseph H.
1966   *Language Universals*. The Hague: Mouton.
Haiman, John
1985   *Natural Syntax*. Cambridge: Cambridge University Press.
Hammarberg, Björn
1996   Examining the processability theory: The case of adjective agreement in L2 Swedish. In: Eric Kellerman, Bert Weltens and Theo Bongaerts (eds.), *EUROSLA 6, A Selection of Papers*, 75–88. Amsterdam: ANéLA.
Hammarberg, Björn
1999   Manual of the ASU Corpus, a longitudinal text corpus of adult learner Swedish with a corresponding part from native Swedes. Stockholm University, Department of Linguistics.
Hammarberg, Björn
2000   A polyfunctional word in native usage and L2 acquisition: The Swedish neutral pronoun "det". In: Johan Falk, Gunnar Magnusson, Gunnel Melchers and Barbro Nilsson (eds.), *Kontraster i språk/Contrasts in Languages*, 103–129. (Stockholm Studies in

Modern Philology 12.) Stockholm: Almqvist & Wiksell International.

Hammarberg, Björn
2001   Roles of L1 and L2 in L3 production and acquisition. In: Jasone Cenoz, Britta Hufeisen and Ulrike Jessner (eds.), *Cross-Linguistic Influence in L3 Acquisition: Psycholinguistic Perspectives*, 21–41. Clevedon/Philadelphia: Multilingual Matters.

Hammarberg, Björn, and Åke Viberg
1977   The place-holder constraint, language typology, and the teaching of Swedish to immigrants. *Studia Linguistica* 31: 106–163.

Haspelmath, Martin
1999a   External possession in a European areal perspective. In: Doris L. Payne and Immanuel Barshi (eds.), *External Possession*, 109-135. Amsterdam/Philadelphia: John Benjamins.

Haspelmath, Martin
1999b.   Explaining article-possessor complementarity: Economic motivation in noun phrase syntax. *Language* 75: 227-243.

Hawkins, John
1978   *Definiteness and Indefiniteness: A Study in Reference and Grammaticality Prediction*. London: Croom Helm.

Hawkins, John
1991   On (in)definite articles: Implicatures and (un)grammaticality prediction. *Journal of Linguistics* 27: 405–442.

Heine, Bernd
1997   *Possession. Cognitive Sources, Forces, and Grammaticalization*. Cambridge: Cambridge University Press.

Holmberg, Anders (ed.)
1992   *Papers from the Workshop on the Scandinavian Noun Phrase*. University of Umeå, Department of General Linguistics, report 32.

Hyltenstam, Kenneth
1984   The use of typological markedness conditions as predictors in second language acquisition: The case of pronominal copies in relative clauses. In: Roger W. Andersen (ed.), *Second Languages*, 39–58. New York: Newbury House.

Hyltenstam, Kenneth
1986   Markedness, language universals, language typology, and second language acquisition. In: Carol W. Pfaff (ed.), *First and Second Language Acquisition Processes*, 55–78. New York: Newbury House.

Klein, Wolfgang, and Norbert Dittmar
1979   *Developing Grammars: The Acquisition of German Syntax by Foreign Workers*. Berlin/New York: Springer-Verlag.

Klein, Wolfgang, and Clive Perdue
1997 The Basic Variety (or: Couldn't natural languages be much simpler?). *Second Language Research* 13: 301–347.
Koptjevskaja-Tamm, Maria
2001 Adnominal possession. In: Martin Haspelmath and Ekkehard König (eds.), *Handbuch der Typologie.* Berlin: Mouton de Gruyter.
Koptjevskaja-Tamm, Maria
forthc. a Genitives and possessive NPs in the languages of Europe. To appear in: Frans Plank (ed.), *The Noun Phrase in the Languages of Europe.* Berlin: Mouton de Gruyter.
Koptjevskaja-Tamm, Maria
forthc. b "A woman of sin", "a man of duty" and "a hell of a mess": Nondeterminer genitives in Swedish. To appear in: Frans Plank (ed.), *The Noun Phrase in the Languages of Europe.* Berlin: Mouton de Gruyter.
Lakoff, George, and Mark Johnson
1980 *Metaphors We Live By.* Chicago/London: The University of Chicago Press.
Langacker, Ronald W.
1991 *Foundations of Cognitive Grammar.* Vol.II. Stanford: Stanford University Press.
Langacker, Ronald W
1995 Possession and possessive constructions. In: John R. Taylor and Robert E. MacLaury (eds.), *Language and the Cognitive Construal of the World*, 51-79. Berlin/New York: Mouton de Gruyter.
Lehmann, Christian
1998 *Possession in Yucatec Maya.* München: LINCOM.
Lyly, Erika
1996 *En bild av Picasso* eller *en bild på Picasso*? [A picture "av" Picasso or a picture "på" Picasso?]. In: *Språket lever! Festskrift till Margareta Westman den 27 mars 1996*, 202-207. Stockholm: Svenska språknämnden.
Lyons, Christofer
1986 The syntax of English genitive constructions. *Journal of Linguistics* 22: 123–143.
Mobärg, Mats
1998 Om gestalttext. [On gestalt-text.] *Språkvård* 1-1998: 10–14.
Norde, Muriel
1997 The history of the genitive in Swedish: A case study in degrammaticalization. Doctoral dissertation. Amsterdam: University of Amsterdam.

Perdue, Clive (ed.)
1993 *Adult Language Acquisition: Cross-Linguistic Perspectives.* Vol. 1-2. Cambridge: Cambridge University Press.

Perdue, Clive, and Wolfgang Klein
1992 Why does the production of some learners not grammaticalize? *Studies in Second Language Acquisition* 14: 259–272.

Perridon, Harry Christian Bernard
1989 *Reference, Definiteness and the Noun Phrase in Swedish.* Academic Proefschrift, Universiteit van Amsterdam.

Pfaff, Carol W.
1992 The issue of grammaticalization in early German second language. *Studies in Second Language Acquisition* 14: 273–296.

Pitkänen, Antti
1979 *Binominala genitiviska hypotagmer i yngre svenska.* [Binominal genitive hypotagms in younger Swedish.] (Skrifter utgivna av svenska litteratursällskapet i Finland 484.) Doctoral dissertation, Helsinki.

Plank, Frans
1995 (Re-)Introducing Suffixaufnahme. In Frans Plank (ed.), *Double Case. Agreement by Suffixaufnahme*, 3–110. New York/Oxford: Oxford University Press.

Pustejovsky, James
1991 The generative lexicon. *Computational Linguistics* 17: 409-441.

Seiler, Hansjakob
1983 *Possession as an Operational Dimension of Language.* Tübingen: Narr.

Serzisko, Fritz
1984 *Der Ausdruck der Possessivität im Somali.* (Continuum – Schriftenreihe zur Linguistik 1.) Tübingen: Narr.

Skiba, Romuald, and Norbert Dittmar
1992 Pragmatic, semantic, and syntactic constraints and grammaticalization: A longitudinal perspective. *Studies in Second Language Acquisition* 14: 323-349.

Stolz, Thomas with Sabine Gorsemann
forthc. Island possessions: Pronominal possession in Faroese and the parameters of alienability/inalienability.

Taylor, John R.
1996 *Possessives in English. An Exploration in Cognitive Grammar.* Oxford: Clarendon Press.

Teleman, Ulf, Staffan Hellberg, and Erik Andersson
   2000   *Svenska Akademiens grammatik*, Vol. 3: *Fraser*. [Grammar of the Swedish Academy. Vol. 3. Phrases.] Stockholm: Svenska Akademien & Norstedts ordbok.

Ultan, Russell
   1978   Towards a typology of substantival possession. In: Joseph Greenberg (ed.), *Universals of Human Language*, Vol. 4: *Syntax*, 11-50. Stanford: Stanford University Press.

Wijk-Andersson, Elsie
   1993   Bestämda nominalfraser i inlärarsvenska. [Definite noun phrases in learner Swedish.] In: Anne Golden and Anne Hvenekilde (eds.), *Nordens språk som andrespråk*, 191-197. Oslo: University of Oslo, Department of Linguistics.

Gerunds as optional categories in second language learning

Anna Giacalone Ramat

1. Introduction

This paper illustrates the acquisition of the gerund by learners of Italian, a topic which so far has been neglected in second language studies. The gerund is a relatively frequent nonfinite verb form both in written and spoken Italian for which, however, there exists in many cases a corresponding finite construction that might be used in its place. Then the gerund is by no means an indispensable element in the same way as inflections for person or the marking of tense and aspect on the finite verb are "obligatory".

This seems to be a reason why the task of acquiring gerunds has specific features which need deeper investigation. If it is true that both natives and L2 learners can use other (more "basic"?) forms in the same contexts to mark interclausal connection, the process which leads to the acquisition of gerunds has to be motivated at some level of linguistic explanation. The aim of this study is to identify patterns and regularities in acquisition and to propose explanations for such patterns correlated to the semantic and pragmatic functions gerunds can express.

A typological description of gerunds is preliminary for our study, since typological generalisations form the basis for predictions for L2 acquisition (Braidi 1999: 79ff). On the other hand, we hope that the study of acquisition will help highlight some inherent aspects of this category.

In the present paper the main features of gerunds and related constructions from a typological point of view are illustrated in Section 2; the gerundial constructions in Italian are outlined in Section 3; the development of acquisition and the main problems encountered in learner productions are described in Section 4. Subjects and data analyses are presented in Section 5 and the results are discussed in Section 6.

2. General typological information about gerunds

According to a widely accepted opinion, Italian gerunds belong to the category of converbs, which is a recently defined cross-linguistic grammatical category (Haspelmath and König 1995). We will take Haspelmath's definition as a starting point: a converb is "a nonfinite verb form whose main function is to mark adverbial subordination" (1995: 3). This formal (morphological) and functional (semantic) definition fits quite nicely to gerunds in Italian as well as to gerunds in other Romance languages. Other types of nonfinite verb forms such as participles (verbal adjectives) and infinitives (verbal nouns) will not be dealt with here. Converbs are part of the inflectional paradigm of verbs and share the notion of nonfiniteness, as stated by Haspelmath. Although criteria for defining finiteness may be controversial (Koptjevskaja-Tamm 1994, Klein 1998), in this paper I use a morphologically based notion of finiteness: those verbal forms which lack specifications for one or more of the following properties of verbs are nonfinite: tense, aspect, mood as well as agreement with their arguments. Nonfinite forms are usually not used as main predicates in independent clauses and in finite subordinate clauses: they may be used in nonfinite subordinate clauses or in periphrastic constructions in association with an auxiliary.

3. Gerunds as adverbial constructions in Italian

As said above, converbs function as subordinate clauses with some nonspecific adverbial relation to the main clause. In many cases this relation can be made explicit by means of a paraphrase with a temporal, causal or conditional subordinate clause. In others a coordinative structure is more adequate. This kind of translation is however not always possible with predicate gerunds with modal or instrumental interpretation.[1]

A global characterisation of the formal and semantic properties of Italian gerunds has been offered in a number of studies both in the functional typological and generative framework (Nespor 1978, Pusch 1980, Lonzi 1991, Solarino 1996, Dinale 1997). In what follows a number of criteria that are relevant to the functional framework of this study will be discussed.

Although there has been much controversy over the semantic analysis of converbial constructions (Pusch 1980, Nedjalkov 1995: 106ff, König 1995: 57ff), the view accepted here is the one followed by König, namely that converbs are essentially vague and unspecific forms which are interpreted on the basis of several syntactic, semantic and contextual factors. In the case of Romance gerunds this position also has a historical motivation, since there is evidence that Romance gerunds are the outcome of several Latin forerunners: gerunds (as inflected verbal nouns), gerundives and participles (Dinale 1997) along a grammaticalisation path.

The notion of "semantic space of interclausal relations" as suggested by Kortmann (1997: 137ff) may fruitfully be applied here. The main assumption is that the semantic domain of interclausal relations is structured in three networks of temporal, modal and CCC (=causal, conditional and concessive) relations and that such relations are cognitively basic. Languages differ significantly to the extent to which the individual interclausal relations are coded by means of conjunctions (subordinators) introducing finite clauses or converbs (cf. note 2). The properties of Italian gerunds confirm universal tendencies but seem to give also rise to specific preferences (Ceglia 2002).

With regard to temporal relations, simultaneity is by far the most frequent relation expressed by gerunds, but also anteriority or posteriority with respect to the main clause verb are possible. Consider the following examples (from Solarino 1996), showing that gerunds are fully capable of denoting time intervals preceding or following the one of the main verb:

(1) *passeggiavano   conversando   amabilmente*
     they-walked   talk-GER   pleasantly
     "they walked talking pleasantly"

(2) *partendo   alle otto   arriverai   in tempo*
     leave-GER   at eight o'clock   you-will-arrive   on time
     "if you leave at eight o'clock you will arrive on time" (anteriority)

(3) *l'auto ha travolto   un pedone,   finendo   contro un*
     the car has run over a pedestrian   end up-GER   against a
     muro
     wall
     "the car has run over a pedestrian and ended up against a wall" (posteriority)

The position of the clause containing a gerund is not fixed: it may precede or follow the main verb; in some cases, however, the position may be relevant for interpretation. If the temporal relation between the gerund and the main verb is of posteriority the gerund must follow the main verb (as in example (3) above). As Solarino (1996: 28) observes, there is clearly an iconic order which follows the flow of events. As expected, in the case of simultaneous relations gerunds may be placed in any position.

In providing criteria for the description of gerunds structural properties have also to be taken into account. A distinction based on syntactic criteria has been drawn between "predicate gerunds" which modify the VP and preferably express temporal, modal, instrumental and accompanying circumstance relations, and "sentence gerunds" expressing causal concessive conditional relations (Lonzi 1991: 572ff).

Other descriptive classifications of Italian gerunds are proposed by Serianni (1989: 485) and Dinale (1997: 35), but apart from terminological additions, the main categories and functions of gerunds remain those of predicate and sentence gerunds, with a category oscillating in between, the one of gerunds expressing temporal relations (Solarino 1996: 107).

Subject reference is a crucial parameter in the literature on gerunds: the gerundial subject is generally implicit and it is controlled by an argument of the main clause. The prototypical (unmarked) situation is that the (unexpressed) subject of the gerund is coreferential with the subject of the main clause, as in (1), (2), (3) and (4). Less frequently, however, the control may be determined by some other argument in the main clause (as in 5). This situation confirms universal tendencies predicting that same-subject converbs are more frequent than different subject converbs (Kortmann 1995: 227).

It is also possible for gerunds to have an explicit subject which is different from the main clause subject as in (6). Converbial constructions with an explicit subject are often called "absolute constructions" (*gerundio assoluto*: Serianni 1989: 485).[2]

Consider the following examples (from Ceglia 2002):

(4) *tornando   a casa devo   fare   la spesa*
     come-back-GER home   I.have to do   the shopping
     "coming back home I have to do the shopping"

(5) *tornando   a casa mi   ha   fermato   la polizia*
     come back-GER home   me   has   stopped   the police
     "the police have stopped me while I was coming back home"

(6) *tornando   Luigi a casa devo   fare   la spesa*
     come back-GER Luigi home   I.have to do   the shopping
     "as Luigi comes back home, I have to do the shopping"

So-called compound gerunds formed with the help of an auxiliary are considerably less frequent than simple gerunds and semantically more restricted: they predominantly give rise to a causal reading (Solarino 1996: 117, Lonzi 1991: 580). The main features are temporal value of anteriority and aspectual value of perfectivity, as in the following example:

(7)   *essendo stato aiutato   da Giovanni,   Paolo è riuscito*
      help-COMPOUND GER   by Giovanni,   Paolo   managed
      a far ripartire   la macchina
      to start again   the car
      "having been helped by Giovanni, Paolo managed to start the car again"

Compound gerunds are scarcely used in spoken language (Serianni 1989: 484) and practically absent from our corpus: therefore they are not discussed in detail here.

As said above, from the formal point of view, the Italian gerund has its origin in the ablative of the Latin gerund, but in the course of time it took over many functions of present participles and developed into a semantically undetermined adverbial modifier (Rohlfs 1969: 109). The use of gerunds is well attested throughout the history of Italian (Ferreri 1983, Dinale 1997). In Old Italian it was even less restricted than in contemporary Italian, as shown by its ability to combine with prepositions. Basing their views on written samples of Old and Modern Italian, Policarpi and Rombi (1983) have argued that the gerund is a declining structure ("una struttura in declino" 1983: 317). The claim is challenged by Solarino (1996: 116) who also notes that it is not surprising that the gerund is expanding in contemporary Italian because of its semantic polyfunctionality and syntactic transparency.

In order to come to terms with these conflicting claims we would need reliable analyses based on representative corpuses of different types of written and oral discourse. Frequency of use would be an important descriptive tool to compare gerunds with finite subordinate clauses. As said above, there is cross-linguistic variation between languages which use gerunds or similar converbial constructions quite frequently and languages which do not. Unfortunately, statements of this type in the literature are usually not based on information derived from text analyses and represent only rough tendencies, as noted by Kortmann (1995: 190). Kortmann, however, provides some interesting quantitative information on English.[3]

To get a more precise idea of the use of gerunds in present-day Italian, the frequency of gerunds has been calculated on the corpus of spoken Italian entitled LIP (De Mauro et al. 1993). The corpus was collected in four big cities (Milan, Florence, Rome and Naples). It is subdivided in five discourse genres, each of them including roughly 100.000 words:

A texts: communication face-to-face;
B texts: conversations on the phone;
C texts: communicative exchanges governed by turn-taking rules (meetings, exams, interviews);
D texts: unidirectional communication in the presence of the recipient: lessons in different educational contexts, addresses in tribunal, sermons, election rallies, etc.;
E texts: communication at a distance, radio and TV.

Occurrences of gerunds were calculated for each type of texts; contexts which were not comprehensible were eliminated.

Table 1. below shows the distribution of gerunds. Percentages are calculated over the total sum of occurrences of gerunds in the LIP corpus (=1218). A fundamental distinction is drawn between gerunds as part of the progressive periphrasis of the type *sta mangiando* "he is eating" and converbial gerunds expressing adverbial subordination as in (1) to (7). It is not surprising to find that converbial gerunds tend to increase across discourse genres, since D texts are stylistically more elaborated than conversations. It is more interesting to remark that scores are not low even in the case of face-to-face communication and phone conversations. This means that gerunds are by no means declining in spoken Italian both in the progressive periphrasis[4] and in converbial function. Converbial gerunds which include predicate and sentence gerunds would need a more detailed investigation in order to answer the question of which type of interclausal relations is preferably expressed by them. A distributional analysis of all contexts in which gerunds appear is beyond the scope of this study, however it is possible to add a few rough statements, which at least capture clear tendencies and sharp contrasts. The modal (see below section 4 for more details) interpretation appears to be by far the most frequent (about 54% of all converbial gerunds according to Ceglia 2002: 288ff).[5]

Table 1. Distribution of gerunds in LIP according to discourse genres

Type of text	A Total	ger %	B Total	ger %	C Total	ger %	D Total	ger %	E Total	ger %
gerunds in progr. per.	120	9.9	168	13.8	120	9.9	110	9	134	11
converbs	104	8.5	74	6.1	132	10.8	171	14	85	4
Total	224		242		252		281		219	

Total of occurrences of gerunds: 1218
Total of progressive periphrases: 652 (53.6%)
Total of converbs: 566 (46.4%)

3.1. Gerunds in periphrastic constructions.

In many languages gerunds and other nonfinite forms are also used as part of periphrastic aspectual constructions in association with auxiliary verbs, generally a locative or existential copula, as in the following example (Haspelmath 1995: 43ff, Bisang 1995):

(8) *Kumaar   enkal   vitt-il   tank-i*
     Kumar   we:OBL   house-LOC   stay-CONV
     iru-kkir-aan   (Tamil)
     be-PRES-3SG.M
     "Kumar is staying in our house"

In Italian motion verbs *andare* "go" and *venire* "come" and postural verb *stare* "stand, be in a certain position" are used with gerunds. The periphrasis with motion verbs has a durative meaning; in present-day Italian it is not frequently used and it is mostly restricted to written language (Giacalone Ramat 1995b).

On the contrary, the periphrasis with *stare* is frequently used to convey the idea of progressivity. It is, however, not obligatory as in the case of the *–ing* form in English because the simple imperfective tenses (present, imperfect) may take a progressive reading.

The compatibility of the progressive construction with the semantic classes of verbs (Vendler 1967) was the topic of a long standing debate: the following is a brief summary of some of the results. It is highly recommended to distinguish between progressive as a semantic notion and as a morphosyntactic device (Bertinetto 1986, 2000, among others). On the one hand, progressive aspect may be conveyed by general imperfective tenses, as is the case in Romance, and on the other hand a specific periphrasis like *–ing* in English may appear in contexts which have little to do with the aspectual notion "progressive" (the English progressive is moving toward an imperfective, as Comrie noted years ago: 1976: 37ff).

As for the four Vendler's classes, activities and accomplishments may readily combine with progressive *stare* + gerund. A considerable growth of the use of achievements was also recently noticed (Bertinetto 2000: 567, 596 note 11): these verbs, when occurring in the progressive, do not contain an endpoint or a culmination point, rather denote an action or an event that is imminent, but has not yet occurred (*sto partendo* "I am leaving"). States are not compatible, however stative verbs like *conoscere* "know" or *capire* "understand" may sometimes undergo a recategorisation as activities (*sto conoscendo sempre meglio Maria*: "I am knowing Mary better and better" (Giacalone Ramat 1997).

Prototypical contexts for progressive may be found in cases of "focalised" progressive (Bertinetto 2000: 564), where an event overlaps with a simultaneously ongoing process, as in (9). However conditions of use are partially a matter of speakers' choice, as shown by native speakers judgements of equivalence between the progressive and the simple forms:

(9)   *alle 8 quando Giovanni è arrivato Anna stava ancora lavorando/ lavorava ancora*
        "at 8 o'clock, when Giovanni came, Anna was still working"

The periphrasis *stare* + gerund represents a case of grammaticalisation in which both the verb *stare* has lost its lexical meaning of "be in a certain position" and the gerund has no longer the original function of predicate modifier. Both forms together make up a single predicate which has taken a progressive meaning. As it is well known, loss of categorial properties and desemanticisation of lexical verbs is a typical feature of grammaticalisation processes (Heine 1993, Giacalone Ramat 1995b).[6]

4. The acquisition of gerunds

As we said, the use of gerunds represents one possibility from a set of alternatives (more specifically, finite subordinate clauses and in some cases coordinate clauses).[7] Thus, gerunds are optional structures which can be treated as cases of language-internal variation. In the following paragraphs I will explore both typological and acquisitional principles and motivating factors that can shed light on the relation between gerunds and finite subordination.

A preliminary remark on the optionality issue is in order here. Optionality in grammars is a phenomenon that has received increasing attention in linguistic theory and in developmental linguistics. Linguistic theory has mainly treated optionality in mature grammars as competition between different grammars that can be evaluated on economy principles. Optimality theory is one candidate in providing a measure to rank different variants (Gilbers and de Hoop 1998).

The optionality of gerunds in native Italian, both as converbial constructions and as part of a periphrastic construction with postural verb *stare* and motion verbs *andare* and *venire*, is a type of stable optionality. The grammar of native speakers normally includes both constructions. However, there are discourse pragmatic constraints and semantic constraints on the distribution of optional forms which sometimes make optionality more apparent than real. Clearly, then, such perspective diverges from research on optionality in L2 grammars, where optionality has been taken so far in the sense of the manifestation of incompleteness in near-native grammars. In this view it is assumed that the dispreferred non target option is never completely expunged (Sorace 2000). In our terms, on the contrary, optionality is couched in native grammars and the successful acquisition of a native competence entails the acquisition of optionality in the ways natives would use it.

Then the interesting question in the perspective of acquisition is at what stage and for what purpose optional constructions are attained. A first answer could be that learners develop gerunds in order to solve more complex communicative tasks. For instance, learners may encounter problems in managing lexical means for temporal contextualisation. In order to provide background to an event in the topic component, beside the all purpose conjunction *quando,* more specific lexical expressions may be required. These include *mentre* "while", *appena* "as soon as", *dal momento che* "since", *nel momento in cui* "at the (exact) moment when", *ogni volta che* "every time (that)". In such cases gerunds may help to override problems of choice among explicit subordinators, though maintaining a hierarchical information structure in the complex sentence. In terms of interclausal connection it is noteworthy that, as noted by Pusch (1980: 62), a context that favours gerunds is the position between subject and finite verb within the appositive relative clause. Consider the following example from the LIP corpus (De Mauro et al. 1993):

(11) *degli incontri che noi abbiamo svolto con queste due*
of the meetings that we have held with these two
società che essendo società per azioni
societies which being limited companies
non hanno azione eh caratteristiche
do not have stock eh characteristic
"of the meetings we held with these two societies which, being limited companies, do not have proper stocks" (MIC223)

That gerunds resolve conflicts at the discourse planning level was also noted by Berman (1998) in a cross-linguistic study on the development of connectivity (=interclausal connection) in children and adults. She explicitly states that in languages like English and Spanish nonfinite constructions represent "later" acquisitions to express a more varied and semantically more complex range of relations. Hendriks (this volume) also notes that gerunds may be used to avoid a breakdown of the referential chain. In sum, the choice of gerunds also depends on pragmatic and information structure grounds, not only on their syntactic and semantic properties.

In order to understand the development of gerunds the relationship with finite subordinate clauses has to be taken into consideration, since both devices compete in expressing certain types of interpropositional relationships, as noted by Kortmann (1995: 192).

In the following I wish to explore whether markedness theory as used in typological research provides a means of determining what the relative markedness of gerunds and finite subordination is. As a first step I will not consider acquisitional data, but I will compare both constructions in native Italian. The notion of markedness differs widely in linguistic approaches, from Prague School to Greenberg (1966), Croft (1990), Eckman, Moravcsik, and Wirth (1986). For a discussion regarding markedness criteria I will rely on Croft (1990: 70ff) who proposes three subsets of criteria:

1. the structural criteria: the realisation of the marked value will involve at least as many morphemes as the realisation of the unmarked value.
2. the behavioral criteria "are any sort of evidence from the linguistic behavior of the elements in question that would demonstrate that one element is grammatically more "versatile" than the other and hence is unmarked compared to the other".
3. the frequency criteria are based on occurrences of the value in question in texts. They require quantitative texts analyses.

The above mentioned criteria all support the markedness of the progressive construction compared with simple imperfective forms (Giacalone Ramat 1995, 1997). Hence gerunds as part of such constructions are also marked. However, markedness criteria do not yield a quite clear picture in the case of adverbial subordination.

The structural criterion is related to the number of morphemes that the elements in question involve (the smaller the number of morphemes, the less marked the element considered). The identification of the basis for comparison can, however, be problematic. The markedness relationship is meant to hold for the same grammatical category: for instance the category "person" could not be selected in our case in order to claim a markedness relationship, since gerunds do not express person. But both gerunds and finite forms express aspect and, at least to some extent, time. Thus, simple gerunds expressing imperfective aspect can be compared to the present tense and to the imperfect. Moreover, gerunds expressing time in relation to the main clause (relative time reference) can be compared with finite forms. On such a basis the structural criterion can apply: the morphemes to be counted for gerunds are: the verbal lexeme + the morpheme *–ndo*: V+*ndo*. Finite verbs do not need more morphemes to signal the tense and aspect category: the imperfect *am-av-a* shows root + stem of the imperfect *av/ev/iv* + 3sing. Thus, in the light of the structural criterion one cannot determine the markedness status of gerunds.

The behavioral criteria can be divided into two general subtypes: the morphological and the syntactic one. The morphological (or inflectional) criterion pertains to the number of distinctions that a particular grammatical category possesses (Croft 1990: 77). It shows that gerunds are more marked because they bear less distinctions with respect to finite verbs: no person distinction and no mood distinction. The distributional behavior involves the number of syntactic environments in which the elements in question occur. Gerunds can occur only in subordinate clauses, while finite verbs occur in main and subordinate clauses: thus, gerunds are more restricted and more marked. Moreover, the same subject constraint generally holds in case of gerunds, while finite subordinates may freely have different subjects. This means that a finite causal clause introduced by *perché* can occur in a larger number of syntactic environments. Thus, the behavioral criterion provides us with evidence for the markedness of gerunds compared to adverbial finite clauses.

As for the textual frequency criteria, it appears that gerunds are less frequent and more marked than finite subordinates. Indeed, if we take into consideration the data from LIP (De Mauro et al. 1993), showing 566 converbial gerunds in all, there is no doubt that their frequency is lower than that of finite subordinate clauses. A cursory check of A-texts (conversations) including about 100.000 words has given 745 occurrences of *perché* introducing a reason clause. In the same text type Table 1 shows 104 occurrences of converbs which besides reason relations also include other semantic values.

On the whole, markedness criteria as used in typological studies seem to support the conclusion that gerunds as means for adverbial subordination are more marked than finite forms.

In second language research it has been generally assumed that markedness provides a hierarchy with respect to the sequence in which competing structures are acquired: unmarked structures are acquired before marked ones (White 1966, Eckman 1985, Battistella 1996: 117, Braidi 1999). Markedness considerations allow to predict that gerunds as marked forms will develop later than finite verbs. At first sight this prediction is confirmed by the scarcity of gerunds found in early learner languages.

The assumption that forms adopted by learners depend on markedness considerations does not exclude the possibility that we may consider other possible motivating and interacting factors. For example, it may be argued that gerunds meet the requirements of economy since they are reduced forms of subordination not associated with conjunctions, while finite subordinates meet the requirements of explicitness. These factors represent competing motivations that have been claimed to be universally valid and influence both language change and language development (Haiman 1983, Haspelmath 1999).

Based on the discussion so far we expect that:

- temporal, causal, concessive conditional relations will be expressed first by means of a specific conjunction followed by a finite verb form. Unfortunately we can only rely on a restricted number of studies on how interpropositional relations are expressed by learners of Italian. Giacalone Ramat (1999a) has described the clause combining strategies of three German learners. The acquisitional patterns that have resulted from this study show a number of hierarchies: adverbial clauses introduced by explicit subordinators are the first type of subordination to emerge; within the set of adverbial clauses, causal and temporal clauses by far outnumber other types, the order of the two structures being however different for the learners observed. With the exception of purpose clauses that are codified from the start by means of preposition *per* + infinitive (as in the target language: see Giacalone Ramat 1999b for a discussion)[8], adverbial subordinate clauses are overwhelmingly explicit. Similar results on the emergence of subordination in learner Italian have been obtained by Chini (1998), Ferraris (1999), Berruto (2001). Ferraris and Berruto have confirmed the very early emergence of explicit subordinate clause along the sequence: causal> temporal > conditional.

- simple imperfective tenses such as the present tense and the imperfect will appear before the progressive periphrasis. This prediction has been equally borne out by Giacalone Ramat (1995a, 1997): it will be checked with reference to the larger corpus considered for the present study.

5. Subjects and data analysis

In order to obtain evidence on the emergence and use of gerunds in L2 Italian, I have used a corpus of L2 Italian available at the University of Pavia, including learners of different proficiency levels and various linguistic backgrounds.[9] The corpus on which the present study is based is larger than the one used in previous work and includes intermediate and advanced learners. The converbial use of gerunds is analyzed here for the first time for the entire corpus. A list of all subjects considered with some essential information is provided in Appendix 1. Part of the learners were followed longitudinally from the beginner stage when they arrived in Italy for six months to one year, for others the data collection was cross-sectional.

All subjects (except for those of the Caruana corpus)[10] lived in Italy at the time of recordings and all received some kind of formal instruction, which for some was reduced to some form of attendance at classes of Italian for foreigners. The corpus also includes students attending classes at the University of Pavia.[11] Although tutored and untutored (or minimally tutored) learners differ in their patterns of contact with the host environment, they were not kept apart in this study. The corpus is rich in personal narratives, descriptions of illustrated stories and retellings of two silent films: a four-minute film on a lost wallet *Il portafoglio* and an excerpt from *Modern Times*. The last task was also used by researchers of the European project "The structure of learner varieties" (Dietrich, Klein and Noyau 1995), thus providing adequate material for cross-linguistic comparison.

All data considered were checked for gerunds, and every instance of gerund was analyzed in its context. The pattern of emergence of gerunds was examined for each learner and comparisons among learners were outlined.

Some of the subjects considered for this study did not exhibit any instance of gerunds. These subjects were neither capable of showing a productive use of distinctive morphological features (number on nouns, person on verbs, tense/aspect oppositions). They were in what Klein and Perdue (1997) refer to as the "basic variety". The learners were: CH, FD, WZ, first language Chinese, all in the beginner stage, HG, first language Tigrinya, FR, first language German, a fossilised learner, EO, first language English. They are not included in Appendix 1. This fact allows us to formulate a first conclusion: learners who have not developed the means to mark finiteness, or at least do not regularly mark tense on the finite verb, do not show nonfinite forms such as gerunds. It must be noted that gerunds need to be dissociated from other types of nonfinite constructions such as infinitives, which are present from the very beginning in learner productions and are sometimes used as main predicates.

Leaving aside those subjects who did not use gerunds at all, learners were grouped according to their use of gerunds in the following subsets:

A) Learners who show a few, mostly inaccurate, attempts to use gerunds. In this group JO and FI, both speakers of English were placed. In the following excerpt JO first attempts to use a gerund where the infinitive would be required, then asks the native speaker for confirmation and finally discovers that the gerund is equivalent to the English *–ing* form:

(11)
JO:	*all'inizio*	*vo/vogliamo* ++*ehm*	*andando*		*a*
	first	we.want	go-GER		to
	Sardenia	*andando*	*?sì?*		
	Sardinia	go-GER	yes?		
Int.:	*andare+*	*vogliamo*	*andare*		
	go-INF	we.want	go-INF		
JO	*ah+*	*andare+*	*andando*	**it's going*_	*andare*
	ah	go-INF	go-GER	it's going	go-INF
	vogliamo	*andare*			
	we.want	go-INF			

"first we want going to Sardinia....going, yes?" "to go, we want to go" "oh, to go! *andando* it's *going*, to go, we want to go"

TU, speaker of Chinese, exhibits two instances of *–ndo* forms which are apparently used as verbal nouns:

(12)
	poi	*sempre*	*ridere*	*come*	*ti chiama*	*sempre*
	then	always	laugh-INF	how	do you say	always
	scherzando no?					
	joke-GER					

"then always laughing, how is it, always joking" (TU means to say that she likes comic films, where one can laugh, amuse oneself).

(13) *sempre   tipo   poesia scherzando   però   li/molto*
       always   like   poetry joke-GER   but   very
       intirissante
       interesting
       "always types of playful poems but very interesting..."
       (talking about her favourite books, TU affirms that she likes poems which are amusing).

In one case FI uses a gerund that can be interpreted as predicate modifier:

(14)
   FI: *abbiamo   passato   la mattina   seduti ehm*
       we.have   spent   the morning   seated
       a la/ a la)   porta (=il porto)   guar/?guardando?
       at the   harbour   look at-GER
   Int.: *Sì*
   FI: *guardando   la/il mare*
       look at-GER   the sea.
       "we spent the morning sitting at the harbor watching?" "yes" "watching the sea"

Summing up:

Table 2. Initial uses of gerunds

Learner	tokens	types	probable function
JO	6	1 andando	verbal complement
FI	2	2 guardando lavorando	predicate modifier uninterpretable
TU	2	1 scherzando	verbal noun
Total	10		

B) learners who exhibit the progressive periphrasis *stare* + gerund. I have calculated the overall rate for each learner. This individual procedure was not applied to the Maltese corpus subdivided in spontaneous (SL) and tutored learners (TL), nor to the FS (*Frog story*) and

ModTim (*Modern Times*) corpus. A distinction between tokens and types seemed necessary because of the predominance of a restricted set of lexical verbs.

Table 3. Distribution of progressive forms across learners and semantic verb classes

Learner	token/type	distribution across actionality classes			
		activities	states	accomplishments	achievements
AB	22/14	12		7	3
MK	30/18	25		4	1
TE	19/8	17		1	1
MT	8/8	2		5	1
UL	4/4	2		2	
AN	1				1
AL	4/2	4			
FA	3/3	2		1	
XI	24/10	24			
BB	24/15	16		7	1
FS	8/8	4		4	
ModTim	38/21	24		13	1
Maltese TL	90/38	57	5	19	9
Maltese SL	86/35	53	3	20	10
TOTAL	361	242	8	83	28

As argued in Giacalone Ramat (1995a, 1997), the highest rate of progressive forms appears with activity verbs. Utterance verbs and propositional attitude verbs are also used in the progressive, as in native Italian. Accomplishments place second, achievements are scarce and states absent, except for Maltese learners. On the whole, the subjects who were investigated for the first time for the present study, such as the Maltese learners and the German learners of FS and ModTim, fully confirm the predictions made in previous studies (Giacalone Ramat 1995a, 1997).

It must be noted, however, that the Maltese learners show some overuse of the progressive periphrasis to stative contexts where it would be inappropriate in Italian, as in (15) and (16) where the imperfect *reggeva* and *sedeva* would be required:

(15) SL 1

e	c'era	un pezzo	di legname	che
and	there was	a piece	of wood	that

stava reggendo	un nave
hold-PROGR-IMPF	a ship

"and there was a piece of wood that was holding a ship"

(16) TL 24

e poi	quello che	stava sedendo	vicino a lui+
then	the one who	sit-PROGR-IMPF	close to him

uno grosso+	voleva il pane
a big one	wanted the bread

"then the big guy sitting near him wanted the bread"

The extension of progressive to states is probably due to the influence of English. The circumstance that the Maltese corpus was elicited in Malta may be responsible for a pattern of use of progressive which was not observed in the data examined.

All learners show a pattern of expansion from a prototypical use of progressive with activities to gradual increase of accomplishments and achievements, according to the most typical uses of natives (Bertinetto 2000: 567).

C) learners who use the gerund in converbial constructions. Below the distribution of gerunds across the learners is reported.

Table 4. Distribution of converbial gerunds

learners	predicate gerunds	sentence gerunds
MT	8	13
AN	2 (3)	/
AL	5	/
FS	5	2
ModTim	11 (+10 participial uses)	2
Maltese TL	7	1
Maltese SL	1	2
Total of converbial gerunds in the corpus: 70	50	20

Production of gerunds in converbial constructions is limited to a few learners who belong to advanced proficiency levels. Note that some learners listed in Table 2. on progressive are not present in Table 3. on converbs: AB, TE, MK, XI, BB.

The German subjects of FS and ModTim are all University students: they were grouped by Chini (1998) at different levels of proficiency: proficiency was determined according to the rate of appropriate use of tense/aspect morphology, subjunctive, clitic pronouns, agreement of past participles. Occurrences of converbs were found in the learners of the advanced group. The tutored Maltese learners (TL) show 8 instances of converbs (of these 5 are produced by the same learner), the spontaneous learners (SL) only 3. Both spontaneous and tutored learners belong to the advanced group according to the grouping adopted in Caruana (2001).

MT – also a University student – shows a remarkable range of appropriate use of subordinate structures; the proportion of subordinate clauses with respect to the total number of clausal units is 37,3% (Giacalone Ramat 1999b: 536), close to the proportion found in data of spoken Italian by Berruto and Bescotti (1995: 468). MT's subordinates are distributed over completive clauses, relatives, purpose clauses and adverbial clauses introduced by subordinators.

I will now discuss the function of converbial gerunds according to the parameters proposed in section 3. The question we need to ask is: what is the prototypical function of gerunds as clause combining strategy? As noted earlier, converbial constructions are compatible with a wide variety of semantic interpretations. In the many controversies regarding the semantic analysis of converbs, a highly relevant contribution was the distinction between "manner" or modal and "accompanying circumstance" (Pusch 1980:108, König 1995: 64ff). As observed by König, the label "modal" should be used for sentences describing two aspects or dimensions of only one event, e.g. a type of motion, or a way of speaking.

Our data show a strikingly high number of such cases which suggest that this is the "prototypical" use which enters the learner language:

Consider the following examples :

(17) TL93:
> *il poliziotto.... ha corso riprendendo la ragazza*
> the policeman has run catch up-GER again the girl
> "the policeman ran and managed to catch up with the girl"

(18) TL93:
> *la donna che l'aveva visto insisteva dicendo*
> the woman who had seen him insisted say-GER
> *che era la ragazza*
> that it was the girl
> "the woman who had seen him insisted by saying that it was the girl"

(19)
> AL: *poi la notte di Pasqua si rompe questo digiuno*
> then the night of Easter is broken this fastening
> *facendo una specie di ....eh.... una festa insomma...*
> do-GER a kind of party
> "then on the eve of Easter this period of fastening is broken by organising some sort of party"

(20)
> AN: *se si lasciano giù traversando il balcone*
> if they.let themselves down cross-GER the balcony
> *che brucia..*
> on fire
> "if they let themselves down crossing the balcony on fire"

(21)
> FS: *si diverte attaccando la cassetta delle api*
> he amuses himself attack-GER the box of the bees
> "he amuses himself by attacking the box of the bees"

The term "attendant (or accompanying) circumstance" "should be used for cases in which two independent events or actions are involved, either of which could be stopped without affecting the other, but which manifest a unity of time and place and thus also a "perceptual unity" (König 1995: 66). This can be illustrated by example (1) above and by the following:

(22)
    FS: *cadono   tutti e due   nell'acqua   cercando*
         they.fall   both   into water   look-GER
       dov'è...
       where it is...
       "they both fall into water while they were trying to find where it is"

(23)
    AL: *il tronco   cadendo   gli è finito sul torace*
        the log   fall-GER   has ended on his chest
    "when the log fell it ended up on his chest"

(24) TL93:
    e poi   gli ha dato   un certificato
    and then   he has handed him   a certificate
    dicendolo   che   da lì   può   avere   un lavoro
    say-GER-to him   that   from it   he.can   get   a job
    "and then he gave him a certificate telling him that he could get a job by it"

(25) ModTim:
    la prossima scena   si vede   Charlie Chaplin
    the next scene   one can see   Charlie Chaplin
    che   se ne va del/del prigione   cercando   un lavoro
    who   is leaving the prison   look-GER   for a job
    "in the next scene one may see Charlie Chaplin who is leaving prison in order to look for a job"

Both subtypes are cases of predicate gerunds associated with the same subject constraint. In (25) the unity of time is questionable, since a relation of posteriority might hold between leaving prison and looking for a job.

For temporal gerunds it is not easy to assess the degree of integration with the main predicate. The distinction between "detached" and "nondetached converbs" (König 1995: 85ff) may be relevant in this regard. Nondetached converbs form one tone group with the main clause and typically express manner or attendant circumstance relations in which the converb is integrated in the main clause. Detached converbs form a tone group of their own as indicated by the pause by which their use is accompanied and may express the background to some event, as in the two examples below:

(26)
   MT: *poi   arrivando   al campeggio   doveva*
        then   arrive-GER   to the camping site   he.had to
      dare   i documenti
      hand in the documents
      "then when they arrived to the camping site he had to hand in the documents"

(27)
   MT: *la sera   arrivando   dalla stazione siamo tornati*
        that evening,   arrive-GER   from the station we returned
      a casa
      home
      "that evening when we arrived from the station we returned home"

In our data causal, conditional and concessive converbs are scarcely represented. A dozen of causal and conditional converbs have been registered only in the corpus of the learner MT (examples 30-33), whereas in the utterances of other learners they are quite rare. They usually manifest an iconic word order, that is gerunds with causal interpretation precede the main clause, while explicit subordinate clauses introduced by *perché* "because" follow the main clause, thus reversing the iconic order.

(28)
   FS: *pensando   che   sono   i rami   di un albero*
       assume-GER   that   they.are the branches   of a tree
      si va   avanti
      he goes ahead
      "assuming that they are branches of a tree he goes ahead, ahead"

(29) SL 168:
      Charlie Chaplin   scambiandola per   la   bottiglia
      Charlie Chaplin   take-GER it   for   the   bottle
      del sale   ha messo   un po' nel suo piatto e
      of the salt   has put   a bit   on his dish   and
      nel suo pane
      on his bread
      "Charlie Chaplin mistaking it for the bottle of salt put some on his dish and on his bread"

(30)
   MT: *avendo   fretta ha messo   il portafoglio in tasca*
      have-GER   hurry, he.has put   the wallet   into pocket
      "because he was in a hurry, he put the wallet into his pocket

(31)
   MT: *sentendo   tutta questa felicità   dentro di noi e*
      feel-GER   all this happiness   within us   and
      essendo   innamorati   ci siamo baciati
      be-GER   in love   we kissed
      "feeling all this happiness with us and being in love we kissed"

(32)
   MT: *magari   sbaglio di meno   non facendoci caso*
      perhaps   I make less mistakes   not pay-GER attention
      "perhaps I would make less mistakes if I don't pay attention"

(33)
> MT: *il rischio   di morire   prendendo   queste sostanze*
>   the danger of dying take-GER this stuff
> "the danger of dying if one assumes this stuff"

The following case could be given a concessive interpretation, though it is also compatible with a temporal interpretation of simultaneity "while he was trying to lean against the wall...".

(34) ModTim:
> *cade   anche   nell'acqua   volendo appoggiarsi*
> he falls also   in water   want-GER to lean
> *al muro*
> against the wall
> "he also falls in water, though trying to lean against the wall"

Combinations of clauses expressing sequential relations, again with iconic word order, were also found:

(35) SL 172:
> *e lei   l'ha spinto   facendolo   cadere*
> and she has pushed him make-GER him fall
> *sull'altra parte   della macchina*
> on the other side   of the car
> "she pushed him towards the other side of the car"

Noteworthy is a set of cases registered in several learners, but seemingly preferred by German learners (10 occurrences in ModTim) in which the gerund is used as a noun modification: this function is not allowed in Italian which would use a (pseudo-)relative construction.
The restriction of the Italian gerund which has no participial use is not acquired by some learners. This may be attributed to first language influence, since German has participles both in attributive and adverbial function, or perhaps to the influence of the English –*ing* form, since all University students of our corpus can speak English:[12]

(36)
MT: *a fianco   seduto   su una panchina   c'è   il padre*
    by the side   sitting on a bench   there is the father
    della ragazza osservando (= che osserva) *bene   tutto*
    of the girl   look-GER   well   all
    quello che succede
    that is happening
    "by the side, sitting on a bench, there is the girl's father who is observing well all that is happening"

(37) ModTim:
    prima scena   si vede   Charlie Chaplin
    first scene   one may see   Charlie Chaplin
    camminando (=che cammina) *molto triste eh*
    walk-GER   very sad
    sulle strade
    on the streets
    "in this first scene one may see Charlie Chaplin who is walking very sadly in the street"

All these gerunds are associated with perception verbs *vedere, osservare* or the existential *c'è* "there is".

6. Discussion and conclusions

Let us briefly recapitulate the main results of this study on gerunds as adverbial modifiers in learner Italian.

This study has provided evidence by means of which we may answer the question: at what stage do learners of Italian develop gerunds? It was shown that gerunds appear after the morphological marking of finiteness is acquired. Learners who exhibit gerunds have developed a verbal system including present tense, auxiliaries, past participles and, partially, imperfect. Among nonfinite verb forms gerunds appear later and are much less frequent than infinitives and past participles. A reason for the earlier emergence of infinitives might be that, except for the initial learner use as main predicates, infinitives generally function as verb arguments, while gerunds function as adverbial subordination, which is external to the main clause and may be signaled by other means. Past participles too belong to the main verb structure and as such are learned earlier.

The second question regarded the purposes for which gerunds are developed. The distribution of gerunds across the learners investigated has shown a frequency scale between the progressive periphrasis (total of 361 occurrences in the data examined) and converbial gerunds (total of 70 occurrences). Moreover, an implicational relation seems to hold, since no learner has developed converbial uses without having developed the progressive periphrasis. In other words, some learners show only occurrences of the progressive periphrasis, others have also developed predicate gerunds, others finally also use sentence gerunds: thus, the data suggest a hierarchy that predicts which uses are likely to emerge first:

progressive periphrasis > predicate gerunds > sentence gerunds

In learner languages converbial constructions typically are predicate modifiers, the function of which is to express modal or accompanying circumstances.[13] The earlier emergence of the progressive periphrasis provides a confirmation of the prominence of predicate gerunds. Consider that the origin of the periphrasis is to be traced back to an adverbial modifier associated with the postural verb *stare* via a grammaticalisation process of both the postural verb and the adverbial modifier. Literally *sta guardando* means something like "he is standing (and) looking": both verbs are related to the same event or action. Then, the progressive periphrasis can be considered to be the earliest use of predicate gerunds in second language learners.

This fact deserves however some attention: one might ask why the first emergence of gerunds in acquisition is within the progressive periphrasis rather than as predicate modifiers, which seems to be the prototypical function of gerunds (as stated above). The answer could be the following: from the point of view of language change the reanalysis associated with the grammaticalisation process had the effect of transforming the complex clause formed by *stare* + predicate gerund into a single structure functioning as a main verb. From the point of view of acquisition main clauses are acquired earlier than complex clauses involving means and strategies of clause connection. Then the acquisition would start for gerunds in the main clause and would be subsequently extended to the clause connection function. These considerations suggest divergent paths between grammaticalisation processes which are familiar from historical linguistics and stages which learners go through in building their second language grammar.

In our earlier discussion on markedness (section 4) we concluded that gerunds on the basis of current typological criteria are more marked than finite subordinate forms. In the acquisitional perspective some further considerations should be added. Formally, gerunds are simple: the morpheme *–ndo* is added to the verb stem (root + thematic vowel): *and-a-ndo, tem-e-ndo, part-e-ndo*. The formation is transparent to the learners, errors are few: I have found only a pair of attempts to take the full infinitive form as the base form: *partir-ando* in place of *part-endo*. Despite their formal simplicity and transparency, gerunds are not promptly learned and are neither frequently used, even by advanced learners. What are the possible motivations for the very limited use of gerunds, beyond the answer supplied in the markedness framework? According to Dietrich, Klein and Noyau (1995) learner languages show a tendency "from simple to complex": the authors clarify that they refer to simplicity of expression. Actually, the development of gerunds does not fall into this trend: the reason might be that gerunds though formally simple are not transparent as far as the relation meaning and form is concerned. The opacity of gerunds is due to the clustering of possible interpretations that they may have. Research on learner languages has shown that also learners tend to follow a "one-form-one meaning principle" (Andersen 1984) which represents a universal of human language (Haiman 1985) aiming at transparent relations between surface structures and meaning. Then, the character of "general-purpose subordination" or in other words semantic vagueness does not favour gerunds. This tendency is however in contradiction with what is usually thought for the conjunction *che* "that" which is used as an all-purpose clause combining strategy.

The factors considered, i.e. typological markedness and transparency vs. opacity in form/function can be in conflict with each other. Although less marked finite structures are learned earlier than gerunds in the domain of subordination, as shown by the data analyzed, a tendency which leads from explicit to implicit seems to emerge as proficiency in the second language moves forward. Advanced learners may choose the possibility of leaving the semantic nature of adverbial relations implicit by using reduced verb forms such as gerunds because they know well enough what can be left to pragmatic inferencing.[14] This is indeed what natives do, since they know that communication may very well work without being explicit about interclausal relations. Under this interpretation the use of gerunds may be economically motivated: economy is achieved by subsuming different meanings under a single form. Note that it must not come as a surprise that guiding principles change in the course of acquisition: in the competition between markedness principles, favouring finite forms, and economy principles one of them may prevail over the other in some moment of the linguistic development (Haiman 1985: 253). Thus, what functional explanations may suggest in the case of gerunds is that variation is to be expected where competing motivations are at work.

As shown above, many subjects in this study have acquired gerunds, however in organising information for expression they do not choose the option of gerunds as often as native speakers are likely to do. Some interesting comparative evidence on this point can be gathered from a set of retellings of *Modern Times* produced by 13 Italian subjects, all University students living in Lombardy.[15] Data from this set have been compared with the retellings of *Modern Times* produced by the 8 German learners considered in this study (=ModTim) (Appendix 1). Table 5 shows that the rate of appropriate gerunds is lower in L2 learners than it is in natives. It also shows that the percentages of finite reason clauses is higher in learners than in natives (Chini 1998). Intermediate learners, even advanced learners, are strongly involved in the construction of grammar: they have become able to master a number of grammatical features and generally prefer to resort to explicit forms. Only some of them start using a less explicit textual type present in native input. The choice of gerunds is ultimately motivated at the information structure level and the discourse construction level which usually guarantee a non ambiguous understanding of the utterance.

Table 5. Distribution of converbial gerunds and finite subordinate clauses in retellings from *Modern Times*: a comparison between L1 and L2

	German learners of Italian (8 subjects)		Native speakers (13 subjects)	
	raw scores	%	raw scores	%
complement clauses	78	34,2	148	28,8
relative clauses	50	22	134	27
adverbial clauses	87	38,2	190	38,2
(reason clauses)	(41)	(18)	(52)	(10,5)
(temporal clauses)	(16)	(7)	(49)	(9,8)
gerunds	3 (+ 10 inappropriate)	1,3 (+4,3)	25	5
total of subordinate clauses	228		497	

Questions to be investigated in future studies concern: 1) possible constraints favouring gerunds in the distribution between gerunds and finite forms; 2) the extent to which the pattern of development observed for Italian can be extended to other languages.

The findings of this study are relevant from a double perspective. For acquisition research they help to answer the question of how learners construct interclausal relations. For general linguistics the data examined may suggest something about the nature and dynamics of converbial constructions and provide insights on the specific features developed by Italian. As shown, modal and accompanying circumstance gerunds, the subject of which is controlled by the subject of the main clause, emerge first and are preferred by learners. These elements give some evidence in favour of the prototypicality of this type, while other types of converbs (different subjects or absolute constructions) are marginal members of the category. This picture is also known from descriptive studies on Italian, for which acquisitional data provide an independent confirmation. Generalisations about converbs that have been developed by typological studies (Haspelmath and König 1995) have also pointed to the general preference in languages for converbial constructions which are predicate modifiers.

These suggestions may turn out to be relevant to the study of linguistic variation in its different manifestations, language acquisition, cross-linguistic typology and historical linguistics.

Appendix 1

Learner, age, sex	First language	Education/activity	Length of stay in Italy (at 1st recording)
AB, 21, f	Tigrinya	Secondary school in Eritrea	1 year
MK, 20, m	Tigrinya	Secondary school in Eritrea	1 month
TE, 16, m	Tigrinya	Secondary school in Eritrea	2 months
MT, 22, m	German	University student	2 months
UL, 33, f	German	Teacher of German	3 months
AN, 20, f	German	Secondary school	2 months
AL, 21, m	French and Moré	Secondary school in Berlin	2 years and 6 months
FA, 29, m	Moroccan Arabic, French	Secondary schools	2 years
TU, about 40, f	Chinese (wú)	Secondary school in China	4 years
XI, 12, f	Chinese (wú)	Elementary school in China	18 months
BB, 17, m	English	Student	2 months
FI, 26, f	English	Teacher of English	5 months
JO, 27, m	English	Teacher of English	1 month and a half
FS*, 20-30, m/f (8 subjects)	German	University students	From 1 to 8 months
ModTim*, 20-30, m/f (8 subjects)	German	University students	From 1 to 8 months
SL **,14-15, m (26 subjects)	Maltese	Junior Lyceum students	
TL **,14-15, m (26 subjects)	Maltese	Junior Lyceum students	

*The same 8 German students produced retellings of *Modern Times* and described the booklet *Frog, where are you?* Their initials are: KAR, COR, FRA, ALE (advanced level), ANT, GIS, WOL, CHR (intermediate level). All students were living in Pavia since 1 to 8 months and attended courses of Italian at the University (Chini 1998).

** The Maltese corpus consists of recordings of 52 subjects, 26 spontaneous learnes of Italian (=SL) and 26 who received instruction in Italian (=TL): all were shown the *Modern Times* film. The recordings were done in Malta as part of the doctoral dissertation of Sandro Caruana (2001) on the impact of television on the diffusion of Italian in Malta.

Notes

1. Dinale (1997) notes that some gerunds can not be paraphrased by explicit adverbial clauses, but rather by means of adverbials or prepositional phrases. She quotes the following Old Italian (XIII century) example, where a possible paraphrasis would be *in lacrime* "in tears", but the observation is true also for Modern Italian:
   (i) *e la donna piangendo   li chiese mercede e disse*
       and the woman cry-GER   pleaded him for mercy and said
       "and the woman crying pleaded him for mercy and said"
2. There are several constraints on the use of absolute gerunds: first of all the explicit subject takes postverbal position. Moreover, this type belongs to an elevated style of speech and written language (Lonzi 1991: 572).
3. Prototypical converb languages are Korean or Nivkh. In English adverbial subordination by means of *–ing* converbs plays a significant role, especially if one compares other Germanic languages. To give a rough idea, English employs five times as many adverbial participial clauses per 10.000 words as German does (Kortmann 1995: 192).
4. Bertinetto (2000: 559ff) provides a descriptive and comparative outline of the progressive periphrasis in Romance languages and in English. Villarini (1999) has analyzed the LIP corpus and commented on the use of *stare*+gerund across all text types.
5. Information organisation is also a relevant factor for the use of gerunds: sentence gerunds are generally used to code topic or presupposed information. This function is not distinctive for gerunds however, since it is implemented by finite causal, concessive, conditional clauses as well. Therefore the issue will not be discussed further here.
6. The grammaticalisation process is not completed in Italian because *stare* undergoes morphosyntactic and semantic constraints. It has not reached the full copula function typical of Spanish *estar* (Bertinetto, Ebert and de Groot 2000: 521).
7. A more marginal, literary register nonfinite adverbial construction is article+ preposition + infinitive, as in:
   (ii) *nel guardarlo, Anna trasse ancora un sospiro profondo, quasi dolorante*
        in.ART look-INF-at.him, Anna sighted in a deep almost painful way
        (quoted in Renzi and Salvi 1991: 568)
   This type was not found at all in our data. Crosslinguistic remarks in Berman (1998: 217).
8. It does not come as a surprise that purpose clauses codification differs from that of causal, concessive and conditional clauses. Purpose clauses show fea-

tures of semantic integration with the main clause, high degree of control by the subject of the main clause and predetermined time reference: in languages these factors may favour a reduced morphosyntactic coding of the dependent clause (Cristofaro 1998).

9. The Pavia corpus includes data from several interuniversitary projects supported by the Italian Ministero dell'Università e della Ricerca Scientifica e Tecnologica (MURST). An account of the design and contents of the Pavia corpus can be found in Bernini 1994, a more recent description including a choice of texts in Andorno (2001) at the website: http://unipv.it/wwwling.
10. The Caruana corpus consists of recordings of 52 subjects, 26 spontaneous learners of Italian (=SL) and 26 who received instruction in Italian (=TL): all were shown the *Modern Times* film. The recordings were done in Malta as part of the doctoral dissertation of Sandro Caruana (2001) on the impact of television on the diffusion of Italian in Malta.
11. Marina Chini elicited a corpus of oral narratives from 8 German students at the University of Pavia. The students watched an excerpt of *Modern Times* (=ModTim) and a picture booklet *Frog, where are you?* (FS=Frog Story) (Chini 1998).
12. In written texts produced by students of Italian at the University of Zürich Berruto, Moretti and Schmid (1989: 20) also found a number of overextensions of gerunds in place of present participles or relative clauses: *una educazione meno specifica portando con sé una consapevolezza...* " a less specific education which implies a consciousness...".
13. This conclusion is supported by Ceglia (2002) who analyzed a group of Arab-speaking migrants living in Turin and by Ferraris (1999).
14. Gerunds and participial constructions are defined "rhetorical options" for textual connectivity by Berman (1998). Their use is also signalled in children aged from 3 to 9 years, speakers of English, Spanish, Hebrew and Turkish.
15. I thank Mary Carroll (Heidelberg) and Marina Chini for making these data accessible to me. The subset collected by Chini includes 3 students in Pavia (Chini 1998, Giacalone Ramat 1999b), the subset provided by Carroll includes 10 students living in Milan.

References

Andorno, Cecilia
    2001   Italiano L2. Banca dati di italiano seconda lingua. Università di Pavia. Dipartimento di Linguistica. http://unipv.it/wwwling.
Battistella, Edwin L.
    1996   *The Logic of Markedness*. Oxford: Oxford University Press.

Berman, Ruth
1998 Typological perspectives on connectivity. In: Norbert Dittmar and Zvi Penner (eds.), *Issues in the Theory of Language Acquisition. Essays in Honor of Jürgen Weissenborn*, 203-224. Bern: Peter Lang.

Bernini, Giuliano
1994 La banca dati del "progetto di Pavia" sull'italiano lingua seconda. *Studi Italiani di Linguistica Teorica e Applicata* 23: 221-236.

Berruto, Gaetano
2001 L'emergenza della connessione interproposizionale nell'italiano di immigrati. Un'analisi di superficie. *Romanische Forschungen* 113: 1-37.

Berruto, Gaetano, Bruno Moretti, and Stephan Schmid
1988 L'italiano di parlanti colti in una situazione plurilingue. *Rivista Italiana di Dialettologia* 12: 7-100.

Berruto, Gaetano, and Katia Bescotti
1995 Sulla complessità/semplicità sintattica dell'italiano parlato. *Studi Italiani di Linguistica Teorica e Applicata* 24: 461-477.

Bertinetto, Pier Marco
1986 *Tempo, aspetto e azione nel verbo italiano. Il sistema dell'indicativo*. Firenze: Accademia della Crusca.

Bertinetto, Pier Marco
2000 The progressive in Romance, as compared with English. In: Östen Dahl (ed.), 559-593.

Bertinetto, Pier Marco, Karen H. Ebert, and Casper de Groot.
2000 The progressive in Europe. In: Östen Dahl (ed.), 517-558.

Bisang, Walter
1994 Verb serialization and converbs – differences and similarities. In: Martin Haspelmath and Ekkehard König (eds.), 137-188.

Braidi, Susan
1999 *The Acquisition of Second-Language Syntax*. London and New York: Arnold.

Caruana, Sandro
2001 Mezzi di comunicazione e input linguistico. L'acquisizione dell'italiano L2 a Malta. Doctoral Dissertation. University of Pavia, Department of Linguistics.

Ceglia, Luca
2002 I converbi nelle lingue del Mediterraneo: convergenze areali e implicazioni universali. Doctoral Dissertation. University of Pavia, Department of Linguistics.

Chini, Marina
1998 La subordinazione in testi narrativi di apprendenti tedescofoni: forma e funzione. *Linguistica e Filologia* 7: 121-159.

Chini, Marina
1999 Riferimento personale e strutturazione di testi narrativi in italofoni e in apprendenti tedescofoni di italiano. In: Norbert Dittmar and Anna Giacalone Ramat (eds), *Grammatik und Diskurs/ Grammatica e discorso. Studi sull'acquisizione dell'italiano e del tedesco/ Studien zum Erwerb des Deutschen und des Italienischen*, 213-243. Tübingen: Stauffenburg Verlag.

Comrie, Bernard
1976 *Aspect*. Cambridge: Cambridge University Press.

Cristofaro, Sonia
1998 Toward a typology of subordination strategies. *Sprachtypologie und Universalienforschung* 51: 3-42.

Croft, William
1990 *Typology and Universals*. Cambridge: Cambridge University Press.

Dahl, Östen (ed.)
2000 *Tense and Aspect in the Languages of Europe*. (Empirical Approaches to Language Typology 20-6.) Berlin/New York: Mouton de Gruyter.

De Mauro, Tullio, Federico Mancini, Massimo Vedovelli, and Miriam Voghera
1993 *LIP. Lessico di frequenza dell'italiano parlato*. Milano: EtasLibri.

Dietrich, Rainer, Wolfgang Klein, and Colette Noyau
1995 *The Acquisition of Temporality in a Second Language*. Amsterdam: John Benjamins.

Dinale, Claudia
1997 Sintassi del gerundio italiano antico tra tipo latino e tipo romanzo. Doctoral Dissertation. III Università degli Studi di Roma.

Eckman, Fred R.
1977 Markedness and the contrastive analysis hypothesis. *Language Learning* 27: 315-330.

Eckman, Fred R.
1985 Some theoretical and pedagogical implications of the markedness differential hypothesis. *Studies in Second Language Acquisition,* 7: 289-307.

Eckman, Fred R., Edith A. Moravcsik, and Jessica R. Wirth (eds.)
1985 *Markedness*. New York-London: Plenum Press.

Ferraris, Stefania
1999 *Imparare la sintassi*. Vercelli: Edizioni Mercurio.

Ferreri, Silvana
1983/86 The evolving gerund. *Journal of Italian Linguistics* 8: 25-66.

Gass, Susan M.
1979 Language transfer and universal grammatical relations. *Language Learning* 29: 327-344.

Giacalone Ramat, Anna
1995a L'expression de l'aspect progressif en italien langue seconde. *AILE (=Acquisition et Interaction en Langue Étrangère)* 5: 47-78.

Giacalone Ramat, Anna
1995b Sulla grammaticalizzazione di verbi di movimento: *andare* e *venire* + gerundio. *Archivio Glottologico Italiano* LXXX: 168-203.

Giacalone Ramat, Anna
1997 Progressive periphrases, markedness, and second language data. In: Stig Eliasson and Ernst Håkon Jahr (eds), *Language and its Ecology. Essays in Memory of Einar Haugen*, 261-285. Berlin/New York: Mouton-De Gruyter.

Giacalone Ramat, Anna
1999a Functional typology and strategies of clause connection in second language acquisition. *Linguistics* 37: 519-548.

Giacalone Ramat, Anna
1999b Le strategie di collegamento tra proposizioni nell'italiano di germanofoni. Una prospettiva di tipologia funzionale. In: Norbert Dittmar and Anna Giacalone Ramat, *Grammatik und Diskurs/ Grammatica e discorso. Studi sull'acquisizione dell'italiano e del tedesco/ Studien zum Erwerb des Deutschen und des Italienischen*, 13-54. Tübingen: Stauffenburg Verlag

Gilbers, Dicky, and Helen de Hoop (eds.)
1998 Optimality Theory. *Lingua* 104, 1/ 2. Special issue.

Greenberg, Joseph
1966 Language universals, with special reference to feature hierarchies. (Janua Linguarum, Series Minor, 59.) The Hague: Mouton.

Haiman, John
1985 *Natural Syntax. Iconicity and Erosion.* Cambridge: Cambridge University Press.

Haspelmath, Martin
1995 The converb as a cross-linguistically valid category. In: Martin Haspelmath and Ekkehard König (eds.), 1-55.

Haspelmath, Martin, and Ekkehard König (eds.)
1995 *Converbs in Cross-Linguistic Perspective.* (Empirical Approaches to Language Typology 13.) Berlin/New York: Mouton de Gruyter.

Heine, Bernd
1993 *Auxiliaries: Cognitive Forces and Grammaticalization.* New York-Oxford: Oxford University Press.

Klein, Wolfgang
1998   Assertion and finiteness. In: Norbert Dittmar and Zvi Penner (eds.), *Issues in the Theory of Language Acquisition: Essays in Honor of Jürgen Weissenborn*, 225-245. Bern: Peter Lang.
Klein, Wolfgang, and Clive Perdue
1997   The basic variety. *Second Language Research* 13: 301-347.
König Ekkehard
1995   The meaning of converb constructions. In: Martin Haspelmath and Ekkehard König (eds.), 57-95.
Koptjevskaja-Tamm, Maria
1993   Finiteness. In: Ron E. Asher and James M. Simpson (eds.), *Encyclopaedia of Language and Linguistics*, vol.3, 1245-1248. Oxford: Pergamon.
Kortmann, Bernd
1995   Adverbial participial clauses in English. In: Martin Haspelmath and Ekkehard König (eds.), 189-237.
Kortmann, Bernd
1997   *Adverbial Subordination. A Typology and History of Adverbial Subordinators Based on European Languages.* (Empirical Approaches to Language Typology 18.) Berlin/New York: Mouton de Gruyter.
Lonzi, Lidia
1991   Frasi subordinate al gerundio. In: Lorenzo Renzi e Giampaolo Salvi (a cura di). *Grande grammatica italiana di consultazione*, Vol.II, 571-592. Bologna: Il Mulino.
Nedjalkov, Vladimir P.
1995   Some typological parameters of converbs. In: Martin Haspelmath and Ekkehard König (eds.), 97-136.
Nespor, Marina
1978   The syntax of gerunds in Italian. In: Maria-Elisabeth Conte, Anna Giacalone Ramat and Paolo Ramat (eds), *Wortstellung und Bedeutung. Akten des 12.Linguistischen Kolloquiums*, 103-111. Tübingen: Niemeyer.
Policarpi, Gianna, and Maggi Rombi
1983   Altre metodologie per la sintassi: tipi di gerundio e tipi di participio. In: Federico Albano Leoni, Daniele Gambarara, Franco Lo Piparo and Raffaele Simone (a cura di), *Italia linguistica: idee, storia, strutture*, 309-331. Bologna: Il Mulino.
Pusch, Luise F.
1978   *Kontrastive Untersuchungen zum italienischen ‚gerundio'.* Tübingen: Niemeyer.

Renzi, Lorenzo, and Giampaolo Salvi (a cura di)
1991 *Grande grammatica italiana di consultazione.* Vol.II. Bologna: Il Mulino.

Rohlfs, Gerhard
1969 *Grammatica storica delle lingua italiana e dei suoi dialetti. Sintassi e formazione delle parole.* Torino: Einaudi.

Sorace, Antonella
2000 Syntactic optionality in non native grammars. *Second Language Research* 16: 93-102.

Serianni, Luca
1989 *Grammatica italiana. Italiano comune e lingua letteraria.* Torino: UTET.

Solarino, Rosanna
1995 *I tempi possibili. Le dimensioni temporali del gerundio italiano.* (Quaderni Patavini di Linguistica. Monografie 15.) Padova: Unipress.

Vendler, Zeno
1967 *Linguistics in Philosophy.* Ithaca, N.Y.: Cornell University Press.

Villarini, Andrea
1999 Analisi delle occorrenze della perifrasi *stare*+gerundio all'interno di un corpus di italiano parlato. In: Massimo Vedovelli (a cura di), *Indagini sociolinguistiche nella scuola e nella società italiana in evoluzione,* 27-49. Milano: Franco Angeli.

White, Lydia
1986 Markedness and parameter setting: some implications for a theory of adult second language acquisition. In: Fred R.Eckman, Edith A. Moravcsik and Jessica R. Wirth, (eds.), 309-327.

Iconicity and finiteness in the development of early grammar in French as L2 and in French-based creoles

Daniel Véronique

0. Introduction

This paper is devoted to a study of the typology of form-function relations in French as a second language (FSL) and in French-based Creoles (henceforth FBC). It is hypothesised that Creolisation is SLA under specific circumstances and that the same organisational principles govern Basic learner Varieties and early pre-creole and creole grammar. An attempt is made to assess the part played by iconicity and finiteness in the development of early grammar in FBC and in FSL. It is generally acknowledged that iconicity – isomorphism and motivational iconicity (Croft 1990: 164-192) – shapes in some measure grammar in language use and in the course of language acquisition and of language change. Although this claim has been put forward mainly by functional linguists, Newmeyer (1992), in the generative persuasion, demonstrates quite convincingly that "[...] iconicity has played a major role in shaping the grammatical properties of human languages" (Newmeyer 1992: 789), and that multileveled generative syntax is in a position to represent iconically "the expression of predicate-argument and quantification relations", i.e. motivation as one aspect of 'structure-concept iconicity'. In the domain of language acquisition, Radford's contribution to the study of the acquisition of early lexical-thematic grammar in L1 makes a similar point (Radford 1990: 239-262). Both formal and functional approaches to language acquisition and language change have also emphasised the importance of finiteness in the development of L1 and

L2 syntax (Jordens (ed.) 1995, Meisel 1994, 1997, DeGraff (ed.) 1999). Although finiteness is defined differently in formal and functional schools of linguistics, (see Klein 1998 and forthcoming), there is some measure of agreement as to its contribution to the development of grammar, namely its role in sentence construction.

Iconicity may be best described as a set of cognitive requisites mapping the form-function relation in language (see Croft 1990: 164-192, and Swiggers 1993, Danon-Boileau 1993, Kleiber 1993 for a discussion of the notion of iconicity), or as a set of principles governing non-arbitrary form-function relations pervasive in all the functional realms coded by language (Givón 1984: 30-32). It shapes linguistic change because non-arbitrary form-function correlations stand in need of restoration as language evolve (Heine, Claudi, Hünnemeyer 1991: 212-215). Iconicity is not of the same order as functional or morphological finiteness. Finiteness belongs in Givón's terms to the realm of propositional semantics as coded by syntax (Givón 1984: 41-44). Functional finiteness, defined by Klein (1998, forthcoming) as a conceptual linguistic category, may be determined by iconicity but the two categories are not on a par. It is expected that both iconicity and finiteness operate in their own terms during the processes of grammaticalisation and reanalysis. For instance, paradigmatisation resulting from grammaticalisation may be at odds with iconic motivation (Croft 1990: 164-192). However, in the course of grammaticalisation, as Haspelmath (1999: 1050) correctly notes, an iconic relationship may exist between form and meaning: "as an item is desemanticized, it is also formally reduced and nobody would expect an element to become formally reduced but semantically enriched".

In this paper, an attempt is made to assess the part played by both iconicity and finiteness in the development of early grammar in French-based Creoles and in French as a second language. It examines the development of existentials, of negation and of temporality in FBC and FSL as resulting partly from grammaticalisation and reanalysis. This comparison is a contribution to the study of the typology of form-function relations in FSL and FBC (Croft 1990: 155-192). It is expected to shed some light on the similarities and dissimilarities between the development of pidgins and creoles and of learner varieties in second language acquisition and to uphold the view that pidginisation and creolisation at their inception are forms of SLA. Section 1 of the paper is devoted to a survey of the major issues involved in the comparison between the development of FBC – the pidginisation/creolisation issue – and the acquisition of FSL – the SLA issue. Section 2 is devoted to the study of some aspects of grammatical development in FSL and FBC. In each subsection, data on the acquisition of FSL is first analyzed, followed by a discussion of data from FBC. Section 3 brings together and discusses the major findings of the study.

1. The comparison of FBC and FSL: theoretical issues
1.1. Pidginisation/creolisation and SLA

"ALA (Adult Language Acquisition) is a halfway house between language change end creolisation ... In language change, lexical items functioning within an already grammaticalised system get bleached, ... whereas in creolisation, the learner creates phrasal constraints in the absence of input" (Sankoff and Laberge 1973). In both these cases, what needs to be explained is the choice of categories which speakers grammaticalise, and in the latter case, their respective order. In ALA on the other hand, the learner is almost always dealing with grammatical input (as opposed to foreigner talk) and what needs to be explained is both the order of the TL phrasal constraints that *are* acquired, and also why some grammaticalised categories of the TL are *not* acquired: the process is not inevitable." (Klein and Perdue, 1993: 260-261).

This quotation aptly summarises some of the issues raised in the comparison of SLA and Creolisation but contains one long-standing error, at least in the case of FBC. It is certainly incorrect to state that FBC have been elaborated in the absence of any input whatsoever (see Hazaël-Massieux 1996: 119-136). Grammaticalisation for one may be an on-going process partly carried over from the lexifier language (Bruyn 1995).

As various researchers have pointed out (Andersen 1983, DeGraff 1999), SLA may be described as a process of language genesis and language change at a micro-level whereas pidginisation and creolisation are cases of language development and change at a macro-level. Some researchers, Bickerton (1983) for instance, have argued that the two processes cannot be compared for that specific reason while Chaudenson (1992) and Mufwene (1996) maintain the opposite view based on the argument that pidgins and creoles grew out of individual acts of communication and of approximations of the Target Language (TL). According to Mufwene 1996, the least marked communication strategies used by the slave population, based on factors such as regularity, invariability, transparency and perceptual salience, may explain the emergence of early creole grammar. Haspelmath (1999) proposes a similar explanation, called the invisible-hand theory, to explain the irreversibility of grammaticalisation.

From the current state of knowledge, it seems that contact languages form a language continuum from jargons to stabilised forms of pidgins and creoles (Mühlhäusler 1986, 1997, Thomason (ed.) 1997). It is generally agreed that some creoles may have developed without a preceding pidgin phase and that creole or pre-creole varieties, at least in the case of FBC, have been carried over from one colony to the next, at least in specific geographical areas (Parkvall 1995, Jennings 1995, Arends ed. 1995, Mufwene 1996). As opposed to the view propounded by Thomason and Kauffman (1988) that creolisation is a case of abnormal language transmission and of rapid and abrupt language change, other researchers provide evidence of gradual language change (Arends 1993, Mufwene 1996). If the latter case is correct, then such linguistic processes as transfer, reanalysis and grammaticalisation should be active in the creole outcome.

The case in favour of pidginisation/creolisation as a gradual process is based partly on socio-historical evidence. Chaudenson (1992) and Baker and Corne (1982) have produced accounts of creole genesis where they insist on the importance of demographic factors. According to both authors, the first major demographic event for creole genesis is the outnumbering of the white settlers by the imported slaves and the duration of that process. The onset of this demographic modification may be due to transition to plantation economy. In some French colonies, this change, called *Event 1* by Baker, occurred within ten to fourteen years of the beginning of the settlement (Mauritius, Guyane) and in others it took longer, fifty years in the case of Réunion (cf. Mufwene 1996). *Event 2* takes place when colony born slaves outnumber the settlers. This event happened 140 years after the establishment of a colony in Réunion, and 90 years after *Event 1*. The same process took some 50 years in Mauritius. According to Baker, the 'jelling' of a creole occurs in the interval between *Event* 1 and the end of the introduction of new slaves in the colony, termed *Event 3*. According to these accounts, the development of a creole language is gradual and lasts approximately some fifty years.

A wide range of theories and models have been put forward to account for pidginisation and creolisation (see amongst others Véronique 1994a for a discussion of some of these proposals). Many of these explanations, from Bickerton (1977) to Chaudenson (1978) and Arends (1995) focus on language acquisition or language creation *qua* linguistic communication. As the socio-historical facts of colonial settlements in settings where creole languages developed are unveiled, two features emerge. Firstly, the social matrix of the creoles known to date vary to a large extent. The sociohistorical facts of FBC development are quite different from those of Atlantic English-based Creoles or Pacific English-based Creoles (Winford 1993, Roberts 1998). Secondly, it seems clear that many, if not all, creoles emerged out of second language adult acquisition under specific social circumstances. This does not rule out the subsequent influence of first language acquisition in the process of creolisation. Reanalysis as observed in first language acquisition might explain Posner's claim that creolisation implies typological change within the same language family (see Posner 1985).

1.2. Iconicity in SLA

Andersen (1984) (but see also some of D. Slobin's operating principles) posits that during early SLA, learners are seeking a one to one relationship between TL forms and semantic and pragmatic functions (see also Pfaff 1987). Early learner varieties are thus shaped by iconicity. Klein (1989) maintains that learner utterances are shaped by semantic and pragmatic principles of transparency, salience, diagrammatic iconicity and isomorphism. However, resorting to iconicity implies neither a simplification of TL (see Valli 1986) nor the use of simplification strategies. Meisel (1977, 1983) establishes that learner varieties are marked by both restrictive – reducing TL complexity – and elaborative simplification – rendering the learner variety more complex.

1.3. Finiteness and SLA

Finiteness as a formal property of verbal morphology related to agreement and tense is deemed to contribute to the development of child grammar by subcategorising VP. The development of finiteness is the first stage of the unfolding of syntactic structure in terms of growth of IP (Meisel 1994). However, the possible role of morphological finiteness in SLA is more open to debate (Meisel 1997). Klein (1998, forthcoming) posits that finiteness is the carrier of an abstract operator "Assertion" which has implications for the marking of tense, for topic-focus structure and for word order. Klein and Perdue (1997) hold that the development of finiteness is one possible avenue for learner varieties that grammaticalise. Otherwise they tend to fossilise at the basic variety level.

1.4. Grammaticalisation and reanalysis in SLA

Since Meillet's founder article in 1912 (Meillet 1921), various features of diachronic grammaticalisation have been enhanced: semantic bleaching, paradigmatisation and obligatoriness, loss of syntactic autonomy etc. (Lehmann 1983, 1991). In his introduction to the special issue of *Studies in Second Language Acquisition* devoted to *Grammaticalisation in Second Language Acquisition*, Dittmar (1992) insists on the fact that little study has been devoted to grammaticalisation in the realm of SLA. According to this author, two pragmatic processes of grammaticalisation, metaphorisation and informativeness, should prove particularly relevant. Strengthening of informativeness as well search for metaphorical, digrammatic and imagic iconicity (Hopper and Traugott 1993: 26-27) are factors that may motivate grammaticalisation and reanalysis (Heine, Claudi, Hünnemeyer 1991: 215-228.).

Giacalone Ramat (1992) and Pfaff (1992) do not wish to conflate grammaticalisation as a process of language change and grammaticalisation in learner varieties. Although there might be some similarities between the outcome of both processes, Giacalone Ramat insists that grammaticalisation in language change is conducive to the emergence of new grammatical items, whereas in SLA, it leads the learner to conform to TL norms. As Giacalone-Ramat (2000: 122-125) shows, the principle of unidirectionality of change from lexical to grammatical categories might be shared by both SLA and language change but grammaticalisation *per se* is not equivalent to language acquisition.

Haspelmath (1998), following Heine, Claudi, and Hünnemeyer (1991: 215-220), insists on the fact that reanalysis should be carefully separated from typological or universal grammaticalisation. According to Haspelmath, reanalysis is produced by abduction and entails a change in the hierarchical structure of the sentence, leading to a new bracketing of constituents. Reanalysis is a process related to perception in language acquisition which results in a new structural description of a given sequence whereas grammaticalisation involves an unidirectional and gradual change based on production.

1.5. The Basic Variety hypothesis

In this paper, it is assumed that the emergence of FBC is the result of SLA under the specific social circumstances of slavery and plantation economy. It is expected that the pragmatic and semantic organisational principles identified by Klein and Perdue (1992) and Klein and Perdue (1997) shaped early FBC utterances. These organisational principles are determined by such factors as:

- Dependence on immediate context,
- Maximising use of linguistic means available,
- Search for transparency and simple form to function relation,
- The highest controller comes first in a specific utterance,
- Information in focus is last , i.e. in salient position,
- Simple is mastered before complex.

Thus, early FSL grammar just as early FBC grammar is shaped by iconicity.

The development of FSL grammar is based, amongst other factors, on the acquisition of finiteness as claimed by Klein and Perdue (1997). Reanalysis and grammaticalisation produce different outcomes in the case of FBC and FSL. It is hypothesised that early FBC grammar is shaped by the same organisational principles as the basic variety in SLA while later FBC grammars diverge from post-basic learner varieties.

2. Analysis of data on the development of grammar in FSL[1] and FBC[2]

Data for the study of the acquisition of French as a second language have been provided by the Moroccan learners of the ESF project (Perdue 1984) and data on the development of early grammar in FBC from available texts from Atlantic and Indian Ocean FBC. It might be argued that the Moroccan Arabic learners of French produce too specific learner varieties in French and that a greater diversity of learner varieties from varied L1 backgrounds might be more helpful. However, the line of thought defended in this paper is that the comparison of any particular case of FSL development with any particular FBC early grammar will suffice to illustrate the similarity of form-function relations in both language continua.

2.1. Existentials in FSL and FBC.
2.1.1. Il y a (There is) and c'est (It is) in FSL

One of the phrasal constraints posited by Klein and Perdue (1997) for the Basic Variety runs as follows:

$$\left\{ \begin{array}{c} V \\ Cop \end{array} \right\} - NP_2.$$

It is in this type of string that *il y a* (there is) and *c'est*[3] (it is) are found in FSL. These items share propositional functions such as:

- clefting,
- acting as a carrier of negation and of temporal information,

and discursive functions such as :

- topic introduction,
- contrasting foreground-background in texts.

il y a expresses mainly existence and possession whereas *c'est* is identificational (Duff 1993).

During one of the first encounters with Malika B., while her learner variety is mainly based on codeswitching between Moroccan Arabic L1 and tentative French, she produces the following utterance in a picture description (see Véronique 1994b):

(1)
    I(nvestigator): *et ça qu' est-ce que c'est ça?*
                   'What is this?'
    MB: /se/ *al bajda*
          'It's eggs'

    I: *voilà où est le chat?*
       'where's the cat?'
    MB: /e/ *le table*
          'is the table'.

/e/ + X is a productive device as can be seen in the following extract from an early encounter with MB:

(2)
    I: *à la poste+   comment   ça se passe*
       'at the post-office + how   do you manage
       à la poste?+   quand tu veux téléphoner?
       at the post-office?   When you want to phone?'
    MB: /e/ *la maison*
           'is the house'
    I: *oui? quoi?*
       'yes? What?'
    M: /tilifuni/   *de la poste*   /e/ *la maison*
        'call   from the post is the house'
    I: *tu téléphones à la poste*
       'you call   from the post-office?'
    M: /e/ *la maison*
          'is the house'.

/jãna/ + X (there is) is used to mark existence and possession (see Duff 1993):

(3)
    I: *tu travailles chez Madame F?*
       'You work at Madam F.'

MB: *Madame F + Madame F*
'Madam F + Madam F'
I: *oui*
'yes'
MB: *moi /li/ bar*
'me (the/she) bar'
I: *hm hm*
MB: */li/ bar moi +++ toi /jãna li/ café*
'(the) bar me you have (the/she) coffee'

(*sa*) *se* + X is used as a presentational as in 4:

(4)
I: *qu' est-ce que tu fais avec le savon?*
'What did you do with the soap?'
MB: */sa se le sabon/*
'That's the soap.'

2.1.2. *Il y a* and *c'est* in learner language development

Il y a or rather *jãna* is found in all learner varieties. It marks possession as well as existence, although the existential value tends to predominate in the more advanced learner varieties. In 5, the first token of *jãna* is an existential and the second expresses possession,

(5)
AE: *voilà /jãna/ deux personnes /iveni/ /ʃerʃe/ avec*
'Ok there are two personnes (they) come search with
quelqu'un /jãna/ des drogues +
somebody has drugs'
voilà /eveni/ euh voilà /ja/ rien /itrap/ avec l'autre qui /mãz/ à
'Ok come there's nothing catch the other who is eating
quelqu'un
besides...'
(Cycle 2, encounter 5 = 2.5).

jãna is extensively use for clefting in more advanced learner varieties leading to proto-relatives (see Véronique 1997a), as in the following example where the contrast between *jãna* and *se* is quite striking:

(6)
    AB: */jãna une femme /se/ une vieille /iladi/ non /se/ pas le monsieur /se/ le fille* (3.5)
    'there's a lady it's an old (woman) (she) says no it's not the man it's the girl'.

In 7, *se* acts as a resumptive pronoun:

(7)
    AE: *le médecin chef se dur avec moi* (3.4)
    'the chief doctor he is hard on me'

2.1.3. *Il y a* (There is) and *c'est* (It is) in FBC

In early texts from Mauritius, the marker expressing existence and possession is *y en a* (there is / have). First tokens of the item are found in texts dating from ca. one century after the settlement of the island (see 1.1 above):

(8)   1804. *Mo y en a femme*
        'I have a woman' (Chaudenson 1981: 81)

(9)   1804. *Y en a ça qui bon y en a ça qui mauvais*
        'There are those who are good, there are those who are bad' (Chaudenson 1981: 81)

Early quotations from Réunion Creole show that the item expressing existence in that creole is *n'en a*:

(10) 1799. *Mon ami n'en a un travail que nous y faut faire ce coup ci*
'My friend, there's a job we must do this time' (Chaudenson 1981: 5).

In the course of evolution, Mau. *y en a* is eroded to *iéna* (Baissac 1880) and to contemporary *ena* while Réu. *n'en a* is modified to *nana* (1864) (Chaudenson 1981: 59).

Se (c'est) is quite rarely found in texts from Mauritius (see 10), or Réunion:

(11) 1828. *Péchés qui y-en-a dans licaire, sé quand moi oblié Bon Dieu*
'Sins I have in the heart, it's when I forget God' (Chaudenson 1981: 109)

It is more frequent in Seychelles Creole, although this marker is different from *se* in Atlantic FBC (Baker and Corne 1982: 40-41). Note that the equivalent of Mau. *ena* and Réu. *nana* in Seychelles Creole is *ana*.

The use of *y en a*, *n'en a* and *ana* in Indian Ocean FBC provides an example of reanalysis in creole genesis. Subsequent erosion provides a clue as to the grammaticalisation of the reanalyzed forms.

Se in Atlantic FBC occurs in equational sentences and seems to have beeen reanalyzed along different lines from Indian Ocean Creoles. In contemporary Atlantic FBC, it is analyzed either as a copula (Valdman 1978: 237-240) or a resumptive pronoun (DeGraff 1992: 168-209).

2.1.4. Summary

Il y a/jãna and *se* are reanalyzed and used along similar lines in early Indian Ocean FBC texts and in early learner varieties. In the course of development, presentationals in learner varieties tend to follow TL norms whereas in FBC various trajectories of grammaticalisation may be observed.

2.2. Temporality in FSL and FBC
2.2.1. The development of time reference in FSL: from pre-basic varieties to post-basic varieties

A contrastive analysis of L1 (Moroccan Arabic) and L2 (French) temporal systems yields the following predictions about the development of time reference in the learner varieties examined:

- Recourse to adverbs and pre-verbs is to be expected.
- Recourse to lexical aspect is also to be expected.
- The left part of V should be the locus of morphological innovation.
- Anteriority should be the first temporal distinction to be marked.

2.2.1.1. Temporality in pre-basic and basic varieties

Previous work shows that pre-basic varieties make use of lexico-pragmatic means and discourse principles before any emergence of verbal morphology (Andersen (ed.) 1984, Pfaff (ed.) 1987, Bardovi-Harlig 1999). Despite progress in L2, these first indirect means are maintained.

a) Recourse to scaffolding by the TL speaker and reliance on contextual inference as in 12:

(12)   (Zahra describes the classes she attends) (1.2)
   Z: *et après le livre*
        'and the book'
   I: *le livre ouais? et qu'est-ce que vous faites? un livre*
        'the book yes? What do you do with the book?'

Z: /e/ la dame la cassette comme ça
'the lady (puts) the cassette like this'
I: oui
'yes'
Z: /e/ / iparle/
'and she speaks'
I: ah d'accord
'ah OK'
Z: /kompri/?
'Understood'
I: oui
'yes'
Z: /e/ après /e/ le livre comme ça /e/ la cassette /iparle/ comme la dame
'and the the book is like this and the cassette speaks like the lady'
I: oui
'yes'
Z: moi /iparle/ comme la cassette
'me speak like the cassette'
I: oui
'yes'
Z: /e/ après /e/ la dame tou / tous la dame /iparle/ pour le livre
'and afterwards the lady, all the ladies speak for the book'

Zahra's narrative is intelligible because of shared world knowledge (what is a typical classroom activity) and because of cooperation on the part of the native speaker who provides assistance in the organisation of the narrative.

b) Use of the iconic principle of natural order:

(13) (Abdelmalek recounts his arrival to France, 1.1)
  I: *tu peux / oui alors tu peux me dire quand c'est / depuis combien de temps tu es là?*

'Can you / yes O.K can you tell me when / since how long you are here?'
AE: *comment le problème comme /ãtre/ la France?*
'how the problem for coming to France?'
I: *ouais par exemple ouais*
'Yes eventually yes'
AE: *ah ouais parce que moi /liãtre/ la France /jana/ pas de passeport /jana/ pas de rien*
'Oh yes because me (I) enter France there's no passport there's nothing'
I: *ouais*
'Yeah'
AE: *parce que /ãtre/ la France /e/ la montagne*
'because enter France (is / and) the mountain'
I: *tu es passé par la montagne?*
'You went through the mountain?'
AE: *ouais*
'Yeah'
I: *ah*
AE: */jana/ cinq jours /e/ la montagne après /lãtre/ la France /lepase/ la douane de France /komjes/? quinze kilomètres*
'There's five days (in) the mountain then come to France go through the customs of France how much? Fifteen kilometers'
I: *à pied?*
'On foot?'
AE: *ouais /lapje/ /e/ après /ilaparte/ l'autoroute /jana/ pas des sous /jana/ rien après /jana/ /e/ le stop après /leveny/ le gendarme*
'yeah on foot after go with the speed way there's no money there's nothing then there's hitch-hiking then come the police'.

Explicit reference to a time span preceding time of speech [+anterior] is mainly marked through the questions and the scaffolding provided by the investigator. The iconic principle of natural order applies and

[+ anterior] time intervals are marked by connective *après* (after). Chronological order is also fostered through the use of calendaric information /jana/ *cinq jours* (there is five days) and through indirect lexical means like motion verbs /ãtre/ (enter), /lepase/ (pass), /ilaparte/ (go away), /leveny/ (come) *and* specific nominals *montagne, douane, autoroute*. The action verbs exhibit long forms *(li/e)* +*Ve*. Only one stative verb /jana/ (there is) is present in this extract. The verbs exhibit formal variation either in pre-verbal position Ø/le/ila/li (which corresponds to the position of the clitic pronoun and the auxiliary in TL) or in post-verbal position (corresponding to the verbal ending in TL) Ø/e/i/, without any explicit correlation between form and meaning (see also Klein, Dietrich, Noyau 1993: 171-172).

c) Use of lexical information and formulaic expressions

In the following story, Zahra rounds off the narration with conclusive /saje/ (it's over) used in some other narratives also:

(14)
Z: /jãna/ /lekase/ l'assiette /e/ la dame comme hafida zahra /røgard/ "/e/ ça /lekase/? /e/ toi /lekase/?" "oui madame /e/ moi /eskyz/ moi /lekase/" /e/ après /saje/ /laʒelete/ la poubelle.
"there's breaking of the plate the lady like hafida looks at Zahra 'and this is broken?' 'Did you break it?' "yes madam, me excuse me break" and afterwards it's finished, it's overthrow it in the dustbin"

d) Use of adverbs and adverbials

This has been well illustrated by Starren and Van Hout (1996), and Starren (1996). Thus *toujours* expresses habituality in 15, iteration in 16 and continuity in 17:

(15)
    Z: *toujours toujours l'ardoise*
        'always always slate'
    I: *oui d'accord? chaque fois?*
        'yes O.K ? Each time?'
    Z: *non toujours l'ardoise le premier (...)/e/ après le livre*
        'no always slate first (...) and after the book'

(16)   *deux mois moi toujours /telefone/ papa* (2.4)
        two months me always call daddy

(17)   *un mois moi toujours mal la tête* (1.8)
        one month me always headache

The difference betwen iteration and continuity is related to the *Aktionsarten* of the verbs involved.

2.2.1.2. Complexifying the expression of temporality

More grammaticalised means may also be used such as:

a) *Expression of TT through temporal subordinate clauses as in 18:*

(18)
    Z: *ton mari ta copine /eleparti/ le Maroc à vacances le/ la dame ne /se/ pas /e/ tous les papiers à la maison /e/ ton mari la femme tous les papiers passeport /e/ après /kølø/ /parti/ le Maroc*
        '(the/ your) husband of (your/ my) friend has left for Morocco on holidays the lady does not know and all the official documents at home and (your/the) husband the woman all the documents passport and after when he arrives in Morocco
        ----
        /kølø/ /ilparti/ au Maroc /e/ après le /kominis/ /e/ après /saje/

when he arrives in Morocco and then (he will visit) the judge and then it's over'

b) Verbal morphology

Inflection is explored from the start by learners but they master TL verbal morphology very slowly. By the end of the third cycle of data collection, most Moroccan Arabic learners have identified the copula, the auxiliary *e/a* and at least two basic verb forms $V+\emptyset$ et $V+e$, which express different aspectual and temporal values. In 19:

(19)
    I: *vous n'y allez pas souvent? (à l'école)*
       'you do not visit (school) often?'
    Z: *une fois pour hanan /tõbe/ à l'école (...) mais /jãna/ les os /gõfil/ comme ça après moi /parti/ avec hanan pour /levwar/ l'institutrice*
       'Once for Hanan fallen in school (...) but bones swollen like this then me go with hanan to meet the teacher
       -----
    Z: *après moi /le parti/ mon docteur pour /il a fe/ les radios pour ma fille*
       then me go (to) my doctor for he x-rays my daughter'.

2.2.2. Temporality in FBC
2.2.2.1. Verb morphology

In the first sentences of Atlantic FBC noted by travellers, colonists or priests, verbs are written in the infinitive form like *tenir* in this sentence from Saint-Christophe (Mongin ca. 1682 quoted by Jennings 1995: 72):

(20)   *Si moi pas tenir Louis moi mourir de faim*
       'If I didn't have Louis, I would die of hunger'

or in an ambiguous Ve form as *iurer, dérober* and *aller* in the following text from Pelleprat 1655:

(21) *Seigneur, toy bien sçave que mon frère luy point mentir, point luy iurer, point dérober, point aller luy à femme d'autre*
'Lord, you know very well that my brother hasn't lied, hasn't sworn, hasn't stolen hasn't been with woman of another'

Note also in this text *sçave* which exhibits a Vstem form.

The same holds true for Indian Ocean Creoles where in the first written quotations of the language (see Chaudenson for 1981 for IOC texts), verbs appear in V stem form or in long form Ve or in the infinitive:

(22) *Si nou n'a pas gagné malheur, ça bon*
'If we get no evil thing, that's good' (1768)

(23) *Moi voulé baiser ça négresse la*
'Me want (to) make love (to) that negress' (1777).

As the last written sentence suggests modals like *voulé* are found earlier in verbal predicates in creole texts than other pre-verbal markers (see Véronique 1995, Hazaël-Massieux 1996: 209-220).

As far as it can be assessed, it would seem that in the first FBC texts temporality is mainly expressed by the very means identified for pre-basic and basic learner varieties in SLA: reliance on context and pragmatic means, on diagrammatic iconicity (the principle of natural order) and the lexical meaning of verbs. Possibly, aktionsart explains the distribution of V stem and Ve verb forms as in learner varieties. The development of the expression of tense, aspect and modality is a late development where both reanalysis and grammaticalisation played their part. This will be illustrated by an analysis of the development of some pre-verbal markers of FBC.

2.2.2.2. FBC pre-verbal markers

Time reference in FBC is mainly expressed through a set of pre-verbal markers derived from periphrastic verbal means in use in dialectal varieties of French (Goodman 1964, Gougenheim 1929). However, different French-based Creoles have reanalyzed these forms in differing ways, leading to partially different systems for conveying temporal information (Goodman 1964, Valdman 1978, Hazaël-Massieux 1996).

a) être / été (à) > te, ti

Goodman (1964) points out that forms derived from Fr. *été*, with a +anteriority value, are found both in Atlantic and Indian Ocean FBC. The most frequent form of the morpheme is *te*, *ti* being found only in Mauritian Creole (henceforth MC). Baker and Corne (1982) mention that the first tokens of temporal *été* in MC occur in texts written between 1779, i.e. approximately 50 years after the beginning of French settlement in the island, and 1835-39. *té* is observed as from 1816 onwards. Present day *ti* is found as from 1839 according to Baker and Corne, and as from 1850 following Chaudenson (1981), i.e. approximately one century after *Event 1* and at the end of *Event 3* in Baker's theory (see section 1.1 above).

In early written testimonials of MC, only four pre-verbal markers, are found besides modals, Ø- early examples of verbs in V stem and long forms are preceded by no markers, except for modal verbs – *été* (+anterior), *fini* (+perfective) (1734) and *va* (+prospective) (1777). The use of *té* instead of *été* in early nineteenth century text in MC occurs at practically the same time as the first combination of pre-verbal markers in written text, *te fini* (1816), *té va* (1855), *té pour* (1855) – *pour* as a preverbal marker is found in a 1818 text –, *té après* (1850) – *après* as a pre-verbal marker dates back to 1822.

It can be gathered from these data that early MC temporal marking is mainly iconic and indirect. In a second stage, markers reanalyzed from the French periphrastic markers *être après, être pour* and from *finir* are used to express temporal and aspectual values. 1850 marks a turning point in the Mauritian Creole system as a result of grammaticalisation. Pre-verbal markers combine in a fixed order: temporal *té* followed by aspectual markers *après, fini, va*. The semantic and syntactic reorganisation of the pre-verbal markers is marked by the erosion of *fini* > *fin* and by the substitution of *ti* to *té*.

In the case of Haitian Creole (henceforth HC), according to Baker and Corne (1982, marker *té* is observed in a 1776 text – i.e. ca. one century after the start of French settlement in St Domingue –, *étois* (1785), *étois après* (1785), and *té après, té fini, t'a* (Fr. etymon *être à* 'to be in the process of') in 1802. Approximately 200 years after the French settlement of Saint-Domingue, Baker and Corne (1982) report erosion of *après* as *apé/pé* and clustering of markers such as *ta va* (possibly *té+ a+ va* = anterior + progressive + prospective, or *té + ava* = antérior + progressive). In her analysis of Ducœurjoly's *Manuel des habitans de Saint-Domingue* (1802), an introduction to life in Saint-Domingue for the settlers, Fattier (1992) shows that in HC Ø is +anterior and confirms Baker and Corne (1982)'s findings. The reanalysis of French periphrastic verbal clusters and their subsequent grammaticalisation seem to follow approximately the same path as in MC. However, *été* maintains its status as copula in early FBC grammar and Atlantic FBC tend to differenciate *va* and *allé* (see below).

Hazaël Massieux (1996: 221) draws a picture of the development of temporal and modal marking in FBC from the lesser Antilles (Guadeloupe) akin to that MC and HC. He notes early Ve forms or verbs in the infinitive combined with modal verbs. He concludes to a first distinction between V forms and pre-verbal markers + V forms. Early pre-verbal markers include *té* and *qu'à/ka* (progressive) in the case of lesser Antilles FBC. Combination of markers such as *té qué* (anterior + prospective), *té va* (anterior + prospective), *té ka* (anterior + progressive) are found in texts dating from the interval between 1815 and 1848, i.e. some 200 years after French settlement in the Lesser Antilles (Hazaël-Massieux: 212). Reanalysis of French periphrastic verbs and subsequent grammaticalisation follow approximately the same path in Lesser Antilles FBC as in HC and MC. However, like the other FBC, Lesser Antilles Creoles develop specific markers, for instance *ka* and specific restructuring of the semantic values of the system of pre-verbal markers (Hazaël-Massieux 1996: 237-240).

b) The grammaticalisation of French periphrastic verbs and its subsequent evolution pour/être pour > pu *et* aller/va > alé/va

Historical accounts of French grammatical evolution show that as early as old French, *por* (lat. *pro*) is used as a marker of the agent, the cause or the beneficiary in the context of an animate NP instead of its original spatial meaning (cf. for instance Brunot and Bruneau 1949, Moignet 1976). Subsequently up to the 15th century, *pour* conveys resultative meaning. As from the 16th century on, *être pour* conveys the meaning of a near future together with modal nuances (Gougenheim 1929).

Pour is found in early FBC texts with the same resultative meaning as in the French etymon. It seems to combine primarily with Ø + *V* to convey modal meaning (Hazaël-Massieux 1996: 213-214). Note that in HC *alé* and *va / a* as prospective markers occur as early as 1776. In Lesser Antilles, *ka alé* yielding subsequently *ke* as a prospective marker is found as early as the 1815-1848 period. *pour* has acquired in modern HC and in Lesser Antilles FBC a modal deontic value besides its functional value as a complementiser.

In MC, the use of *va* and *pour* dates back to 1805 and 1818 respectively. Reanalysis of *pour / être pour* and subsequent grammaticalisation has placed both *pu* and *va* in the TMA paradigms as markers of future time reference, with deontic value in the case of *pu* and epistemic value in the case of *va* (Hazaël-Massieux 1993 and Baker 1993).

2.2.2.3. Summary

FSL and FBC data on time reference exhibit similar processes of reanalysis *qua* simplification of the TL verb morphology, and the same reliance on diagrammatic iconicity. Differences in input – periphrastic verbal forms may be less frequent in contemporary input to foreign workers than in dialectal French adressed to slaves – may partly explain the development of pre-verbal markers in FBC against morphological development in FSL. The process of development of pre-verbal markers provides a typical case of on-going grammaticalisation in French, carried over in FBC, reanalyzed and later grammaticalised anew (Véronique 1999).

Following Klein and Perdue (1997), it can be assumed that finiteness develops in FBC as soon as the first pre-verbal markers combine with the lexical verb. First written testimonials are found at a time interval of approximately 50 to 100 years after the start of colonial settlement, but in actual speech, some form of finiteness may have been present in individual lects earlier.

2.2.3. Negation in FSL and FBC
2.2.3.1. The acquisition of negation in FSL

a) Pre-basic varieties

In a prebasic learner variety (Malika B), *non* is by far the most productive item, and *pas* occurs in some rote-learned expressions such as */se/ pas* (know not) or *ça va pas* (not OK). Anaphoric *non* in focus position is often associated with a lexical topic as in 24:

(24)
   I: *oui? vous pouvez me l'écrire* (1.3, role play)
      'Yes? Can you write this for me'
   MB: (produces a gesture of negation)
   I: *non?*
      'no'
   MB: *non français non*
      'no French no'.

Pas is found in formulaic chunks as in 25:

(25)
   MB: *moi + petit whisky +/se/ pas* (1.3).
      'me small whisky don't know'

As from encounter 6 of cycle 1 of data collection, when N (V) N strings tend to be more frequent, *pas* replaces *non* as clausal negator, with variable placement as in 26 and 27:

(26)
   MB: */li/ pas l'école* (1.6)
      'he / she no school'

(27)
   MB: */jãna/ pas* (1.6).
      'there is not'

non is the main negator in Malika B.'s pre-basic variety. It is an external item, used holophrastically, often in focus position. The development of *pas* is linked to the development of the predicate in focus position.

b) Negation in the basic variety

In the basic variety, *pas* and *non* are both found, *pas* being first observed in rote learned expressions such as *je /kõprã/ pas* (I don't understand), *je /se/ pas* (I don't know), or in stereotyped presentational formulae like */jãna/ pas + X* (there isn't X) et */se/ pas+ X* (it isn't X). Gradually, the use of *pas* extends to the context of lexical verbs. One of the major stage from the pre-basic variety to the basic variety is the replacement of anaphoric negator, *non*, often used in focus position, the topic being a nominal entity (see 28), to the left of the negator, by *pas* is as a post-predicate marker (see 29 below):

(28)
   Z: *la théâtre?* (1. 2)
        'theatre?'

I: *oui*
'yes'

Z: *la théâtre non*
'theatre no'

(29)
Z: *heureusement euh les enfants /jãna/ pas de l'école aujourd'hui* (1. 2)
'Happily the kids do not have to attend school today'.

Table 1. Zahra – Tokens of *pas* per cycle of data collection

	je /kɔ̃prã/ — (X)	*je* /se/ —	/jãna/ — (X)	/se/ — (X)	other verbs	Total
Cycle 1	53 (29, 3 %)	2 (1, 1 %)	7 (3, 9 %)	64 (35, 4 %)	55 (30,4 %)	181
Cycle 2	39 (13, 9 %)	4 (1, 4 %)	14 (5 %)	151 (53,9 %)	70 (25 %)	280
Cycle 3	30 (8 %)	28 (7, 4 %)	23 (6, 1 %)	137 (36,3 %)	158 (42 %)	377
Total	122	34	44	352	283	828

In the course of linguistic development, *pas* is used with an increasing number of different verbs. Only one token of discontinuous negation has been observed in the whole range of data produced by Zahra.

(30)
Z: *oui oui les femmes ne /travaj/ pas*
'yes yes women do not work'

c) Negation in basic-postbasic varieties : Malika H and Abdelmalek

Table 2. Abdelmalek: Tokens of *pas* per cycle

	X pas	pas X	Ne pas X[4]	Aux. pas X	Other[5]
Cycle 1	246	64	18	2	39
Cycle 2	337	59	10	10	21
Cycle 3	347	28	3	9	31

Table 3. Abdelmalek: Tokens of pre-posed *pas*

	(je) pas V	pas /kõprã/	pas /kompri/	Total
Cycle 1	49 (76,5%)	3 (4,6%)	12 (18,75%)	64
Cycle 2	54 (91,5%)	4 (6,7%)	1 (1,7%)	59
Cycle 3	28			28
Total	137	7	13	157

Table 4. Abdelmalek: Tokens of post-posed *pas*

	(je)[6]/kõprã	(je) /se/ —	/jãna/[7] — (X)	/se/ —(X)	other verbs	Total
Cycle 1	14 (5,7%)	16 (6,5%)	111 (45,12%)	68 (27,6%)	37 (15,04%)	246
Cycle 2	27 (8,01%)	26 (7,7%)	68 (20,17%)	126 (37,38%)	90 (26,7%)	337
Cycle 3	38 (10,95%)	29 (8,35%)	46 (13,25%)	97 (27,95%)	137 (39,48%)	347
Total	74	71	225	290	264	930

Differently from both Zahra and Malika H., Abdelmalek places *pas* in pre-verbal position in the early phases of data collection except in rote-learned expressions. However, by the end of the data collection period, *pas* is placed in post-verbal position following TL norm. The basic-post-basic varieties of Malika H. and Abdelmalek present both strong similarities and points of difference in the use of negator *pas*. In both varieties, *pas* is first found in the same rote learned expressions as with other Arabic speaking informants. In Malika H.'s data, the placement of *pas* is varied as shown in examples 31 and 32.

(31)
   MH:/*iladi*/ *pas hein?* (1. 2)
      'he did not say it hey?'

(32)
   MH:/*ile*/ *pas bon alors euh moi* /*fe*/ *pas* /*zami*/ (1. 2).
      'he is no good then I do not make friends'

As soon as VP is analyzed, *pas* is post-posed to the verb. In 33, the auxiliary /*ete*/ is properly analyzed and tensed as well as the modal verb /*vø*/, the placement of *pas* before non finite /*rãtre*/ is target-like:

(33)
   MH:*je* /*lave*/ *il* /*ete*/ *maintenant trop petit il* /*vø*/ *pas* /*rãtre*/ (2.9).
      'I washed it was now too small it does not fit'

One peculiarity of Abdelmalek's use of negator *pas* is the preposition of the negator to VP as in 34 and 35, where VP is in topic position:

(34)
   I: *tu connais Aix?* (1. 1)
         'You know Aix?'
   AE: *non pas* /*kon*/ *Aix*
         'no not know Aix',

(35)
   I: *tu comprends?* (1.1).
         'You understand?'
   AE: *non pas* /*komprã*/
         'no not understand' (= no I don't understand)

The preposition of *pas* to VP seems to be related to the absence of a grammatical subject, either pronominal or nominal, and to discourse genre. Preposed *pas* seems to occur mainly in reported speech and in narratives.

In the early stages of Abdelmalek's basic variety, /napa/ X and
pas X alternate freely as in 36:

(36)
AE: /saje/ ça /napakompri/ ça pas /kompri/ (1. 2).
'OK that not understood that not understood (i.e I have not)'

The TL like placement of *pas* is related in Abdelmalek's data, as in the case of other informants, to a proper analysis of VP and to the development of inflection and subject marking. This is well illustrated by one of the early examples of TL like placement of *pas* by Abdelmalek.

(37)
I: *oh mais tu vois des/tu parles français quelquefois*
'Oh but you see / you speak French sometimes'
AE: *même jamais je /parl/ le français*
'even never I speak French'
I: *mais quand tu vas au bar?*
'but when you visit the bar?'
AE: *chaque fois*
'each time'
I: *ouais?*
'yes?'
AE: *où je /part/ / jamais je /part/ avec un bar + français même je /part/ euh/par exemple je /parl/ avec toi le français /se/ tout hein + les autres je /parl/pas* (1. 6)
'where I go never I go with a bar + French even I go for example I speak French with you that's all + I don't speak with the others'.

As in the case of other Arabic speaking informants, post-position of *pas* is first observed with presentationals. However, as the use of /se/ and /jãna/ extends, the tokens of negative presentational clauses tend to decrease. In the course of the development of Abdelmalek's interim grammar, during cycles 2 and 3 of data collection, the following alternation may be observed: postposed *pas* cooccurs with the stem form of the verb whereas preposed *pas* is found in the context of the suffixed verb.

(38)
    AE: *non non je /kraʃ/ pas non non je /sufl/ pas non non je pas /sufle/* (2. 6)
    'no no I do not spit no no I am not breathless no I am not breathless'

(39)
    AE: *même euh je pas /parte/ toujours hein une fois par semaine + chaque fois je /part/ pas hein* (2. 7)
    'even I not go always hey once a week + each time I do not go'

This alternation may result from an indirect influence of L1.

When the TL auxiliary becomes salient for the informants, *pas* is placed according to TL use between the auxiliary and the non-finite verb, in pre-verbal position:

(40)
    AE: *parce que /tu/ la journée /ʒe/pas /mõʒi/ alors parce que je /travaj/pas* (2. 6).
    'because all the day I have not eaten then because I do not work'

Data from Abdessamad, an advanced Moroccan Arabic learner, confirms the developmental sequence of acquisition of the negation found in the other learner varieties described. In formulaic and rote-learned expressions and with presentationals, Abdessamad uses postposed *pas*, hence */jana/ pas* (there isn't) and *je /kõprã/ pas* (I don't understand). Post-posed *pas* is also used by this informants with other thematic verbs as in 41:

(41)
    AD: *je /ʒue/ pas parce que l'autre /ile ʒue/ à mimoun* (1. 2).
    'I played not because the other one he played with Mimoun'

However, *pas* is also preposed to VP in clauses such as 42:

(42)
    AD: *je pas /travaj/ comme aujourd'hui samedi* (1. 1)
    'I do not work since today (is) Saturday',

but placed as in TL in examples such as 43:

(43)
    AD: */ʒe/ pas /mõte/* (1. 2)
    'I have not gone up'

2.2.3.2. Negation in FBC

In early written testimonials of Atlantic FBC, or possibly pidginised or pre-creole varieties, preposed negation is frequent. *Non, point, pas* are found in such preverbal position,

(44)   *Luy mouche manigat. Mouche manigat mon compère moy non faché à toy*
        'He is much skillful. You are much skillful mate. I am not angry against you' (Bouton 1640, in Prudent 1993)

(45)   *Seigneur toi bien savé que mon frère lui point mentir, point lui jurer ... Toi pas connaître moi*
        'Lord you well know that my brother him no lie, no him swear...you don't know me' (Mongin 1682, in Prudent 1993)

(46) *Compère na pas tenir peur, si canot tourner toi tenir coeur fort*
'Friend do not have fear, if the boat overturns you keep (your) heart steady' (Labat 1722, in Prudent 1993)

Hull (1975) mentions, following G.C Robin (1807), *Voyage dans l'intérieur de la Louisiane*, the existence of constructions such as *moi pas connais* (I do not know), *moi pas capable* (I am not able) in Louisiana Creole. Valdman (1996) and Speedy (1995) also quote some early cases of negative items in Louisiana FBC where the preposed negator includes the TL auxiliary or single *pas*,

(47) Loui. *Cela n'est pas bon, s'y toy mourir seuls et n'y a pas faire mourir monde qui n'y a rien faire avec toy* (1748)
'It's not good if you die by yourself and do not get people killed who had nothing to do with you'

(48) Loui. *Vous pas mire donc Maître à moi, ça Caïman qui mange monde?* (Bossu 1777, *Nouveaux voyages dans l'Amérique septentrionale*, in Speedy 1995)
'You have not seen my Master, the caiman that eats everybody'

Referring to a later period of Louisiana Creole, A. Hull (1975) notes, quoting Mercier (1880) *L'habitation Saint-Ybars ou Maîtres et esclaves en Louisiane*, and Fortier (1895), an alternation in the position of the negator according to verb morphology, hence *mo sot pa* (I jump not) vs *mo pa sote* (I do not jump). He signals the existence of negative verbs *napa* (have not), *fopa* (must not), *vepa* (want not). Goodman (1964: 92) adds that in Louisiane FBC *pas* follows preverbal markers *te, sa, se*, derived from the French copula and modal *savoir*, and precedes *(a)pe, (a)le* grammaticalised from periphrastic tense forms.

The expression of negation in Atlantic FBC at least, is initially based on the reanalysis of French *Neg. + Auxiliary* to form a compound pre-verbal negator. In a first stage *pas* and *n'a pas/n'est pas* etc. seem to alternate. There does not seem to be a distinction between negator *n'a pas* and the negative verb *n'a pas* (It does not exist). Post-position of *pas* with certain modals can also be observed. At an intermediate stage, *pas* is inserted between marker *te* and the verb (Hazaël-Massieux 1996: 175ff.). Alternation of the position of the negator following verb morphology and pre-position to some, if not all TMA markers seem to be a late development, following a reanalysis of TL verb morphology (see above).

The general picture drawn for Atlantic FBC is confirmed by data from Haïti, Guyane and the Lesser Antilles. The following quote from Juste Chanlatte, *L'entrée du Roi en sa capitale* (1818),

(49)   *N'a pas pitit chanté ça ...Valentin ...n'a pas pitit composé li va composé dans tête à li ... n'a pas pitit roulé n'a roulé bamboula*
'It's not a small song that (...) Valentin (...) It's not a small song writing he is going to write in his head, it's no small drumming drumming bamboula'
Valentin :*...to pas dire nous à rien de bel pitit Prince Royal à nous ... Nous té pas connai que métier procureur là fait li maître nous*
'you tell us nothing of our beautiful young Prince we did not know that our master was attorney',

illustrates the state of negation in early creole from Haiti/Saint-Domingue.

Early negation in Indian Ocean Creoles develops along a path similar to that of Atlantic FBC, at least in the case of Mauritius. The early form of the negator for Mauritius FBC is *n'a pas/ napas*:

(50)   Mau. *ça n'a pas bon, Monsié* (Bernardin de St.-Pierre 1773, in Chaudenson 1981)
'It is not good Sir'

(51)   Mau. *moy n'apa été batté ça blanc là* (1779, in Chaudenson 1981)
'I have not hit that white man'

(52)   Mau. *zautres pretes na pas été instruire zautres* (Le Brun 1816, in Baker and Syea 1991)
'Your priests have not taught you'

(53)   Mau. *Blancs napas laçarité pour malhérés* (Baissac 1880).
'White people are not kind to the poor'

It is difficult to distinguish between the negator and the negative verb meaning non-existence. Cases of post-posed negation in formulaic expressions are also observed as in the case of the Atlantic FBC,

(54)   *Moi vé-pas souffri davantage* (F. Chrestien 1820, in Chaudenson 1981)
'I do not want to suffer more'

Although Reunion Creole shares *n'a pas* with Mauritius Creole (Chaudenson 1981: 6), it has developed mainly post-posed negator *pas*. Réunion Creole shares with Atlantic FBC (mainly Haitian Creole, Alleyne 1996: 107) the fact that the negator *pas* cannot be combined with future as marked by *va* + *V*. Hazaël-Massieux (1996: 177) argues that the existence of a negative future distinct from the positive *va* future should also be interpreted as a clue that both *va* and *été* maintained their status as auxiliary verbs at the inception of the Atlantic FBC time reference system. Baker and Corne (1982: 222-224) avail of a difference in the expression of the negation between Reunion and Mauritius FBC to argue that the two creoles are genetically unrelated. Although alternation of preposed *n'a pas* and postposed *pas* is found in early texts from Réunion FBC, it should be remembered that post-position of *pas* may also be found to some degree in all FBC.

At an intermediate stage of development, Atlantic and Indian Ocean FBC differ in their placement of negator *pas*. This is partly related to the reanalysis of French *été*, which differs from one creole to another. Hazaël-Massieux (1996: 175) shows that between 1797 and 1872, in texts from Guyane, Louisiane and the Lesser Antilles, *té* precedes *pas*:

(55) Guy. *Vou té pas tiré aucun profit di vou travail* (Burnet 1797, Hazaël-Massieux 1996)
'You obtained no benefit from your work'

(56) Guy. *Mo té pa briga* (St-Quentin 1872, Hazaël-Massieux 1996)
'I was not a thief'

(57) Loui. *li té pa gê sulyé* (Hazaël-Massieux, 1996)
'he had no shoes'.

Similarly, Alleyne (1996: 102) shows that in Haitian Creole both preverbal markers and the negator are post-posed to copula *se*:

(58) Haï. *li se te yon rafinatè*
'he was a refiner'

(59) Haï. *i se pa yon rafinatè*
'he was not a refiner'

(60) Hai. *li **se te** pa mèt lekòl*
'he was not a teacher'.

However, Alleyne notes that in 60, *se* tends to be omitted. According to Hazaël-Massieux (1996: 103), the post-position of *pa* to *té* should be interpreted as the fact that *(é)té* maintained its status as a copula in FBC before being reanalyzed as a pre-verbal marker. For Mauritius FBC, Baker and Syea 1991 show that the use of *été* as a copula is a late development, the first use of that item being to mark +anterior tense.

2.2.3.3. Summary

In FBC, the development of a pre-verbal negator is linked to the reanalysis of French *Neg + Auxiliary*, to the simplification of verb morphology leading to an alternation of the placement of the negator and to reanalysis and subsequent grammaticalisation of the French auxiliary system. A change in the expression of finiteness leads to a modification in the placement of the negator. One striking feature surfaces when the acquisition of negation in FSL is compared to the development of negation in FBC, the modification of verb morphology has far-reaching consequences in both cases.

3. Discussion

In previous papers, FBC and FSL have been compared in the domains of NP and VP (Véronique 1994a), in the domain of modality (Véronique 1995) and in the domain of prepositions and temporal markers (Véronique 1997, 1999). The findings reported in this paper confirm that the organisational principles that lie behind the Basic Variety in adult language acquisition may have been active in the FBC continuum. Two majors shaping factors have been identified, iconicity leading to a simple form-function relation in the domain of reference to existence and possession or for reference to time and finiteness shaping negation marking.

Under the proviso that input are at least structurally identical in contemporary FSL and during the emergence of FBC, the development of early grammar in both sets of data exhibit identical form-function relation marked by isomorphism and 'structure-concept' iconicity. In the course of the gradual development of FBC though, grammaticalisation is carried over from the lexifier language to the emergent system. This is well illustrated in the domain of the development of the pre-verbal markers. Reanalysis interacts in a subtle way with the on-going grammaticalisation as shown by the processing of French *Neg + Auxiliary*. The TL sequence is reanalyzed as a single morpheme (*napa* in nineteenth century Mauritius FBC, *nãpwê* in contemporary Haitian FBC, Fattier 1998: 939) before semantic bleaching of the constituents and phonic erosion. However, the erosion of *Aux* does not follow similar lines in Atlantic and Indian Ocean FBC; *été* is re-interpreted differently in both sets of FBC, leading to partially different time reference systems.

It is in early grammar that FSL and FBC share common properties under the partial influence of iconicity. As grammaticalisation sets in, FBC turn into autonomous language systems that tend to develop along different lines. Differences between the linguistic systems resulting from creolisation are caused by many factors including diffusion, grammaticalisation and search for non-arbitrary form-function correlations.

Notes

1. Data have been provided by the following informants:

	Abdel-malek (AE)	Abdes-samad (AD)	Abder-rahim (AB)	Zahra (Z)	Malika. H (MH)	Malika. B (MB)
Age (1983)	20	24	26	34	20	18
Civil Status	Bachelor	Bachelor	Bachelor	Married	Bachelor	Married
Education	Primary School	None	None	None	None	None
Date of arrival	Sept. 81	Oct. 81	Sept. 81	1981	Oct.81	Oct. 82
French Courses	1h /week (7 months)	1h /week (7 months)	None	1h /week (4 months)	4h /week (7 months)	None
Other languages	Some Written Arabic, some Spanish	None	Some Spanish	None	None	None
Occupation	Fisherman	Fisherman	Dish-washer	Cleaning lady	Cleaning lady	Bar maid

2. The data analyzed come from the Atlantic Creoles i.e. Lesser Antilles Creoles (Hazaël-Massieux 1991, 1996, Bernabé 1983, Prudent 1993), from Louisiana Creole (Neumann-Holzschuh 1987), and from Indian Ocean Creoles (Chaudenson 1981). The data are quoted in the orthography used in the published documents. Whenever dates are given, they should be used with caution as written testimonials of FBC are rare. The scarcity of written documents should be borne in mind to avoid hasty conclusions and argumentation *ex silentio*: absence of a given form does not mean non-existence of that item. Some of the early FBC utterances may belong to a pre-creole rather than to a fully-fledged language. Following Valdman 1996 and Speedy 1995, it should be remembered that Louisiana FBC is not a unified language but presents a diversity of dialects. Here are the dates of French settlement in FBC areas: St Christophe/St Kitts (1627), Guadeloupe and Martinique (1635), Louisiane (1672-1763), St Domingue/Haiti (1659-1804), Bourbon/Réunion (1665), Ile de France/Mauritius (1721-1814), Seychelles (1770-1814).
3. *il y a* et *c'est* occur under various phonetic guises in the data: /ja/, /jãna/, /se/ /sete/.
4. Included here are items such as /nepakompri/, /napakompri/ (not understood) used by Abdelmalek during the first interviews.
5. Include contexts where *pas* co-occurs with a non-verbal item.
6. Brackets () mark the optionality of the constituent.
7. This morpheme may be realised as /jana/, /jan/, /jãna/ and /ja/ (see note 3 above).

References

Alleyne, Mervyn
    1996   *Syntaxe historique créole.* Paris: Karthala/Schoelcher: Presses Universitaires Créoles.

Andersen, Roger W.
    1983   A language acquisition interpretation of pidginization and creolization. In: Roger W. Andersen (ed.), *Pidginization and Creolization*, 1-56. Rowley (Mass.): Newbury House.

Andersen, Roger W. (ed.)
    1983   *Second Languages. A Cross-Linguistic Perspective,* Rowley (Mass.): Newbury House.

Andersen, Roger W.
    1984   The one-to-one principle of interlanguage construction. *Language Learning* 34: 77-95.

Arends, Jacques
 1993 Towards a gradualist model of creolization. In: Francis Byrne and John Holm (eds.), *Atlantic Meets Pacific. A Global View of Pidginization and Creolization*, 371-378. Amsterdam: John Benjamins.

Arends, Jacques
 1995 Introduction. In: Jacques Arends (ed.), ix-xv.

Arends, Jacques (ed.)
 1995 *The Early Stages of Creolization*. Amsterdam: John Benjamins.

Baissac, Charles
 1880 *Etude sur le patois créole mauricien*. Nancy: Berger-Levrault.

Baker, Philip
 1993 Contribution à l'histoire du futur en créole mauricien. *Etudes Créoles* 16: 87-100.

Baker, Philip, and Chris Corne
 1982 *Isle de France Creole: Affinities and Origins*. Ann Arbor: Karoma.

Baker, Philip, and Anand Syea
 1991 On the copula in Mauritian Creole, past and present. In: Francis Byrne and Tom Huebner (eds.), *Development and Structure in Creole Languages. Essays in Honor of Derek Bickerton*, 159-175. Amsterdam: John Benjamins.

Bardovi-Harlig, Kathleen
 1999 From morpheme studies to temporal semantics: Tense-aspect research in SLA. *Studies in Second Language Acqusition* 21: 341-382.

Bernabé, Jean
 1983 *Fondal-natal. Grammaire basilectale approchée des créoles guadeloupéen et martiniquais*. 3 volumes. Paris: L'Harmattan.

Bickerton, Derek
 1977 Pidginization and creolization: Language acquisition and language universals. In: Albert Valdman (ed.), *Pidgin and Creole Linguistics*, 49-69. Boomington: University of Indiana Press.

Bickerton, Derek
 1983 Comments of Valdman's *Creolization and Second Language Acquisition*. In: Roger W. Andersen (ed.), *Pidginization and Creolization*, 235-240. Rowley (Mass.), Newbury House.

Brunot, Ferdinand, and Charles Bruneau
 1949 *Précis de grammaire historique de la langue française*. Paris: Masson.

Bruyn, Adrienne
 1995 *Grammaticalization in Creoles: The Development of Determiners and Relative Clauses in Sranan*. Amsterdam: IFOTT.

Chaudenson, Robert
 1978 *Les créoles français*. Paris: Nathan.

Chaudenson, Robert
1981   *Textes créoles anciens (La Réunion et Ile Maurice). Comparaison et essai d'analyse.* Hamburg: Buske.

Chaudenson, Robert
1992   *Des hommes, des îles, des langues.* Paris: L'Harmattan.

Croft, William
1990   *Typology and Universals.* Cambridge: Cambridge University Press.

Danon-Boileau, Laurent
1993   De quelques préjugés relatifs à l'usage des notions de motivation et d'iconicité. *Faits de Langues* 1: 79-87.

DeGraff, Michel
1992   Creole grammars and the acquisition of syntax: The case of Haitian. Ph.D dissertation, University of Pennsylvania.

DeGraff, Michel (ed.)
1999   *Language Creation and Language Change. Creolization, Diachrony and Development.* Cambridge (Mass.): The MIT Press.

DeGraff, Michel
1999   Creolization, language change, and language acquisition: A prolegomenon. In: Michel DeGraff (ed.), 1-46.

Dittmar, Norbert
1992   Grammaticalization in second language acquisition. *Studies in Second Language Acquisition.* 14: 249-257.

Duff, Patricia
1993   Syntax, semantics, and SLA: The convergence of possessive and existential constructions. *Studies in Second Language Acquisition* 15: 1-34.

Fattier, Dominique
1992   Un fragment de créole colonial: le *Manuel des habitants de Saint-Domingue* de S.J Ducœurjoly, 1802. Paper given at the *7e Colloque International des Etudes Créoles*, Mauritius, manuscript.

Fattier, Dominique
1998   Contribution à l'étude de la genèse d'un créole: L'Atlas Linguistique d'Haïti, cartes et commentaires. Thèse de doctorat d'État, Université de Provence.

Giacalone Ramat, Anna
1992   Grammatical processes in the area of temporal and modal relations. *Studies in Second Language Acquisition* 14: 297-322.

Giacalone Ramat, Anna
2000   Typological considerations on second language acquisition. *Studia Linguistica* 54: 123-135.

Givón, Talmy
    1984   *Syntax. A Functional-Typological Introduction.* Vol. 1. Amsterdam: John Benjamins.
Goodman, Morris F.
    1964   *A Comparative Study of Creole French Dialects.* The Hague: Mouton.
Gougenheim, Georges
    1929/1971 *Etude sur les périphrases verbales de la langue française.* Paris: Nizet.
Haspelmath, Martin
    1998   Does grammaticalization need reanalysis? *Studies in Language* 22: 49-85.
Haspelmath, Martin
    1999   Why is grammaticalization irreversible? *Linguistics* 37: 1043-1068.
Hazaël-Massieux, Guy
    1991   Genèse ou histoire de la modalité verbale en créole de Guadeloupe. In: Colette Russier, Henriette Stoffel and Daniel Véronique (eds.). *Modalisations en langue étrangère*, 17-30. Aix-en-Provence: Publications de l'Université de Provence.
Hazaël-Massieux, Guy
    1993   L'expression du futur en créole mauricien. *Etudes Créoles* 16: 61-75.
Hazaël-Massieux, Guy
    1996   *Les créoles. Problèmes de genèse et de description.* Aix-en-Provence: Publications de l'Université de Provence.
Heine, Bernd, Ulrike Claudi, and Friederike Hünnemeyer
    1991   *Grammaticalization. A Conceptual Framework.* Chicago: University of Chicago Press.
Hopper, Paul, and Elizabeth Closs Traugott
    1993   *Grammaticalization.* Cambridge: Cambridge University Press.
Hull, Alexander
    1975   On the origin and chronology of the French-based creoles. Paper given at the International Conference on Pidgins and Creoles, Honolulu.
Jennings, William
    1995   Saint-Christophe: Site of the first French Creole. In: Philip Baker (ed.), *From Contact to Creole and Beyond*, 63-80. London: University of Westminster.
Jordens, Peter (ed.)
    1997   Introducing the basic variety. *Second Language Research* 13: 289-300.

Kleiber, Georges
   1993   Iconicité d'isomorphisme et grammaire cognitive. *Faits de Langues* 1: 105-121.

Klein, Wolfgang
   1989   *L'acquisition de langue étrangère*. Paris: Armand Colin.

Klein, Wolfgang
   1994   Learning how to express temporality in a second language. In: Anna Giacalone Ramat and Massimo Vedovelli (eds.), *Italiano lingua seconda/lingua straniera. Atti del XXVI Congresso della Società di Linguistica Italiana, Siena 5-7 Novembre 1992*, 227-248. Bulzoni: Roma.

Klein, Wolfgang
   1998   Assertion and finiteness. Manuscript.

Klein, Wolfgang
   Forthc.   On Finiteness. Manuscript

Klein, Wolfgang, Rainer Dietrich, and Colette Noyau
   1993   The acquisition of temporality. In: Clive Perdue (ed.), *Adult Language Acquisition: Cross-Linguistic Perspectives*, Volume II: *The Results*, 73-118. Cambridge, Cambridge University Press.

Klein, Wolfgang, and Clive Perdue
   1992   *Utterance Structure (Developing Grammars Again)*. Amsterdam: John Benjamins.

Klein, Wolfgang, and Clive Perdue
   1993   Concluding remarks. In: Clive Perdue (ed.), *Adult Language Acquisition: Cross-Linguistic Perspectives*, Vol.II, 251-272, Cambridge, Cambridge University Press.

Klein, Wolfgang, and Clive Perdue
   1997   The basic variety. *Second Language Research* 13: 301-347.

Lang, Jürgen, and Ingrid Neumann-Holzschuh (eds.)
   1999   *Reanalyse und Grammatikalisierung in den romanischen Sprachen*. Tübingen: Niemeyer.

Lehmann, Christian
   1985   Grammaticalization: Synchronic variation and diachronic change. *Lingua e Stile* 20: 303-318.

Lehmann, Christian
   1995/1982 *Thoughts on Grammaticalization*. München-Newcastle: Lincom Europa.

Meillet, Antoine
   1921   *Linguistique historique et linguistique générale*. Paris: Honoré Champion.

Meisel, Jürgen
1977 Linguistic Simplification: A Study of immigrant workers' speech and foreigner talk. In: Samuel Pit Corder and Eddy Roulet (eds.), *Actes du 5e Colloque de Linguistique Appliquée de Neuchâtel*, 88-113. Genève: Librairie Droz.

Meisel, Jürgen
1983 Strategies of second language acquisition. More than one kind of simplification. In: Roger W. Andersen (ed.), *Pidginization and Creolization as Language Acquisition*, 120-157. Rowley (Mass.), Newbury House.

Meisel, Jürgen
1994 Getting FAT: Finiteness, agreement and tense in early grammars. In: Jürgen Meisel (ed.), *Bilingual First Langauge Acquisition. French and German Grammatical Development*, 89-129. Amsterdam: John Benjamins.

Meisel, Jürgen
1995 Principles of universal grammar and strategies of language learning: Some similarities and differences between first and second language acquisition. In: Lynn Eubank (ed.), *Point Counter Point Universal Grammar in the Second Language*, 231-276. Amsterdam: John Benjamins.

Meisel, Jürgen
1997 The acquisition of the syntax of negation in French and German: Contrasting first and second language development. *Second Language Research* 13: 227-263.

Moignet, Gérard
1976 *Grammaire de l'ancien français*. Paris: Klincksieck.

Mufwene, Salikoko.S.
1996 The founder principle in Creole genesis. *Diachronica* 13: 115-168.

Mühlhäusler, Peter
1986 *Pidgin and Creole Linguistics.* Oxford: Blackwell.

Mühlhäusler, Peter
1997 *Pidgin and Creole Linguistics.* London: University of Westminster.

Neumann-Holzschuh, Ingrid (ed.)
1987 *Textes anciens en créole louisianais*. Hamburg: Buske.

Newmeyer, Frederick J.
1992 Iconicity and generative grammar. *Language* 68: 754-796.

Parkvall, Mikael
1995 The role of St Kitts in a new scenario of French Creole genesis. In: Philip Baker (ed.), *From Contact to Creole and Beyond*, 41-62. London: University of Westminster.

Perdue, Clive (ed.)
1984   *Second Language Acquisition by Adult Immigrants: A Field Manual.* Rowley (Mass.): Newbury House.
Pfaff, Carol (ed.)
1987   *First and Second Language Acquisition Processes.* Rowley (Mass.): Newbury House.
Pfaff, Carol
1992   The issue of grammaticalization in early German second language. *Studies in Second Language Acquisition* 14: 273-296.
Pfaff, Carol
1987   Functional approaches to Interlanguage. In: Carol Pfaff (ed.). *First and Second Language Acquisition Processes*, 81-102. Rowley (Mass.): Newbury House.
Posner, Rebecca
1986   La créolisation – altération typologique? *Etudes Créoles* 9: 127-134.
Prudent, Lambert-Félix
1993   Pratiques martiniquaises: genèse et fonctionnement d'un système créole. Thèse pour le Doctorat d'État: Université de Haute Normandie.
Radford, Andrew
1990   *Syntactic Theory and the Acquisition of English Syntax.* Oxford: Blackwell.
Roberts, Sarah J.
1998   The role of diffusion in the genesis of Hawaiian Creole. *Language* 74: 1-39.
Speedy, Karen
1995   Mississippi and Tèche Creole: Two separate starting points for Creole in Louisiana. In: Philip Baker (ed.), *From Contact to Creole and Beyond*, 97-114. London: University of Westminster.
Starren, Marianne
1996   Temporal adverbials as a blocking factor in the grammaticalization process of L2 learners. In: *CLS Proceedings of the opening of the academic year 1996/1997*, 1-16.
Starren, Marianne, and Roland van Hout
1996   Temporality in learner discourse: What temporal adverbials can and what they cannot express. *Zeitschrift für Literaturwissenschaft und Linguistik* 104: 35-50.
Swiggers, Pierre
1993   Iconicité: un coup d'oeil historiographique et méthodologique. *Faits de Langues* 1: 20-28.

Thomason, Sarah G. (ed.)
1997   *Contact Languages. A Wider Perspective.* Amsterdam: John Benjamins.
Thomason, Sarah G., and Terrence Kaufman
1988   *Language Contact, Creolization and Genetic Linguistics.* Cambridge: Cambridge University Press.
Traugott, Elizabeth C., and Bernd Heine
1991   Introduction. In: Elizabeth C. Traugott and Bernd Heine (eds.), Vol. 1:1-14.
Traugott, Elizabeth C., and Bernd Heine (eds.)
1991   *Approaches to Grammaticalization.* Volumes 1 and 2. Amsterdam: John Benjamins.
Valdman, Albert
1978   *Le créole: structure, statut et origine.* Paris: Klincksieck.
Valdman, Albert
1996   La diffusion dans la genèse du créole louisianais. Communication au 8ème Colloque International des Etudes Créoles, Pointe-à-Pitre, Guadeloupe.
Valli, André
1986   Le traitement de la variation linguistique dans l'étude de l'acquisition des langues secondes. In: Alain Giacomi, Daniel Véronique (éds.), *Acquisition d'une langue étrangère: perspectives et recherches,* 541-558. Aix-en-Provence: Publications de l'Université de Provence.
Véronique, Daniel
1994a.   Naturalistic adult acquisition of French as L2 and French-based creole gensis compared: Insights into creolization and language change? In: Danny Adone and Ingo Plag (eds.), *Creolization and Language Change,* 117-137. Tübingen: Niemeyer.
Véronique, Daniel
1994b   Premières étapes de l'émergence des constructions grammaticales en français, langue étrangère. In: Anna Giacalone Ramat and Massimo Vedovelli (eds.), *Italiano lingua seconda/lingua straniera. Atti del XXVI Congresso della Società di Linguistica Italiana, Siena 5-7 Novembre 1992,* 139-15. Roma: Bulzoni.
Véronique, Daniel
1995   Acquisition des modalités en français langue étrangère et développement des modalités dans les créoles français. In: Anna Giacalone Ramat and Grazia Crocco Galèas (eds.), *From Pragmatics to Syntax. Modality in Second Language Acquisition,* 59-82. Tübingen: Narr.

Véronique, Daniel
1997   Le devenir des "petits mots": *pour* dans quelques créoles français. *Faits de langues* 9: 61-70.

Véronique, Daniel
1999   L'émergence de catégories grammaticales dans les langues créoles: grammaticalisation et réanalyse. In: Jürgen Lang, Ingrid Neumann (eds.), *Reanalyse und Grammatikalisierung in den romanischen Sprachen*, 187-209. Tübingen: Niemeyer.

Winford, Donald
1993   *Predication in Caribbean English Creoles*. Amsterdam: John Benjamins.

Lexicalisation of aspectual structures in English and Japanese*

Yasuhiro Shirai and Yumiko Nishi

1. Introduction

Inherent aspect categories of Achievements, Accomplishments, Activities, and States (Vendler 1957), and the semantic features that define these categories (stativity, telicity, and punctuality) have been so central in the study of aspect that it is impossible to discuss aspectual phenomena without reference to them (e.g. Smith 1997, Tenny 1994). Although the universality of these semantic categories has been emphasised in the linguistic literature, not much attention has been paid to the crosslinguistic differences in how these aspectual notions are lexicalised across languages. In this paper, we make a first systematic attempt to investigate the crosslinguistic variation by conducting a case study comparing English and Japanese to explore how aspectual notions are lexicalised in these languages. This crosslinguistic variation also has important implications in the acquisition of tense/aspect morphology among second language learners, which so far has been completely neglected in this area (e.g. Andersen and Shirai 1996; Bardovi-Harlig 2000).

The paper is organised as follows. First, we define four inherent aspectual classes of verbs, which is the basis of the current study. Second, we briefly discuss the correspondence patterns between Japanese and English in terms of how the same concept is expressed in these two languages, and propose the hypothesis that stativity is differently expressed across languages, whereas Activities are similarly lexicalised crosslinguistically. In the next section, we report on a study which tested the hypothesis based on an analysis of 100 most frequent verbs in English and Japanese, and we argue that the hypothesis is supported. Finally, we discuss the implications of the findings for second language acquisition of aspectual morphology. To avoid confusion, we should note here that this paper focuses on how aspectual structure is expressed differently across languages at the lexical level (i.e. inherent/lexical aspect, aktionsart, or actionality). How viewpoint/grammatical aspect (e.g. English progressive or Romance imperfective past) is expressed differently across languages has been investigated in many studies (e.g. Smith 1997, Shirai 1998a).

2. Inherent aspect

First, we briefly summarise the inherent aspectual classes based on Vendler (1957). Vendler's semantic categories of verbs are State, Activity, Accomplishment, and Achievement. State terms (e.g. *love*) describe a situation that is viewed as continuing to exist unless some outside situation makes it change. Activity terms (e.g. *run*) describe a dynamic and durative situation that has an arbitrary endpoint, i.e. it can be terminated at any time. In contrast, Accomplishment terms (e.g. *make a chair*) describe a situation that is dynamic and durative, but has a natural endpoint after which the particular action cannot continue. Finally, Achievement terms describe an instantaneous and punctual situation, i.e. one that can be reduced to a point on a time axis. These are represented in Figure 1 (Andersen 1990).

State	————————	*love, contain, know*
Activity	~~~~~~~~~	*run, walk, play*
Accomplishment	~~~~~~~x	*make a chair, walk to school*
Achievement	x	*die, drop, win the race*

Figure 1. Schematic representation of four inherent aspect classes

In this diagram, the solid line is used to represent State, which is to last timelessly, without a beginning point or endpoint in its focus. The wavy lines for Activity and Accomplishment indicate the dynamic duration of an action, while x for Accomplishment and Achievement represents the punctual point of change of state. That is, x signals telicity. States are [-dynamic], [-telic], [-punctual]; Activities are [+dynamic], [-telic], [-punctual]; Accomplishments are [+dynamic], [+telic], [-punctual]; Achievements are [+dynamic], [+telic], [+punctual] (Andersen 1989, 1991). This inherent aspect classification based on the temporal schemata of the situation described by the verb nicely predicts the aspectual meanings that aspectual markers (e.g. 'be V-ing' in English) carry (Smith 1997).

3. Aspect in Japanese

As noted by Kuno (1973: 140) and Kageyama (1996: 56), Japanese does not have as many State verbs as English. Shirai (2000) suggests that a common way of denoting stativity is by attaching the durative aspect marker *-te i-(ru)* to Achievement verbs, as in examples (1) and (2):[1]

(1) *Asoko-ni   booru-ga   oti-te i-ru*
There-LOC   ball-NOM   fall-ASP-NPST
'The ball has fallen there (and it is there now)'

(2) *Ken-wa   sin-de i-ru*
Ken-Top   die-ASP-NPST
'Ken is dead'

A most interesting example is the asymmetry between English and Japanese concerning a very common concept of {knowing}. English denotes the state of {John knows Mary} by using the non-progressive aspectual form (that is, unmarked zero form) of the state verb *know* as in (3) below. In contrast, Japanese denotes the same stative situation by using an Achievement verb, *siru* 'come to know', inflected for durative aspect *-te i-(ru)*, as in (4).

(3)   *John knows Mary*

(4)   Ken-wa   Naomi-o   sit-te i-ru
      Ken-Top   Naomi-Acc   come:to:know-Asp-Nonpast
      'Ken knows Naomi'

In fact, Japanese does not have a State verb that corresponds to *know* in English. Here, we define State verbs as those verbs that can have non-iterative meaning in simple nonpast tense (Dowty 1979, Shirai and Andersen 1995). Based on this criterion, we can identify State verbs in Japanese (Shirai 1993) – for example, *aru* 'exist', *iru* 'need', *dekiru* 'be able', *mieru* 'be visible', *wakaru* 'understand', etc. If we apply this test, it is clear that the Japanese equivalent of *know* – *siru* – is not stative, but dynamic, in this case Achievement. The direct translation of *Ken knows Naomi* in Japanese cannot refer to a non-repetitive state of Ken knowing Naomi. Instead, it has future meaning.

(5)   Ken-wa   Naomi-o   siru.
      Ken-Top   Naomi-Acc   know:nonpast
      'Ken will know Naomi'

Japanese does not have a future tense marker, and therefore dynamic verbs in simple nonpast tense form in an unmarked reading signify either a habitual situation or future. (Of course, like other languages, Japanese has marked uses of the present/nonpast form such as 'sportscasters present' or 'narrative present'.)

What is interesting is that this typological variation is not random. For one thing, many of these State verbs in Japanese are also lexicalised as stative predicates in English (e.g. *aru* 'exist/be', *iru* 'be necessary', *mieru* 'be visible'). Second, some of these verbs can denote not only "state" itself when used as a State verb (as in *Wakaru* 'I understand') but also "entry into state", when used as an Achievement verb (as in *Wakatta!* 'I got it!'). Note here, the discrepancy in the case of *siru* and *know* pointed out earlier is not as conspicuous as it may seem, since English *know* can refer to entry into state, e.g. *Then I knew it!* (Vendler 1957) even though it is clear that in general *siru* is an Achievement verb and *know* is a State verb. Therefore, there seems to be some level of commonalty in how stative notions are lexicalised, and at the same time variation is seen with respect to what phase of a situation can be expressed by individual verbs. Both *wakaru* and *understand* can refer to the entry into a state as well as the state itself. In contrast, although both *siru* and *know* can refer to entry into state, only *know* can refer to state. This correspondence pattern is represented in Figure 2.

	state	entry into state
wakaru understand	*wakaru.* I understand.	*sonotoki wakatta.* Then I understood.
siru know	*?kare-o siru.* I know him.	*sonotoki sitta.* Then I knew it.

Figure 2. Two different correspondence patterns of State verbs in Japanese and English

Activity verbs, on the other hand, tend not to show much crosslinguistic variation. Typical activity notions such as *running, walking, playing the guitar, singing* are mostly lexicalised as Activity verbs in both English and in Japanese. The correspondence, however, may not hold for less typical Activity verbs such as *sit* and *stand*, which are often referred to as posture verbs. These notions are expressed by Activity verbs in English[2], since they have habitual interpretation in simple present tense, and can be used with adverbials of duration such as *for thirty minutes* (e.g. *Ken sat there for 30 minutes*). In contrast, these notions are lexicalised not as Activities but as Achievements in Japanese, since the equivalent sentence in Japanese is marginal.

(6)　　*?Ken-wa*　　*soko-ni*　　*30-pun*　　*suwat-ta*
　　　　Ken-Top　　there-Loc　　30-minutes　　sit-Past
　　'Ken sat there for 30 minutes'

Interestingly, these posture verbs are lexicalised as State verbs in Mandarin Chinese (Li and Shirai 2000: 117), which suggests that these are non-prototypical, marginal Activities, and tend to show crosslinguistic variation.

Although these are interesting observations, there has not been any study which systematically investigates in terms of aspectual structure how the same concepts or situations are described using different types of verbs across different languages. The present study analyzes the 100 most frequent verbs in English and Japanese, compares them systematically by applying linguistic tests proposed by Vendler (1957), Dowty (1979), and others, and establishes a pattern of correspondence. We hypothesise that (1) State verbs in English correspond to State verbs, adjectives, and Achievement verbs in Japanese, thus exhibiting considerable variation, and that (2) Activity verbs tend to be Activities in both languages, although some verbs do not follow this pattern.

4. The study
4.1. The data

In order to investigate the distribution of verbs and crosslinguistic variations in English and Japanese according to the four-way classification of inherent aspect of verbs, we analyzed the 100 most frequent verbs in English and Japanese texts. The verbs were identified in the frequency lists in English (Francis and Kucera 1982) and in Japanese (Kokuritu kokugo kenkyuuzyo 1962). Some verbs were excluded from the original lists, because for various reasons it was not possible to assign their specific inherent aspectual values. These include auxiliary verbs, pro-verbs, and homonyms. In English, the verbs *be, do, lie, bear*, and *apply* were excluded because it was not possible to assign to each of them a typical meaning and its inherent aspect. In Japanese, *suru* 'do', *yoru* 'be based on, rely', *taisuru* 'face', *tuku* 'attach', *oku* 'put', *kansuru* 'concern', *sitagau* 'obey', *hiku* 'pull', *nasaru* 'do (honourific)', *itasu* 'do (humble form)', and auxiliary verbs *-reru* (passive), *-rareru* (passive), and *-saseru* (causative) were excluded.[3] To get 100 verbs for each language, we added more verbs from the list below the frequency rank of 100.

4.2. Analysis

Many of these high-frequency verbs are polysemous. Since inherent aspect can vary depending on the specific meaning of a particular verb, we needed to identify one most typical meaning for each verb. For all 200 verbs, we determined the prototypical meaning of each verb using dictionaries. We chose the first definition in the entry of each verb in the dictionary as its prototypical meaning. We used the *Cobuild English Dictionary* to identify the prototypical meanings of English verbs, and *Iwanami Kokugo Ziten* (Iwanami Dictionary of Japanese) for Japanese verbs, as these two dictionaries list the most common meaning or usage as the first sense in each entry. However, when the entries of the dictionary contradict the intuition of both of the authors, we followed our intuition.[4]

We then categorised the 200 verbs into four categories of inherent lexical aspect by applying linguistic tests proposed by Vendler, Dowty, and others. The linguistic tests from Shirai and Andersen (1995) were used for the analysis of English verbs, and the tests from Shirai (1998b) were applied for the analysis of Japanese verbs. These tests are listed in the Appendix.

Next, in order to compare the lexical aspect of the verbs in English and Japanese qualitatively, we determined the equivalent verbs in each language. For each of the 100 English verbs, we identified a Japanese verb which is semantically equivalent to the prototypical meaning of the English verb, and assigned it an inherent aspect category. The same was done for the 100 Japanese verbs, in that equivalent English verbs and their inherent aspect values were identified. The equivalent expressions were determined by the researchers' intuition and by dictionaries as needed.

5. Results and Discussion

Results of the analysis are summarised in Table 1.

Table 1. Distribution of inherent semantics of the 100 most frequent verbs in English and Japanese.

	English	Japanese
Achievement	47	63
Accomplishment	7	4
Activity	22	25
Stative	24	8

When we compare the distribution of the inherent semantics of the 100 most frequent verbs in English and Japanese, the numbers of Accomplishment verbs and Activity verbs are very similar for English and Japanese. However, we found that Japanese has fewer State verbs but has more Achievement verbs compared to English. This finding supports Kuno's (1973) and Kageyama's (1996) observation that there are not many State verbs in Japanese.

One might wonder whether the findings in this study truly represent the frequencies of verbs of different aspectual categories. For example, the current analysis concerns the type analysis of the most frequent verbs, but Japanese may use the same State verbs many times, and thus token analysis may find that Japanese use as many State verbs as English. Nishi and Shirai (2000) addressed this question by analyzing the English and Japanese translations of a French novel (*The Little Prince*), and compared the token frequency counts. The results were similar: Japanese had more Achievement verbs than English, whereas English State verbs outnumbered Japanese State verbs.

The correspondence patterns of inherent aspect for 100 most frequent verbs in English and their equivalents in Japanese are summarised in Table 2.

Table 2. Correspondence patterns of inherent aspect for 100 most frequent verbs in English and their equivalents in Japanese.

English verbs		Corresponding Japanese Verbs	
Achievement	47	Achievement	46
Accomplishment	7	Accomplishment	7
Activity	22	Activity	20
		Achievement	2
	stand	→ tatu	
	sit	→ suwaru	
State	24	State	14*
		Achievement	6
	have	→ motu	
	know	→ siru	
	live	→ sumu	
	remain	→ nokoru	
	indicate	→ simesu	
	remember	→ oboeru	
		Activity	4
	see	→ miru	
	keep	→ tamotu	
	hear	→ kiku	
	continue	→ tuzukeru	
Total	100	Total	99**

*This includes two cases of adjectives in Japanese.
**One English word (let) was excluded here because it was not possible to identify an appropriate translation.

Achievement verbs, Accomplishment verbs, and Activity verbs in English correspond to Achievement verbs, Accomplishment verbs, and Activity verbs in Japanese respectively, with the exception of two Activity verbs (*stand* and *sit*), which correspond to Achievement verbs in Japanese (*tatu* and *suwaru*). On the other hand, many of the State verbs in English do not correspond to Japanese State verbs. Out of 24 State verbs in English, only 14 have correspondence to Japanese State verbs, while the remaining correspond to Achievement verbs or Activity verbs. This result supports the hypothesis of the present study that there are fewer State verbs in Japanese compared to English.

Table 3. Correspondence patterns of inherent aspect for 100 most frequent verbs in Japanese and their equivalents in English.

Japanese verbs		Corresponding English Verbs	
Achievement	63	Achievement	56
		Activity	3
	tatu	→ stand	
	kakaru	→ hang	
	noru	→ ride	
		State	3
	siru	→ know	
	nokoru	→ remain	
	odoroku	→ be surprised	
Accomplishment	4	Accomplishment	3
Activity	25	Activity	21
		State	3
	tuzukeru	→ continue	
	tuzuku	→ continue	
	komaru	→ be in trouble	
		Achievement	1
	kataru	→ tell	
State	8	State	8
Total	100	Total	98*

*Two Japanese verbs *dekiru* 'be able' and *okonau* 'conduct' were excluded here because it was not possible to identify an appropriate translation equivalent.

The correspondence patterns of inherent aspect for the 100 most frequent Japanese verbs and their equivalents in English also support the hypothesis (see Table 3 above). All the State verbs in Japanese correspond to State verbs in English, whereas English State verbs correspond to the verbs of different inherent aspect values in Japanese. This suggests that State verbs in Japanese are a subset of State verbs in English.

We also found that some of the Achievement verbs and Activity verbs in Japanese correspond to State verbs in English, whereas none of the Achievement and Activity verbs in English correspond to State verbs in Japanese. However, it should be noted that two of the three Activity verbs in Japanese that correspond to State verbs in English (i.e. *tuduku* 'continue', and *komaru* 'be troubled') are low in dynamicity in the sense that the grammatical subject is not an agent of volitional action. These are not the prototypical Activity verbs (e.g. Smith 1997), and thus support our hypothesis that only less prototypical Activities are lexicalised as non-Activities across languages. A similar asymmetry is also observed in Table 2, where Activity verbs in Japanese correspond to State verbs in English (*see*, *keep*, *hear*, *continue*), and these are also non-prototypical Activities. Furthermore, another class of Activity verbs that lack correspondence across languages is the posture verb (such as *stand*, *sit*, *hang* and *ride* as observed in both Tables 2 and 3). These verbs are also non-prototypical Activities. In fact, Smith (1997) and Talmy (1985) suggest that these are stative predicates. This observation supports our original hypothesis that Activities tend to be universally lexicalised as Activities, and that when they are not, they are non-prototypical Activities lacking dynamicity.

Although we did not predict this trend, it is clear from the results that Accomplishment verbs are stable crosslinguistically. All the seven Accomplishment verbs in English correspond to Accomplishment verbs in Japanese. Accomplishment verbs in Japanese also correspond to Accomplishment verbs in English except for one item *okonau* (a formal equivalent of *suru* 'do')[5] which was excluded because it was not possible to assign inherent aspect value to its equivalent *do*.

Quantification of the degree of correspondence for each verb class is represented in Table 4. The ratio of discrepancy here is calculated as follows: First, the total number of the verbs in each inherent aspect class from both languages is calculated. Then this number is divided by the number of verbs whose equivalent in the other language has a different aspectual value. For example the total number of Achievement verbs in English and Japanese combined is 110, of which 6 have non-Achievement verbs as their lexical equivalent. Thus, the ratio of the discrepancy is 5.5. A low figure indicates a close correspondence for the two languages. As the table shows, Accomplishment verbs have the lowest degree of discrepancy. In contrast, State verbs have the highest discrepancy ratio (31.3) because the Japanese equivalents for many English State verbs are not always State verbs – some equivalents are Activities, and some are Achievements. Thus the degree of discrepancy is in the order of: Accomplishment → Achievement → Activity → State. This is consistent with the pattern of correspondence discussed in relation to Tables 2 and 3.

Table 4. The ratio of discrepancy in four verb classes between English and Japanese

	Achievement	Accomplishment	Activity	State
Total of English and Japanese verbs	110	11	47	32
Number of verbs whose equivalent verbs have different aspectual values	6	0	6	10
Ratio of discrepancy	5.5	0	12.8	31.3

Why, then, are there more State verbs in English than in Japanese? As noted earlier, this is a direct consequence of the fact that what is denoted by the simple present form of State verbs in English is often expressed in Japanese by an Achievement verb plus the durative imperfective form *-te i-(ru)*. As Talmy (1985: 85) suggests, States in Vendler's sense can be considered as 'being in a state' and Achievements can be considered as 'entering into a state'. That is, Achievement can be treated as the beginning point of a state. As indicated by the fact that State verbs often denote both 'state' and 'entry into state', State and Achievement are not completely distinct. Talmy (1985: 86-87) further pointed out that English treats posture verbs as State verbs, and they are lexicalised as 'being in a state' type verbs, whereas in Japanese they are 'entering into a state' type verbs. He suggests that the same concept is lexicalised differently across languages, with several patterns observed. All these point to the claim that the similarity between States and Achievements is real, and that Japanese Achievement verbs are frequently used to describe states whereas in English State verbs are normally used to describe states.

The next question we need to ask is: where does this difference come from? What typological difference between Japanese and English is the cause of such difference in perspective taking on the same situation of 'being in a state'? One interesting proposal has been made by Kageyama (1996).[6] He suggests that English takes a result-oriented perspective whereas Japanese takes a process-oriented perspective. He illustrates this point by the following examples:

(7)
a. *And then there were none*
b. *Sosite   daremo   inaku-nat-ta*
   And:then   anyone   not:exist-become-Past
   'And then everybody disappeared'

(8)
a. *Boil for 3-4 minutes until (it is) syrupy*
b. *Siroppuzyoo-ni-naru made   3-4-pun   yude-ru*
   syrupy-Dat-become   until   3:to:4:minute   boil-Nonpast
   '(You are supposed to) boil 3 to 4 minutes until it becomes syrupy' (Kageyama 1996: 10, emphasis in the original)

In these examples, Japanese sentences focus on the process of the change by using the verb *naru* 'become', whereas English sentences focus on the result state itself, disregarding the process of change, by using stative verbs (i.e. the copula). If Kageyama is correct, it is not surprising that Japanese prefers to describe stative situations as a resultant state by using Achievement verbs plus -*te i-(ru)* because this makes it possible to refer to not only the state but also the change itself. In contrast, English prefers to use State verbs, which can focus only on the state without reference to how it came about. Thus, the results of the present study, which made clear the difference between Japanese and English concerning lexicalisation of aspectual structure, can also be regarded as a data-based, quantitative support to Kageyama's proposal concerning the difference between Japanese and English in their perspective-taking on events.

6. Implications for the second language acquisition of aspect

Finally, we discuss the implications of the findings in this study for the second language acquisition of aspect. We suggest that learners will have more difficulty acquiring verbs in cases where a perfect correspondence cannot be found, such as *siru* vs. *know*. This is a matter-of-fact observation, but we would like to point this out since research on L2 aspect acquisition has neglected this fact.

Although the discussion so far has only focused on the resultative meaning of the Japanese durative imperfective marker -*te i-(ru)* when it is attached to achievement verbs, it can also have action-in-progress meaning when it is attached to dynamic durative verbs (i.e. Accomplishment and Activity verbs) (Shirai 1993, 2000). Recent research on the acquisition of the -*te i-(ru)* form by second language learners has repeatedly found that the resultative state meaning of the -*te i-(ru)* form, which is obtained when it is combined with Achievement verbs, is more difficult for L2 learners than the action-in-progress meaning, which obtains when it is combined with Activity verbs (e.g. Shirai and Kurono 1998, Sheu 1997, Koyama 1998, Shibata, 2000; see Li and Shirai 2000, Ch. 6 for review). This observation was interpreted as a support for the Aspect Hypothesis, which claimed that learners universally associate progressive marking with Activity verbs, and perfective and past marking with Achievement verbs (Andersen and Shirai 1994, 1996, Bardovi-Harlig 2000, Shirai and Kurono 1998). However, the results of the present study indicate that the difficulty for L2 learners may also be due to the L1-L2 discrepancies often observed in the expression of stativity in Japanese and other languages, which presumably makes it difficult to acquire the aspectual structure of these verbs.

Let us take an example of learners whose native language is English. To express the notion of action in progress, what they need to do is simply translate what they have in their L1 (for example, *Ken is running*) to Japanese (*Ken-wa hasit-teiru*), by applying progressive marker to the verbs, since most Activity verbs in English are also Activity verbs in Japanese. Thus, a simple one-to-one translation strategy works quite well. In contrast, the way we refer to stative situation in Japanese is quite different from that in English. First, as shown in the present study, there are far fewer State verbs in Japanese, and thus a simple translation strategy does not work. In fact, teachers of Japanese often hear errors of this type, such as (9).

(9)   *Oisii   resutoran-o   siri-masu
      tasty   restaurant-Acc   come:to:know-Nonpast:Polite
      (intended meaning) (I) know a good restaurant

(9) is probably a direct translation of *know a good restaurant*. Since the use of *-te i-(ru)* is obligatory here, (9) results in an ungrammatical sentence. This is a direct consequence of the typological difference we found in the present study – many stative situations expressed in English by State verbs are expressed by an Achievement + *-te i-(ru)* form in Japanese.

There is a straightforward mapping between L1 and L2 when learners are trying to express the notion of action in progress, whereas this does not apply when they try to denote a stative situation because applying progressive marker to denote stative sitaution is not common in English, thus it is quite foreign to English speakers. This is a difficulty that L1 English speakers encounter at the grammatical level (i.e. at the level of grammatical aspect). Furthermore, the present study shows that there is another complication at the lexical level. That is, concepts denoted by State verbs in English are often lexicalised as Achievements in Japanese. For example, the State verb *know* has a Japanese equivalent *siru*, which is an Achievement verb.

Although these two levels of difficulty are not mutually exclusive, and thus may both contribute to the difficulty of acquiring the resultative use of *-te i-(ru)*, it is worthwhile to test the possibility that the difficulty of the lexical level is the real cause underlying the observation in previous studies that the resultative meaning of *-te i-(ru)* is much more difficult to acquire than the progressive meaning. This can be done in an experiment such as the following. We can present four different types of predicates involving *-te i-(ru)* based on two dimensions: Meaning (result-state vs. progressive) and discrepancy in L1-L2 lexical aspect, as shown in Figure 3.

		Resultative State		**Progressive**
+discrepancy	(A)	sit-te i-ru (ACH) 'know' (ST)	(C)	komat-te i-ru (ACT) 'be troubled' (ST)
–discrepancy	(B)	oti-te i-ru (ACH) 'fall' (ACH)	(D)	hasit-te i-ru (ACT) 'run' (ACT)

Figure 3. Four types of predicates with *-te i-ru* for L1 English learners of Japanese.

If there is no effect of meaning type, we would find no difference between result-state and progressive if we control for the factor of [+/-discrepancy]. On the other hand, if there is no effect of L1-L2 differences in lexical aspect, and the learner's difficulty is purely based on the fact that the Achievement + *-te i-(ru)* combination to denote stativity is more difficult, then we would find no difference between [+discrepancy] items vs. the [–discrepancy] items. It may be that both variables are at work, and in that case we will find that A is the most difficult, and D is the easiest, and B and C fall in between.

In conclusion, this study shows, on the basis of quantitative evidence, that there are far fewer State verbs in Japanese than in English, and that Japanese may be compensating a lack of State verbs by referring to result-state by Achievement verbs combined with the durative aspect marker *-te i-(ru)*. Furthermore, we found that stative verbs in English are often lexicalised as dynamic verbs in Japanese, whereas Activities, Achievements and Accomplishments are relatively stable across the two languages, although non-prototypical Activities do show crosslinguistic differences in lexicalisation. For future research, we should extend the comparison to different languages, to test whether the pattern observed here are universal tendencies. Do State verbs in English often correspond to other verb types in other languages as well? Are Activities relatively more stable across languages? For example, Giacalone Ramat (1997: 278) notes that L2 learners' progressive marking in Italian develops first with Activity verbs in Vendler's terms, which includes "mental state verbs" such as *pensare* 'think'. This suggests that these verbs, although lexicalised as State verbs in English, are less typical State verbs closer to Activities in Italian, or perhaps they may in fact be Activities. It would be interesting to replicate the present study in Italian to see whether Italian has fewer State verbs than English, and if that is the case, how does Italian refer to stative situation? Is it a language which tends to focus on change, as in Japanese, or on result-state itself, as in English? Such studies will further contribute to the understanding of the system of how human language refers to aspectual structures of situations, and add a new dimension to linguistic typology.

The results of the present study also indicate that there is another level of difficulty in aspect acquisition, to which little attention has been paid in previous research – the difficulty of acquiring inherent aspect when there is a discrepancy in the learner's L1 and L2. Based on the current analysis, we should investigate the acquisition of Japanese aspect by L1 English speakers. Furthermore, we should extend the scope of research to the acquisition of Japanese by learners from different L1 groups after a careful analysis of correspondence patterns in their L1-L2 inherent lexical aspect. Such research will shed light on the effect of L1 transfer in aspect acquisition, which has tended to be neglected in previous research in SLA.

Appendix: Linguistic tests used to classify verbs

English (Shirai and Andersen 1995)

Step 1: State or non-state?

Does it have a habitual interpretation in simple present tense?
    If no----> State (e.g., *I love you*)
    If yes---> Non-state (e.g., *I eat bread*) ---> Go to Step 2

Step 2: Activity or non-activity?

Does 'X is Ving' entail 'X has Ved' without an iterative/habitual meaning? In other words, if you stop in the middle of Ving, have you done the act of V?
    If yes---> Activity (e.g., *run*)
    If no----> Non-activity (e.g., *run a mile*) --> Go to Step 3

Step 3: Accomplishment or Achievement

[If test (a) does not work, apply test (b), and possibly (c).]

a) If 'X Ved in Y time (e.g., 10 minutes)', then 'X was Ving during that time'
    If yes----> Accomplishment (e.g., *He painted a picture*)
    If no-----> Achievement (e.g., *He noticed a picture*)

b) Is there ambiguity with 'almost'?
    If yes----> Accomplishment (e.g., *He almost painted a picture* has two readings; i.e., he almost started to paint a picture, and he almost finished painting a picture)
    If no-----> Achievement (e.g., *He almost noticed a picture* has only one reading)

c) 'X will VP in Y time (e.g., 10 minutes)' = 'X will VP after Y time'
    If no -----> Accomplishment (e.g., *He will paint a picture in an hour* is different from *He will paint a picture after an hour*, because the former

can mean that he will spend an hour painting a picture, but the latter does not)

If yes----> Achievement (e.g., *He will start singing in two minutes* can have only one reading, which is the same as in *he will start singing after two minutes*, with no other reading possible)

Japanese (Shirai 1998)

Step 1: State or non-state?

Can it refer to present state in simple present tense without having a habitual or vivid-present interpretation?
    If yes---------> State (e.g., *Tukue no ue ni hon ga aru* 'There is a book on the table')
    If no-----------> Non-state (e.g., *Boku wa gohan o taberu* 'I will eat rice')
    ----> Go to Step 2

Step 2: Activity or non-activity? (Telic or atelic)

If you stop in the middle of the action, does that entail that you did it?
    If yes-------> Activity (e.g., *aruku* 'walk')
    If no--------> Non-activity (e.g., *eki made aruku* 'walk to the station')
    -----> Go to Step 3

*If it is difficult to distinguish between 'punctual verbs denoting resultative state' and 'activity verbs denoting action in progress', use the following tests (a), (b), (c) and/or (d).

(a) Is it possible to say X wa Y (Y=time; e.g., 10 minutes) V-ta without iteration involved?
    If yes-----> activity (e.g., *John wa sanzyuppun hanasita* 'John talked for 30 minutes')
    If no ------> resultative state (e.g. **John wa sanzyuppun sinda* 'John died for 30 minutes')

(b) Is it possible to say 'X wa Y (=place) de V-teiru', and if so, is it more natural than to say 'X wa Y ni V-teiru'?

    If yes to both questions ---------> activity (e.g., *John wa soko de neteiru* 'John is sleeping there')

    If no -----------> resultative state (and therefore the verb is Achievement) (e.g., *John wa soko ni/?de taoreteiru* 'John fell down and is lying there')

(c) Is it possible to say V-hazimeru without iteration involved?

    If yes -------> activity (e.g., *hanasi-hazimeru* 'start talking')

    If no --------> resultative state. (e.g., **suwari-hazimeru* 'start sitting')

(d) Does it have a 'simultaneous activity' reading in the frame 'V-nagara'?

    If yes ---------> activity. (e.g., *hanasi nagara.* 'while talking')

    If no -------> may be resultative state (e.g. *siri nagara* 'although knowing') – but not necessarily, since this test also involves 'agency'

Step 3: Accomplishment or Achievement? (Punctual or non-punctual)

<u>If test (a) does not work, apply test (b), and possibly (c).</u>

a) If "X wa Y de V-ta" (Y=time; e.g., 10 minutes), does that entail X was involved in Ving (i.e., V-teita) during that time?

    If yes-------> Accomplishment (e.g., *Kare wa zyuppun de itimai no e o kaita* 'He painted a picture in ten minutes')

    If no--------> Achievement (e.g., *Kare wa itimai no e ni kizuita* 'He noticed a picture in ten minutes')

b) Can 'V-teiru' have the sense of "action-in-progress"?

    If yes-------> Accomplishment (e.g., *Kare wa oyu o wakasiteiru* 'He is heating water till it is hot')

    If no--------> Achievement (e.g., *Kare wa sono e ni kizuiteiru* 'He has noticed the picture')

c) "X wa Y de V-daroo" (Y=time; e.g., 10 minutes) = "X wa Y-go-ni V-daroo"

    If no -------> Accomplishment (e.g., *Kare wa itizikan de e o kakudaroo* 'He will paint a picture in an hour' is different from *Kare wa itizikan go ni e o kakudaroo* 'He will paint a picture after an hour', because the former can mean he will spend an hour painting a picture, whereas the latter does not)

If yes-------> Achievement (e.g., *Kare wa nihun de utai hazimeru daroo* 'He will start singing in two minutes' can have only one reading, which is the same as in *Kare wa nihun go ni utai hazimeru daroo* 'He will start singing after two minutes', with no other reading possible)

Notes

* We would like to thank Kevin Gregg for his helpful comments on the paper. This chapter is based on the paper presented at the 2nd International Conference on Practical Linguistics of Japanese (San Francisco State University, April, 2000), which appeared in the conference proceedings in Japanese (Nishi and Shirai 2001).
1. See also Talmy (1985: 85-93) for a related discussion.
2. Posture verbs such as *stand* are sometimes treated as State (e.g. Comrie 1976; Talmy 1985). This also suggests that they are not typical Activity verbs. However, we argue that they are in fact dynamic verbs since *He sits on the chair* cannot refer to the present state of his sitting, but his habit of sitting on the chair regularly. Note that *the statue stands on Third Street* is State, even though it is a posture verb because of its permanence. For example, compare **The statue is standing on Third Street* with *The policeman is standing on Third Street*.
3. Many of these Japanese verbs excluded here are in fact already grammaticised postpositions. For example, *tuku* 'attach' is often used as *-ni-tsuite* (locative postposition *-ni* plus the non-finite connective form of the verb). Many postpositions in Japanese are created by this process (Matsumoto 1999).
4. For English, there was no case where our intuition did not match that of the dictionary.
5. It may sound odd that the verb meaning 'do' is an Accomplishment. However, the formal variety of 'do' in Japanese involves a clear sense of goal-orientedness because *Ken-wa sore-o okonat-te i-ta* 'Ken was doing it' does not necessarily entail *Ken-wa sore-o okonat-ta* 'Ken did it'.
6. See also Matsumoto (1996: 148-149) for a related discussion.

References

Andersen, Roger W.
1989 La adquisición de la morfología verbal. *Lingüística* 1: 89-141.
Andersen, Roger W.
1990 Unpublished lecture in the seminar on the acquisition of tense and aspect. Applied Linguistics, University of California, Los Angeles.
Andersen, Roger W.
1991 Developmental sequences: The emergence of aspect marking in second language acquisition. In: Thom Huebner and Charles A. Ferguson (eds.), *Crosscurrents in Second Language Acquisition and Linguistic Theories*, 305-324. Amsterdam: John Benjamins.
Andersen, Roger W., and Yasuhiro Shirai
1994 Discourse motivations for some cognitive acquisition principles. *Studies in Second Language Acquisition* 16: 133-156.
Andersen, Roger W., and Yasuhiro Shirai
1996 Primacy of aspect in first and second language acquisition: The pidgin/creole connection. In: William C. Ritchie and Tej K. Bhatia (eds.), *Handbook of Second Language Acquisition*, 527-570. San Diego, CA: Academic Press.
Bardovi-Harlig, Kathleen
2000 *Tense and Aspect in Second Language Acquisition: Form, Meaning, and Use*. Oxford: Blackwell.
Comrie, Bernard
1976 *Aspect*. Cambridge: Cambridge University Press.
Dowty, David R.
1979 *Word Meaning and Montague Grammar: The Semantics of Verbs and Times in Generative Semantics and in Montague's PTQ*. Dordrecht: Reidel.
Francis, W. Nelson, and Henry Kucera
1982 *Frequency Analysis of English Usage: Lexicon and Grammar*. Boston, MA: Houghton Mifflin.
Giacalone Ramat, Anna
1997 Progressive periphrases, markedness, and second-language data. In: Stig Eliasson and Ernst Håkon Jahr (eds.), *Language and Its Ecology: Essays in Memory of Einar Haugen*, 261-285. Berlin/New York: Mouton de Gruyter.
Kageyama, Taro
1996 *Doosi Imiron* [Verb semantics]. Tokyo: Kurosio Publishers.

Kokuritu Kokugo Kenkyuzyo [National Language Research Institute]
1962 *Gendai Zassi 90-syu no Yoogo Yoozi,* Vol. 1: *Sooki to Goihyoo* [Use of words and characters in 90 present-day magazines, Vol. 1: General description and word list]. Tokyo: Shuei Shuppan.
Koyama, Satoru
1998 Nihongo gakusyuusya ni yoru tensu asupekuto no syuutoku [The acquisition of tense-aspect by learners of Japanese]. Paper presented at the 9th National Meeting of the Japanese Association of Second Language Acquisition, Nagoya University, December.
Kuno, Susumu
1973 *The Structure of the Japanese Language.* Cambridge, MA: MIT Press.
Li, Ping, and Yasuhiro Shirai
1987 *The Acquisition of Lexical and Grammatical Aspect.* Berlin/New York: Mouton de Gruyter.
Matsumoto, Yo
1996 Subjective-change expressions in Japanese and their cognitive and linguistic bases. In: Gilles Fauconnier and Eve Sweetser (eds.), *Spaces, Worlds, and Grammar,* 124-156. Chicago: University of Chicago Press.
Matsumoto, Yo
1999 Constraints on the development of adpositions from verbs: Japanese perspectives. Paper presented at the 6th International Cognitive Linguistics Conference, University of Stockholm, Sweden, July.
Nishi, Yumiko, and Yasuhiro Shirai
2000 The lexicalization of aspectual structures: A case study on English and Japanese. Paper presented at the 9th International Conference of EAJS (European Association for Japanese Studies). Lahti: The University of Helsinki, August.
Nishi, Yumiko, and Yasuhiro Shirai
2001 Asupekuto koozoo no goika ni okeru fuhensee to sai: Eego to nihongo no baai [Universals and variations in the lexicalization of aspectual structures: A case study on English and Japanese]. In: Masahiko Minami and Yukiko Sasaki Alam (eds.), *Gengogaku to Nihongo Kyooiku II* [Linguistics and Japanese language education II], 75-92. Tokyo: Kurosio.
Sheu, Shiah-pey
1997 Tyuu-zyookyuu taiwanzin nihongo gakusyuusya ni yoru teiru no syuutoku ni kansuru oodan kenkyuu [A cross-sectional study of the acquisition of *-te iru* by intermediate and advanced Taiwanese

Shibata, Miki
2000   learners of Japanese]. *Nihongo Kyooiku* [Journal of Japanese Language Teaching] 95: 37-48.
2000   Comparing lexical aspect and narrative discourse in second language learners' tense-aspect morphology: A cross sectional study of Japanese as a second language. Doctoral dissertation, Second Language Acquisition and Teaching Program, University of Arizona.

Shirai, Yasuhiro
1993   Inherent aspect and the acquisition of tense/aspect morphology in Japanese. In: Heizo Nakajima and Yukio Otsu (eds.), *Argument Structure: Its Syntax and Acquisition*, 185-211. Tokyo: Kaitakusha.

Shirai, Yasuhiro
1998a   Where the progressive and the resultative meet: Imperfective aspect in Japanese, Korean, Chinese and English. *Studies in Language* 22: 661-692.

Shirai, Yasuhiro
1998b   The emergence of tense-aspect morphology in Japanese: Universal predisposition? *First Language* 18: 281-309.

Shirai, Yasuhiro
2000   The semantics of the Japanese imperfective *-teiru*: An integrative approach. *Journal of Pragmatics* 32: 327-361.

Shirai, Yasuhiro, and Roger W. Andersen
1995   The acquisition of tense-aspect morphology: A prototype account. *Language* 71: 743-762.

Shirai, Yasuhiro, and Atsuko Kurono
1998   The acquisition of tense-aspect marking in Japanese as a second language. *Language Learning* 48: 245-279.

Smith, Carlota S.
1997   *The Parameter of Aspect*. Second Edition. Dordrecht: Kluwer.

Talmy, Leonard
1985   Lexicalization patterns: Semantic structure in lexical forms. In: Timothy Shopen (ed.), *Language Typology and Syntactic Description*, Volume III: *Grammatical Categories and the Lexicon*, 57-149. Cambridge: Cambridge University Press.

Tenny, Carol L.
1994   *Aspectual Roles and the Syntax-Semantics Interface*. Dordrecht: Kluwer.

Vendler, Zeno
1957   Verbs and times. *The Philosophical Review* 66: 143-160.

Using nouns for reference maintenance: A seeming contradiction in L2 discourse

Henriëtte Hendriks

1. Introduction

In the last decade, quite a number of studies on the construction of discourse, and more specifically on anaphoric linkage within discourse, have shown that, irrespective of source-target language pairs, L2 learners, with increasing proficiency in the L2, are more explicit in reference maintenance than native speakers of the target language. In other words, the L2 speakers are over-explicit. For example, Chini (1998) looked at Germans learning Italian; Ahrenholz (1998) looked at Italian and Polish natives learning German; Muñoz (2000) looked at Spanish learning English, and all came to the same conclusion.

The phenomenon of over-explicitation in L2 acquisition feels somewhat contradictory. Principles governing discourse organisation and especially the use of anaphoric means in discourse have been studied for a large number of languages, i.e., by Givón (1983, 1993), Hickmann (1995), Lambrecht (1994). These studies have shown that more or less universal principles play a role in the interaction between linguistic means used to refer and the accessibility (givenness) of the entity referred to. Thus, when information is "new" to the listener, the speaker will, in most languages, mark this newness, for example through indefinite articles (West-European languages) or through position (Chinese); having been introduced, the information now "given", may be more or less accessible and more or less activated (Givón, 1983; Lambrecht, 1994). Accordingly, fuller or leaner forms will be used. Although the number of forms covering the new/given range may differ according to the language in question, the correlation *more accessible – less full* form vs. *less accessible –*

fuller form is never reversed, as can be seen below in the overview of forms available in the languages in this study:

new	given	more given	most given
Nominals		Pronominals	
indefinite	definite	explicit	zero anaphor
a dog	the dog	it	0
un chien	le chien	il	0
ein Hund	der Hund	er	0
yì-zhī gǒu	(zhèi-zhī) gǒu	tā	0
one-CL dog	(this-CL) dog	3p	0

Assuming that an adult second language learner "knows" the principles governing the so-called information flow/discourse organisation in his L1, and given that these principles are more or less universal as the mentioned studies and above schema suggest, it would seem that the learner should not need a lot of proof (input) in the L2 to come to the conclusion that similar principles govern discourse organisation in his L1 and in the L2. There is no reason, logically, for the learner to assume that the L2 uses full forms where the L1 licenses a zero anaphor or vice versa. And yet, data suggest that L2 learners do exactly that, i.e., use fuller forms than expected given the forms that are allowed in the L1. Hence the contradiction we alluded to and the research question of this paper.

Note that this phenomenon of over-explicitation in the L2 data arrives at an *intermediate* stage. In *initial stages* of L2 acquisition obligatory major syntactic arguments, often topics of the discourse, are frequently omitted in spontaneous speech production. Different types of explanation have been offered for this phenomenon. Within the UG approach it has been suggested that the setting for the pro-drop parameter in the L1 may have an influence on the initial construction of utterances in the L2. Thus, if a source language is a +pro-drop language, then we should more likely find utterances with missing subjects; if the source-language is –pro-drop the missing subject phenomenon in learner data should be negligible. However, it has been shown that the omission of subject occurs in L2 languages irrespective of source and target language (White, 1985).

Studies in a more functional approach have also looked at missing topic phenomena, contrasting mainly topic-prominent and subject-prominent languages, the prototypical feature of topic-prominent languages being null-elements in topic positions. Results show that, although on the whole, speakers coming from topic-prominent languages learning subject-prominent languages indeed tend to "drop" the topic element in early production as expected, learners with a subject-prominent L1 learning another subject-prominent language will also drop more topics in their early L2 productions than native speakers. However, learners with a subject-prominent L1 learning a topic-prominent language such as Chinese show less null elements than one would expect given the combination of languages (Jin, 1994). Null elements in the Chinese variety are found to be rare in low-proficiency learners, and its use seems to have to be learned over time.

Gundel and Tarone (1983) tested if the pragmatic condition of anaphora, i.e., "the use of a pronominal anaphor will be felicitous if and only if its reference is activated" is abided to in L2 learner language, and found that it is never violated in their L2 data. Researchers in the ESF project on second language acquisition by adult immigrants have similarly argued that learners will omit topics only when they are well established and inferable from discourse. Thus, the following utterance by an Italian learning German is perfectly understandable in the context. There is an agent, since *komme* denotes an action, and it is *clear from the context* that Charlie Chaplin is the agent. Klein and Perdue (1992) argue that having access to verbs in the second language allows the speaker more freedom in the sense that he can use the argument structure of the verb to indicate missing arguments to the listener. The intended meaning can thus be deduced as being "Chaplin comes to a building site". Data in the ESF project shows that all language pairs involved know the phenomenon of missing topics.

(1) *komme in eine baustell*
'Come in a building site' (Example from Klein and Perdue, 1992: 24)

In short, in L2 acquisition we find a movement from an initial stage in which reference is too implicit to reference being over-explicit at some later point of development. That the phenomenon of under-explicitation and over-explicitation both occur during the process of second language acquisition may point to a dilemma basically all speakers have continuously when constructing discourse, i.e., how to find the balance between a minimalisation of redundancy and a search for hyper clarity (Williams (1988)). The search for clarity may seem even more pronounced in adult learners of a second language, given that they are aware of their "short-comings" in the L2.

It seems clear to us that in any case, over-explicitation has to do with a concern for communicative success. Two questions therefore arise: 1) one wonders if communication in the phase of under-explicitation is functioning at all, and in how far becoming over-explicit is related to earlier problems of miscommunication while being under-explicit; 2) in the case of speakers of a language that licences zero anaphora, such as Chinese, where speakers know that communication can very well work without referring to topics explicitly, the first question is even more relevant, since one has to wonder what makes those learners switch from under- to over-explicitation.

A number of explanations for over-explicitation in L2 learner data that take the question further than just communication problems has been suggested by Véronique, Carroll and von Stutterheim, 2000:

1. "Given that learners tend to acquire lexical means before grammatical means it might be that at the point in development in which we find the over-explicitation, learners only have access to nouns". If this were a true assumption, stories should all look similar to example (2) below in the stage of over-explicitation, strictly speaking. These examples are, however, clear exceptions to the rule. Most stories show a combination of full nouns, pronouns and zero forms.

(2) ce07hor.cod
>
> There is ***a horse***. There comes ***a horse***
> ***The horse*** *want*
> *to cross a fence*
> *ehm on the on the other side there is **a cow***
> *and ehm and there is **a bird** on the fence*
> *and the ehm **the horse** is thinking*
> *if he - he can cross the fence*
> *and eh after few minutes **the horse** wants*
> *to try*
> *so **the horse** ehm try ehm*
> *the the **the horse** across the fence*
> *but ehm but ehm **the horse** broken the fence*
> *and ehm fa - and ehm fell down*

2. The second explanation, although related to the first in that linguistic means are still what is basically lacking, hints at the construction of discourse taking place "at a lower organisational level", that is, chunks are being linked, but linguistically and conceptually the learner does not manage to construct one coherent whole. As a result, larger referential chains keeping the topic constant (topic persistency) will fail to occur, resulting in less optimal conditions for the use of pronominal forms.

In this paper, I would like to explore the over-explicitation of topic elements in some more detail. The major questions that will guide this study are 1) is over-explicitation indeed a language independent phenomenon, and 2) what elements, if any, in source and target language seem to have an influence on the over-explicitation phenomenon? Is it the overall organisation of discourse that has a main influence, are there language-specific linguistic means that enhance or hinder the use of leaner forms, etc.? In order to allow us to answer the questions we will look at yet another set of language-pairs, in which the source language, a +pro-drop, topic-prominent language (Mandarin Chinese) is kept constant, but target languages, even though all –pro-drop and all more or less subject-prominent (English, French and German) vary.

2. Method and data

The data I will present concern native speakers of Mandarin Chinese (Mainland or Taiwanese) learning either German, French or English, in a semi-guided situation. The data will be compared with those of native speakers (monolinguals) of Chinese, English, French and German as reported in Hickmann et al. (1996) and Hickmann and Hendriks (1999). The monolingual data come from a larger database containing adult and child data as collected by Maya Hickmann, and each language group contains 10 speakers. The L2 data consist of rather unequal groups for the moment: 40 Chinese learning German at 4 different levels of proficiency; 20 Chinese learning French; and 10 Chinese learning English. All learners are students in one of the three European countries, majoring in different subjects (languages or linguistics excluded). Learners of German and French had no knowledge of the L2 prior to their arrival in the country. It was not possible to find Chinese learning English without any prior knowledge of the language. All 10 subjects in this group had had English at high school (zhōngxué) level.

The data were elicited by means of two picture sequences, a Horse story and a Cat story (see Appendix 1). Note that the two stories differ in terms of number and importance of protagonists. The Horse story has one clear main protagonist who enters the scene first, is agentive in most of the story, and is present in all five pictures. In contrast, it is much harder to decide upon a "main protagonist" in the Cat story.

Subjects were asked to tell an unknown, absent adult interlocutor "what happened". It was explained to them that the listener would hear the story from audio tape and should be able to understand it without having access to the pictures. Informants were thus encouraged to rely maximally on linguistic means, avoiding uses of deictic means such as pointing, etc.

3. Typological characterisation of the source and target languages

Typological differences between the source language, Mandarin Chinese, and the target languages of this study, German, French and English, are manifold, but the discussion here will focus only on those points relevant for our questions about anaphoric linkage.

Chinese, in contrast to the three European languages concerned, allows for so-called null elements; null subjects and null objects. Such languages are also called pro-drop languages. To account for null subjects occurring in Chinese and in a typologically quite different language like Italian, Jaeggli and Safir (1989) proposed the "morphological uniformity principle". That is, "null-subjects are permitted in all and only languages with morphological uniformity" (p. 29). Languages like Italian license null subjects because **all** verbs are systematically inflected, Chinese licenses null subjects because **no** verbs are inflected. English, German and French have a so-called mixed inflectional paradigm with some inflected forms and some bare forms, and do not licence null subjects.

The licencing of null subjects has been discussed from other points of view as well. Thus, it has been frequently argued that Chinese is a topic-prominent language, in contrast to the target languages here concerned which are subject-prominent languages (Li and Thompson, 1976; Huang, 1994). In subject prominent languages such as English, all sentences must have a subject. In Chinese, subjects are not obligatory elements of the sentence. In contrast, if one wants to explain the structure of typical sentences in, then the concept of topic appears to be crucial (Li and Thompson, 1976, p. 16). This difference can be illustrated best in cases in which English requires a "dummy" subject, i.e., in weather predicates, where Chinese sentences can do very well without, as shown in example (3):

(3)   **It** is going to rain

       Kuài yào xià-yǔ le
       Soon will down rain le

Given that Chinese is very much discourse-oriented (Huang, 1984, as reported in Yuan, 1997) and that it furthermore has a topic NP deletion rule, topics may be deleted whenever they are identical with a topic in a preceding utterance. The result of such a deletion process has been called a Topic Chain (Huang, 1984). An example of a topic chain is given below:

(4) *Nà   tā   nàge   tā -- tā   qīzi   gān   shénme*
    Uhm   3p   uhm   3p -- 3p   wife   do   what
    ne?
    NE[1]?
    Uhm what does his wife do?

   Tā   qīzi   ma   zuò   gōngrén
   3p   wife   MA[2] be   worker
   His wife is a worker

   0   sùliào chǎng   l   gōngzuò
        plastics plant   in   work
   (She) works in a plastic factory

   0   yě   bǐjiào máng
        also   quite   busy
   (She) is quite busy as well
   (Example from Huang, 1994: 224)

Note that English, French and German do know topicalisation, but that "topic-drop" as featuring in the above example is not possible. The typological differences as sketched here obviously lead to a different treatment of the referential system in source language and target languages, which explains our interest in the specific combination of source and target languages here presented.

4. Results
4.1. Linguistic means used for reference maintenance

In the following, we shall be looking at the distribution of linguistic means for reference maintenance only. By reference maintenance, also called subsequent mentions in this paper, we mean all linguistic expressions referring to a protagonist after the first act of referring to that particular protagonist. In a first instance we will not be looking at different coreferential contexts in reference maintenance. Thus, the following two instances are treated similarly even though one is in a local coreferential relation (example (5)) and one is not (one clause intervening between 2 references to the horse) (example (6)). In all of the paper, we will restrain our analyses to animate referents.

(5) local coreference:
 The horse comes to a fence
 and *he* wants to jump over

(6) no local coreference:
 The horse comes to the fence
 There is a cow on the other side of the fence
 and *the horse/he* wants to jump over

We will first look at the distribution of linguistic means used for reference maintenance by native speakers of the four languages concerned in this paper. The findings reported here were published earlier by Hickmann and Hendriks (1999). In that previous study, the patterns summarized in Table 1 were found. Comparing the Chinese data to the European data, it was clear that Chinese native speakers use a higher proportion of pronominal forms (57%), including personal pronouns and zero anaphora, than speakers of the three European languages (English 46%; French 47%; German 44% (additionally including relative pronouns)). This phenomenon can be explained by the fact that Chinese, as mentioned above, licenses the use of zero anaphora in a much broader range of contexts than the European languages. Constraints are purely of the discourse-type, not the structural type (as for example in English or German).:

Table 1. Forms used to maintain reference to animate referents (native speakers) (Adapted from Hickmann and Hendriks, 1999).

	Chinese	French	English	German
zero pronoun	31%	7%	11%	26%
pers. pronoun	26%	27%	32%	10%
rel. pronoun	--	13%	3%	6%
noun + def art	--	49%	48%	46%
noun + dem. art	19%	1%	1%	5%
bare noun	22%	--	1%	1%
other forms	2%	3%	4%	6%

Nominals in Chinese, which does not have an article system, consist of nouns without any determiner (22%) (bare nouns) or nouns preceded by a demonstrative determiner (19%).

Comparing subsequently the French data to the data of the Germanic languages, we find very few zero anaphora in this Romance language (7%). Relative pronouns, in contrast, occur in relatively high proportions in French when compared to the other languages (13%), and are especially triggered in narratives, by constructions such as:

(7) *Il y a **un oiseau**, **qui** va chercher ..*
    There is a bird that goes to look for ...
(8) *C'est **la vache qui** met un pansement*
    It's the cow that puts a bandage

Bare nouns do not exist in the French native adult data. Proportions are low in the Germanic languages as well but instances do exist as in examples (9) and (10). Note that the category of bare nouns includes proper names such as Elsie in example (11). One final difference between French on the one hand and English and German on the other (not visible in Table 1) is the usage of dislocations by French speakers. Although adults do not use any in the present data, dislocations (as in example (12)) are extremely frequent in the oral input.

Comparing finally English and German, within the pronominal forms, the proportion of zero anaphora is much more important in German (26%) than in English (11%).

(9) *And meanwhile **Mother bird** is coming back with a worm for **Baby birds***

(10) *Und **Muttervogel** kommt schnell zurück*
And Mother bird comes back quickly

(11) *And then the horse decided well he's gonna jump over the fence to play with **Elsie***

(12) *Et **la maman elle** revient avec un ver de terre*
And the mother she comes back with an earthworm

With the first analysis of the second language learner data we tried to establish what forms are used for reference maintenance by the Chinese learners of English, French, and German. Given different theories of L2 acquisition, one might expect similar patterns in all three learner languages if one assumes a major impact on the learner varieties through transfer of the L1; if one assumes the target language to have an influence on the learner variety, or the combination of source and target language influence, then the three learner languages should show different patterns in use of forms for reference maintenance. Important differences were found in the three learner varieties (cf. Table 2): One main difference occurs between German as an L2 on the one hand and French and English L2 on the other in the quantity of nominal forms, more specifically in the quantity of definite noun phrases (German 48%, French 39%, and English 41%).

Table 2. Forms used to maintain reference to animate referents (learner data).

	French	English	German
zero pronoun	2%	8%	9%
pers. pronoun	42%	39%	25%
rel. pronoun	6%	<1%	<1%
noun + def. art	39%	41%	48%
noun + dem. art	3%	1%	6%
bare noun	<1%	9%	10%
other forms	7% (dislocs)	1% (dislocs)	1%

We furthermore find bare nouns in English (9%) and German L2 (10%), as exemplified in (13) and (14) but not in French. The proportions of bare nouns in the learner varieties are bigger that in the target native data. In German and English, Chinese learners have found this form in the input which is form- and function-wise very similar to a source-language form (the bare noun in Chinese covers the same part of the new-given scale: subsequent mentions). As a result, Chinese learners have readily incorporated the "familiar" form into their learner variety. In French, where the form does not occur at all in the target, Chinese learners have not tried to transfer bare nouns into the learner variety.

(13) ce00cat.cod
 *But ehm **cat** think **dog** is not right*

(14) cg0434hor.cod
 *Aber **Kuh** hat sich irgendwie entschuldigt*
 But cow somehow made her apologies

The French L2 data show a remarkably high proportion of dislocations. In this language, Chinese learners seem to have found not so much a familiar form, but rather a familiar function in the form of topic promotion. French has been claimed to be a language which is midway on the subject-prominent, topic-prominent continuum (Lambrecht, 1981). In this language, the dislocation has been shown to execute the function of topic promoter (Lambrecht, 1981; Hickmann and Roland, 1990; Hendriks, 2000). Again, Chinese do not try to promote topics through dislocations or any other constructions in English and German, but, when the specificities of the target input allows for similar forms and / or functions these similarities are reflected in the learner language, as in French. As is the case with bare nouns in German and English, Chinese use higher proportions of dislocations, when compared to proportions in the target language.

4.2. Establishing the amount of over-explicitation

After this general analysis of forms used for reference maintenance in the L2 data, we now proceed to our actual question: do Chinese learners of French, German and English use more explicit forms in reference maintenance than native speakers of those three European languages? Table 3 summarises the forms used by native speakers and learners, adding up all nominal forms on the one hand and all pronominal forms on the other.

Table 3. Proportions of nominal/pronominal forms used for reference maintenance by native speakers and Chinese learners.

	native speakers			learners	
	nominals	pronominals		nominals	pronominals
Chinese L1	43%	57%			
English L1	54%	46%	English L2	52%	48%
French L1	53%	47%	French L2	50%	50%
German L1	55%	45%	German L2	64%	35%

A first observation that can be made on the basis of Table 3 is the fact that Chinese do not reproduce proportions of pronominals and nominals in their learner variety similar to the source language. Formulated differently, Chinese are definitely more explicit in the learner variety than in their native tongue. In other words, they rely less on discourse organisation when referring in the second language than in their own language. This general statement is true for all three learner varieties. If we compare proportions of learner varieties with the respective target languages, we can conclude that no disproportionate use of nominal forms is found in English L2 (52%) compared to English L1 (54%). In detail, however, as mentioned before, we find more bare nouns, and less definite nouns in the learner data than in the target language, and we find a smaller proportion of zero anaphora in the learner data than in the target language data.

For French, again, an overextended use of nominal forms is clearly not attested in the learner variety (50%) compared to the target (53%). In detail, we do find, as in English L2, a smaller amount of zero anaphora than in the native speaker data and furthermore the already mentioned slightly exaggerated use of dislocations.

In German, proportions of nominals in the learner variety are disproportionate (64%) compared to the native speaker data (55%). Or, over-explicitness does seem to occur in this last learner variety. Returning to the earlier two tables, we notice furthermore a relatively high proportion of zero anaphora in the native German data, in principle a familiar form with familiar functions for Chinese learners (overlapping with the same part of the given-new scale in Chinese and German), which is, however, not at all manifested in those learners' data.

Thus, looking merely at over-explicitness in terms of using nominal forms instead of pronominal forms, this does not seem to be a correct way to describe the English and French data at hand. In German, however, over-explicitness is attested. More nominal forms are used in the learner variety than in German L1, and within the use of pronominal forms, explicit pronouns are more frequently used than zero anaphora, in contrast to German L1.

In sum, the previous analyses show that over-explicitation indeed occurs in learner data, but that the extent to which it occurs varies across source-target language pairs. The feature clearly cannot be the result of L1 transfer, given that the Chinese native data are overall less explicit than the learner varieties. Logically, therefore, the language-specific factors of the different target languages influence the amount of over-explicitation, but it is in no way clear what specific elements in the target language allow for the present results. Finally, Chinese learners seem to search familiar linguistic means and functions while in the process of getting to grips with the new language. This can be shown for dislocations in French, and bare nouns in German and English. However, it does not seem to influence the Chinese learner's use of zero anaphora. We will get back to this latter point later.

4.3. Coreferentiality and its influence on linguistic means used

As we mentioned above, accessibility and active-ness have an influence on the exact form chosen by the speaker to refer to a certain referent. Several ways of measuring the status of accessibility/activeness of a referent have been proposed. One is: are we talking about cases of local coreference (cf. Hickmann and Hendriks, 1999), that is, is the protagonist referred to in two consecutive utterances as shown in example (5) above, in which the protagonist is considered to be highly active, or has the protagonist referred to been referred to previously in discourse but at a certain distance from the present instance of reference in which case he is accessible but not necessarily active? Another way of measuring involves topic persistence (Givón, 1983, 1993). Givón states that "topic persistence is a reflection of the topic's importance in the discourse, and thus a measure of the speaker's topical intent (p.14)". Givón operationalises the notion as "the number of clauses to the right – i.e., in the subsequent discourse from the measure clause – in which the topic/participant continues an uninterrupted presence as a semantic argument of the clause (p. 15)". We will, in the following, be looking at both factors, but note that we will be using the concept of topic persistence in a slightly different way than Givón originally used it. Topic persistence automatically involves coreference, but a narrative can contain a high proportion of coreferential situations and still not have a high topic persistency.

As far as the influence of local coreference on referential expressions is concerned, Hickmann and Hendriks (1999) have reported that when there is no coreference, that is, in *non-coreferential* contexts such as in example (6) above, around 90% of the linguistic means used are of the nominal form irrespective of the target language analyzed. In *coreferential* contexts, the three European languages show a very similar 26% of nominal forms used, all others being pronominal forms. Within the pronominal forms, Germans use most zero anaphora (34%), English fewer (20%) and French uses of zero anaphora are very constrained (12%), as we have seen before.

Comparing the learner data presented in table 4 with the native speaker data just discussed, French learner data look remarkably similar to the target language data in both coreferential and non-coreferential contexts. In non-coreferential contexts 87% of the forms are nominals, in coreferential contexts 28% of the forms are nominals, 60% are explicit pronouns and 12% of the forms are zero anaphora. English learner data are very close to the target language data as well, although here we find 10% more nominal forms in coreferential contexts than in native English (36% vs. 26%), and a lower proportion of zero anaphora in the learner data (13%) than in the English native speaker data (20%). Finally, the German learner data are very different from the native speaker data as far as the distribution of forms in coreferential contexts is concerned. The learners use 42% of nominal forms (vs. 26% in the native speakers) and only 11% of zero anaphora in coreferential contexts vs. 34% in the native speaker data. In non-coreferential contexts uses of pronominal vs. nominal forms do not seem to differ. Again, we find the same pattern as before: even in felicitous contexts in which reference is coreferential, Chinese learning German are more explicit than German natives. Chinese learning French are very much like speakers of the target language, and Chinese learners of English again show a slight tendency to over-explicitation in coreferential contexts.

Table 4. Forms used for reference maintenance as a function of coreferentiality.

		nominals	expl. pronouns	zero anaphora
English L2	CO	36%	51%	13%
	NOCO	86%	14%	--
French L2	CO	28%	60%	12%
	NOCO	87%	13%	--
German L2	CO	42%	47%	11%
	NOCO	92%	7%	1%

In order to understand the extent and reasons of diversity from one language pair to the other, we have decided on a further, more detailed analysis of the data. A number of assumptions underlie this analysis.

1) The ideal context for the use of pronominal forms involves a high topic persistency in the sense of the number of clauses in which the protagonist continues an uninterrupted presence as a semantic argument of the clause (a referential chain).
2) A high topic persistency puts the protagonist involved high on the accessibility scale, and, as said, results in a high number of coreferential contexts.
3) The ideal context is to some extent controlled by the picture sequence offered to the subjects. Thus, the horse story allows the creation of such ideal contexts easier than the cat story. The horse, being present in all pictures of the picture sequence can in principle continue an uninterrupted presence as a semantic argument of the clause all through the narrative. Note that the horse story *allows* such a more optimal environment. It does not mean that learners have all the linguistic means available to create these ideal contexts, which leads us to the fourth assumption:

4) Subjects might have problems on the discourse level, possibly on a conceptual level, as found for children learning their first language, who do not necessarily conceive of the series of pictures as a coherent sequence of events forming a story, but rather of a processing kind, the production of a narrative task overtaxing the learner's processing abilities and therefore masking some of their linguistic abilities. For example, if we re-examine the example (2) repeated here for convenience and we compare that example with example (15), then it should be obvious that the reason for a lack of less-explicit forms in the two examples is not the same. Example (2) creates a context where less-explicit forms would be possible, but for some reason the learner does not have access to those forms. In contrast, the production in example (15) is not a story in the sense that there does not seem to be a coherent sequence of events organised around a main protagonist. We are dealing here with a description of a sequence of pictures, rather than with a narrative. In the second example I would be tempted to say that the problem is a discourse construction level problem, whereas in the first example a problem of a lack of linguistic means is much more likely.
5) We feel that there is no obvious reason why Chinese would construct a less coherent story in one target language rather than in another. Therefore, we will argue that any difference should have a language-specific explanation, not a purely developmental one.

(2) ce07hor.cod

*There is **a horse**. There comes **a horse***
***The horse** want*
to cross a fence
*ehm on the on the other side there is **a cow***
*and ehm and there is **a bird** on the fence*
*and the ehm **the horse** is thinking*
if he - he can cross the fence
*and eh after few minutes **the horse** wants*
to try

*so **the horse** ehm try ehm
the the **the horse** across the fence
but ehm but ehm **the horse** broken the fence
and ehm fa - and ehm fell down*

(15) cf04hor.cod

*Il y a quatre fleurs et **un cheval** dans une premier picture
et le deuxieme il y a trois animaux ehm **un cheval** et un - **une vache**
le le troisième c'est ehm **le cheval** ehm
oh c'est difficile
et **de vache** regarde le de la de **la cheval** et **le bird** aussi
et dans le même place dans le quatre picture ehm **le cheval** ehm
déménage
vache regarde **to lui**
oui et de dernier picture le **le vache et le cheval***

There are four flowers and a horse in the first picture. And the second there are three animals ehm a horse and a cow. The the third it's ehm the horse ehm. Oh it's difficult. And the cow looks at the the horse and so does the bird. And in the same place in the fourth picture ehm the horse ehm moves. Cow looks at him. Yeah and the last picture the cow and the horse.

4.4. *Referential chains and linguistic means used*

In this analysis we will thus be looking at the influence of discourse organisation on the usage of forms in a more detailed way. For this analysis we looked exclusively at the *Horse story* data. A number of features of discourse organisation were calculated, such as number of referential chains (referring to the horse) per story, mean length of the referential chains found per story, and the number of pronominal forms actually found within the referential chain. Again, some assumptions concerning these calculations:

1) we assume that a story with a higher number of referential chains is a more fragmented, less coherent story, thereby creating a less favourable context for the use of pronominal forms.
2) we assume that the length of the referential chain contributes to the number of pronominal forms used within the chain. The longer the chain, the more ideal the context for pronominals.

Table 5. Overview of referential chains in learner varieties.

	chains per story	mean length of chain	pron forms in chain
French L2	1.2	4.7	100%
German L2	1.6	3.6	86%
English L2	2.3	3.8	94%

Examining first the number of referential chains per narrative, we conclude that Chinese learners of French construct Horse stories with a lower mean number of referential chains per story (1.2) than Chinese learning German (around 1.6) and Chinese learning English (2.3). Or, Chinese learners of French seem to build the least fragmented narratives, followed by Chinese learning German, and Chinese learning English. However, this measure should be seen in combination with the results on the calculation of mean length of referential chain. This second measure shows the same tendency, in that the mean length of referential chain is higher in French L2 (4.7) than in English and German L2 (3.8 and 3.7 respectively). L2 English and German do not really differ in this respect.

One of the main elements breaking up referential chains in German and English in this story is the introduction of cow and bird as can be seen in examples (16) and (17). In both examples, the story seems to jump back and forth between the different protagonists. As can be seen very clearly in example (17), this prevents the learner from using pronominal forms for referring to the horse. Thus, as soon as the horse is introduced in the first utterance, the learner turns to pronouns to maintain reference to the horse, but only until the cow and bird are introduced in lines 3 and 4 after which reference to the horse is taken up again with a nominal form, *der Pferd läuft*.

(16) cg0110hor.cod

Es ehm es gibt eine ehm breite Wiese mit eh lange Zaun
*und ehm ... darinne lauft **eine Pferd***
ehm da außen daraus da außen wanderte ein Rinder um
auf der auf dem auf dem Zaun eh steht eh eine kleine Vogel
***der Pferd** moechte*
There is a large meadow with a long fence and ehm in it walks a horse. And eh outside walked an ox. On the on the fence stands a little bird. The horse wanted

(17) cg0127hor.cod

*Eh **ein Pferd** lebt in ein eh wie heißt das - Garten*
***se** sehr glücklich*
*und ja neben **ihm** gibt's auch ein Kuh*
und dann irgendwann kommt auch ein Vogel
*ja, **der Pferd** läuft*
ja und de Kuh und de Vogel haben den Pferd ja gesehen
*Oj! Ja aber **der Pferd** hatte Pech*
*Sie hat eh **er** hatte eh gefallen ja ja er hat gefallen*
*und **er** hat auch eh verletzt, eh eh er wird verletzt*
ja und de Kuh hatte dem Pferd geholfen
Ehm a horse lives in a what's it called, garden. She is very happy. And next to him there is also a cow and then one day comes a bird. Yeah, the horse walks yeah and the cow and the bird have seen the horse. Oj! But the horse had bad luck. She has he has he fell down and he hurt himself, he gets hurt. Yeah and the cow had helped the horse.

There are linguistic means to avoid this breakdown in the referential chain. For example, subordination of the information about cow and bird, or the use of gerund forms, as shown by the example of a native French adult in (18). It may argued that subordination and gerund constructions are linguistic means that learners of a second language master only relatively late in the acquisition process, and that therefore they have no way of avoiding a breakdown of the referential chain. However, easier strategies exist as well, and these are indeed used, in particular by Chinese learning French, as shown in example (19). In this example, cow and bird are introduced through the horse's perspective instead of through the narrator's perspective. In order to do so, the verb *voir* is chosen, which allows horse, cow and bird to all be semantic arguments to the same verb, and as a result, to be all mentioned in the same utterance. As a consequence, the referential chain is prolonged.

(18) fad11hor.cod

[...] Le cheval,
voyant le taureau
eut envie d'aller le rejoindre
et 0 sauta par-dessus la barrière.
Il se retrouva donc dans le champ du taureau
avec les quatre fers en l'air
The horse, seeing the bull felt like joining him and jump over the fence. He ended up in the bull's meadow his legs up in the air.

(19) cf02hor.cod

ehm il y a très longtemps il y a un cheval
qui se promène dans le champs
il courait partout
*et soudain **il voit** une vache avec un corbeau*
il voulait
leur montrer le saut
donc il a sauté
mais il n'était - il n'avait pas fait attention
donc il s'est cassé - il est tombé
il s'est cassé le pied
et finalement c'est le corbeau qui est allé chercher des médicaments

Ehm a very long time ago there is a horse wandering around in the meadow. He ran everywhere and suddenly he sees a cow and a crow. He wanted to show them his jump so he jumped. But it wasn't he hadn't paid attention so he's broken himself, he has fallen and he has broken his foot. And finally it's the crow that left looking for medication.

If we now look at the linguistic means used within the referential chain (the first reference of the chain is excluded for obvious reasons) then we find the highest proportion of pronominal forms used by Chinese learning French (100%); Chinese learning English use pronouns in these highly ideal contexts in 94% of the cases, and Chinese learning German use pronouns in only 86% of these cases.

In sum, this analysis shows that Chinese learning French manage to build the most coherent narratives, thereby creating more optimal contexts for the use of pronominal forms. Moreover, once the optimal contexts created, they do indeed use the highest proportions of pronouns compared to the other learner groups. Chinese learning German create more optimal contexts for the use of pronominal forms than Chinese learning English, but they are less likely to use pronominal forms when favourable contexts are created (86% vs. 94%). As mentioned before, we feel that there should be linguistic reasons both for the creation of less coherent narratives, and for a less frequent use of pronouns in optimal situations.

4.5. Ambiguous reference and the use of gender

In highly optimal (coreferential, topic persistent) contexts, one reason to resume to nominal forms may be the competition between a number of referents for the same referential expression. Thus, imagine a situation in which the horse is the main protagonist, where cow and bird have been introduced and in which the narrator has stated that "the horse, the cow and the bird looked at each other". In any following utterance, speakers may want to avoid the pronoun *he* because of the ambiguous reference created by means of that pronoun in English in the given situation (*he* could refer to all three protagonists). However, in German, where the horse differs in gender from the bird and the cow, i.e., *das Pferd* (neuter), *der Vogel* (masculine) and *die Kuh* (feminine), the correct use of pronouns will avoid the ambiguity in this case and the described situation does not result in a problematic context for the use of a pronominal. As we have reported, however, the German learner variety knows the highest proportion of nominal forms for reference maintenance, suggesting that somewhat more complicated is going on than we just proposed.

As a consequence, our last set of analyses looks at the gender systems in English, French and German, and their disambiguating force, and at its use by the learners in the various learner varieties.

English does not have grammatical gender, only biological gender. That is, if the biological gender of a protagonist is known, i.e., because the protagonist is a girl, a man, or a bull, then one is obliged to choose the masculine or feminine pronoun in accordance with biological gender. However, for a large number of animate and inanimate entities one can basically choose what gender to attribute. Speakers of English can thus choose a gender for the animal protagonists in the *Horse story*. It is not clear how many speakers actually consciously make choices in order to avoid ambiguities, but, if chosen consciously and/or cleverly, the choice may result in a narrative as in example (20) by a Chinese learner of English where most situations are disambiguated because of the cat being *she* and the dog being *he*. This is a device learners will have to acquire, especially our Chinese learners who do not make a distinction between *tā* 'he' and *tā* 'she' in their native spoken language.

(20) ce05cat.cod

and ehm ehm in this time a naughty cat come in
the naughty cat walked near the tree
*and **she** noticed*
[...]
*and so **she** crawl up on the tree*
*as far as her - as **she** want*
and ehm suddenly a dog is coming

*and **he** noticed that what has happened here*
ehm so the dog ehm bite ehm bite the tail of the cat
*and try **his** best*
to pull the cat down from the branch of the tree
*the cat try **her** best to touch the nest*
*and **she** nearly get the top of the nest*
and the dog bite the tail seriously hurt
*try **his** best to pull the cat down*
the cat can't bear the pain
*so **he** dropped down - **she** dropped down from the tree*

Note, however, that ambiguity does not seem to worry Chinese learners of English greatly, as should be clear from example (21) where gender is not used to distinguish between cat and dog and where some utterances such as *and he came near the tree* are only disambiguated in a later utterance. Although comprehension is clearly at risk in this narrative, the speaker does not seem to hesitate, change gender, or resort to nominal forms for clarity once.

(21) ce09cat.cod

a cat on the ground saw	
the mother bird flying away	
***he** thought*	CAT
well that would be a very nice meal for me	
*so **he** quietly climbed up the tree towards the nest of the little birds*	CAT
*but **he** does not know*	CAT
*something is happening just behind **him***	CAT
a dog saw	
*what **he** was doing*	CAT
*and **he** came near the tree*	DOG
and just before the cat reached the nest	
***he** bit his bit the cat's tail*	DOG
*and dragged **him** down*	CAT

French and German both assign gender grammatically. All learners of French have to learn that *chat* 'cat' is a masculine word and all learners of German have to learn that *Pferd* 'horse' has neuter gender. In a number of cases, grammatical gender accords with biological gender. Thus, *vache* 'cow' in French and *Kuh* 'cow' in German both have feminine gender. In French, the horse story consists of two protagonists with masculine gender, *le cheval* 'the horse' and *l'oiseau* 'the bird'. The cow is feminine. To some extent, therefore, possible ambiguities in the story between cow and horse can be avoided simply by applying gender, as exemplified below in (22) by a Chinese learner of French. This presupposes, however, that the speaker has acquired gender.

(22) cf05hor.cod

eh eh dans un champ il y a un petit poney
il *joue très bien dans son dans son champs tous les jours*
il *est heureux d'être dedans*
mais de l'autre côté il y a un autre champs de la vache
*la vache **elle** vit bien aussi*
elle *est dans son champs*
et tous les deux bêtes ils se parlent pas
*mais un jour le poney **il** veut*
<travers> la barrière
*pour saluer **le - la** vache*
*mais **il** a fait tombé*
*et **il** s'est cassé des pattes*
*et la vache **elle** est très gentille*
elle *a fait bandage sur les pattes du poney*

Ehm in a field there is a little pony. He always plays well in his field. He is happy to be in it. But on the other side there is a field of the cow. The cow she is happy as well. She is in her field and the two animals do not talk to each other. But one day the pony he wants to jump over the fence to say hi to the cow. But he fell and he broke his legs and the cow she is very nice. She puts a bandage around the pony's legs.

In German, all three protagonists in the Horse story have a different gender:

***das** Pferd*	(the horse)
***die** Kuh*	(the cow)
***der** Vogel*	(the bird)

If acquired, gender in German can therefore allow for even more disambiguation than the other two languages. *If acquired* is the crux of the matter, however. Apart from the three way gender distinction, pronouns get inflected for 4 cases in German, leading to a total of approximately 10 different forms of personal pronouns. Note that the number of declensions is not the only factor that complicates the acquisition of the German gender system. Researchers such as Kempe and MacWhinney (1998), in a comparison of the acquisition of Russian and German case marking, have argued that the declensions in German are less informative than the Russian declensions (which are even more numerous) because of the overlap between some of the forms, or, as they call it, they have a lower cue validity. In their paper, they show that German case marking frequently neutralises the distinction between nominative and accusative (for feminine, neuter and plural nouns) which always results in ambiguities. As a result, English learners of German can use gender cues less often in comprehension, and they acquire the system in a slower fashion than English learning Russian. Note that Kempe and MacWhinney focus on comprehension only, and that they clearly state that production might be dependant on the number of declensions rather than on their cue validity. In both cases, however, German is clearly the most complicated system of the three languages compared here.

The combination of facts makes the German gender system more difficult to acquire for our Chinese learners than the French system, which can be concluded on the basis of examples such as (23) to (25) in which the learners are clearly struggling to find the target language appropriate pronominal form in L2 German. Similar searches for the correct pronominal form in French as an L2 simply do not occur in our data. Of course, when one does not know the gender of a protagonist, one runs the risk of making a text ambiguous, rather than disambiguating it. Therefore, in cases of ignorance, it is safer to use the nominal form than a pronominal form. Learners of German resort to this strategy in many more cases than Chinese learning French, resulting in the higher proportions of pronominal forms used in the latter learner variety.

(23) *Und ehm **eine Horst er** lauft in die Wiese. Und **sie sie nicht sie er** und **er** hat eine Kuh gesehen.*
And a horse runs in the meadow. And she she not she he and he has seen a cow.

(24) *Und er möchte **sie sie ehm eh diese kleine Vögelchen** vielleicht essen.*
And he probably wanted to eat them them the little birds.

(25) *Ein Pferd ... lauft auf eine Wiese. Und ehm ... plötzlich .. trifft **er ... der ... oder sie**, weiß ich nicht **des Pferd** an eine Zaun.*
A horse runs in a meadow. And suddenly he he or she I don't know the horse gets to a fence.

Thus, Chinese learning German are extremely aware of their problems with the gender system, and, presumably, also of the possible communicative problems arising through the misuse of gender. Example (25) shows how hesitation about gender may make the learner change strategy from using a pronominal form to a nominal form. Moreover, once starting to doubt, lower proficiency learners will stick with the nominal strategy from there on, avoiding all pronouns, as shown in example (26). Only more advanced learners (example (27)) will, after initial hesitation, let higher level discourse organisation prevail over lower level sentence organisation and return to the use of pronouns at the risk of ambiguity but with the advantage of more discourse cohesion.

(26) cg0226hor.cod

und ehm eine vielleicht junge Pferd läuft gerade
*vielleicht will **er - diese Pferd** versuch*
diese Zaune überzugehen
und im andere Seit ist noch eine Kutsch une auch eine kleine Vogel
auf die Zaune
*jetzt bleibt **diese Pferd** ruhig*
*vielleicht hat hatte **diese Pferde** nicht geschafft*
diese Zaune überzugehen
*Danach werde **diese Pferde** noch mal versucht*
*aber **dieser Pferd** ist nich in die Lage*
diese Zaune übergehen
And eh the little horse just walks maybe he wants to - this horse tries to go over the fence. And on the other side is a cow and a little bird on the fence. Now the horse keeps quiet, maybe the horse did not make it the go over the fence. Afterwards the horse tried once more but this horse is not capable to go over the fence.

(27) cg0305hor.cod

*ehm **ein Peferd** ehm läuft auf eine Wiese*
*und eh ehm plötzlich trifft **er ... der oder die weiß ich nicht des Pferd***
an eine Zaun
*und ehm **der Pferd** will*
über diese Zaune springen
*aber **er** hat es nicht gelungen*
ehm a horse runs on the meadow. And ehm suddenly he he or she I don't know the horse gets to a fence. And this horse wants to jump over the fence. But he didn't make it.

5. Conclusion

In this paper we have investigated the contradictory finding of overexplicitation of topic elements in L2 learner discourse. The discourse-pragmatic principles governing the introduction and maintenance of reference in narratives have been shown to follow more or less universal patterns. As a consequence, adult learners of a second language should be familiar with these principles through the knowledge of their mother tongue. It would seem that, given these prerequisites, a learner of a second language should not need much input of the L2 to realise that L1 and L2 discourse pragmatic rules are similar. Findings so far have shown, however, that adults do not benefit from their L1 knowledge, and go through a stage at which they use more explicit linguistic means than necessary for successful communication, and, more specifically, more explicit means than the native speaker of the target language would use.

Why do adults not benefit from this universal knowledge? Children around 4-5 years of age show the same "symptom" of over-explicitation (cf. Hickmann, 1995). The explanation in their case is that they have not yet fully acquired the discourse pragmatic rules, and therefore are not completely aware of the given-new contract. They have furthermore been shown to have problems conceptualising a sequence of pictures as a story, resulting in a description of each of the pictures as a separate element, rather than in a narration. As a consequence, children do not create optimal conditions for the use of leaner forms, and are therefore more explicit than the adult speakers of their language. However, these explanations are not valid in the case of adult second language learners.

In order to get more information on the phenomenon, we looked at yet another set of language-pairs; speakers of Mandarin Chinese learning English, French or German. The specific questions we asked were: 1) does over-explicitation indeed occur in all learner varieties, irrespective of source-target language pairs, and 2) what elements, if any, in source and target language seem to have an influence on the over-explicitation phenomenon?

Hypotheses were that if Chinese learners would construct discourse as in their L1, they should produce narratives that show under-explicitation when compared to the European languages, and that if Chinese geared their output towards the target languages, we should find variation such as a more pronounced use of zero anaphora in German than in English and French.

Results showed that narratives are not constructed as in Chinese, but that they are also not constructed as a direct image of the target language. However, differences between language pairs exist in this respect. Thus, Chinese are clearly better at using target like proportions of available linguistic means in French, than in English or German. Moreover, only in German can we really speak of over-explicitation. We investigated several facets of the produced narratives in order to find an explanation for the variation across language pairs. We showed that Chinese learners of French construct the *Horse story* taking the horse's perspective. This allows them to keep referential chains referring to the horse going, thereby creating optimal conditions for the use of pronominals. Chinese learning English and German usually take a narrator's perspective when narrating the *Horse story*, resulting in having to interrupt the referential chain referring to the horse, thereby creating a more fragmented story which is less felicitous for the use of pronominal forms.

An important question to be asked here is: why do Chinese produce a different kind of narrative structure in French than in German. A variety of perspectives is possible and occurs in Chinese. It has been shown that languages tend to conventionally chose a certain perspective when narrating events (Carroll and von Stutterheim, 1993) so it might be that Chinese adjust to the particular perspectivisation of the target language. The problem with this hypothesis is, however, that it has been shown that becoming native-like in this particular domain (perspectivisation) is one of the latest developments in an L2 (Carroll and von Stutterheim, this volume). We will need more detailed analyses about the influence of perspective taking on the use of linguistic means on the one hand, and the difficulty of acquiring those linguistic means on the other, before we can give a satisfying answer to this question.

The fact that the French learner narratives are most coherent, resulting in most frequent use of pronominal forms validates the second suggestion of Véronique et al. (2000) that the construction of the narrative will influence over-explicitation. However, their suggestion works only up to a certain level: the next finding is the fact that learners of French, once felicitous conditions are created, use pronominal forms 100%, whereas learners of German, even in these felicitous conditions use pronominal forms in only 86% of the cases. We showed that this result is related to the fact that learners of German have a harder time acquiring the German pronominal system than learners of French and English. Thus, the finding seems to validate Véronique et al.'s 1st suggestion, i.e., that lexical means are acquired before grammatical means. We would like to note here, however, that the means as such (pronouns) have been acquired, but that their use is hindered by the fact that pronouns in German have to be marked for gender and case. Adult learners, being very much aware of possible ambiguity problems when using a wrongly marked pronominal form, will resort to nominal forms in a much higher proportion of the cases in German than in French or English.

A final finding deals with variation across target languages concerning a preference for certain form-function pairs. Thus, our Chinese learners took up the use of bare nouns to maintain reference in English and German where these forms do also occur in the input, and the use of dislocations in French with the function of topic-promoting. This observed variation shows that second language learners are highly sensitive to corresponding forms and functions in source and target language.

The important question to be asked related to this finding is: given that they are highly sensitive to corresponding forms between source and target, why do Chinese not use more zero anaphora in German where they consist of 26% of the forms? The answer to this question may be twofold: First, the use of zero anaphora in German is highly constrained and much more likely to occur in narrative situations of the type we are looking at than in everyday speech. As a result, Chinese may not have had as much input data containing such uses of zero anaphora. Second, having gone through an earlier period where they omit elements, Chinese may at this later stage have realised that the licencing of zero anaphora in European languages is more restricted than in Chinese.

In sum, this paper found that over-explicitation indeed occurs in learner varieties, but that the importance of the over-explicitation is variable depending on source-target language pairs. A large number of factors seems to play a role in the level of over-explicitation found, such as the way in which the discourse is constructed and the difficulty of particular linguistic means necessary for reference maintenance and disambiguation. A number of questions, such as, "why is it easier for a learner to construct a more coherent narrative in French than in German" remains, and will be taken up in future studies.

Appendix

Description of the picture sequences

Horse story

(1) A horse is running in a meadow in the direction of a fence.
(2) He arrives at the fence and stands still. There is a bird on the fence and a cow on the other side.
(3) The horse is jumping over the fence. The bird and the cow are watching.
(4) The horse is lying down on the other side of the fence. One rail of the fence is broken. The bird and the cow are watching.
(5) The horse is standing. The cow is bandaging one of his legs. The bird is holding a first-aid kit.

Cat story

(1) There is a nest on the branch of a tree with three baby birds in the nest and a mother bird standing on the nest.
(2) A cat has arrived at the bottom of the tree and is looking at the nest. The mother bird is flying away.
(3) The cat is sitting down, still looking at the nest.
(4) The cat is climbing up the tree. A dog appears in the background.
(5) The cat has reached the nest. The dog has grabbed it by the tail. The mother bird is coming back to the nest, holding a worm in its beak.
(6) The mother bird is back on the nest. The dog is chasing the cat away.

Notes

1. NE: a sentence final particle marking that sentence is a question.
2. MA: topic marker

References

Ahrenholz, Bernt
1998 *Modalität und Diskurs. Instruktionen auf deutsch und italienisch.* Tübingen: Stauffenburg Verlag.

Carroll, Mary, and Christiane von Stutterheim
1993 The representation of spatial configurations in English and German and the grammatical structure of locative and anaphoric expressions. *Linguistics*, 31: 1011-1042.

Chini, Marina
1998 L'emploi de la subordination chez des apprenants germanophones d'italien: entre agrégation et intégration. Paper presented at the Euroconference: The structure of learner language. From pragmatics to syntax: Organizational principles of second language acquisition. Maratea, September.

Givón, Talmy
1983 Topic continuity in spoken discourse. In: Talmy Givón (ed.) *Topic Continuity in Discourse: A Quantitative Cross-Language Study.* Amsterdam: John Benjamins.

Givón, Talmy
1993 *English Grammar: A Function-Based Introduction.* Amsterdam: John Benjamins.

Gundel, Jeannette, and Elaine Tarone
1983 Language transfer and the acquisition of pronominal anaphora. In: Susan M. Gass and Larry Selinker (eds.), *Language Transfer in Language Learning.* London/New York/Tokyo: Newbury House.

Hendriks, Henriëtte
2000 The acquisition of topic marking in L1 Chinese and L1 and L2 French. *Studies in Second Language Acquisition*, 22: 369-397.

Hickmann, Maya
1995 Discourse organization and the development of reference to person, space, and time. In: Paul Fletcher and Brian MacWhinney (eds.), *The Handbook of Child Language.* Oxford: Blackwell.

Hickmann, Maya, Henriëtte Hendriks, Françoise Roland, and James Liang
1996 The marking of new information in children's narratives: A comparison of English, French, German and Mandarin Chinese. *Journal of Child Language*, 23: 591-619.

Hickmann, Maya, and Henriëtte Hendriks
1999 Cohesion and anaphora in children's narratives: A comparison of English, French, German and Mandarin Chinese. *Journal of Child Language*, 26: 419-452.

Hickmann, Maya, and Françoise Roland
1990   Topiques et sujets dans les récits d'enfants français. Paper presented at the third conference of the Réseau Européen de Laboratoires sur l'Acquisition des Langues, Bielefeld, Germany.

Huang, James
1984   On the distribution and reference of empty pronouns. *Linguistic Inquiry*, 15: 531-574.

Huang, Yan
1994   *The Syntax and Pragmatics of Anaphora: A Study with Special Reference to Chinese*. (Cambridge Studies in Linguistics, 70.) Cambridge: Cambridge University Press.

Jaeggli, Osvaldo, and Ken Safir
1989   The null subject parameter and parametric theory. In: Osvaldo Jaeggli and Ken Safir (eds.), *The Null Subject Parameter*, 1-44. Dordrecht: Kluwer.

Jin, HongGang
1994   Topic-prominence and subject-prominence in L2 acquisition: Evidence of English-to-Chinese typological transfer. *Language Learning*, 44: 101-122.

Kempe, Vera, and Brian MacWhinney
1998   Acquisition of Russian and German case marking. *Studies in Second Language Acquisition*, 20: 543-587.

Klein, Wolfgang, and Clive Perdue
1992   *Utterance Structure: Developing Grammars Again*. Amsterdam: John Benjamins.

Lambrecht, Knud
1981   *Topic, Antitopic and Verb Agreement in Non-Standard French*. Amsterdam: John Benjamins.

Lambrecht, Knud
1994   *Information Structure and Sentence Form: Topic, Focus and the Mental Representations of Discourse Referents*. (Cambridge Studies in Linguistics, 71.) Cambridge: Cambridge University Press.

Li, Charles, and Sandra Thompson
1981   *Mandarin Chinese: A Functional Reference Grammar*. Berkeley: University of California Press.

Muñoz, Carmen
2000   The over-explicitation of personal reference in L2 narratives. Paper presented at the Euroconference: Information structure, linguistic structure and the dynamics of acquisition, San Féliu de Guixols, October.

von Stutterheim, Christiane and Monique Lambert
    forthc.   Crosslinguistic analysis of temporal perspectives in text production. In: Henriëtte Hendriks (ed.), *The Structure of Learner Varieties*. Berlin/New York: Mouton de Gruyter.

Véronique, Daniel, Mary Carroll, and Christiane von Stutterheim
    2000   Anaphoric linkage. Paper presented at the Euroconference: Information structure, linguistic structure and the dynamics of acquisition, San Féliu de Guixols, October.

White, Lydia
    1985   The "pro-drop" parameter in adult second language acquisition. *Language Learning*, 35: 47-61.

Williams, John
    1988   Zero anaphora in second language acquisition. A comparison among three varieties of English. *Studies in Second Language Acquisition*, 10: 339-370.

Yuan, Bo-ping
    1997   Asymmetry of null subjects and null objects in Chinese speakers' L2 English. *Studies in Second Language Acquisition*, 19: 467-497.

Crosslinguistic comparison and second language acquisition: an approach to Topic and Left-detachment constructions from the perspective of spoken language

Rosanna Sornicola

1. Introduction

This paper will discuss a perspective of research on Topicalisations and Left-Dislocations (henceforward TNs and LDs, respectively)[1], which brings together results from different domains. These structures, in fact, have been extensively and separately studied in various areas of linguistics, such as analysis of individual spoken languages – or spoken language *tout court* – typology and language acquisition. The approach presented here will possibly show the bias of research interests in spontaneous spoken language, which over time have been reoriented towards cross-linguistic analysis and therefore towards typology. This partiality is perhaps inevitable, but may turn out to be not entirely misleading.

The position endorsed here is that the integration of the three domains is highly desirable, although it may prove controversial. One of the major difficulties in interdisciplinary work is the comparison of unrelated frameworks, which requires singling out and translating similarities and dissimilarities in assumptions, analytic tools and objectives. For example, in the framework of the research group on "the structure of learner language", TNs and LDs have been considered as a particular aspect of "referential movement", a choice betraying a number of theoretical assumptions that are not without implications on the results obtained and their use in other domains. However, in general the results gathered in this area of research display interesting convergence with those achieved in the area of spontaneous spoken language.

The structures in question pose a number of descriptive and interpretative problems, the more so in that there is no unitary theoretical and methodological framework underlying their investigation. Here the discussion will concern:

(a) the typology of constructions with TN or LD;
(b) a critical assessment of three functional models that have been widely used for their study, i.e. Li and Thompson's, Chafe's and Lambrecht's;
(c) some possible implications of points (a) and (b) for the acquisition of L2.

2. The typology of TN and LD structures

TN and LD structures will be examined here from three angles: (1) their formal properties, (2) their cross-linguistic occurrence in typologically different languages, (3) their pragmatic properties.

2.1. Formal properties of TN and LD structures

A major problem in the study of formal properties of TN and LD structures is the determination of a cross-linguistic grid balancing two diverging prerequisites: on the one hand such grid should include sufficient constraints to avoid that patterns with a loose similarity can be grouped together, on the other hand it should have sufficient flexibility to accommodate the diverse patterns from various languages into a unitary frame. This, in fact, is a general difficulty in typological research, obviously with an important theoretical dimension. Of special interest, for example, seems the setting of the cut-off point for structural diversity. But there are empirical dimensions as well. Not only does the determination of a suitable grid of formal properties set criteria for class inclusion, it also provides a tool for further description of empirical phenomena that have been never observed before.

A few considerations concerning the structural analysis of TNs and LDs can help clarifying these points. Both types of constructions show a very general property in typologically different languages, which may be described in terms of a given constituent that happens to be outside the proper sentence domain, in what has been defined in generative literature "the leftmost sentence periphery/edge". This is hardly a theory-"neutral" account, if there may be any. First of all, the expression "happens to be" has been used here to dodge the old thorny theoretical question of whether the topicalised/left-dislocated constituent is in situ and consequently whether it implies movement from another sentence position. Whatever the treatment of TNs and LDs in recent generative works, this problem has fuelled controversies for years and one might agree that the dispute has an interesting theoretical content, which goes beyond the more technical aspects of the generative models (see here § 3; cf. also Sornicola 2001). In this paper the "happen-to be" and the "leftmost sentence periphery" formulations will be used in their most intuitive contents of – respectively – a constituent being in a certain position and the sentence space beyond that determined by the Subject - Predicate relationship. Accordingly, the terms "detachment/detached" instead of "dislocation/dislocated" will be used. These formulations are broad enough to accommodate the diversity of typological data presented here.

Languages differ as to the categorial nature and the number of constituents that can occur in the leftmost sentence periphery. They also differ in the morphological markings of constituents in that position. Finally, languages vary as to the degree of grammaticalisation of TN/LD structures.

Although the constructions taken into account as candidates to represent TN/LD structures show a certain amount of microstructural diversity, they share at least two properties, of formal and pragmatic nature, respectively, which can be defined as follows:

Formal property
A given constituent finds itself isolated/confined to the leftmost periphery of the sentence.

Pragmatic property
In both TN/LD constructions the constituent in the above mentioned position is a centre of attention, i.e. it conveys an highlighting function.

Thus the set of constructions that will be examined ranges from "hanging topic" to LDs of various kinds. Sentences such as (1) and (2) will not be included in this analysis, in that they have a constituent in P1 position that is still part of the proper sentence domain; in both cases this constituent occupies a non-canonical position in an anterior area of the sentence proper domain; moreover in both cases the constituent in P1 is a focus of contrast, not a highlighted element.

(1) *Das habe ich nicht gesagt*
     'THAT isn't what I said'

(2) *Tuo   fratello   ho incontrato, non   tua   madre*
     your   brother   I.have met   not   your   mother
     'I met YOUR BROTHER, not YOUR MOTHER'

Although TNs and LDs differ in their structures, they share the property of having a constituent outside the sentence proper domain. This seems to be correlated to an interesting macro-structural (textual) property, which is reflected in a large number of different languages: TNs/LDs mark the sentence orientation towards the left context (as well as RD structures mark the sentence orientation towards the right context). Possibly, this is an iconic property, as are prosodic properties with a wide distribution across languages, like the occurrence of a pause and/or a change in the intonational contour to mark the fact that the topicalised/detached constituent belongs to the leftmost sentence periphery. One could think, in fact, that these prosodic devices are spontaneous "natural" tools for delimiting different sentence areas.

However, the languages investigated here differ in their microstructural formal properties, that is in the syntactic means they exploit to code the relationship between the topicalised/detached constituent and the sentence proper domain. These means offer an appropriate case for identifying typological differences.

2.2. TNs and L/RDs in the languages of the world

TNs and LDs occur in Indo-European languages in all diachronic stages for which we have documentation. TNs conform to the structure in (3):

(3)   X // YWZ

where X is the constituent isolated in the leftmost sentence periphery, YWZ is an unspecified string of constituents defining the sentence proper domain. Note that in current descriptions no anaphoric relation between X and any of the constituents YWZ is envisaged (for an attempt to recognise here special coreferential relations, of a "part-whole" type, see Sornicola 1984). However, between X and at least one of the constituents of the string YWZ (which represents the sentence proper domain) a relation of semantic contiguity holds (for example a part-whole relation) or one of "sloppy identity co-reference" (cf. Sornicola 1984). The semantic role of X may be that of a "peripheral" element, carrying the semantic role of a Locative or Cause/Instrument (cf. (4a), (4b), respectively). However, often no exact relation between X and any of the constituents in the sentence proper domain can be determined:

(4)   a.   *La scuola //*   *hanno*   *fatto*   *delle*   *palazzine*
           the school   they-have   made   some   buildings
           nuove
           new

'At school, they have made some new buildings'

b.   *La benzina //   è   scoppiato   un   incendio*
       the petrol   is   broken out   a   fire
'The petrol, a fire has broken out'

In modern Indo-European languages, type (3) seems confined to informal/unplanned styles of spoken languages or to written texts of poorly educated speakers.

LDs can be represented by a structure like (5):

(5)   X // Y Pro Z

where X and Pro are coreferential, Y and Z stand for any string of constituents. This structure has been widely investigated for both Romance and Slavonic languages, especially in their contemporary synchronic stages, where it is characteristic of – though not uniquely confined to – spoken registers:

(6)   a.   *Cet élève // je l'aime bien*
              'This pupil, I love him very much'
      b.   *Mio   marito //   lo   amo   molto*
              my   husband   him   I.love   much
              'My husband, I love him much'

(7)   a.   *A   Lena // ona   skoro   pridet*
              But   Lena   she   soon   will.arrive:3SG
              'But Lena, she soon will arrive'
      b.   *Miša // emu   vse   ravno*
              Miša   to.him   all   equal
              'It is all one to Miša' (Zemskaja 1973: 239)

The structure (5) is also documented in spoken registers of contemporary Germanic languages:

(8) a. *Den Kerl, den habe ich zu oft gesehen*
'That guy, I have seen him too often now'
(Scherpenisse 1986: 45)
b. *Q: What are the people like to work with, the drivers and that*
A: The driver, he is really friendly (Miller and Weinert 1998: 238)
c. *John, I haven't met him recently*

LDs also occur in Indo-European languages with VSO basic order, though under special conditions: for example, in Irish sentences with the structural representation (5) appear only when the X constituent has a heavy structure with an embedded relative sentence; on the other hand, in Welsh they do not seem to be constrained by this restriction; they are, however, rather rare:

(9) *Fy   stumog   i   mae   hi*
    my   stomach   Aux. Pro is   Pro 3SGF
    fel   crempog
    like pancake
'My stomach, it's like a pancake' (Watkins 1991: 334)

Among VSO languages type (5) is in no way confined to Celtic languages. Thus the evidence from Arabic shows that (5) is not only frequent, but also plays a fundamental role in determining the well-known SV(O) pattern which is concurrent to VS(O), as in (10a):

(10) a. *Bini   h'lāl,   rḥal[at]   sab^c isnīn*
        Bani   Hilāl   travelled.3MSG[3FSG] seven   years
        'The Bani Hilāl, [they] wandered for seven years'
     b. *il-'ḥilim,   a^{c}ād[-ah] ^{c}ala   ux-ūh*
        the-dream   related.3MSG[-it]   to   brother-his
        'The dream, he related it to his brother' (Ingham 1991: 723-724)

Type (3) may be found in various Arabic dialects:

(10) c.   'iḥna, ykūn   al-ᶜiris   ib-šaṭṭ
             we   must.be.3MSG   the-wedding   at-Shaṭṭ
             iz-zaḥāmi
             al-Zaḥāmi
             'We, the wedding should be at Shaṭṭ al Zaḥāmi' = 'Our wedding should be...' (Ingham 1991: 726)

It has been argued that in languages with V-initial structures as basic/dominant orders, TNs/LDs are crucial for the determination of concurring S/O-initial orders. As is well known, such concurring orders are fairly normal in V-initial languages (cf. Greenberg 1963). A further confirmation is provided by Iaai, a Melanesian language spoken in Ouvéa, one of the Loyalty islands (New Caledonia). In Iaai V-initial orders are dominant, but structures with a NP in the leftmost sentence periphery also frequently occur, with NP resumed by a pronoun in the sentence proper domain, which carries S-function:[2]

(11)   wanakat //   a   me   walak
        child   he   AspM   play
        'The child, he is playing' (Ozanne-Rivierre 1976: 132)

The pattern in (11) conveys a PF of highlighting, while (12a) is the unmarked sentence:

(12)   a.   a me walak wanakat
              'The child is playing' (Ozanne-Rivierre 1976: 132)

Type (5) is not confined to inflectional languages, as is clear from its occurrence not only in Iaai, but also in many African languages. In Zarma (according to Greenberg's classification, a Nilo-Saharian language) the syntactic type in (12b) has the function of highlighting a given constituent:

(12)   b.   wándíó   bé:ròó à   néè
                 girl   big   she   say-PERF
                 'The big girl, she said' (Tersis 1972: 195)

Similar structures exist in Banda-Linda (an Ubanguian language, belonging – in Greenberg's classification – to the Adamawa-Eastern sub-group of the Niger-Congo family). Differences may occur as to the GF carried by the anaphoric pronoun. In Zarma detachment structures are found only when the GF of the resumptive pronoun is S, while in Banda-Linda any GF can be involved in the anaphoric chain.[3]

(13) a. cè   nje   cè   wis   n   wi
         he   too   he   PERF.know   it   NEG.know
         né
         EMPptc
         'He too doesn't know at all'
    b. m   bàle   m   ì
        I   alone   I   IMPERF.resist
        'I alone, I resist' (Cloarec-Heiss 1986: 255)

The wide occurrence of structure (5) in morphologically and syntactically different language types could make one think that it is almost universal. But this may prove to be a premature conclusion. The functionalist literature of the Seventies called attention on the fact that Chinese and Japanese lack structure (5) and only have structure (3), as in examples (14) and (15), respectively:[4]

(14) Neì-xie   shùmu shù-shēn   dà
     those   tree tree-trunk big
     'Those trees, the trunks are big' (Li and Thompson 1976: 462)

(15) Gakkoo-wa   buku-ga   isogasi-kat-ta
     school-TM   I-SM   busy-PST
     'School, I was busy' (Li and Thompson 1976: 462)

The typological situation of these and other Far-Eastern languages, however, may be more complicated. Topic "Chinese-style" was defined by Chafe (1976: 50) as the sentence element that "sets a spatial, temporal, or individual framework within which the main predication holds". Chafe also observes that "Chinese seems to express the information in these cases [i.e. cases like (14)] in a way that does not coincide with anything available in English" (1976: 50). This definition has influenced recent grammatical descriptions of other Far-eastern languages like Japanese and Korean. As to Japanese, Hinds (1986: 161) notes that "it is difficult to argue that dislocation in the sense of Ross 1967 [i.e. dislocation as a movement phenomenon, where the moved constituent leaves a trace behind it] actually exists in Japanese. Many examples of what appears to be dislocation may be adduced, but it is quite possible that these are merely stutter starts or other types of disfluency". He quotes the following example, posing the problem of whether the NP *kono shashin* can be really considered a "moved element" and *kore wa* its "trace":

(16) *kono   shashin,   aa,   kore   wa   saki   hodo*
     this   picture   uh   this   TM   before   extent
     no   shinkansen   no,   konoo, okuri   no
     LK   train   LK   uh   send-off   LK
     tsuzuki   mitai   desu   kedo   ne
     continuation   seems   COP   but   EM
    'This picture, ah this one looks like it's a continuation of that send-off picture (we saw) before, doesn'it' (Hinds 1986: 162)

Examples like (16) show the difficulty that has to be faced when one takes into account the intermediate levels between competence and performance, which are crucial for the study of spontaneous spoken language. In fact, in such cases a clear-cut dividing line between "false start" and full grammaticalisation of a given construction may not always be traced.

Korean, like Chinese and Japanese, has TN-constructions of type (3), i.e. constructions without anaphoric relations between X and any constituent in the proper sentence domain. Such structures are often characterised by a relation of semantic contiguity, as is clear in (17):[5]

(17) Yongho-ka   kho-ka   khu-ta
     Yongho-NM   nose-NM   big-DC
     'As for Yongho, his nose is big' (Sohn 1994: 193)

More generally, the T-element establishes the set of predication:

(18) Minca, æ   Minca-ka   kyothong-sako
     Minca ah   Minca-NM   traffic-accident
     na-ss-eyo
     occur-PST-POL
     'Minca, ah, Minca had a traffic accident!' (Sohn 1994: 188)

(Note that in addition to its case-marking value, the -*ka* marker may be a topic-marker, like in (17) or a focus-marker, like in (18) [cf. Sohn 1994: 193].)

The following examples show once again the difference between TN- and LD-types of structure: whatever the semantic role of X, this constituent has no anaphoric resumption in the subsequent part of the sentence:

(19) Ku   totwuk-un   nay-ka cap-ass-ta
     The   thief-TC   I-NM   catch-PST-DC
     'As for that thief, I caught him' (Sohn 1994: 192)

(20) mikwuk-ulo-pwuthe-nun   manh-un   sangphwum-i
     America-DIR-from-TC   much-MD   commodity-NM
     swuip-toy-ess-ta
     import-become-PST-DC
     'From America, many commodities were imported' (Sohn 1994: 192)

However, an example like (21) shows that structures may be found with an anaphorical relation defined between X and one of the constituents in the proper sentence domain. Such structures resemble the LD type. What is involved in this case is not a pronominal anaphor, but a repetition (copy) of the whole NP; this therefore appears twice, in the leftmost periphery with a T-marker and in one of the positions of the sentence proper domain with an accusative marker:

(21)   *I*   *sacin-un,*   *nay-ka caknyen-ey*   *i*   *sacin-ul*
      This   photo-TC   I-NM   last-year-at   this   photo-AC
      ccik-ess-eyo
      take-PST-POL
      'As for this picture, I took it last year' (Sohn 1994: 195)

As in the case of the Japanese example, however, the degree of grammaticalisation of this type is not clear. It is perhaps not entirely implausible to consider that anaphorical relations are a secondary property of detached constructions, in that they are possibly related to specific different pronominalisation strategies of languages, rather than to TN or LD processes as such.

2.3. Pragmatic properties of TN and LD structures: some critical considerations

In 2.1. for both TNs and LDs the pragmatic property was defined whereby the constituent in the leftmost sentence periphery is a centre of attention, i.e. conveys a highlighting function. This generalisation, however, is far from being self-evident, as comparability of PFs is even more controversial than that of GFs. The first difficulty is that – in order to be ascertained – functions like 'highlighting' require a macro-structural analysis. But crosslinguistic comparison of macro-structures is not an obvious operation, for various reasons. A second difficulty is that we do not know to what extent the structural coding of PFs is a purely natural strategy: it is reasonable to think that – at least partially – this is determined by "cultural" factors, like rhetorical or stylistic normativisation. Finally, the coding of PFs is highly variable across speakers of the same language (cf. 4.2.1.). For all these reasons the generalisation about the highlighting value of TNs and LDs should be considered tentative.

3. Three models for the explanation of TN and LD structures

In this section three functional models will be reviewed that have tried a new departure from the traditional conception of the sentence as a structure with the basic grammatical relations of Subject, Predicate and Object. Although sharing a number of general assumptions and a more or less pronounced interest in typology, they have offered different "explanations" of TNs and LDs.

The rationale for confining the discussion to functional models is that these have tried to integrate the various levels of syntax, semantics and pragmatics into a broader analysis, instead of assuming an autonomous level of syntax as the main locus for the study of grammatical relations. This multi-level perspective, in fact, seems more fruitful for the interdisciplinary approach proposed here.

A review of the three models does not seem an unmotivated digression, as it will allow us to single out some theoretical problems that have some implications not only for the study of TNs and LDs but also for the study of the syntax-pragmatics interface in research on typology, spoken language and second language acquisition.

3.1. Li and Thompson's model

Li and Thompson (1976) proposed a main typological partition of languages in "Subject-prominent" and "Topic-prominent" (henceforward referred to as SPL and TPL, respectively). They identified a set of grammatical characters implied by the two properties and differentiating the two groups of languages:

(i)   Surface Coding: TPLs have surface coding for T, but not necessarily for S;
(ii) Incidence of Passive Construction: in TPLs PCs do not occur or are marginal, while they are common among SPLs;
(iii) Dummy Subjects can be found in SPLs, but not in TPLs;
(iv) Pervasive Double Subjects (i.e. structures x, y) only occur in TPLs;

(v)   Control of co-reference in TPLs is triggered by T, not by S;
(vi) V-final feature is more typical of TPLs;
(vii) Constraints on Topic constituent: in SPLs there are severe constraints on the accessibility of a constituent to T-function, while these lack in TPLs ;
(viii) Basicness of Topic - Comment sentences: in Li and Thompson's words, "Perhaps the most striking difference between a TPL and a non-TPL is the extent to which the Topic - Comment sentence can be considered to be part of the repertoire of basic sentence types in the former but not in the latter" (1976: 471).

These properties have different logical status. (i), (v) and (vii) are statements about structural properties, while all the remaining characters concern frequency. Some properties can be inferred from others: (vii) is perhaps presupposed by (viii) and (iv) is presupposed by (vii). We have already observed here that the so-called "double-subject" construction can be frequent (though perhaps not pervasive) in spontaneous spoken registers of languages considered to be S-prominent. This not only disproves (iv), but also weakens the validity of (vii) and (viii).

More generally, properties (i)-(viii) can be questioned as criteria for typological identification of SPLs and TPLs. A first problem concerns their empirical adequacy: they were possibly selected – at least in part – on the evidence of simplified data from idealised written styles. This obviously infirms typological modelling. As a consequence, the actual classification shows areas of inconsistency, which makes it necessary to resort to the use of "S-prominency" and "T-prominency" as features with a [+/-] specification. Thus Filipino languages are reported to be neither SP nor TP, Korean and Japanese both TP and SP. But such ad-hoc solution trivialises the dichotomy itself. A second problem concerns the nature of the implicational relation between properties (i)-(viii) and the features of S-prominency and T-prominency. It is possible to ask to what extent the occurrence of passive constructions and dummy subjects is correlated to S-prominency in a significant way, i.e. to what extent this correlation has an explicative import or is a mere coincidence. For example, the fact that Chinese does not have anaphoric chains, which is supposed to be true in SPLs, may be due to specific strategies of pronominalisation without any systematic correlation with the TP feature:[6]

(23) xià   chē   yǐhòu, Ø   xiān   dào   Dàhuá Fàndiàn,
     descend vehicle after   first   arrive Dahua hotel
     xiūxi   yǐhuǐr, Ø   chī   le   wǔ   fàn,
     rest   a while   eat   PRF   afternoon   food
     jiù   Ø   qù   kāi   huì,   sàn   le   huì,   Ø
     then   go   open   meeting adjourn PRF   meeting
     méi   shì   le,   Ø kěyǐ   dào   hú   biān   kàn
     not   matter PRF   can   to   lake   side   see

'After (we) get off the train, (we)'ll go to the Dahia Hotel first and rest a while. After we eat lunch, (we)'ll attend the meeting. When the meeting ends, (we) have nothing to do, so (we) can go to the lake' (Li and Thompson 1981: 660)

The same question could be posed for the V-final property in T-prominent languages. Statement (v) is a mere observation about frequency of V in final position in TPLs, but V-finality cannot be considered a diagnostic tool for class inclusion, as there are many SOV languages that definitely do not meet the other conditions envisaged for T-prominency. In Kannada, a Dravidian language with SOV basic order, both types (3) and (5) are documented: see examples (24) and (25)-(26), respectively:[7]

(24) Nimma   manege   baralikke:no   iSTa
     you-POS   home-DAT   come-INF-DAT-TOP   liking
     'As for coming to your house, (I / we) certainly like it' (cf. Sridhar 1990: 144)

(25) naTara:juna:?   avanu ella: tinnuttane
     Nataraju-QCl   he   all   eat-PST-3SG
     'As for Nataraju, he eats everything' (Sridhar 1990: 144)

(26) | *S'aŋkara* | *avanige* | *sa:la* | *koTTavaru* | *ya:ru* |
|---|---|---|---|---|
| Shankara | he-DAT | loan | give-PST-they | who-INC |
| *iduvaregu:* | *va:pas paDedilla* | | | |
| so far-INC | back get-PST-NEG | | | |

'Shankara, no one who has lent him (money) has got it back yet' (Sridhar 1990: 145)

The picture is made more complicate by the possibility of structures like (27), where X is anaphorically resumed by a copy of NP:

(27) | *eLeni:ru* | *andare* | *tipaTu:rina* | *eLeni:re,* |
|---|---|---|---|
| tender-coconut | TM | Tipatur-GEN | coconut-EMP |
| *swami* | | | |
| sir | | | |

'As for tender coconut, Sir, (there is) only the Tipatur one' (Sridhar 1990: 143)

Types like (26) and (27) may be due to spontaneous universal processes like the one exemplified in the French sentence (28):

(28) *Cette tête là // je pense que j'ai déjà vu cette grande blonde-là quelque part* (Hirschbühler 1975, quoted from Altman 1981: 26)

It is true that observations like those presented so far only falsify the truth of possible statements like: "If a language is SOV it must be T-prominent" and not of statements like "If a language is T-prominent, it must have SOV order". However, Li and Thompson's model was built on a too restricted corpus of languages to allow the latter implicational generalisation.

3.2. Chafe's model

In addition to defining Topic "Chinese style", Chafe (1976: 51-53) also introduced the notion of Ts as "premature subjects", with examples from a *corpus* of narrative texts in Caddo, an American Indian language spoken in Oklahoma. The fundamental idea is that "a topic would be – or might have originated as – a subject which is chosen too soon and not as smoothly integrated into the following sentences" (1976: 52). What is presented here is a *genetic* or *dynamic* model of TN processes, which is built on hypotheses about how speakers organise "chunks of knowledge" into a sentence.

According to Chafe, the speaker would first divide the global mental content in sentence-seized pieces and would then proceed to build up the sentence, choosing the case frame of the sentence and the noun included in the case frame as the subject of the sentence. Chafe's hypothesis is that these two options are implemented more or less simultaneously. The assumption that they are interdependent seems a delicate point: "the choice of a case frame provides candidates for subject status, while conversely the choice of a subject constrains the possible case frames". Therefore it is claimed that "a speaker is able to think simultaneously of the most effective framework of cases to express what he has in mind and the most effective way to package it in terms of subject" (1976: 51). However, Chafe admits that "it is not unusual... for speakers to depart from this simultaneity by choosing – and in fact uttering – the subject before the case frame has been chosen" (1976: 51). He then reports a few instances of what he considers "premature subjects". These exhibit various degrees of integration of the noun into the case frame, ranging from a premature subject which is later inserted in the sentence case frame, to the complete non-integration of the subject in the following sentence. In terms of our discussion the examples conform to either structure (5) or (3).

Chafe's concluding remarks are especially interesting in a perspective of research that tries to combine theoretical and applied aspects of TN and LD constructions:

One might think of calling such prematurely chosen subjects topics, or even speculating that the origin of topics as distinct from subjects lies in this kind of aberration in the timing of the processes of sentence construction... Some languages seem to allow their speakers to do quite easily what was illustrated for Caddo above. Caddo speakers seem to put sentences together in this fashion quite frequently, and not to be disconcerted by it. On this basis Caddo might be regarded as at least one kind of "topic-prominent" language, but in a quite different sense from Chinese (Chafe 1976: 52-53).

Chafe's model – like Li and Thompson's – is built on the syntactic notion of 'sentence'. TNs and LDs, however, can be studied from the vantage point of the pragmatic notion of 'utterance', as this has an inherent linear and dynamic dimension that is absent in the syntactic notion of sentence. As is well known, one of the differences between "utterance" and "sentence" is that the first is closer to the level of processual arrangement of speech, i.e. to actual speech production, while the latter deals with the abstract and static levels of grammatical relations and with their mapping onto constituent structure. The two notions therefore imply different conceptions of linearity, in that "utterance" involves the more empirically oriented representation of constituents occurring one-after-the-other, while "sentence" concerns the representation of abstract templates or patterns of order. The processual dimension of linearity, in fact, plays an important role in the formation of TDs and LDs and thus can contribute to a better understanding of these structures.

The functional models under examination collapsed the utterance vs sentence distinction as they projected the static representation of the sentence role frame onto utterance arrangement. As a consequence, structures like (3) and (5) are considered "aberrations" instead of the results of phenomena interesting per se and with their own specific reasons. There are other problematic consequences, however. One concerns the adequacy of the structural description: the constituent isolated in the leftmost periphery is necessarily assigned a canonical GF, like S, O etc., as it should necessarily have one of these relations if it were integrated into the proper sentence domain. Yet such an assignment can be only based on a (disputable) conceptual equivalence between two different structures.

The typological implications of the model require further remarks. The fact that structures like (3) and (5) are considered "aberrations" confined to particular languages – like Caddo or others – does not help the recognition that they are widely diffused in spontaneous spoken registers of many typologically different languages, i.e. that they cross typological groupings. Apart from this general observation, two additional objections could be raised. Phenomena like those described for Caddo are seen as a peculiar potentiality of some languages, but it is not clear whether this potentiality is determined by internal (i.e. structural) or external (i.e. cultural) factors. Moreover, the postulation of a different kind of T-prominency from that of Chinese makes a global understanding of the general property of T-prominency more problematic.

The perspective adopted here is that (a) TNs and LDs are not the results of language-specific potentialities; (b) there are not different forms of T-prominency; (c) cultural factors play a fundamental role in the way universal strategies of spontaneous spoken languages are grammaticalised.

3.3. Lambrecht's model

Though apparently presenting a radically alternative perspective, Lambrecht's model has hidden similarities with Chafe's. The starting point of the discussion is that

> against what seems to be a widespread assumption, ... the grammatical topic-marking construction referred to as NP "detachment" or "dislocation" is not some kind of structural anomaly which tends to develop under the pressure of historical change and which grammars strive to eliminate by absorbing it into the canonical sentence model in which all semantic arguments of a predicate appear as syntactic arguments in a clause (1994: 192).

This observation is to welcome, as it is fully consistent with the logic of spoken languages. Lambrecht is aware that "languages with an apparently well-established SVO or other canonical constituent pattern have a strong tendency to violate this pattern under specific pragmatic conditions by placing lexical topic NPs, especially potential subjects, outside the clause... In certain languages, including spoken French, this tendency is so strong that the canonical pattern is hardly ever used in spontaneous speech" (1994: 195). Accordingly, he quotes several examples from SVO languages; of particular interest is the discussion of English data from spontaneous spoken corpora, like the following English ones:

(29) *That isn't the typical family anymore. The typical family today, the husband and the wife both work* (from a TV interview; Lambrecht 1994: 193)

(30) *Tulips, you have to plant new bulbs every year?* (Lambrecht 1994: 193)

(31) *Other languages, you don't just have straight tones like that* (from a lecture in an introductory course; Lambrecht 1994: 193)

These examples provide further evidence to the idea that TNs and LDs can be found across different language types.

However, Lambrecht's assumption that "it is the reinterpretation of detached NPs as "regular" subjects that constitutes the anomaly" seems too extreme. This view is related to the basic hypothesis that TNs and LDs conform to the "Principle of the Separation of Role and Reference", according to which "the lexical representation of a topic referent takes place separately from the designation of the referent's role as an argument in a proposition...The communicative motivation of this principle can be captured in the form of a simple pragmatic maxim: "Do not introduce a referent and talk about it in the same clause" " (1994: 185).

Two distinct but interrelated justifications of the maxim are provided. The first is speaker-oriented and presents the psycholinguistic tenet that it is easier to build a complex sentence if the referential coding of a topic is independent from the syntactic coding of the proposition. The second justification is hearer-oriented and is based on the conjecture that the understanding of a message is easier if the identification of the topic is performed independently from the task to interpret the proposition about the topic (1994: 185). Thus Lambrecht comes to the conclusion that the reinterpretation of detached NPs as "regular" subjects and its generalisation across languages "would contradict the functional motivation for the detachment construction, which is precisely to keep lexical topic constituents outside the clauses in which their referents play the semantic and syntactic role of argument" (1994: 192).

Although different at a first sight, paradoxically Lambrecht's model presents the same problems discussed here for Chafe's. However, Lambrecht goes to the other extreme in considering that the canonical sentence is an anomaly. His functional principle of the Separation of Role and Reference poses several difficulties. It is too rigid and cannot account for a process that seems to have a more intricate origin in spoken language production and in which the role of the listener's understanding seems irrelevant. Its pragmatic justification, which relies on the greater ease of construction for the speaker and of understanding for the listener, seems a speculation unsupported so far by psycholinguistic evidence. Its typological and historical domains of application are equally unsubstantiated by significant statistical evidence. Furthermore, this model is also so general and abstract to be vacuous: it cannot explain, for example, why – although occurring across many different languages – TNs and LDs are more frequent in some languages than in others. This problem can hardly be tackled without dealing with sociolinguistic and individual differences among speakers of a given language, as well as with historical factors like the impact of traditions of written language (which are supported by schools, academies, etc.), ideologies, and so on. Lambrecht's principle pushes the potentialities of spoken language too far and without distinctions. It is matter for reflection, for example, that research on spoken languages like French and Italian has independently pointed to a sensible amount of cross-speaker variability. The perspective endorsed here is that the analysis of such variability is a better starting point to try to understand the nature and origin of TNs and LDs than extremely general functional principles (cf. 4.2.2. and 4.2.3.).

A further problem with Lambrecht's model is that the structural description of TNs and LDs is underspecified. The author denies the status of constituent to the detached NP, at least in some languages:

> in some languages at least, the detached topic NP cannot be a constituent – whether argument or adjunct – of the clause with which it is pragmatically associated. Rather it must be analyzed as a syntactically autonomous, extra-clausal element, whose relationship with the clause is not the grammatical relation of subject or object but the pragmatic relation of aboutness and relevance (Lambrecht 1994: 192-193).

Thus no structural relation at all is assigned to detached NPs, which are only endowed with the semantic property of aboutness. This seems an opposite choice to that of forcing GFs into detached NPs, as in Chafe's model. But the claim of syntactic autonomy of detached NPs, at least in some languages, is unconvincing: syntactic connectedness is not exclusively related to closely integrated GFs. Rather, it seems that connectedness of a special kind is at work here, which is most frequently coded by "part-whole" relations (cf. Sornicola 1984).

4. TN and LD structures in the studies of acquisition of L2
4.1. Some results emerged in the studies of acquisition of L2

Although research on TNs and LDs in the acquisition of L2 is not abundant, it raises issues which come across some theoretical and methodological aspects of the study of spoken language. Therefore it seems opportune to summarise its results, as they emerge in the works by Trévise 1986, Perdue, Deulofeu, Trévise 1992, Hendriks 2000.

In the studies mentioned above there is a consensus on the idea that TNs – and in particular LDs – develop at a stage beyond the acquisition of Basic Variety (but note that "topicalisation" here covers a broader class of syntactic phenomena than the term which has been used in this paper; it has in fact primarily a pragmatic and functional meaning).

In Trévise's words, "to study the potential influence of the devices used to structure utterances in spoken French on the acquisition/learning of a second language, it is necessary to look at the spontaneous speech of fairly advanced speakers who have gone beyond the pragmatic mode and who master enough of L2 syntactic structures to be able to alter the neutral SVO linear ordering" (1986: 193). Trévise also observes that "in the spontaneous acquisition of French as an L2... acquirers use subject topic + anaphoric subject pronoun from very early on, a device frequently used in French native input" (1986: 201; on this problem cf. also Perdue, Deulofeu and Trévise 1992: 297). However, the general trend emerged may require further evidence, as in three cases out of four the studies mentioned consider French as L2 and the range of L1 languages – though greater – is limited to Chinese, Spanish, English and Arabic.

The speakers investigated do not show a great amount of transfer phenomena from their L1 structures. Hendriks (2000: 384-387) observes that "learners of French tend not to use those constructions typical of a topic-prominent language"; moreover "transfers of clearly Chinese constructions are very rare in French L2". Trévise has more general considerations on this point: "transfer can never be a clear-cut explanation for a given morphosyntactic feature, but only one of the possible factors at play for some learners and some languages" (1986: 186). This view is attuned to the broader conclusions elaborated by Klein and Perdue, who maintain that "the interaction between intrinsic and contrastive (Source Language-Target Language) factors is then that the latter facilitate acquisition more or less, but structures are not acquired *simply* because the SL and TL are close in some respect: SL-TL comparisons will only get you some of the way – they are mediated by other factors, such as meaning and context" (1992: 335). These conclusions differ from Meisel's (1981: 47), according to whom L2 acquirers "are using the underlying canonical WO of L1 as a starting point in L2 acquisition and speech processing in the second language".

Trévise's work opens a stimulating scenario:

> The hypothesis would then be that French learners of a foreign language will typically not transfer everyday spoken French dislocations, but will rather resort to more 'neutral' topicalisation devices such as locative/existential or identificational constructions with the 'feeling' that there is a hierarchy in the transferability of various devices, in terms of L1-specificity or 'neutrality' (1986: 192).

Therefore for Trévise,

> Word order... seems to have a special status as far as language acquisition or loss are concerned, as if there were a L1 'hard core' more difficult to acquire in L2 and more readily lost... In short, it may be that informal pragmatic word order is not easily transferred, perhaps because it is not felt to be transferable (1986: 196-197 passim).

This hypothesis is fascinating but should be worked up in its various parts: it is not clear, for example, what it means that dislocations are a L1 "hard core". Moreover such hypothesis is at variance with some results of research in spontaneous spoken language, where it has emerged that: (a) TNs and LDs occur in *impromptu* speech, especially in argumentative textual progressions; (b) TNs and LDs have conspicuous cross-individual variability (cf. Sornicola 1981; Milano (forthcoming)), a point that has also been unsystematically noticed in the works on TNs and LDs in the acquisition of L2. In short, Trévise's hypothesis quoted above may have been influenced by two biases: the exclusive use of a narrative type of text and the limited number of speakers analyzed.

The three studies also agree in evidencing – though with different findings and solutions – that in the development of LDs in L2 a major problem is the form / function relationship. A methodological point that brings these works very close to the problems of research on spoken language is the choice to analyze the function/form relationship in parallel in groups of adult learners of L2 and of children learners of L1, as well as in groups of adult speakers of L1.

As far as function is concerned, according to Perdue, Deulofeu e Trévise (1992: 297) "pronoun-copy variants are a development, motivated by the need to make salient the NP in topic: re-introducing an entity in topic, and disambiguating entities from a preceding utterance who are potential subsequent topics" (this assumption is shared by Hendriks 2000).

Hendriks identifies two main functions of TNs and LDs in the three groups of speakers investigated (native speakers of French, native speakers of Chinese and Chinese speakers of French): (a) the reintroduction of an old referent and (b) making old a new referent. Although Hendriks observes that "the adult learners have no trouble understanding the discourse pragmatic rules that govern the use of dislocations in French", she finds a few cases of TNs and LDs structures with the function of introducing new entities in the group of the adult Chinese learners of French, a fact that is not expected in her model: "Chinese learners of French should not use these structures with introductions at all, assuming they understand the conditions of use of dislocation as a topic marker upon acquiring it" (Hendriks 2000: 388). Her conclusion is that "the combination of functions for which dislocations are used by adult learners is more complex, even though the main overall function is the same as in the target language. Dislocations are used when reference is less presupposed" (Hendriks 2000: 389). The author also maintains that the behaviour of the Chinese learners of French "functionally speaking... results in a usage pattern conform to the target language pattern right from the start. The pattern of acquisition and usage in L2 differs from the pattern in L1 child learners of French in that we find a more extensive use of dislocations in this task for marking contrast than in L1 child data" (Hendriks 2000: 390).

As to form, Hendriks (2000: 393) observes that "in contrast to functions, forms used by adult learners of French do not all coincide with the target language dislocated forms". She finds a few instances of a presentational structure (like *le chat qui grimpe*) in a different context than that which is considered appropriate in French, where it is supposed to require a preceding locative-existential structure (most typically, *il y a*). Hendriks's conclusion is that "the most likely hypothesis is... that the learner acquires this construction without necessarily knowing about or paying attention to these limitations... In sum, the cluster of functionally related forms is readily identified by Chinese L2 learners of French, but the number of constructions in the cluster and their formal similarity result in a situation in which the target language linguistic means is not a stable element in the learner language" (Hendriks 2000: 391).

The impact of spoken and written language is another factor believed important in spontaneous learning of topicalisations in L2 (Trévise 1986: 192, 197; Hendriks 2000: 387). Comparing a group of English students learning French at school and a group of French students learning English in a non-guided context, Trévise observes that in the first group TNs do not occur and that this would be due to "teaching reasons"; the second group, on the other hand, has no transfer of these structures from their L1, "maybe because of the image they have of normative constructions". The author thinks that

> one possible conclusion at this point could be that, word order being a central and functional feature of French, the reason why French students do not transfer it directly lies in their more or less conscious feeling for the French written standard they were (intensively) taught at school. They may have the feeling that this type of canonical word order... is more 'neutral' and thus more transferable than pragmatic non-morphosyntactical dislocations, which they may feel as specific to the spoken norm and thus more language-specific as well as forbidden in an institutional setting (Trévise 1986: 197).

These considerations are interesting, but they put too much emphasis on the role of the speaker's awareness of the written standard as an explanation for the lack of various kinds of TNs at the stages of acquisition of L2 investigated. Moreover the conclusions presented can hardly be generalised, as they are centred on the historical and sociolinguistic situation of French, where two factors have played a special role: (a) the influence on written standards of an old and prestigious grammatical tradition; (b) the high frequency of TNs and LDs in spoken registers. Both factors may induce higher levels of awareness of what is typical of written or of spoken language. But studies on other languages show a different situation: as far as Italian is concerned, for example, not even educated speakers seem to be aware to perform utterances with TNs, LDs or – more in general – other kinds of "cleft" structures (note that here "cleft" is used in a non-technical sense).

4.2. Some considerations on the theoretical and methodological assumptions of the studies on the acquisition of TNs and LDs in L2

The results discussed so far stimulate further considerations on some aspects of the theoretical and methodological backgrounds in which they have been achieved.

4.2.1. The notions of 'Topic', 'Focus' and 'Referential Movement'

The studies examined in 4.1. give a central role to the notion of 'referential movement', a notion which is clearly semantically and pragmatically oriented. The centrality given to semantics and pragmatics is also clear from the definitions of Topic and Focus which have been adopted. On the basis of the *quaestio* model, Focus is defined as "that part of the statement which specifies the appropriate candidate of an alternative raised by the question", and Topic as "the remainder of the answer" (Klein and Perdue 1992: 51-52). Thus the procedure of analysis goes from function to form.

Another aspect worth mentioning is the interest in universal pragmatic principles. Although Klein and Perdue prudently warn against an easy adoption of universal pragmatic principles – like "from known to unknown" – they obviously consider them of central importance (cf. Klein and Perdue 1992: 17, "we think that universals of this sort indeed play an important role in the organisation of learner varieties") and more fruitful for research in second language acquisition than conditions on Universal Grammar and statistical universals of typology (cf. Klein and Perdue 1992: 17). Therefore universal pragmatic principles have largely been resorted to in framing initial hypotheses as well as in getting conclusions (cf. Trévise

1986: 186, who postulates "invariant cognitive features"; Hendriks 2000: 370-71 and 377-79).

This approach, which has been very popular in various routes of functionalism (cf. Sornicola 1994), poses several problems. The first is that notions like Given/New, Known/Unknown, Topic/Focus are far from being uncontroversial and therefore their status as tools for systematic linguistic comparison is disputable. In fact, from how these notions are defined different results can be obtained.

Secondly, it is controversial to what extent the codification of PFs is universal or is typologically differentiated. An answer to this question may prove to be out of range for the present. Generalisations about the universality of distribution of Given and New, or of Topic and Focus seem premature.

A third problem concerns to what extent macro-structures are determined by natural or cultural factors. Macro-structural organisations of texts are heavily influenced by extra-linguistic factors like grammatical and rhetorical traditions, which are especially active on written language, the impact of different educational systems, no less than by psycholinguistic and sociolinguistic differences among speakers. If this is true, research on referential movement in second language learning should not concentrate almost exclusively on internal factors.

A fourth problem stems from a combination of the previous ones: is it really possible to compare informational macro-structures of different languages? If yes, how? This is a tricky problem, for more than one reason: (a) macro-structures differ from micro-structures in both internal organisation and processes of formation; (b) the investigation of how macro-structures are formed in synchrony and diachrony is still in its infancy. The old debate raised by text linguistics in the Sixties and the Seventies could be reopened: to what extent text grammars of individual languages can be built up? This question could be reformulated today in a comparative key: to what extent languages can be compared in their textual grammars? The perspective endorsed here is that of a temperate skepticism: for the time being, we simply do not know.

These difficulties seem to support the point of view that considers preferable in the description of data to identify form first and then to assign function to each form that has been singled out. As is well known, the analysis of spoken data often presents preliminary technical problems in the identification of forms, and the more so the analysis of spoken data of learners of L2. In this case – because of the multiple and unstable paths of structural development – the reduction to form of a given stretch of text cannot rule out the possibility of alternative interpretations. For example, in the studies mentioned above LDs have often been identified as structures with NP + a pronoun copy of NP (like, for example la fille il plor beaucoup). Yet, in corpora of spoken data of learners of L2 the occurrence of this syntactic configuration does not necessarily imply a LD structure, but it may conceal a more "local" phenomenon like the fossilisation of the pronoun agglutinated to the verb, i.e. an imperfect learning of a morphological structure, whereby a sequence Pro + V has been reanalyzed as V. This possibility is especially suggested by the data quoted in Trévise 1986.

4.2.2. On the notion 'learning/acquisition of topicalisations'

A further question that emerges from the literature concerns the notion of 'learning/acquisition of topicalisations'. It has been assumed that such processes can be learned/acquired like any other structure of a given L2. Yet this assumption is controversial. Whatever the reasons that induced Trévise to claim that TN structures in L2 cannot be easily transferred, her opinion is to welcome in that it criticises the idea that syntactic structures have all the same status and thus an equal potentiality to be learned/acquired. Hendriks comes close to this problem when she observes that the capability to control topical and focal information – though believed universal – "is not always a very explicitly marked function in language, and might therefore not stand out to all speakers equally" (Hendriks 2000: 379). Neither Trévise nor Hendriks, however, push their observations to a more general discussion of the psychological status of TNs.

The crucial point in this discussion seems the determination of the speakers's level of awareness in the production of TNs and LDs. Research on spontaneous spoken language of Italian and English has pointed out that TNs LDs are typical of unplanned text production (cf. Sornicola 1981; Miller and Weinert 1998). Thus TNs and LDs can be described as processes of impromptu speech, to which a semantic and pragmatic value of bringing a referent to a centre of attention is often (though perhaps not always) associated. It is highly disputable, however, whether this description can tell us the reason why speakers produce such processes. To make this claim, one should assume that in unplanned spoken language these phenomena reach a high level of crystallisation, which often corresponds to high levels of speakers's awareness of what they perform. But such claim can hardly be made. To understand this point, it is useful to compare the properties of LDs in spontaneous spoken language to their properties in literary or journalistic styles. Studies on Italian written texts of this kind show that in this case the phenomena in question (a) occur in a limited and fixed number of shapes, i.e. they are fully structured and (b) are planned for special stylistic reasons of mise en relief.

A plausible conclusion is that – under the pragmatic and sociolinguistic conditions described – TNs and LDs occurring in spontaneous spoken language do not fit traditional form - function models. As to form, they have a low degree of grammaticalisation and thus a range a variant syntactic configuration; as to function, they are not necessarily motivated by the speaker's intention to establish a "centre of attention" nor by the speaker's will to signal such a "centre of attention" to the listener. The literature on the acquisition of TNs and LDs in L2 has overgeneralised the importance of the listener for the speaker, as well as the assumption that the speaker controls "mutual knowledge" in mature stages of production of these structures. In fact, there is evidence that – even in the development of the communicative competence of L1 – speakers tend to differ in this respect: the acquisition of the competence of monitoring "mutual knowledge" and producing appropriate referential expressions depends on factors like social class, education and – above all – the kind of socialisation processes experienced by the speakers, especially within primary groups like family and school (cf. Sornicola 1978 for an analysis of the phenomenon of "egocentric reference"). Furthermore, the ability to plan referential structures seems variable across the life span of many speakers of a given L1, as it is very sensitive to psychological factors, like emotional states, etc.

On the basis of the previous considerations, the problem of learning/acquiring how to topicalise in L2 may reveal some pitfalls. In many cases learning/acquiring both formal and functional properties of LDs is a target that can only be related to the learning of written language. It cannot be related to the acquisition of spontaneous spoken language, simply because in spontaneous spoken registers of many languages it is no stable and consistent target even for L1 speakers, who produce TNs and LDs automatically and unconsciously in the course of their utterance planning.

4.2.3. The variability of spoken language

The problem discussed in 4.2.2. is related to another issue, which deals with methodological aspects of research on spoken language. The works by Trévise 1986, Perdue, Deulofeu, Trévise 1992, Hendriks 2000 take into account data on spoken languages that are the input to L2 and/or the L1 background of the groups of speakers examined. These data are too homogeneous: they do not reflect the massive variability and irregularity of spoken languages with respect to sociolinguistic and psycholinguistic factors, pragmatic and contextual factors and text genres (they are restricted to narrative text types).

An example of the difficulties that may result from this limited range of data is given by Hendriks's account of the function of presentative structures produced by Chinese speakers acquiring French. In 4.1.3. it has been mentioned that Hendriks elicited presentative structures in a different context from that assumed to be "normal" in spoken French, where an existential-locative structure preceding is expected. Hendriks incidentally observes that "in colloquial French it is claimed to be possible to have the exact same construction without a presentational clause [= existential-locative] in the immediate context" (Hendriks 2000: 391), but she does not elaborate on this point. The possibility of a presentative structure of the kind elicited by Hendriks is confirmed for other spoken Romance languages, where it seems to be unsystematic and oscillating across types of texts and types of speakers.

4.2.4. Typological models in studies of acquisition of TNs in L2

The typological conceptions underlying the works examined so far unproblematically adopts the model of Topic vs Subject-prominency (cf. Trévise 1986: 190, 201; Hendriks 2000: 384, 389). Yet the results that have been obtained provide interesting counterexamples to this model: (a) in Chinese texts produced by Chinese children and adults Topic-prominent structures are found to be very infrequent; (b) in Chinese texts produced by Chinese children an unexpected instance of LD is elicited, which confirms a cross-linguistic distribution of this syntactic type hardly accountable in terms of the dichotomic typological model assumed.

5. Conclusions

The issues which have been discussed in this paper seem to have some consequences not only for the description and functional interpretation of TN and LD structures, but also for the more general problem of language learning.

A fundamental issue debated in the literature on the acquisition of L2 has been why adults do not attain the end-state of primary language acquisition. This question, which has been substantially influenced by the theory of Universal Grammar, has been reversed by Klein and Perdue (1992: 334) in "Why do adults attain the state that they do?". The two scholars observe that "the homogeneous "end-state" hypothesised by some researchers for first language acquisition (represented for our purposes by the grammar of the TL) is not necessarily the best starting point for adult acquisition studies". Their conclusion is that it is possible to recognise a communicative logic in adult language acquisition, which induces the learners to acquire linguistic tools to perform minimal linguistic tasks. These conclusions show a remarkable harmony with some findings that emerge from the research on spontaneous spoken language. As has been observed in 4.2.2. it seems problematic to postulate – for both L1 and L2 – the existence of "targets" related to the development of TNs and LDs. It is perhaps an optical illusion to relate the highly variable and dynamic acquisition processes to an end-state of "complete" maturation of abilities. What emerges for native speakers is that there is no end state, no complete process of maturation. In particular, as far as text planning is concerned, linguistic abilities may attain different levels: they may fossilise at an initial level or they may progress and/or revert over the whole life span of speakers. If linguistic abilities are not conceived as "levels of knowledge", but as "aptitudes to do", it is not surprising that native speakers may reveal non-linear paths of linguistic development. Therefore the notion of 'reaching the target' seems unmotivated as a conceptual background for the study of the acquisition of TNs and LDs, no less than for the study of the emergence of these structures in L1. Independent evidence for this assumption is provided by the high individual variability, which has often been detected in spontaneous spoken language.

Another possible conclusion deals with the use of the notion of 'function' in the study of TNs and LDs. These are most often the results of processes of text planning, which are automatic and below the threshold of awareness. It has been claimed here that such processes cannot be assigned function in the sense of functional models like Lambrecht's. Yet they exist and pose a challenge to our efforts to draw functional models. One of the implications of this perspective is that the often noticed lack of TNs and LDs in Basic Varieties might be due to the fact that at these stages speakers learning a L2 lack those levels of spontaneity and automatisation which are an important condition for these structures to occur. If this hypothesis is plausible, a further step of research should be to try to better understand the relationship between the development of automatic and unaware production of texts in L2 and the emergence of TNs and LDs. The typological evidence provided in 2. seems to give clues to answer the interesting question raised by Trévise:

> Are such dislocations, especially those with no anaphora, still part of a pragmatic mode which is crosslinguistically attested in the first stages of spontaneous second language acquisition, or are they already due to the informal French input the subjects are in daily contact with? (Trévise 1986: 202).

In fact, the crosslinguistic comparison seems to show that TNs and LDs are universal spontaneous processes that are not confined to specific language types. It has been argued, however, that the fact that they have not been found in Basic Varieties may be due to different levels of awareness of speakers in L1 and in L2.

Trévise's question is an instance of a kind of linguistic problem that cannot be approached without an integrated perspective from the fields of second language acquisition, spoken language and typology. This integration is not obvious. What makes the task difficult is that no single perspective should surrender to the others. This perhaps will require new strategies of integrated research. But the three fields have too much to contribute one to the others to give up this effort.

Notes

1. In this paper the following additional abbreviations have been used:
   GF = Grammatical Function;
   PF = Pragmatic Function;
   RD = Right Dislocation.
2. AspM = Aspectual Marker.
3. PERF = Perfective;
   NEG = Negative;
   EMP = Emphatic;
   EMPptc = Emphatic particle;
   PST = Past;
   IMPERF = Imperfective.

4. TM = Topic Marker;
   SM = Subject Marker;
   LK = Linking particle;
   COP = Copula.
5. NM = Nominative particle;
   DC = Declarative Sentence-type suffix;
   POL = Polite Speech suffix or particle;
   DIR = Directional particle;
   MD = Pre-nominal modifier suffix.
6. The symbol "Ø" denotes a null pronoun.
7. DAT = Dative;
   INF = Infinitive;
   QCl = Question Clitic;
   INC = Inclusive Clitic;
   GEN = Genitive;
   POS = Possessive.

References

Altman, Hans
    1981   *Formen der "Herausstellung" im Deutschen.* Tübingen: Niemeyer.
Chafe, Wallace
    1976   Givenness, contrastiveness, definiteness, subjects, topics, and point of view. In: Li (ed.), 25-55.
Cloarec-Heiss, France
    1986   *Dynamique et équilibre d'une syntaxe: Le banda-linda de Centrafrique.* Paris: Societé d'Études Linguistiques et Anthropologiques de France.
Greenberg, Joseph H.
    1963   Some universals of grammar with particular reference to the order of meaningful elements. In: Joseph H. Greenberg (ed.), *Universals of Language*, 73-113. Cambridge (Mass.): The MIT Press.
Hendriks, Henriëtte
    2000   The acquisition of topic marking in L1 Chinese and L1 and L2 French. *Studies in Second Language Acquisition* 22: 369-395.
Hinds, John
    1986   *Japanese.* London: Routledge.
Hirschbühler, Paul
    1975   La dislocation à gauche comme construction basique en français. In: Christian Rohrer and Nicholas Ruwet (eds.), *Actes du colloque*

Franco-Allemand de grammaire transformationelle, I: Études de syntaxe, 9-17. Tübingen: Niemeyer.

Ingham, Bruce
1991   Sentence structure in Khuzistani Arabic. In: Alan S. Kaye (ed.), Semitic Studies in Honor of W. Leslau on the Occasion of his 85th Birthday, I, 714-728. Wiesbaden: Harrassowitz.

Klein, Wolfgang, and Clive Perdue (ed.)
1992   Utterance Structure. Amsterdam: John Benjamins.

Li, Charles N. (ed.)
1976   Subject and Topic. New York: Academic Press.

Li, Charles N., and Sandra A. Thompson
1976   Subject and topic: A new typology of language. In: Li (ed.): 457-490.

Meisel, Jürgen M.
1981   The role of transfer as a strategy of natural second language acquisition/processing. Paper presented at the first Eunam workshop on crosslinguistic SLA research, Lake Arrowhead.

Milano, Emma
forthc. Le dislocazioni in italiano parlato. Ph.D. Dissertation, University of Heidelberg.

Miller, Jim, and Regina Weinert
1998   Spontaneous Spoken Language. Oxford: Clarendon Press.

Ozanne-Rivierre, Françoise
1976   Le Iaai. Langue mélanésienne d'Ouvéa (Nouvelle Calédonie). Phonologie, morphologie, esquisse syntaxique. Paris: Societé d'Études Linguistiques et Anthropologiques de France.

Perdue, Clive, José Deulofeu, and Anne Trévise
1992   The acquisition of French. In: Klein and Perdue 1992, 225-300.

Ross, John
1967   Constraints on variables in syntax. Doctoral Diss., MIT. Bloomington: Indiana University Linguistic Club.

Scherpenisse, Wim
1986   The Connection between Base Structure and Linearization Restrictions in German and Dutch. Frankfurt am Main: Peter Lang.

Sohn, Ho-min
1994   Korean. London: Routledge.

Sornicola, Rosanna
1978   Egocentric reference as a problem for the theory of communication. Journal of Italian Linguistics 4: 7-63.

Sornicola, Rosanna
1981   Sul parlato. Bologna: Il Mulino.

Sornicola, Rosanna
    1984   Indeterminate relations and the notion of "quasi-government". *Folia Linguistica* 18: 379-408.
Sornicola, Rosanna
    1994   The many routes of functionalism. *Rivista di Linguistica* 5: 157-176.
Sornicola, Rosanna
    forthc.   Basic word-order from a pragmatic perspective. In: Giuliano Bernini (ed.), *Pragmatic Organization of Discourse in the Languages of Europe*. Berlin: Mouton de Gruyter.
Sridhar, Shikaripur N.
    1990   *Kannada*. London: Routledge.
Tersis, Nicole
    1972   *Le Zarma. Étude du parler Djerma de Dosso*. Paris: Societé d'Études Linguistiques et Anthropologiques de France.
Trévise, Anne
    1986   Is it transferable, topicalization? In: Eric Kellerman and Michael Sharwood-Smith (eds.), *Crosslinguistic Influence in Second Language Acquisition*, 186-206. Oxford: Pergamon Press.
Watkins, T. Arwyn
    1991   The function of cleft and non-cleft constituent orders in Modern Welsh. In: James Fife and Erich Poppe (eds.), *Studies in Brythonic Word Order*, 329-351. Amsterdam: John Benjamins.
Zemskaja, Elena Andreevna
    1973   *Russkaja razgovornaja reč'*. Moscow: Nauka.

Typology and information organisation: perspective taking and language-specific effects in the construal of events

Mary Carroll and Christiane von Stutterheim

1. Introduction

In order to convey meaning through language, speakers do not simply acquire a set of lexico-grammatical elements with rules or conventions which determine their possible combinations. In acquiring such means they also discover the principles whereby representations of states of affairs are typically paired with the lexico-grammatical structures which each language provides. This process of transformation is referred to here as organising information for expression. Language users learn to establish a conceptual framework which provides a blueprint for the kinds of decisions required in selecting and anchoring what is to be expressed in context. It proceeds on the basis of principles which guide speakers in tasks such as the segmentation of a body of information into propositional units, the location of content within an appropriate spatio-temporal frame, the specification of a principle which guides the order of mention (linearisation), etc. (cf. Levelt 1989). In this sense the information at issue is transformed into units which are amenable to expression in a linear medium with respect to a specific communicative goal.

In this paper we present evidence for the role which grammatical means play in determining the underlying principles which speakers follow, focusing on those found in both fully-fledged languages (English, French, German, Italian, Spanish) and learner varieties (L1English-L2German, L1German-L2 English, L1Spanish-L2 German). Analyses show that in complex tasks such as descriptions and narratives speakers tend to follow principles which are linked to obligatory grammatical categories. Categories such as the *syntactic subject* and the *morphosysntactic structure of spatial expressions* are central to the principles found in spatial descriptions and grammaticised features such as *tense, aspect*, which are relevant in the construal of events, play a crucial role when organising information for expression in narratives (cf. Gumperz and Levinson 1996; Berman and Slobin 1994; Myhill 1992).

These findings on information organisation raise a number of questions which are relevant for both language typology and second language acquisition research. Studies of advanced second language learners offer insights into the nature of the factors involved, since the acquisition of the individual grammatical means of a language does not automatically entail target-language-like principles in information organisation, as the findings reveal. In order to achieve native-like proficiency, second language learners have to uncover the role of specific grammatical features of the target language in information organisation. As shown below, however, learners retain the underlying principles of their source language, and even at very advanced stages of acquisition we find evidence of the way speakers accomodate the grammatical means found in the target language to basic principles of the source language. The problem of analysis for the learner is given by the fact that the determining factors are implicational in nature and their role is revealed only when tracked as a bundle across different domains (time, space, person, etc.). Languages provide different coding options (lexical, grammatical means) and learners not only have to recognise the set of options that are typically chosen in the target language, but the underlying principles which determine their choice. In this sense recognition of these principles constitutes one of the ultimate hurdles in gaining full proficiency in a second language.

2. Perspective taking

Taking a perspective on something means choosing among alternative viewing points, since entities are never perceived in their entirety, but are present in part only, as defined by the actual standpoint of the viewer (Graumann 1989: 96). When organising information for expression speakers encounter the first set of alternatives in deciding whether a state of affairs should be verbalised in the form of a description, a narrative, dialogue, etc. The selection of the alternative at issue can be specified by posing a question or *quaestio* (Klein and von Stutterheim 1987; von Stutterheim and Klein 1989, in press). A question such as *what happened there yesterday?* will lead to the production of a narrative text and with this to the selection and organisation of information in terms of a sequence of events. The question *what was it like there?* calls for a description of the state of affairs, where events generally play a minor role. A text can thus be viewed as a structured body of information which provides an answer to an underlying question. The quaestio model of information organisation specifies clearly defined constraints for the network of conceptual domains (time, space, object, event, modality) and the role they assume in each text type when structuring information and mapping it into form (von Stutterheim and Klein 1989; von Stutterheim 1997).

The selection of a *quaestio* or text type, and with this basic structural requirements for information organisation, does not cover all required decisions, however. There are language-specific preferences in information organisation which are clearly linked to grammaticised meanings (Carroll 1993; Carroll and von Stutterheim 1993; Carroll 1997; von Stutterheim 1999; Carroll et al. 2000; von Stutterheim and Nuese in press). The role of grammaticised means in information organisation is reflected at all levels – in the type of spatio-temporal frame found across different languages, in the linearisation procedure selected, and the principles whereby dynamic situations are segmented into individual events, etc. These findings fall in line with a large body of cross-linguistic evidence which points to the relevance of grammaticised meanings in determining how speakers proceed in verbalising states of affairs (Slobin 1991; Lucy 1992, 1996; Levinson 1997). Studies have been carried out, for example, for both child and adult speakers on differences between speakers of verb-framed versus satellite-framed languages in selecting and coding information on motion events in narratives (Berman and Slobin 1994; Slobin and Hoiting 1994; Slobin 1996; Naigles et al. 1998).

The present paper brings together evidence of language-specific principles in organising information in both spatial and temporal frames of reference, as required in spatial descriptions and narratives. Its focus goes beyond the individual domains and addresses the following question: Are there overreaching principles in narratives which guide the choices made across different domains such as space and time. In a narrative task, for example, we can ask to what extent does the frame of reference selected to link events in time affect the concepts chosen in locating and linking events in space. We first review the findings for a range of cross-linguistic analyses on spatial frames of reference in descriptions (English, French, German, Italian, Spanish) and compare these with principles found when linking information in the domains of both space and time in narrative tasks in the same languages, as well as learner varieties of English and German.

2.1. Methodology

In order to pinpoint the set of factors which determine the coding options selected in language use, we need to have criteria which help assess the relevance of linguistic over other possible factors, such as cultural or contextual factors. One way of isolating such factors is to collect data from languages which share the same cultural background but have different linguistic systems (cf. Pederson 1995). Another is to take different languages and cultural groups (Algerian Arabic, English and Spanish speakers, for example) keeping constant a certain set of relevant linguistic features, such as grammatical *aspect*, *pro-drop/free word order* (Italian, Spanish), *verb second constraint* (German), *fixed word order* (English, French). If grammaticised meanings drive the coding options selected in language use, languages which share a similar grammatical profile should exhibit similar sets of principles in information organisation in the relevant domains. This is the procedure adopted in our cross-linguistic comparisons.

The grammatical factor investigated in the study of information organisation in descriptions concerns the *grammatical subject* and its role in *topic* assignment (in the sense of *topic background*), as well as the *morphosyntactic structure of spatial expressions*. Comparisons were drawn on the one hand between French, Italian, Spanish, and English, where the grammatical subject typically codes topic information (a function grammaticised through fixed position, as in English and French, or pro-drop features in Italian and Spanish). In German, by contrast, the coding of topic information is grammaticised via the verb second constraint for finite verbs in main clauses. This grammatical feature limits the occurrence of constituents before the verb to one only. In German any constituent, in addition to the subject, which typically occurs in the 'Vorfeld' or preverbal slot, created by the verb second constraint, is a potential candidate in coding topic information, thus leaving the subject free to code focus or background information on a systematic scale. The following analyses show how structural differences of this kind affect the choices which speakers make in descriptions and narratives when selecting information for expression and mapping it into form.

3. Information organisation in picture descriptions in English, French, German, Italian, Spanish

The role of grammaticised meanings in information organisation in descriptions will be illustrated in the present section on the basis of the *verb second constraint* in German, since in this case speakers can choose between two options with respect to the role of the syntactic subject in information structure. As mentioned above, the syntactic subject can fill the preverbal slot, or another constituent such as an adverbial, but not both. If speakers select the first option and decide to consistently place the syntactic subject in the preverbal slot, the type of information which maps into the syntactic subject, in a task such as a *picture description*, is the picture itself, as evidenced in the analyses: the syntactic subject occurs in expletive form (*es gibt ..., there is ...*), and utterances coded in this way constitute statements about the picture: *es gibt ..., there is* (topic: picture) *a square* (focus or background). In descriptions the entity (x) has topic status since the text is treated as a body of information which answers the general question or quaestio *what is x like?* (von Stutterheim and Klein 1989).

If speakers decide to systematically map adverbials into the preverbal slot *(hinten im Bild sind Berge, in back in the picture are mountains; rechts ist eine Apotheke, on the right is a drugstore)*, the syntactic subject codes background or focus information, i.e. the set of elements which are located *at the back of the picture* or *on the right hand side*, for example. In this case the picture is divided into spatial regions, and entities are grouped and selected for mention on the basis of the locations which they share. The object under description is represented spatially as a set of regions and these also have topic status.

3.1. Spatially based perspective

In the picture descriptions analysed speakers of German typically direct attention to the spaces on the picture, selecting entities for mention on the basis of the regions of space which they share (18 out of 20 speakers), and adverbials typically fill the preverbal slot or 'Vorfeld'. This leads to a high rate of locationals in reference introduction, as illustrated in the examples above, and in reference maintenance each entity is maintained on the basis of the region of space which it delimits. German is the only language in the present group in which means are grammaticised to express this latter function, with a paradigm of so-called proadverbials (*davor,* there-in-front; *dahinter,* there-behind), for example, which maintain objects in spatial terms.

The two remaining speakers select the alternative option using existentials to introduce referents to the domain of discourse. In this case the expletive subject (*es gibt,* there is) fills the pre-verbal slot, and demonstrative pronouns (*neben dem,* beside that) as opposed to adverbials are used in reference maintenance. Objects are thus maintained as an entity (pronoun) and not as a region of space (*da,* there). This is treated as an object-based perspective (Carroll et al. 2000).

3.2. Object based perspective

In descriptions in English and the Romance languages the syntactic subject occurs in expletive form (*there is a playground near the baroque building*) giving existentials in reference introduction and nominal forms in reference maintenance (*in front of that* ...). With this perspective statements are made about the existence of objects as a characteristic feature of the town and objects are often grouped in terms of inherent features such as function (buildings, vehicles, etc). The central role of the syntactic subject in coding topic information is grammaticised via fixed word order in English and French, or pro-drop features in Italian and Spanish. Similarly, the spatial concepts which are used to divide the picture into sections also follow an object-based pattern in that these concepts are closely linked conceptually to an intrinsic viewing point (cf. in detail, Carroll et al. 2000).

In summary, the cross-linguistic comparison shows that linguistic means used in reference introduction (existentials vs. locationals) share common features with those used in reference maintenance (pronouns vs. adverbials), and these also 'fit' spatial concepts selected to structure the space under description (object based/instrinsic vs. external reference point). These findings reveal that the choice of one linguistic form over another does not only depend on features of the surrounding discourse, or levels of activation of knowledge. A unifying perspective guides the linguistic means selected and the options observed correlate with grammaticised meanings.

3.3. Information organisation in descriptions in learner varieties

So what role do principles underlying information organisation play in developing languages? Are learner varieties characterised by the absence of a unifying perspective in information structure, or do they strive to acquire forms which fit an overall perspective? The second language analyses focus on the fact that although the learner varieties of very advanced learners are characterised by a high degree of formal accuracy, their use of linguistic structures in context, i.e. form function relations, do not correspond to those found in the target languages. In certain cases learners accomodate the grammatical means of the second language to functions and principles of their source langugage. This was found for learners with an object-centered perspective in descriptive tasks in their native language (L1English, L1Spanish), showing that source language constraints on the use of a spatially-based perspective are transferred to the learner variety. Their success in acquiring the spatially-based pattern of information organisation in German correlates with the nature of the constraints in their native language, which are stronger in Spanish than in English.

English learners acquire a spatial perspective in almost all but one respect. Traces of an object-based pattern of information organisation is found in the learner variety in the following form: the area under description is often structured in terms of the concept of *place,* which is defined as the area delimited by an object and its boundaries. In the picture description these are places such as the town square, a playground, a house, etc. In the learner descriptions entities within such places are located as being *da* (there). This means that the relative location between entities within a place is not specified, and proadverbials, which code locations relative to another location (*daneben,* there-beside) are markedly absent. The analyses show, however, that proadverbials are available, but the overall principle of information organisation that warrants their use is not yet fully anchored in the learner variety (Carroll et al. 2000). The object-based concept of *place,* which plays a fundamental role in English but not in German (cf. Carroll 1997, 1993), is still in evidence in the learner language.

The Spanish learners of German – although at a comparable level of formal competence – have not acquired the spatial perspective of the target language to the same degree. An object-based perspective predominates in information structure: in reference introduction learners mainly use existential and other presentational forms, as in their source language. The use of locationals is highly restricted, as in Spanish, and learners maintain the underlying constraint in their learner variety. Locationals are used in Spanish (and Italian) only when the entity in question has already been introduced to the domain of discourse (definite reference), or can be easily identified via world knowledge. This constraint is typically referred to as the *identifiability constraint* or *definiteness effect* (Abbott 1993). The forms used in reference maintenance show that the learners have proadverbials, but they nevertheless play a marginal role in this variety as well, taking the low frequency with which proadverbials occur in the data.

If one of the basic factors driving language acquisition is consistency in pairing form-function relations which span different domains, then the relative unity given by the object-based perspective in L1Spanish-L2German may mean that there is less impetus toward reorganisation of the learner variety, compared to the English learners, who have to take the final step in reassessing the role of the concept of place in information organisation. The L2 speakers must reconceptualise the role played by the conceptual domains (object, space) in information organisation in order to achieve native-like proficiency in the TL. So can English learners recognise that the spatial concept of place has little or no function in spatial descriptions in German? In order to assess the kind of reconceptualisation involved we will take up the discussion with a brief review of the differences in perspectivisation in the source and target languages.

3.4. Shifting perspectives from source to target language principles

The fundamental concept, when giving spatial descriptions in English, is to characterise the nature of the entity which constitutes the place under description (the town and its surroundings, the main square, the playground, etc). In spatial descriptions in English relative locations are defined when linking objects and their places but not necessarily when referring to objects which are viewed as contained or included within another place. In characterising an entity and its place – such as the main square, for example, it may be sufficient to specify what is on it (*there is a bus stop, there is also a cafe, etc*), and one need not necessarily say where these entities are in relation to one another. The use of the relation of inclusion is guided by the concept of place in English, and what is viewed as such (Carroll et al. 2000).

With a spatial perspective, as in German, the entity under description is not just the thing itself, there is a shift in focus to the space it delimits, as mentioned above. Given an overall spatial perspective the primary focus is how parts, areas, and individual entities are linked relative to one another (*close to x is y; in front of y is z; and directly behind is ...* etc.). In order to fulfill the task of structuring and linking all parts, native speakers of German prefer frames of reference which are projected from an external viewing point and *supersede inherent structures* (Carroll 1997, 1993).

In English the spatial structure projected from an external viewing point (coordinate axes) is constrained by inherent features of the entity (Carroll 1997). In other words, speakers of English scan the object for possible inherent reference points in setting up a spatial frame of reference, and the projection of structures is mediated by features of the object being described. Focus is placed on the nature of entities as *things*, and with this their associated features, and the location of any individual part constitutes but one feature among others. In German speakers focus on the nature of the entity as a spatially defined network, and in this case relative locations are at the forefront of attention. Giving a detailed or less detailed spatial description may seem to differ in terms of degree only, but in the underlying frames of reference they reflect different principles in the organisation of information for expression.

4. Information organisation in narratives

In the present section we extend our focus to spatio-temporal frames of reference, as found in narratives based on a picture story book and film re-tellings. One of the main questions concerns the status of unifying principles in information organisation: Do the language specific-principles described for the spatial domain in descriptions of states also apply in spatio-temporal frames of reference where speakers are faced with the task of locating entities as they move from one place to another (motion events), or are spatial frames of reference adapted to accomodate the temporal concepts and relations used to link the events in time? So the analysis of narrative tasks allows us to see if there are unifying principles in information organisation which apply to both spatial and temporal frames of reference in a given task, and thus ensure coherence across these domains. The findings for English and German will be summarised in the following section and used as a basis of comparison in the analysis of an advanced learner variety of English (L1German-L2English).

The material studied consists of narratives based on a picture story book (*Frog, where are you?*, Mayer 1969) and a silent film (Quest)[1] on the adventures of a single protagonist in his quest for water, which takes him through four different worlds. The data base covers 15 speakers of English, 15 speakers of German and 15 L1German-L2English speakers. The majority were university students in their mid-twenties. The 15 learners studied are college students with English as their major, and they had all spent up to one year in an English speaking environment. In terms of exposure to the target language they do not compare, however, with the very advanced learners of German (L1 English) studied for the descriptive tasks. So in this context we roughly distinguish between advanced and very advanced varieties, although length of stay is not a reliable indicator of actual proficiency in all cases.

4.1. Space: frames of reference for paths traced in motion events

Speakers may locate motion events such as *the boy went out of the house and into the forest*

– as a set of events each occurring within a region of space and its boundaries (relation of inclusion within a region of space)
– or as a set of events where each event may reach across regions of space and their boundaries (transition to and across regions of space)

An example of the first case from the film re-tellings runs as follows

(i) motion within places, inclusion: *the figure tries to dig a hole, the sand caves in and the figure starts sliding down with the sand, he disappears and lands in a new world; the boy leaves the house and goes searching in the forest*

In the case of inclusion or 'motion within a region of space', each event is mapped into and contained within the place or region mentioned. The place where the *sliding down* occurs is also the place where *the sand caves in*, for example. It is also the place at which *he disappears*, and a locative is used only when a new location (*in a new world*), which describes the place in which the event *lands* occurs. Changes in place (first place *the hole*; next place *new world*) are thus represented in the underlying frame of reference as a succession of 'bounded place-event units'. If the same place is maintained, as with the place of *the hole* in *sliding down, falling,* and *disappearing,* it need not be repeated. This way of conceptualising a series of motion events is based on the spatial relation of inclusion of an event within a place or region of space, and trajectories are represented as contained within the boundary of the place mentioned (cf. in detail, Carroll 2000).

(ii)   motion to a place/ transition: *the figure tries to dig a hole, the sand caves in and he falls into the hole and down into a new world; he goes out of the house and into the forest*

With 'motion to a place', events and their associated trajectories are conceptualised as crossing or reaching boundaries. As example (ii) above shows, the transition to a boundary or across the boundary from one place to the next is explicitly marked, as with the transition from outside the hole to inside the hole (*falls into the hole*), or across the boundary from the area inside the hole to the place given by the new world: *falls down the hole into a new world.*

In English these distinctions are coded by the contrast between simple versus compound prepositions (*in* vs. *into*) and in German by the dative (*er landet in einer neuen Welt,* he lands in a new world) versus the accusative case (*er fällt in eine neue Welt,* he falls into a new world).

As the comparison between the two frames of reference indicate, the underlying concepts of inclusion versus transition differ fundamentally. If motion to a new boundary or endpoint is at issue, for example, this is represented in the transition frame as, for example, *still looking for the frog, he goes out of the house and walks over to the forest.* The forest does not denote the actual location of the walking event, but the intended one. In contrast, this can be represented as *he leaves the house, and goes searching in the forest* where the places mentioned (*house, forest*) are represented as regions which encompass the actual location of the event mentioned – the event of leaving takes place at the house, and that of searching at the forest. As mentioned above, the representation *falls into the hole and down into a new world* can be alternatively represented in a frame of reference based on inclusion as *slides through the hole, disappears, and lands in a new world,* locating the sliding event as included in the place of *the hole,* and a landing event in that of *the new world.* This frame reflects a high level of detail or granularity in the narrative, and lexical selection is appropriate to the set of individual sub-events (*slides, disappears, lands*), while this change in place is represented in the transition model by a single verb *fall.* As the examples illustrate, the inclusion model entails an advanced level of lexical proficiency for learners of a second language.

4.1.1. Perspective taking in spatio-temporal frames of reference

These two options in structuring space for motion events differ with respect to perspective. A frame of reference based on the relation of inclusion within a place or region of space can be described as neutral, since the relation of inclusion is topological, and thus independent of a viewing point. An entity retains the location 'included in' regardless of the standpoint of an observer, as in *the ball is rolling around inside the goal*. In contrast, the description *the ball is rolling into the goal* codes 'transition across a boundary'. But crossing a boundary does not give the direction in which the transition occurs, i.e. as *out of* or *into the goal*. The specification of one or the other direction is dependent on the position of an observer and his or her viewing point. In the narrative tasks studied this viewpoint is consistent with that of the protagonist or *figure* in motion (Carroll 1996, 2000).

Both English and German have the linguistic means to represent these two frames of reference and to locate motion events on the basis of an inclusion or transition principle, as mentioned above. The analyses of the narrative data reveal that English and German speakers differ in the extent to which they make use of one or the other option. Speakers of German show a clear preference in narrative tasks for a transition principle, and motion events are preferably represented as motion to a goal or across a boundary, with goal points marked via the accusative case. The viewpoint given with the transition principle is thus goal centered and often reflects a *figure* or protagonist-based perspective on the events, as mentioned above. This applies in German both in narratives based on the picture story book and the film re-tellings. In contrast to German narratives, speakers of English use one or the other frame, depending on context (Carroll 1996, 2000).[2] Studies on perspective taking in narratives in English show that it is characterised by a certain degree of variability (Li and

Zubin 1995; Tversky 1996.) As the present analyses indicate, this does not apply to the same extent in German.

These language-specific preferences in selecting a spatio-temporal frame of reference can be illustrated in the film re-tellings when coding the change in place from each world to the next (1) the protagonist going from a desert to a paper world; (2) from the paper world to a stone world; (3) from the stone world to a world run by robots. In the English film re-tellings these changes in place are preferably represented on the basis of inclusion, as illustrated in example (i) above: The relative frequency with which 15 speakers select this option over the three scenes is 88.9%, while representations involving a transition to or across a boundary amount to 11.1%. In German (15 speakers) the inclusion model is selected by 13.3% while representations as a transition to or across a boundary amount to (86.7%) (Carroll 2000).

Comparisons with advanced learners of English with German as their L1 (15 speakers) reveal that they have recognised the required pattern in English.

Table 1. L1German-L2English

Inclusion of motion event within places	53.4%
Transition to and across boundaries	46.6%

However, learners do not yet apply a frame of reference with a neutral perspective, which is based on the concept of inclusion within places or spaces, to the extent found in the English narratives. In a frame based on the relation of inclusion, links between places remain implicit, and the relevance of this emerges when we examine frames of reference used in linking and locating these events in time.

4.2.1. Event time relations

In what follows the focus will be placed first on the role of temporal categories in relation to the representation and textual integration of situations.

Although work on time event relations abounds in the literature, the main body of semantic research – starting with Reichenbach's influential theory on temporal reference – has focused on temporal properties at the propositional level. However, more recent work in the field of temporal semantics has broadened the subject of investigation by taking into account temporal relations between sentences. The notion of *reference time*, which describes a subjectively selected viewing point on a specific event time, already points to temporal information which is provided contextually. The question how this reference point is selected and to what extent temporal coherence reflects a clear set of principles, however, has not been addressed until very recently (cf. the discussion in Roßdeutscher 1999). The idea that there are principles to be discovered beyond the level of propositional semantics has long been rejected by formal semanticists. But work on anaphoric temporal relations has led to the integration of notions such as *perspective* or *subject of consciousness* into formal theories such as *discourse representation theory*.

> Wir sollten also die Konsequenzen ziehen und es aufgeben, Regeln für die temporale Referenz im Kontext vom temporalen Profil (Tempus, Aspekt, Aktionsart C. v. S.) <u>allein</u> zu formulieren. (Roßdeutscher 1999: 9). (We should draw the consequences and stop formulating rules for temporal reference in context which are solely derived from temporal profiles (tense, aspect, aktionsart).

In describing the types of temporal categories which are relevant when establishing temporal relations we draw upon the theory developed in Klein (1994). This distinguishes three basic notions, *time of utterance (TU), time of situation (Tsit)* and *topic time (TT)*, where TU and Tsit correspond to what has been called speech time and event time in the Reichenbach framework. TT, however, cannot be equated with Reichenbach's notion of reference time. In Klein (1994) topic time is defined as the time interval for which an assertion is made. Whereas the situation time Tsit, that is the time for which a situation holds, is objectively fixed, the topic time which holds in a given sentence is a matter of choice. We can therefore say that temporal perspective taking is closely linked to the notion of topic time and different types of relations are involved in constructing a temporally coherent piece of discourse:

- the relation between topic time and event time (this is what has been described under the notion of *aspect* (Comrie 1976) referring to the subjective category of viewpoint).
- the relation between topic time and time of utterance yielding categories of deictic temporal location. These relations have to be decided upon at the propositional level.

Linking situations in order to form a complex information structure requires perspective taking along another dimension. The topic time of a sentence as a contextually given value can be hooked up to the temporal structure of the preceding sentence(s) in several ways.

- the topic time can be linked to the preceding time of situation
- the topic time can be linked to the preceding topic time
- the topic time can be linked to the time of utterance

As will be shown in the examples below, these relations are not established according to separate, individual decisions in text production, but converge in forming a consistent whole. We contend that the different perspectives described above result in specific patterns of *topic time management*. Before coming to the analysis of crosslinguistic aspects of topic time management we will illustrate the notions on the basis of the most pertinent patterns for linking events in discourse.

– pattern 1: TU linked frame
One possible option for relating events is illustrated by the following sequence:

(x) *the figure is starting to dig* $\quad$ TT_x in $Tsit_x$,
$\qquad\qquad\qquad\qquad\qquad\qquad\qquad\;\; TT_x = TU_x$
(y) *he is digging* $\qquad\qquad\qquad\;\;$ TT_y in $Tsit_y$,
$\qquad\qquad\qquad\qquad\qquad\qquad\qquad\;\; TT_y = TU_y$
(z) *he is being sucked down by the sand* $\quad$ TT_z in $Tsit_z$,
$\qquad\qquad\qquad\qquad\qquad\qquad\qquad\;\; TT_z = TU_z$

The three utterances show the same temporal properties with respect to the relations between the three temporal parameters TU, Tsit, TT. The topic time includes the time of situation and overlaps with time of utterance. In short:

$$TU = TT_{x\text{-}z} \text{ is included in } Tsit_{x\text{-}z}$$

In understanding the temporal relation between the situation times, inferences have to be drawn on the basis of the specific relation between TT and Tsit, as well as situational and world knowledge. In order to guide the interpretation of the actual relations between Tsit, the contours of the events can be sharpened by phasal segmentation, using inchoative aspect (*starting to dig*) or imperfective aspect (*is digging*), as in the example. Note that the choice of this temporal perspective often coincides with a presentation of the event without a point of completion or right boundary. If this pattern of TT management is maintained, each Tsit is hooked up to TT independently of some other Tsit. So this gives the general relation:

$$TU = TT = /\text{includes}/\text{follows}/\text{precedes } Tsit_x$$

– pattern 2: shift of topic time
Again an example is used to illustrate this pattern:

(x) *then he walks up to the wet spot* $\qquad\qquad$ $Tsit_x$ in TT_x

(y) *and then he takes a piece of rock*	Tsit$_y$ in TT$_y$ and TT$_y$ after Tsit$_x$
(z) *and then he makes a hole in the ground*	Tsit$_z$ in TT$_z$ and TT$_z$ after Tsit$_y$

In the first utterance the topic time interval is given as the post time of some preceding event, marked by the temporal shifter *then*, and the event time is included in this time interval. The same pattern is apparent in the second and third utterance. Typically, this temporal perspective entails a certain degree of completeness with respect to the situation described. The events are specified for a point of completion, either in the spatial domain (utterance x) or by referring to an affected or effected object (utterance y and z).

In contrast to the first strategy mentioned above, temporal relations are based on a link between topic time and the time of situation established in the preceding utterance. The *then* selects a topic time interval after the time of situation Tsit. The temporal intervals are explicitly related, leaving TU more or less without any relevant function.

(TU=) TT$_x$ follows/precedes Tsit$_{x-1, x+1}$, includes Tsit$_x$

4.2.2. Film re-tellings: TU linked frame and a circumstantial perspective

In the English film re-tellings (Quest) the majority of speakers select a strategy for topic time management where events are linked to TU, as described above under pattern 1. Since the actual temporal relations between situations remain implicit, speakers have to rely on other means in order to convey how situations progress. In doing so they focus on causal links between situations (x leads to y) and often direct attention to the circumstances surrounding events. Although there are few speakers of English who maintain a perspective of this kind throughout the entire narrative, there is a preference across all narratives to supply information on the circumstances surrounding events.[3] This is reflected in the use of causal (*so*) in linking events, and the opposition in English between the simple present (sits) and the progressive (is sitting) is crucial in this frame.

The following examples illustrate how circumstances are viewed as leading in some way to sets of events.

Ex. 1: Circumstances: use of progressive (-ing*)* form # ... #
- a   # *he starts trying to scoop the water up*
- b   *but the water is being absorbed into the surface* #
- c   *and he cannot get any water from that*

switch to simple tense
- d   *so <u>he sits there</u>*
- e   *and <u>looks up</u>*
- f   *to where he thinks they are*
- g   *but there's no more drips*
- h   *they have stopped dripping* (termination of frame)

In Ex. 1 the topic time is given by the deictic *now*. The time of situation of the utterances a-c is hooked up to this TT, and is either simultaneous with TT – as in a – or includes TT – as in b and c. This means that TT is maintained through the first 3 utterances. The temporal interval introduced by the situation *water being absorbed into the surface* functions as TT-interval for the following events. The Tsit of d-g are situated within this frame-time-interval, and nothing more is stated about their temporal location or the way in which they are interrelated. The present perfect form requires a point in time as TT as the point at which an event is terminated, and the post state of the event holds as the point of reference. This point in time can only be given by the deictic *now* as the globally established default TT. The pattern of topic time management for this text is as follows:

a	TT (point in time) = deictic *now*	TT overlaps Tsit
b	TT maintained	TT ⊂ Tsit
c	TT maintained	TT ⊂ Tsit
d	TT (interval) = Tsit	Tsit ⊂ TT
e	TT maintained	Tsit ⊂ TT

f	TT maintained	Tsit ⊂ TT
g	TT maintained	Tsit ⊂ TT
h	TT (point in time) = deictic *now*	TT after Tsit

The next example exhibits the same pattern. The two utterances a and b are hooked up to the deictic centre as their TT. They establish a temporal interval by their Tsit, which functions again as TT interval for the events reported in the following utterances.

Ex. 2: Circumstances: use of -ing form #...#
    a   *# there's no water to be found*
    b   *and he's walking through this area #*

Embedded set of actions which happen while walking; switch to simple tense

    c   *and he hears the drip again*
    d   *and sees this moist area on this piece of paper*
    e   *so he gets excited*
    f   *and he runs over*

Events such as *hears, sees*, and possibly *gets excited* occur within the established time span. The termination of the time span *walking through x* is given with certainty by the event *and he runs over*. So this gives the general pattern of TT management:

$$TU = TT \supseteq Tsit_x$$
$$Tsit = TT \subset Tsit_{x+n}$$

In sum, the pattern followed by the English speakers is temporally complex. The deictically introduced TT provides the anchor for the introduction of a circumstantial frame, characterised by an imperfective view on the activities or processes reported. The frame includes a set of events, and these are accorded some implicit portion of time within the given span where events may overlap or follow each other in time. Although the contrast between progressive and simple tense forms is crucial in indicating progression, the actual temporal relations between the respective Tsit remain implicit. This is underlined by the incompatibility of the form *then* at specific points in these frames, since *then* relates to the boundary of an event: *water is dripping onto the paper* (a continuous event) *and (*then) water is being absorbed into the paper*. The meaning encoded by *then* clashes with the notion of what ongoing events involve, since it sets an unnecessary and often incompatible period of dissociation between them.

As mentioned above, the link between the framing and associated events is often of a causal nature (there is circumstance x: so this leads to y), but causal links can be more or less evident, as in the two examples. With a circumstantial perspective there is no constraint on the type of event which can be used to construct a frame. They may involve activities of the protagonist, *he is looking for water; he is walking around*, or features of the situation in which the actions related occur *there are rocks heading straight for him; there are pieces of paper floating around*.

So what role does the progressive play when linking events in sequence in a narrative context? There is a general consensus that the progressive encodes a speaker's viewpoint on a situation as a continuing event (Brinton 1988). The meaning encoded is *ongoing*, or *continuative*, and ongoing events are anchored on a temporal scale by means of the form *now*, which is closely linked to the viewpoint of an external observer (deictic zero point). In this sense the frame includes both an external reference point as well as circumstances which are inherent to the situations at issue in constructing a frame of reference. There are thus clear analogies in conceptualising and organising information for expression in descriptions and narratives in English for both the spatial and temporal domain.

4.2.3. Analogies between time and space in frames of reference in English

As in spatial descriptions in English, the material at issue in narratives is also processed with respect to inherent features. Speakers who select a circumstantial frame train their sights on the state of affairs surrounding certain types of events, and situations have to be conceptualised in terms which allow the speaker to assess the status of events as candidates for a circumstantial or 'framing' capacity, in contrast to those which qualify for an embedded or inclusive relation. The possibility of inferring implicit shifts in time for events which are included within an ongoing time span does not detract from the fact that the overriding relation is that of inclusion. This echoes the role of the concept of place in spatial descriptions where speakers often specify the location of an entity as included within a *place* (such as a town square) but not necessarily their location in relation to one another within the place in question. Both frames of reference incorporate individuated entities, whether places or events, and the links between them often remain implicit. The relation of inclusion, which can be defined on both a spatial and temporal basis constitutes a suitable representation in spatio-temporal frames of reference which have to accomodate events that are conceptualised as ongoing and often start and overlap in a complex manner. Its role in English re-tellings illustrates the pattern of conceptualisation which German learners of English have to acquire in order to narrate in English with native-like proficiency, since speakers of German show a clear preference for pattern 2 (shift of topic time TT) in construing a temporal frame of reference in the same narrative task.

4.2.4. TT shift: Protagonist based perspective in film re-tellings

In contrast to a circumstantial perspective, complex situations are segmented into events which can be presented as occurring in sequence. The relations are established by mapping the situation onto an external temporal structure, which is reflected in the use of the adverbial *dann* (then).

Ex. 3: a   *die Sandfigur fällt vom Himmel*
             'the creature falls from the sky'
         b   *und landet in einer Wüste*
             'and lands in a desert'
         c   *mit lauter umherfliegenden Papieren*
             'with a lot of flying sheets of paper'
         d   *er umgeht ein grosses Stück Papier*
             'he avoids a piece of paper'
         e   *das auf ihn zukommt*
             'which comes towards him'
         f   *die Figur geht **dann** weiter*
             'the figure **then** goes on'
         g   *er findet eine kleine Pfütze*
             'and finds a small puddle of water'
         h   *und rennt dahin*
             'he runs towards it'
         i   *kniet sich hin*
             'kneels down'
         j   *und verschwindet **dann** wieder*
             'and **then** disappears again'

Here we have the following temporal structure:

a	TT (interval, taken from preceding context)	TT ⊂ Tsit
b	TT post time of Tsit$_a$ (TT shifted)	TT ⊂ Tsit
c	TT maintained	Tsit ⊂ TT
d	TT post time of Tsit$_b$ (TT shifted)	TT ⊂ Tsit
e	TT maintained	Tsit ⊂ TT
f	TT post time of Tsit$_d$ (TT shifted)	TT ⊂ Tsit
g-j	TT post time of Tsit$_{f,g-j}$ (TT shifted)	TT ⊂ Tsit

The adverb *dann* (then), which relates to the notion of boundedness, constitutes one of the basic elements in constructing a sequence of events (von Stutterheim and Lambert in press; von Stutterheim 1997). The general pattern of topic time management can be formulated as follows:

$$\text{Tsit}_x \geq \text{TT} \subset \text{Tsit}_{x+n} \quad \text{(main structure)}$$
$$\text{Tsit}_y \subset \text{TT} \quad \text{(side structure)}$$

The pattern exhibited follows the strategy of linking the current topic time to the preceding time of situation. With this frame the narrative events are temporally linked, and TU is not relevant. The temporal domain provides a tightly knit structure in creating coherence. Significantly, it also requires the selection of event types which meet the criterion of boundedness, in order to define a temporal shift and link a current topic time to the preceding time of situation. In the narratives studied this goes hand in hand with a protagonist-based perspective which focuses on the goals that the protagonist intends to reach.

In sum, the German speakers prefer to view a dynamic situation as an entity with boundaries which can fill a slot on a structured time line. Talking about dynamic events can be regarded as mapping two structures: a temporal structure (abstract interval structure) and an event structure (entities). The following features are characteristic of the texts which are structured according to this perspective:

– Explicit marking of temporal relations by temporal adverbials which are used to establish TT and to link them explicitly to the preceding Tsit.
– A holistic view is taken on the events, including points of completion or results of an event. This provides the anchor point for the shift-relation of the TT interval.
– The perspective chosen follows the event line from the inside, as a participant. Comments from the speaker's point of view or switches to the observer's perspective are rare.

Here we can again draw parallels between spatially and temporally structured texts. When describing space-object-relations in spatial descriptions in German, entities are selected for mention according to the regions of space which they share. The prerequisite in this case is a clearly defined spatial network which allows speakers to select and anchor entities in explicit terms. In metaphorical terms this conforms with the pattern in the narrative texts. Regions of time (intervals) are related to each other, and entities – in this case situations – are selected for mention as the substance which fills these regions, so to speak. As shown for the English speakers, German speakers also follow a consistent perspective in relating entities to spaces and situations to times.

Preparing the ground for the analysis of the learner variety, we will contrast again the two preferred patterns in organising temporal coherence on the basis of the unfolding of topic time:

$TU = TT \supseteq Tsit_x$
$Tsit = TT \subset Tsit_{x+n}$

$Tsit_x \geq TT \subset Tsit_{x+n}$ (main structure)
$Tsit_y \subset TT$ (side structure)

circumstantial perspective
(dominant pattern in the English texts)

protagonist based perspective
(pattern in the German texts)

4.2.6. Perspective taking in film re-tellings in advanced second language varieties (L1German-L2English)

So with English as target language, how do German learners of English proceed, given the task of re-telling what happened in the film? Taking as indicators the two different perspectives we get the following picture: All of the learners of English with German as their first language select a protagonist based perspective – the perspective chosen by native speakers of German. The analyses show, however, that the learners do not simply adapt the linguistic material of the L2 to the requirements of an L1 perspective. The conceptual implications of the format acquired, in particular the aspectual system, lead to form function relations in the L2 texts which evidence a high degree of incompatibility. Examples 5 to 7 were selected to illustrate the different facets of this specific problem.

Ex. 5:
a   *this time it is covered with paper*
b   *and you can see*
c   *sheets of paper floating above the ground*
d   *and **first** the clay figure is unconscious*
e   *but **after that** he comes to*
f   *he stands up again*
g   *and tries to find his way around*
h   *while walking around*
i   *he **suddenly** sees a puddle*
j   *and he kneels in front of it*

a	TT (point in time) = deictic *now*	Tsit ⊂ TT
b	TT maintained	TT overlaps with Tsit
c	TT maintained	Tsit ⊂ TT
d	TT (new, unspecified interval)	TT = Tsit (unbounded)
e	TT post time of $Tsit_d$ (TT shifted)	TT ⊂ Tsit
f	TT maintained	TT ⊂ Tsit
g	TT post time of $Tsit_f$ (TT shifted)	TT ⊂ Tsit
h	TT (cataphorically taken from TT_i)	Tsit ⊂ TT
i	TT (new, after TT_g)	Tsit ⊂ TT
j	TT post time of $Tsit_i$ (TT shifted)	TT ⊂ Tsit

In a-c the speaker uses forms which could serve to code a circumstantial perspective: locate a Tsit in a cataphorical relation to the following TT, dispensing with the temporal frame introduced in a–c. Shifts are coded as in e, although d refers to a situation which is an ongoing state and part of the circumstances. Tsit in i (*suddenly*) provides the TT for the ongoing situation in h, which is also frequently found in protagonist-based patterns.

In the next example evidence is given of problems at two levels. There is no consistent perspective in structuring the information and there is no local compatability of the types of temporal concepts selected, in particular the bounding of temporal frames by adverbials (in c and d below).

Ex. 6 a   ... *there is no water in him*
       b   *he consists of sand*
       c   **then** *he is still searching for water*
       d   *then he is really desperate*
       e   *and he tries to find another hole in the ground*

This example contains an interesting combination of different temporal reference frames, a combination which is not found in native English texts. In a and b the speaker refers to state-like situations, introducing a set of circumstances, while c and d continues with the story line by referring to an ongoing event *the searching for water* and the state of *being desperate*. By means of the adverbial *then* the speaker establishes some topic time interval which follows some preceding event time, which is therefore bounded on its left side and open on the right. The imperfective aspect, however, requires a topic time which is either conceived of as a point in time (e.g. the deictic *now*) or which is specified with respect to both its boundaries. Since this is not provided by the context, the imperfective is not anchored. The incompatible nature of this piece of text can therefore be explained by a clash in perspectives: one which follows the English pattern by taking the deictic centre as the anchor point for the presentations of the event chain, and another perspective which follows the pattern in German by linking topic time to preceding situation times through anaphoric expressions.

The last example illustrates problems which the learners have in constructing and combining the appropriate phasal segments of a complex situation.

Ex. 7 a   *then he gets up*
       b   *and* **starts walking** *around*
       c   **until** *he hears water dripping again*
       d   *he finds a place*
       e   *where there is actually water on the ground*

In a the speaker follows a protagonist-based pattern established in the preceding discourse. Utterance b refers to the starting point of an ongoing situation, as appropriate for a potential circumstantial frame. In c this is bounded explicitly by *until*, where, in violation of the principle of phasal event construal, the speaker links the starting point of an ongoing inchoative phase directly to an endpoint. We interpret this problem as warranted by the underlying temporal frame of the learner variety which is based on topic shift. This fact is further supported by the relations underlying d and e in which the circumstances are hooked up to the event expressed by a subordinate construction.

5. Summary of results

To come back then to the questions posed at the outset of these studies on advanced second language learners – what role does perspectivisation and information structure play in developing languages, to what extent are learner varieties characterised by a unifying perspective in information structure, and do learners acquire and maintain linguistic means which fit an overall perspective?

In producing narrative texts advanced learners are faced with a problem which parallels the patterns found in descriptive texts at an abstract level of conceptualisation. The findings illustrate that it is at the level of perspective taking, as one of the basic steps in the process of language production, where the basis for the inappropriate use of certain linguistic forms lies. In organising information for expression the learners apply forms which are related by implication to a specific perspective without fully implementing the principles which the perspective actually entails. In consequence this leads to a clash between the linguistic representation of a single situation – which in most cases is in itself an adequate formulation – and the overall contextual frame. The flow of information – to use a term introduced by Chafe (1987) – is disrupted by inappropriate selections and combinations of temporal categories. The learners of English have acquired the means to establish a circumstantial frame in narrative retellings but they do not utilise them in this function. This does not mean however that learners simply transfer the L1 principles of information organisation to the L2. In acquiring and using forms such as the progressive and phasal verbs they go beyond what they could express in their L1. They construct single informational units which accord in part only with principles of the target language (TU linked), and run into trouble since they do not construe sets of events as larger units which are linked in causal terms, for example. It would seem that they still rely on L1 principles at a very basic level. So the picture the learner varieties reveal is more complex than what has been described hitherto in the literature. It is not just new forms for old functions which can be described as the typical pattern of transfer still found in advanced varieties, but rather new forms and new functions at a local level, which are not licensed however at a global level of information organisation. The role of the specific linguistic forms in the dynamics of acquisition is evident, on the one hand, but a lot of questions remain unanswered. It is evident that through the acquisition of forms new perspectives are discovered and expressed by the learner. However, since the knowledge which is put to use at a local microscopic level in speaking about single situations is not applied at global levels of planning, this is where basic L1 principles seem highly resistant to reorganisation.

Learners do not recognise the full range of implications of form function relations which hold in information structure in the target languages, or if they do so, they cannot easily reorganise the elaborate L2 system accordingly. So with very advanced systems we may not only be dealing with a problem of analysis but one where the principles in question cannot be implemented since this would undermine the foundations of what are now complex linguistic systems. The relevance of these results for language typology as well as fundamental questions in acquisition studies will be discussed in the next section.

6. Conclusions

We have provided evidence for language-specific patterns of information organisation which hold both within and across different conceptual domains. Taking up once again the question as to the factors which lead to these differences, we have referred at several points to the role of particular patterns of grammaticisation. Grammar expresses a restricted set of meanings which make up the basic schematic framework for conceptual organisation within the cognitive domain of language (Talmy 1988; Slobin 1991). On this basis we claim that the systematic cross-linguistic differences in information organisation are rooted in the grammaticised meanings found in the respective languages. For the temporal domain, for example, aspect constitutes a central category, and notions such as ongoingness or progression are highlighted by morphological means. These notions entail a particular viewing point on the situation or events at issue, and languages which code such options have to accomodate the underlying perspective at many levels and ensure consistency across different domains in information structure (not just time, but space as well, for example).

Further evidence for the role of grammaticised categories comes from the comparison of languages such as Arabic and English, which are typologically unrelated but share the morphological feature aspect. Initial analyses of the re-tellings obtained for the same experiments show that comparable principles hold in both languages with respect to the construal of events in the narratives. The analyses thus underline the role of grammaticised means in constructing representations of states in the world and mapping information into linguistic form.

In first language acquisition aspectual distinctions are the first ones to be marked on the verb in aspect languages (cf. Berman and Slobin 1994). The early grammatical categories lead the speaker to focus on specific components of situations as building blocks in constructing verbal messages. These basic patterns are enriched later by other options. This interpretation of the developmental path is reflected in other terms in the acquisitional sequence found in L1 acquisition in German (cf. Halm 2000).

In describing the semantic basis for grammatical typology Wierzbicka (1995:179) states that far from being an autonomous system, grammar is concentrated semantics and embodies a system of meanings which are treated in a given language as important or essential in the conceptualisation of reality. Grammaticised meanings provide a blueprint for the speaker when pairing representations of states of affairs with the set of linguistic coding options which each language provides.

Significantly, the perspective which is grammatically motivated may in turn become the source for further processes of grammaticisation. In this sense we argue for the relevance in language of a *cognitive typology* which is defined at the level of information structure. Typological features lead to what can be termed *preferred* patterns of information organisation.

So what kinds of linguistic indicators serve to guide the path of analysis for the language learner, showing how form function relations work under a grammatically determined perspective? These questions on principles underlying information structure are not only relevant to language acquisition but to language typology as well. Features such as the role of the syntactic subject in English in coding topic information, or the verb second constraint in German, all lead to language-specific perspectives in information organisation and associated clusters of form function relations in both descriptive and narrative tasks.

The question is what happens when grammar allows a number of options at this level? Speakers of German can select the syntactic subject to code topic information in descriptions, for example, thus giving an object-based rather than a spatially-based pattern of information organisation. Speakers who choose this option select the same form function clusters found in English and the Romance languages (existentials and not locationals in reference introduction; nominal forms and not proadverbials in reference maintenance etc.). But this is not the preferred pattern of perspectivisation used in this language since only two out of twenty speakers select it. The majority of speakers follow the other option provided by the verb second constraint and select spatial information as the carrier of topic or background information, treating the area under description as a network of regions. Taking the preferred perspectives in each language, the analyses reveal that German speakers follow a consistent perspective across descriptive and narrative tasks, thus indicating that use of the same options across both tasks may be motivated by the criterion of consistency (cf. in detail Carroll and Lambert in press). The achievement of a certain degree of consistency in linguistic systems for form function relations in perspective taking may constitute one of the driving forces in diachronic development (e.g. productivity of forms such as proadverbials (*dahinter*, there-behind) in German and their gradual erosion in English).

Conditions for language learning would be optimised if the patterns of grammaticisation which are relevant for perspective taking were consistent and clearly indexed across the different semantic domains. But even if there were unambiguous typological parameters to serve as signposts for the learner in the process of acquisition, the process for the adult learner of a second language differs fundamentally from that of first language acquisition.

Information organisation is relevant in this respect in that it sheds light on knowledge bases which are designed to function dynamically in context. In language use information is organised for expression on the basis of basic processes which are common to all the source and target languages studied (information selection, segmentation into propositional units, selection of a linearisation principle, assignment of topic focus status, selection of principles to structure space and time, etc). The present studies indicate that the different steps required in organising information for expression are coordinated on the basis of a unifying principle which has been termed *perspective taking*. In an abstract sense these general planning requirements are common to all the languages studied, be this the speaker's first or second language.

So the question is how do learners come to recognise the form function entailments involved and the principles which guide perspective taking at this level? Studies of first language development show that the acquisition of grammatical form proceeds at a relatively rapid pace, whereas the recognition of what are then core grammatical features, and how they work in unison when organising information for expression, is an extended process which lasts well into adolescence.

There is ample evidence from studies of adult second language acquisition to show that linguistic knowledge poses both an advantage and disadvantage for the adult learner. The acquisition of new forms in an L2 does not necessarily imply acquisition of their corresponding target language functions. This dissociation not only occurs at the phrase or sentence level (cf. for example, Kellerman and Sharwood Smith (1986) on transfer) but also at the level of more complex constructions.

The present series of studies has examined the extent to which adult learners select forms to fit preordained functions in information structure, showing that the process of acquisition proceeds on a top down basis from the outset. As the learner variety data also reveal, advanced speakers come a very long way and succeed in acquiring the structural forms of the TL, regardless of whether it is a typologically related or unrelated language, but at a very subtle and fundamental level they remain rooted in at least some of the principles of conceptual organisation as constituted in the course of L1 acquisition, leading to the kinds of inconsistencies in the L2s discussed above. The underlying principles constitute a powerful constraint on the types of functions which L2 forms are required to serve. Furthermore, the more elaborate the system becomes the less amenable it will be to large scale processes of reorganisation. So in conclusion there are two types of *critical constraints* whereby second and first language differ, and they are both linked to information organisation.

Notes

1. Copyright Katholisches Filmwerk Frankfurt.
2. Evidence for a *Figure-centered* perspective in transition-based frames is given by use of figure/protagonist as reference point in locating other objects encountered along the way. In frames based on the principle of inclusion, objects encountered along the way are located with respect to the *Ground* or surroundings (cf. Carroll 2000).
3. There is preference across nearly all film retellings to use this frame, and 7 out of 32 speakers use it throughout. Only 6 out of 32 speakers select the other frame (pattern 2, topic shift) for the entire narrative. As with the picture story

book narratives use of one or the other frame is often dependent on the nature of the circumstances.

References

Abbott, Barbara
   1993   A pragmatic account of the definiteness effect in existential sentences. *Journal of Pragmatics* 19: 39-55.

Berman, Ruth A., and Dan I. Slobin
   1994   *Relating Events in Narrative: A Crosslinguistic Developmental Study*. Hillsdale: Erlbaum.

Brinton, Laurel J.
   1988   *The Development of English Aspectual Systems*. (Cambridge Studies in Linguistics 49.) Cambridge: Cambridge University Press.

Carroll, Mary
   1993   Deictic and intrinsic orientation in spatial description: A comparison between English and German. In: Jeanette Altarriba (ed.), *Cognition and Culture: A Cross-Cultural Approach to Psychology*, 23-44. Oxford: Elsevier.

Carroll, Mary
   1996   The acquisition of L2-specific perspectives on paths of motion (L1 English-L2 German). Paper presented at the Euresco conference on adult second language acquisition, Esphino.

Carroll, Mary
   1997   Changing place in English and German: Language-specific preferences in the conceptualization of spatial relations. In: Jan Nuyts and Eric Pederson (eds.), *Language and Conceptualization*, 137-161. Cambridge: Cambridge University Press.

Carroll, Mary
   2000   Representing path in language production in English and German: Alternative perspectives on figure and ground. In: Christopher Habel and Christiane von Stutterheim (eds.), *Räumliche Konzepte und sprachliche Strukturen*, 97-118. Tübingen: Niemeyer.

Carroll, Mary, and Monique Lambert
   in press   Information structure in narratives and the role of grammaticised knowledge: A study of adult French and German learners of English. In: Christine Dimroth and Marianne Starren (eds.), *Dynamics of First and Second Language Acquisition*. Amsterdam: Benjamins.

Carroll, Mary, and Christiane von Stutterheim
1993 The representation of spatial configurations in English and German and the grammatical structure of locative and anaphoric expressions. *Linguistics* 31: 1011-1041.

Carroll, Mary, Jorge Murcia Serra, Marzena Watorek, and Alessandra Bendiscioli
2000 The relevance of information organisation to second language acquisition studies: The descriptive discourse of advanced adult learners of German. In: Clive Perdue (ed.), *Studies in Second Language Acquisition*, special issue, 22/3: 441-466

Chafe, Wallace
1987 Cognitive constraints on information flow. In: Russell Tomlin (ed.), *Coherence and Grounding in Discourse*, 21-51. Amsterdam: Benjamins

Comrie, Bernard
1976 *Aspect: An Introduction to the Study of the Verbal Aspect and Related Problems.* Cambridge: Cambridge University Press.

Graumann, Carl F.
1989 Perspective setting and talking in verbal interaction. In: Rainer Dietrich and Carl F. Graumann (eds.), *Language Processing in Social Context*, 233-276. Amsterdam: Elsevier.

Gumperz, John J., and Stephen C. Levinson (eds.)
1996 *Rethinking Linguistic Relativity.* Cambridge: Cambridge University Press.

Halm, Ute
2000 Planung und Ausdruck von Ereignissequenzen bei Kindern und Erwachsenen. Thesis, University of Heidelberg.

Klein, Wolfgang
1994 *Time in Language.* London: Routledge.

Klein, Wolfgang, and Christiane von Stutterheim
1987 Quaestio und referentielle Bewegung in Erzählungen. *Linguistische Berichte* 109: 163-183.

Kellerman, Eric, and Michael Sharwood Smith (eds.)
1986 *Cross-Linguistic Influence in Second Language Acquisition.* Oxford: Pergamon Press.

Levelt, Willem J. M.
1989 *Speaking: From Intention to Articulation.* Cambridge: The MIT Press.

Levinson, Stephen C.
1997 From outer to inner space: Linguistic categories and non-linguistic thinking. In: Jan Nuyts and Eric Pederson (eds.), *Language and Conceptualization*, 13-45. Cambridge: Cambridge University Press.

Li, Charles N., and D. A. Zubin
1996   Discourse continuity and perspective talking. In: Judith F. Duchan, Gail A. Bruder and Lynne E. Hewitt (eds.), *Deixis in Narrative: A Cognitive Science Perspective,* 287-307. Hillsdale (NJ): Erlbaum.

Lucy, John A.
1996   *Grammatical Categories and Thought.* Cambridge: Cambridge University Press.

Lucy, John A.
1996   The scope of linguistic relativity: An analysis and review of empirical research. In: John J. Gumperz and Stephen C. Levinson (eds.), *Rethinking Linguistic Relativity*, 37-69. Cambridge: Cambridge University Press.

Mayer, Mercer
1969   *Frog, where are you?* New York: Dial Press.

Myhill, John
1992   *Typological Discourse Analysis: Quantitative Approaches to the Study of Linguistic Function.* Cambridge, Mass.: Blackwell.

Naigles, Letitia R., Ann R. Eisenberg, Edward T. Kao, Melissa Highter, and Nancy McGraw
1998   Speaking of motion: Verb use in English and Spanish. *Language and Cognitive Processes* 13: 521-549.

Pederson, Eric
1995   Language as context, language as means: Spatial cognition and habitual language use. *Cognitive Linguistics* 6: 33-62.

Roßdeutscher, Antje
1999   Kohärenz, temporale Anaphorik und Inferenz. Manuscript, IMS. University of Stuttgart.

Slobin, Dan Isaac
1991   Learning to think for speaking: Native language, cognition and rhetorical style. *Pragmatics* 1: 7-26.

Slobin, Dan Isaac
1996   From "thought and language" to "thinking for speaking". In: John J. Gumperz and Stephen C. Levinson (eds.), *Rethinking Linguistic Relativity*, 70-96. Cambridge: Cambridge University Press.

Slobin, Dan Isaac, and Nini Hoiting
1994   Reference to movement in spoken and signed languages: Typological considerations. In: *Proceedings of the 20th Annual Meeting of the Berkeley Linguistics Society*, 487–505.

Talmy, Leonard
1988   The relation of grammar to cognition. In: Brygida Rudzka-Ostyn (ed.), *Topics in Cognitive Linguistics*, 165-205. Amsterdam: Benjamins.

Tversky, Barbara
1996 Spatial perspective in descriptions. In: Paul Bloom, Mary A. Peterson, Lynn Nadel and Merrill F. Garrett (eds.), *Language and Space*, 463-491. Cambridge, Mass.: The MIT Press.

von Stutterheim, Christiane
1997 *Einige Prinzipien der Textproduktion: Empirische Untersuchungen zur Produktion mündlicher Texte.* Tübingen: Niemeyer.

von Stutterheim, Christiane
1999 How language specific are processes in the conceptualiser? In: Ralf Klabunde and Christiane von Stutterheim (eds.), *Representation and Processes in Language Production*, 153-179. Wiesbaden: Deutscher UniversitätsVerlag.

von Stutterheim, Christiane, and Wolfgang Klein
1989 Textstructure and referential movement. In: Rainer Dietrich and Carl F. Graumann (eds.), *Language Processing in Social Context*, 39-76. Amsterdam: Elsevier.

von Stutterheim, Christiane, and Wolfgang Klein
in press Quaestio und l-perspectivation. In: Carl F. Graumann and Werner Kallmeyer (eds.), *Perspectivity and Perspectivation in Discourse.* Amsterdam: Benjamins.

von Stutterheim, Christiane, and Monique Lambert
in press Crosslinguistic analysis of temporal perspective. To appear in: Henriëtte Hendricks (ed.), *The Structure of Learner Language.* Berlin: de Gruyter.

von Stutterheim, Christiane, and Ralf Nuese
in press Processes of conceptualisation in language production, language-specific perpectivation and event construal. In: *Linguistics*, Special Issue: *Processes of perspectivation in language production.*

Wierzbicka, Anna
1995 A semantic basis for grammatical typology. In: Werner Abraham, Talmy Givón and Sandra A. Thompson (eds.), *Discourse Grammar and Typology. Papers in Honor of John W.M. Verhaar*, 179-209. Amsterdam: Benjamins.

Typological comparison and interlanguage phonology: maps or gaps between typology and language learning of sound systems?

Stefania Giannini

1. Introduction

Recent contributions have concentrated the attention of linguists on the theoretical potential of linking study of the diachronic evolution of grammar to the process of acquisition experienced by learners in building their own grammar of a second language. A convergence of strategies and procedures between the historical evolution of languages and individual diachrony has been highlighted, but so far investigation has focused on phenomena of grammaticalisation. The findings have provided empirical confirmation of the principle of unidirectionality (lexicon precedes grammar in the history of languages, as it does in the development of interlanguage) alongside a certain number of specific points of correspondence between the successive phases of the historical evolution of grammatical forms and their appearance and consolidation in interlanguage.[1]

An initial reply to the question Comrie (1984) posed to the scientific community, "Why (do) linguists need language acquirers?", thus comes from diachrony: the reply is contained in a general research project, which focuses both on a typological and language learning perspective. This project is inspired by the conviction that linguists can obtain insight into the way language operates from the contribution offered by research into second language acquisition (SLA).

Comrie's question also implicitly contains an invitation to examine the correlation between universally-distributed tendencies and linguistic category acquisition processes. The methodological proposal is coupled with a precise programmatic declaration: the aspects of a language that are consistent with a linguistic universal should be easier to acquire than those which seem inconsistent. Two subordinate hypotheses derive from this:

a) a property which is consistent with a universal tendency will be acquired more easily than one which is not, even if the native language conflicts with both;
b) a property which is inconsistent with a universal trend will be acquired with more difficulty than one which is consistent, even if the native language is consistent with both.

In other words, the power of attraction and conditioning of the universal principles of language is projected as being stronger than the structural convergence that exists by chance between the (first and second) languages.

The problem of greater or lesser difficulty in acquiring structures nevertheless cannot remain separate from assessment of the markedness of the feature. For this aspect it is equally possible to foresee inversely proportional relationships between the markedness characteristics of a category and the ease with which it is acquired, so that:

1. less marked properties will be easier to acquire (even if the property is found in L2 but not L1);
2. more marked properties will be more difficult to acquire (even if the property is found in both L2 and L1);

with a corollary, which represents the third hypothetical condition:

3. properties common in interlanguage (and therefore not very marked) can be acquired easily even if neither the first nor the second language has them.

The perspective suggested by Comrie casts into serious doubt the interpretive value of SLA if the latter is effected within its own research dimension and divorced from theoretical reference to typological comparison and universal principles.

With regard to typology, it is therefore necessary to go beyond the idea that difficulty in learning a certain category can be measured in the exclusive comparison of L1 and L2 structures. The formulation of predictive hypotheses concerning the strategies which could be adopted sees the inclusion of the concept of interlinguistic markedness as the third and indispensable level of assessment of interlanguage processes.

The challenge promises to be complex but, at the same time, even more stimulating for phonology. Here the persistence of first-language conditioning has, more than in other grammatical domains, obstructed the development of independent SLA projected towards explanatory hypotheses that can immediately be translated into the theoretical and methodological schemes adopted for typological comparison and diachronic evolution.

Further scientific objectives in the phonological field were introduced by Eckman in the early 1980s (cf. Eckman 1984), again in the form of problems to be addressed and solved at the level of empirical research and deeper theoretical study. Here again are those which are still current:

is it possible to characterise the notion of *human interlanguage* in terms of implicational and non-implicational universals?

if so, what is the relationship between these universals and those formulated for first languages?

In Eckman's view, the most reasonable hypothesis to put forward as a starting point is the following: given the body of absolute and typological universals formulated on the basis of first languages, there will be no interlanguage that violates these principles.[2] The state of knowledge that has been reached thus far in SLA allows us to test this hypothesis but not the extreme opinions (that is, whether there exists a relation of identity between first language universals and interlanguage universals, or if specific universals for interlanguages exist).

The remarks summarised in this paragraph justify the theoretical distinction between the learning conditions of L1 and L2:

a. L2 learners find themselves in an individual condition of bilingualism which may (though not necessarily) also lead them to a typological change (in the frequent case that L1 and L2 are typologically distant from each other);
b. the condition of *acquisitional bilingualism* assumes the form of a contact situation, and as such is more subject to the influence of context (as opposed to what happens in the case of the first language);
c. L2 acquisition occupies an interval of time which comprises internal evolution and development. It proceeds in phases which are comparable and commensurate with the historical phases of diachrony *tout court*.

From these premises there derives a theoretical and methodological proposal, the explanatory potential of which has not yet been fully explored either by the typologists or, still less, by the acquisitionalists: to measure the acquisitional data not on the basis of their relationship with the first and second languages, but in comparison with the most general principles which are implied in the realisation of a certain process (e.g. the category of iconicity for syntax and morphology, the naturalness and the greatest perceptive and/or productive simplicity of certain processes for phonology), and to test its correspondence (Giacalone Ramat 2000).

This makes SLA an ideal observatory for interpreting the conditions and forms of linguistic variation. The research objectives are the following:

1. to define a hierarchical scale of access to the linguistic categories to be acquired;

2. to work out a series of hierarchical relationships of an implicational type with reference to the times and manners of entry of such categories into the interlanguage;
3. to establish predictive hypotheses which no longer derive from comparison with the ascertainment of the presence/absence of a given phenomenon in L1 or L2 (or of the gap that separates them in respect of that same phenomenon), but instead stand in relation to its degree of markedness and frequency in the natural languages;
4. an objective which is perhaps still more ambitious, and is certainly bolder (at the present state of knowledge): to succeed in formulating principles of formal restriction of the probability of acquiring a given grammatical category, and the greater or lesser probabilities of change during diachronic evolution.

In this study the above points will be examined and tested at the level of phonology, within the limits of the data which can be deduced from the study of the category of consonant length in Italian L2 in comparison with the diachronic data already available on the development of the feature of consonant length in late Latin.

Partial but convincing results have been obtained in answer to at least some of the questions raised above. Later expansion of the quantitative data and extension of the research to different target languages from Italian will allow wider-ranging generalisations, which cannot be formulated at this stage of research.

2. Phonological typology, universals and sound change

The theoretical areas of reference are represented by the three research subfields which independently have produced methods and principles for the classification and interpretation of the phonological processes:

a. *dynamic and diachronic typology*: the discovery of correlations between individual structural features common to natural languages and the determination of their possible candidature for the status of universals, uniformly and absolutely present in the world's languages (*ergo* absolute), or subordinate universals, indicating the presence of other features (*ergo* implicational). The properties of the linguistic categories directly involved in this type of phenomena are the frequency and markedness factors (naturalness for phonological features);

b. *diachronic phonology*: the study of sound change within the wider theory of language change allows us to formulate generalisations and, in some cases, implicational principles commensurate with the results of research produced in typology;

c. *interlanguage phonology*: the field of study of second-language sound system acquisition strategies has developed in the course of the last twenty years with particular regard to English L2. The peculiarities of second-language phonological acquisition (among others, the greater influence of the first language on errors of replacement and of adaptation to the L2 categories) have made this an area of specialisation which is partially independent within the field of SLA.

In the pages that follow, there will be a concise reminder of the points of contact and the theoretical instruments which the three areas of research provide independently of their disciplinary interaction.

In later paragraphs (cf. below §§ 3–4) concrete application of these instruments will be demonstrated for the case of consonant length in Italian L2, observed during guided learning by adult speakers from various linguistic and geographical origins. The acquisitional data will be compared with the generalisations that can be deduced from the typological comparison for the specific feature and with the analysis of consonant gemination in the historical development from Latin to Romance.

2.1. Dynamic and diachronic typology

Greenberg's diachronic typology decreed the demise of the taxonomic objective in the course of three decades of thorough work on the theoretical model combined with empirical research conducted on wide-ranging *corpora* of languages which vary as to their geographical origins and genetic composition.[3]

Greenberg introduced innovations at the methodological level, supporting a particularistic approach (as opposed to the previous holistic model and with its consequent focus on single grammatical sectors). Furthermore, on the theoretical level his approach was the first to explore the possibility of transforming the individual structural features into a series of implicative relationships. This led in the first instance to a probabilistic list of the models of possible variation.

The objectives pursued and already achieved, if not completely then at least in great part, by Greenberg's typology are well known and are part of the body of technical knowledge of theoretical linguistics:

a. to define the notion of possible human language (on the basis of a set of restrictions which affect the occurrence of individual features);
b. to correlate logically-independent linguistic features;
c. to determine universal principles, both absolute (uniformities valid for all languages) and implicational, ordered hierarchically, with important theoretical consequences on the predictive level;
d. to contribute to clarifying the concept of markedness (and naturalness) of linguistic processes.

Functionally-inspired typology has also addressed classificatory problems in the diachronic dimension, suggesting conditions of uniformity of realisation in linguistic change just as in interlanguage variation. An ambitious goal of this area of typological study is that of establishing a correlation between the various types of changes;

this will hopefully be linked to a forecast of conditions of greater or lesser stability in a language state and the accompanying discovery of the most fragile points which are more exposed to the possibility of change.[4]

In the phonological sphere, research was soon oriented towards the construction of principles of classification of the phonological inventories that characterise and distinguish the languages of the world, selected and grouped into samples which are sufficiently wide-ranging and representative of the various language families. The starting point in this area is the Language Universals Project set up and directed by Greenberg himself and Ch. Ferguson at Stanford University (SPA = *Stanford Phonological Archive*); a debt is owed to this project, in various ways, by the UPSID (*University of California at Los Angeles Phonological Segment Inventory Database*, reference to which is also made in this study: cf. § 3.1 below). The latter remains the widest-ranging and most easily-available typological repository for statistical research into the contents of sound systems (cf. Maddieson 1984).

In his early work on universals, Greenberg (1966) formulated the necessary criteria for determining the conditions for occurrence of marked and unmarked values in a given segment. He thus acknowledged, albeit indirectly, the theoretical priority of the markedness and frequency factors in order to be able to arrive at interlinguistic generalisations on the structure and substance of the phonological classes.[5]

This early model led to implicative hierarchies which are still called upon and valued in the formulation of predictive hypotheses on the probability of the occurrence of a feature, or in relation to the presence or absence of other features in the same language (e.g. the point of articulation, for which the following implicative scale is used: velar < dental/alveolar < bilabial; sonority feature: obstruents < nasals < liquids < glides < vowels).

Even now the statistical and universalistic observations that can be put forward for the classes of sounds benefit from the theoretical framework and the range of monograph studies which Greenberg and his researchers produced on individual phonological categories (cf.

nasals, recently re-examined from a typological and historical viewpoint: cf. Hajek 1997).

Typology supplied the empirical, verifiable evidence for possible reliable generalisations of the universalistic type, with the building up of large databases on a comparative interlinguistic basis and with a wide structural range. It is therefore likely to become a fundamental benchmark for the phenomena of acquisitional and historical variation.

2.2. Diachronic phonology: universals, markedness and frequency of phonological processes

The typological classification of the phonological categories distinguishes between logically-possible processes and that which is present naturally and can be deduced from comparison. In addition, the typological programme is completed by the position stated in Kiparsky (1995): his study defends the phonological nature of sound change through the identification of language-specific interpretive restrictions which affect a speaker's actions and processing principles. In the interpretive area, Kiparsky holds that it becomes necessary to identify a more restricted range of possibilities, established by the phonological system of the language or languages in question (and by linguistic contact, in the SLA sphere), within the body of phonologically-plausible processes. Autosegmental abstractionism, in contrast, places the requirements of acceptability of the formal description on the plane of correctness and of representative consistency; the result is often a descriptive output which is too powerful, capable of predicting logically-possible representations of phonological processes which in reality are never observed.

The hopeful outcome of this type of approach relates to the theoretical possibility of establishing constraints in realisation on sound change and on the access to L2 categories that derive from universalist hypotheses with a typological and comparative basis.

The universal parameters that emerge in the description must then be tested in the light of plausible phonetic explanations. Linguistic reconstruction should therefore be limited to that which is phonetically plausible and empirically verifiable. This also allows separation, on the theoretical and interpretive level, of phonetic 'naturalness' from the derivative adequacy of synchronic phonological rules.

The crucial role in the transmission of sound change is attributed to the listener, without this involving adherence to any teleological positions, which are now foreign to the theory of language change: the empirical phonetic basis instead provides concrete substance, which can be checked experimentally, to justify the passage from segment A to segment B in language X in terms of gradual, minimal and natural movement.

The predominant mechanism of transmission and perception of the phonological categories is of a selective kind. A similar principle enlivened the theoretical debate on evolutionary biology when Jakobson himself adopted the discipline as an epistemological model for historical linguistics (for a restatement of this position, duly updated, see Lass 1997).

In mastering the system of sounds in a second language, the learner actively works on the data: the variants which contrast with the specific structural principles of the target language will be learned with greater difficulty and will have less chance of becoming an integral part of the system. In the case of L2, selection occurs under the double stimulus of the two languages involved (L1 and L2), in the admittedly impartial condition of contact, but also in the observance of hierarchies of access and categorial restructuring that may be revealed as language-independent.

Other controversial diachronic phenomena, such as the phonologisation of redundant features, have also been explained by calling upon the determining action of the selection principle. The process can be defined (as, again, for Kiparsky 1995) in terms of the priming effect: a redundant feature becomes phonologised if the phonological representations have a class node available to accept it.

The cases of compensatory lengthening and assimilation as diachronic strategies of reactive rearrangement are interesting when compared with other segmental transformations. The loss of a consonant causes a lengthening in the word when the language already has an opposition of quantity. Similarly, total assimilation of consonant clusters which may produce geminates are seen mostly (though not exclusively) in languages that already have consonant length as a distinctive feature (well-known examples: Finnish, Ancient Greek, Latin and Italian). Languages which do not have gemination prefer to simplify the clusters by eliminating one of the two consonants (included in this group are English, German, French and Modern Greek). The variationist/selective model explains the mechanisms of sound change, and introduces a framework which is also promising for acquisition, where the hypothetical action of a priming effect on the part of the phonological inventory of the base language would be correlated with the tendency which is typologically the least marked and universally the widest distributed of the category.

In the diachronic and interlinguistic framework summarised here, there is nevertheless an unanswered question: what conditions/factors can encourage, if not actually determine, the onset of the phonological processes? And from there: from what point does selection of the units affected by the change begin?

The problem is an old one, and the suggested solutions have not always appeared entirely convincing for diachrony. Suffice it to recall the diffusionist argument, which continues to field staunch supporters against similarly radical opponents in the international debate on sound change and its means of transmission within languages.[6]

Bybee (2000a, 2000b), in very recent publications devoted to this specific question, shows that the factor responsible for the incipient phase of phonologically-motivated sound changes, i.e. those that operate on the superficial phonetic form (segmental reduction and assimilatory processes, e.g. the elimination of /t/ and /d/ at the end of the word in English), is to be found in the statistical frequency of the lexical units.[7]

The case of elimination of English /t/ and /d/ in word final position is reconstructed in the following way: the sound change is strongly conditioned by frequency and by phonological factors relating to context. *Kept* and *slept* are the verb type most affected due to the superimposition of the labial articulation on the coronal (a factor that obstructs and pollutes the perception of *–t*). This sound change comes about on three levels:, articulatory, perceptive and lexical. On the articulatory level there is a reduction; at the same time, perception of the reduced consonant is masked by the context. The lexical items with a coronal final gradually adapt to the change under way and gradually become restructured, losing the stop completely (cf. Bybee 2000a).

We have therefore come back, in short, to an expression of the substantialist position in the restatement of the importance of the 'phonetic details' of which every phonological process is made up; sound change thus goes back to being in the first instance a concrete event which affects individual lexical units, in real time, in a measure proportional to their frequency of use. On paper, low-frequency words are those which are at the least risk of corruption, and indeed are seen to be less exposed to it in convergent results of the data deduced from diachrony and SLA; those with a high statistical frequency (and with a high rate of incidence in speech) will be affected systematically and in a much shorter time.

Bybee (2000) therefore supports, without theoretical or empirical reservations, a lexicalist vision of sound change:

1. sound change affects the lexicon, advancing gradually, spreading from more frequent to less frequent lexical units and producing gradual changes in the phonetic representation of the lexical units;
2. sound change therefore affects the lexicon permanently, and the lexical units are not represented by an abstract phonemic transcription;
3. phonemes do not exist as units, but rather represent relationships of similarity between the components of phonetic strings.

In diachronic events the central role is assigned to the lexicon as being the crucial vehicle for the transmission and propagation of new rules (whether these are entering the grammar of a community or the individual grammar of a learnt language). This combines with the partial results so far obtained for phonological acquisition,[8] and it automatically leads the explanation back to the pertinent level of the ways the speaker accesses the mental representations of the processes of phonetic variation and variability and, above all, to the criteria of deposit and storage of acoustic information in the memory

On this specific topic some studies of second language learning (cf. Flege, Koster, 2.3 below) supported by perceptive-type experimental data, describe the characteristics of the acoustic memory, which operates in storing the individual segments and is a defining element in the explanation of the selective processes that depend on the listener.

2.3. Interlanguage phonology: perception, selection and restructuring of categories

Interlanguage phonology has witnessed the consolidation of theories and experimental procedures which assign a priority function to the discriminatory processing of the listener. One of the most widely-accepted theoretical and experimental models in the field of interlanguage is that of Flege, based on the idea that interlanguage is a contact situation in which errors are the effects of a restructuring process (interaction hypothesis); Flege's model holds that a great proportion of the errors in production are the results of an erroneous perceptive representation, and the productive potential of the learner is placed in a causal relationship of dependence on these acoustic deformations.[9]

Research into the mechanisms of perception and recognition of second-language categories has thus taken up a legitimate, recognised central position in SLA, thanks to the contributions made by a series of research experiments on the comparative abilities of native and non-native speakers (cf. Koster 1987, Flege 1997). At the time of writing we have a quantity of empirical data available from which we can abstract some provisional conclusions of a general nature on the role of perception in the categorial selection on which correct construction of L2 grammar is based.

Each speaker in the position of oral message receiver/listener has to address the basic problem of recognising words in the speech continuum. Non-native speakers have much greater difficulty due both to the frequent difference in the phonetic realisation of the phonemes in the various languages (and the consequent assignment of a particular segment to another category) and to the conditions of acoustic contamination which often characterise words in sandhi. An extremely high rate of variability in execution, especially at the ends of words and as a consequence of the phonetic context (prosodic features and the speed of the speech produced), further increases the difficulty of establishing the divisions at the beginning and end of words for the non-native receiver.

In the syntagma recognition exercises designed and administered by Koster (1987) to native and non-native speakers of English, it was observed that non-native speakers proceed using conscious attempts to find words that might correspond in some measure to a certain quantity of acoustic elements identified in the utterance (among the many examples: *weights and measures* > *wage emerges*, *dearest you* > *dear stew* etc.)

In detail, the identification tests given to the informant sample included the following:

1. experiments in recognising syntagma made up of two words, where the second is the target;
2. experiments to assess the influence of the phenomenon of assimilation on perceptive and discriminatory performance; it is held that when a word is introduced acoustically the initial part of the acoustic sequence activates all the lexical representations that begin with that particular string. The context does not play any role in the activation of the first part, but has an important effect by helping to reduce the number of words that are candidates to occupy the position.

The differences in performance seen in the data fall within predictions largely taken for granted: thus non-native speakers are seen to be slower in recognising the phonological categories (60 msec more for the phonemes, 200 msec more for words or exercises that require lexical access, Koster 1987), and the sentence context conditions their performance more directly.[10]

The main problem for non-native speakers is not at the phonemic but rather at the lexical level; their errors of perception are linked to the production of syntactically-anomalous sentences, in the constant attempt to give some sense to what they hear, rather than being comparable with the so-called 'slips of the ear' of native speakers.

The lexicon is thus a sort of 'unit of measurement' in the segmentation of speech: the identification of an uncertain/dubious phonological category (which might be attributed to more than one lexical unit) makes it possible to assume that the lexical item has priority in the processes of construction and restructuring of speech, and that the interpretive effort aims to rebuild independent units.

If even the non-native speaker appears to concentrate on the recovery and integration of a phrasal context that satisfies conditions of suitability and 'good' semantic and syntactic construction, and if progressive development of the skills of second-level articulation, like those of perception and discrimination, passes in any case through the filter of the lexical unit, then the existence of word-sensitivity would seem to be acceptable on several levels of the synchronic and diachronic operation of language. Lexicon appears as the primary vehicle for transmission of categorial information and knowledge which do not involve the semantic and morphological levels alone.

The role of the phrasal context in perception and identification of categories in the interlanguage provides further confirmation. Lexical and semantic factors have a strong effect on the identification of the phonetic segments: the consonant clusters at word boundaries, if inserted or capable of being inserted in semantically-suitable word contexts, are identified much better and much earlier (thus the sequence /t#g/ is recognised easily in the syntagma *eight girls*, whilst in *mate guns* it is recognised in 25% of the useful cases, Koster 1987), and the non-native speakers benefit to a greater extent.

Finally, targeted perception tests have demonstrated that the syntagmatic context immediately following the phoneme or cluster in question (the suitability of the syntagma could only be assessed at the end) is also a conditioning factor. Different conclusions have been drawn regarding the possibility of postcategorial correction: for some, it appears improbable that the potential phonetic classifications are changed into classifications that make sense in the case of ambiguous stimuli (because this would imply that acoustic information was stored in echo memory, which is extremely short – less than a second for the stops). As an alternative, it has been suggested that the information and the acoustic stimulus are judged on the basis of the lexical status of the word in which they appear (where by lexical status we mean a function of the interaction between lexical knowledge and phonetic classification).

Some experiments (again from Koster's corpus: e.g. /swik gɜl/ interpreted as *sweet girl*) demonstrate that phonological information can be held in the acoustic memory long enough to allow the speaker to correct the output of the process of phonetic classification. With this operation the learner passes from the phonetic code, which does not produce words, to the phonological code, which in each language governs the development of the system of sounds into portions of sense.

The substantialist and perceptive perspective has also led to a review of the interpretation of some consonantal universals which have been quietly accepted. Under the same conditions, the vowel that precedes a voiced consonant is longer than the one that precedes an unvoiced consonant (the /i/ in *bid* is longer than the one in *bit*). The difference in the length of the vowel segment has been attributed to acoustic differences: speakers internalise a vowel target of greater length before a voiced consonant in relation to a difficulty in immediately identifying the segmental boundary between vowel and voiced consonant (since the feature of sonority passes from one segment to the other).

The learner's search for the criteria of internalisation of the perception target constitutes a promising field of inquiry. In the course of studying consonant length in Italian L2, reference will also be made to this aspect of the process of of classification process of the consonantal feature examined.

3. Case-study: the feature of consonant length in Italian L2
3.1. Classes of sounds and phonological processes

The phonological processes act on the segmental units in ways that vary, sometimes significantly, from language to language, and from period to period if one considers the diachronic evolution of an individual system.

In the opinion of Kay (1989), modern phonology retains two primary scientific tasks, still largely untouched: to understand more fully the nature and function of the phonological processes in the economy of natural languages (What are phonological processes for?); and, as a priority, to discover the general motivation that justifies their existence in all the world's languages (Why are phonological processes present in all linguistic systems?) (1989:40).

Until now attention has concentrated above all on the former question. The phonetic solution holds that phonological processes, not being a logical necessity, exist in virtue of the changes that the segments undergo in subordination to the context. The greater ease of articulation and the tendency to produce ever more 'natural' sequences (as a reaction to the unnaturalness of other sequences which the system eliminates) becomes a basic explanatory principle of the naturalistic model.

On the other hand, a typological review of phonological inventories leads to conflicting conclusions. It can be observed that examples of divergence between the individual natural languages are very wide-spread (thus repudiating the hypothesis of a drift which is uniformly orientated towards the production of articulations with less use of energy); and the hypothesis of the naturalness of the phonological processes would thus seem hard to sustain, at least in its strongest version, on the test-bed of interlinguistic comparison.

The functional motivation of phonological processes has also been sought at the level of formal representations in the course of the deeper theoretical study of the criteria of maximum simplicity and linearity in phonological representations (the question: What is a possible phonological process?), an area to which Kay himself belongs. From this viewpoint it is held that limits and constraints on the types of processes possible are not dictated by physio-motor requirements, but by the existence of domains and configurations above the level of the individual segments. Generative grammar has identified the exclusive target of any type of phonological process in the concept of the natural class (that is, each class of sounds that can be defined with a single matrix of features – the coronals, for example, with inclusion of at least the following points of articulation: dental, alveolar, palato-alveolar and palatal).[11]

In the course of this study we will test the application of this notion during acquisition to confirm the possibility that the phonetic categories are stored and processed in the semantic memory, as already demonstrated for lexicon and morphology. This memory acts on portions of paradigms composed of elements which are differentiated in some properties but can clearly be discriminated and grouped into a single class in the perceptive phase through feature association and analogy and through shared properties. Every natural class is the prime object of a certain set of processes: in the case of the coronals again, the weakening phenomena (substitution and segmental loss, assimilation) are widespread, and not only in a single language (Paradis and Prunet 1991).

The processes of assimilation are an illuminating example. In Italian, for example, sequences of stops derived from Latin have been simplified into geminated consonants as the final outcome of a process of assimilation (cf.: It. *sette* < *septem*; *dottore* < *doctor*, where the two *t*s are actually pronounced; the *tt* in *fatto* is about twice that of *fato*). The muscular effort is greater in the case of the geminated consonant than in that of the simple, but nevertheless languages produce processes that bring these conditions about, with the greatest concentration in some segmental classes (cf. below 3.3).

The second question is central, and still awaits an answer, which could in effect spring from of the contribution made by typological linguistics: why do languages use such a broad spectrum of different processes? The extent of the variety has perhaps been exaggerated. In any case, the 'classical' version of the theory of markedness, dating back to *SPE* (Chomsky and Halle 1968) allowed a theoretical justification to be found in the hierarchical constraints on specification of the features in the matrices: the specification of one feature creates conditions for the specification of other features. An example, the representation of front and back vowels (combined or not combined with the rounding feature), is given here:

i	u	ü	ɯ
[- back	[+ back	[- back	[+ back
- round]	+ round]	+ round]	- round]

In normal (i.e. unmarked) cases these features have the same value: indeed, it is easier to find languages that have the *i* and *u* vowels but not the other two (like Spanish and Arabic). However, we will not find a language that has the *ü* without having *i*, or ɯ [+ back], without *u* (Kay 1989: 62ff.).

The theory of markedness had thus already created theoretical conditions of predictability of the real conditions of feature specification in individual segments. Dynamic typology strengthened these and projected them onto the historical-evolutionary level (predictions about the possible path of sound change in relation to universal human constraints) and onto that of individual learning diachrony.

3.1. Consonant length: typological generalisations, markedness and feature frequency

Some generalisations regarding the consonant length feature can be inferred from the UPSID corpus (cf. above 2.1), in the comparison with Greenberg's hierarchical principles.

The UCLA sample contains 317 languages selected and entered on the basis of admission criteria that reproduce the experience of Stanford and guarantee that they are typologically representative.[12]

In describing the dimensions and the structure of the phonological inventories, Maddieson introduces the general limits within which the languages are usually registered: there are languages with limited inventories (<20), which nevertheless tend to remain stable over time (the Polynesian family is a famous example) *vs.* languages with wide inventories (>40).[13]

Within these numerical confines, UPSID provides confirmation that the phonological inventories are organised according to a well-defined central structural principle. Their structure is subject to hierarchical organisation, which implies wide diversity in the phonological complexity seen from language to language.

For Maddieson, the limits of the dimensions of the inventories are set not only by the theoretical questions of the density of the message and of the tolerance capacity of the channel in processing, but also by socio-linguistic pressures dictated by many contact situations, above all under adult learning conditions. The mechanism of phonological acquisition in these contexts acts through the substitution of each segment which is not connected to a very similar one in L1, or which can not be generated via a simple process of addition of familiar features. This leads to some probabilistic hypotheses for the different learning situations: for example, acquiring /g/ will be easier if L1 already contains /p,b,t,d/ and /k/; similarly, the more limited the L1 inventory, the higher the probability that some segments are generated through replacement, whilst the wider the inventory, the lower the probability that similar segments coincide, and therefore the higher the probability of a simplification of the inventory itself.[14]

The index of frequency of some phonemes compared with others is explained by the fact that the former are more prominent and choice of such phonemes maintains the distance between the segments of the language in question more clear-cut. The implicative hierarchies are scales that include different grades of phonetic prominence, with the most prominent segments in the highest position in the hierarchy and the least distinctive (and distant) in the lowest positions. In this light the concept of phonetic distance or prominence becomes an explanatory factor in the structure of phonological inventories, and also in the creation of interlanguage inventories. Naturally, not all inventories are constructed on the basis of the principle of maximising the phonetic distance: clicks are very prominent, but nevertheless are only used in a small number of languages (about 1% in the UPSID).

Similarly, long consonants are perceptively favoured compared with the corresponding short ones for all the classes of sounds in which they appear, despite a decidedly low statistical incidence. By assessing the incidence of C: for classes of sounds in the UCLA sample, the following distributional pattern is observed:

Table 1a. The distribution of C: in the UCLA sample.

C	Distribution	C:	Distribution
/p/	263	/p:/	7
/b/	198	/b:/	5
/t/	72	/t:/	2
/d/	53	/d:/	2
/k/	283	/k:/	9
/g/	175	/g:/	4
/ts/	46	/ts:/	3
/dz/	10	/dz:/	0
/tʃ/	141	/tʃ:/	5
/dʒ/	80	/dʒ:/	2
/s/	131	/s:/	4
/m/	299	/m:/	11
/n/	55	/n:/	4
/ɲ/	107	/ɲ:/	2
/r/	52	/r/	2
/l/	122	/l:/	4

The feature of consonant length is spread thinly through the languages in the UPSID sample and is marked for every class of sound (with an absolute percentage index of presence in the sample of 3.3%). One can only note a certain correlation between the length in the system of nasals and the length in other segments of the consonantal inventory (with the exception of three languages: Chuvash, Ocaina, !Xũ): 11 languages have /m:/ and 9 /p:/ or /b:/, or both. In these two groups 8 are the same, that is they have both /m:/ and the stop. The probability these segments have of co-occurring in the hypothesis of random distribution is about 0.0001. Applying this principle to the UPSID corpus, we would expect 1/900 languages to show this correlation, whereas in fact the index of frequency is about 1/40. The numbers are nevertheless too few to be able to assign a direction to the association between long consonants and nasal phonemes.

Italian (at least in its standard form on a central geographical basis) is in a situation of typological markedness: it is the only one of the Romance languages to have long consonants for 15 phonemes /p b t d k g tʃ dʒ f v s m n l r/, albeit with different criteria of synchronous productivity (the function is auxiliary for the dentals /ts dz/ in the contexts of V_V, V_j, w, and for the palatals /ɲ ʎ/ and the postalveolar /ʃ/ in the context of V_V) (Giannini and Costamagna 1998).

The preferential syllabic and prosodic context is of the type *matto*, in which the C: occupies the post-tonic position in syllabic coda, which is permitted to few other consonant phonemes in Italian (in particular: nasals liquids or sibilants, Mioni 1993: 101 ff.).

3.2. Acquisition of consonant length in Italian L2

The study of long consonant acquisition by adult learners in a guided context is part of wide-ranging research into the interlanguage phonology of Italian L2 which was initiated at the Perugia University for Foreigners in 1997.

The first data relating to consonant acquisition procedures, with particular reference to the case of the long consonant and limited to a corpus elicited from 3 learners with different native languages (Brazilian Portuguese, Modern Greek and French) have so far given the following results (cf. Giannini and Costamagna 1998):

1. consonantal gemination concentrates to the maximum in the interlanguage of the 3 subjects observed in a syllabic and prosodic pattern of the type ['VC:-CV] (It.: *mat-to, fat-to*), that is to say bisyllables with gemination in the post-tonic position;

2. the phonological scheme coincides with clearly-identifiable lexical classes: prepositions (It.: *della, nella, dalla*); verbal forms (It. past part.: *fatto, detto, messo*; pres. ind.: *hanno, fanno, sanno*); modifiers (It.: *tutto, bello, quello, stesso*).
3. the lexicon therefore represents the primary vehicle for spreading the category in the interlanguage, in a similar way to some mechanisms of distribution and propagation of sound change.

The body of data we present to complete the picture described above regards acquisition of consonant length by 11 adult learners studied longitudinally (from a minimum of 6 months to a maximum of 11 months) and subjected to a systematic programme of elicitation of data aimed at investigating the perceptive and productive mechanisms of C: (free conversational analysis and spontaneous speech; guided interview; perception and production tests for the discrimination, identification and imitation of words and phrases containing geminated consonants, cf. Giannini and Costamagna 1998: 67 ff). In this paper we will discuss the results of the productive tests.

During the period in question, each speaker was recorded for an average 6/7 times (from a minimum 4 sessions to a maximum 11, depending on availability) at regular intervals (minimum 1 week, maximum 3 weeks between one interview and another). The interviews were always carried out by the same researcher to ensure a certain familiarity with the informants and uniformity of method. The average time of recording for each learner was approximately 130 minutes.

The content of the recordings has been transcribed and encoded in IPA through the CHILDES (*Child Language Data Exchange System*) method of data processing.

Encoding in CHILDES has enabled us to collect and examine both the types and the tokens of each lexical form containing C:, in unstressed and stressed position for all types of consonantal segments (according to the typology in standard Italian: *palla, pallone, avvocato*). Finally, the auditory analysis allowed us to quantify the presence of C: in the types and tokens in relation to the syllabic types, classes of sounds and morphological and lexical classes implicated in the process of acquisition of the category.[15]

The first languages involved in the study are, in order: Spanish (Victoria) Venezuelan Spanish (Amelia), Modern Greek (Anthoula and Sofia), German (Ines, Laura, Maike and Thomas), French (Maguelonne and Robert) and Brazilian Portuguese (Luiz). None of these have consonant length as a distinctive feature.[16]

The characteristics of typological markedness of the feature combine with the contrast between the language systems of the base and target languages; the difficulties in acquisition will therefore be predictable independently of the characteristics of the learners' native language. On the basis of comparison with the UPSID typological data, the nasals should, in theory, represent a reference class, considering their distribution in the corpus.

The quantitative data relating to the existence of long consonants in the interlanguage of the individual learners were processed on the basis of the following classification criteria:

A. Analysis of the correct forms actually produced (percentage values of the occurrence of C: in the tokens):

Table 1b. Analysis of the correct forms actually produced

	(1)	(2)
Amelia (Venezuela)	48.0	46.0
Anthoula (Greece)	12.0	52.0
Ines (Germany)	54.0	28.0
Laura (Germany)	59.0	43.0
Luiz (Brazil)	30.9	44.0
Maguelonne (France)	17.5	59.9
Maike (Germany)	65.1	47.3
Robert (France)	28.0	51.4
Sofia (Greece)	15.8	55.7
Thomas (Germany)	32.9	49.2
Victoria (Spain)	22.0	34.8

(1) average values of the presence of C: per learner (obtained by calculating the ratio of correct forms to number of potential occurrences for tokens in the individual interlanguage of each learner)
(2) percentage values of the incidence of bisyllables in the tokens containing C

B. Analysis of the incidence of C: by types:

1. progressive and average percentage values relating to the presence of C: in individual development of interlanguage (from the first to the last recording session).

Table 2. Incidence of C: by type

Amelia (Venezuela)	39.0	23.0	43.0	44.0	48.0	53.0				
Anthoula (Greece)	18.0	12.0	5.0	2.2	10.0	20.0	12.5	21.5	7.0	
Ines (Germany)	40.0	46.0	54.0	68.0	48.0	55.0	55.0	40.0	57.0	
Laura (Germany)	45.0	41.0	44.0	62.0	57.0	68.0	64.0	62.0	69.0	59.0	69.0
Luiz (Brazil)	34.5	42.2	25.2	25.5	29.4	35.5	31.7	51.0		
Maguelonne (France)	18.7	15.4	13.9	13.2	24.2	25.4	27.7			
Maike (Germany)	55.0	63.7	65.6	65.0	62.0					
Robert (France)	37.3	27.5	26.1	34.9	31.5	37.6	23.9			
Sofia (Greece)	31.5	15.5	3.0	14.0	20.8	30.2	15.0			
Thomas (Germany)	34.4	35.5	25.6							
Victoria (Spain)	36.0	23.3	27.7	24.1	24.6	25.4	32.1			

428 *Stefania Giannini*

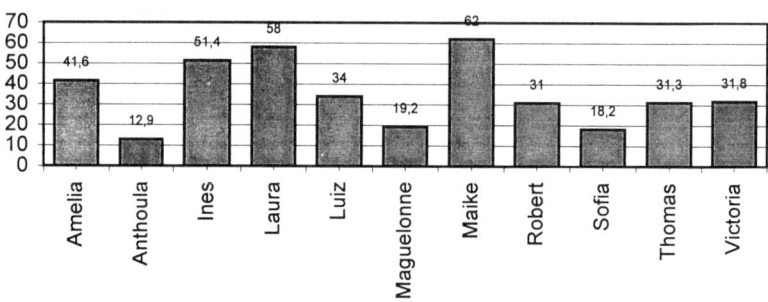

Figure 1.

C. Analysis of the occurrence of C: by classes of sounds:

1. incidence of C: by individual classes of sounds (percentage values obtained by calculating the ratio of the number of instances of production of C: for each phoneme to the overall number of tokens in which C: appears) for each learner:

Table 3. Incidence of C: by classes of sounds

	t	s	l	r	n	m	nasals
Amelia (Venezuela)	23.0	19.4	15.0	7.0	2.6 +	1.9 =	4.5
Anthoula (Greece)	35.0	14.0	17.0	0	5.7 +	1.4 =	7.1
Ines (Germany)	29.4	20.4	9.0	0	8.0 +	2.3 =	10.4
Laura (Germany)	18.0	23.7	17.4	0	8.4 +	0.6 =	8.9
Luiz (Brazil)	21.2	37.7	8.5	1.8	4.0 +	1.0 =	5.1
Maguelonne (France)	27.9	23.0	12.0	0.4	6.4 +	0.8 =	7.2
Maike (Germany)	28.9	17.9	11.4	0.8	8.5 +	3.6 =	12.1
Robert (France)	39.2	14.3	23.3	1.2	2.5 +	0.3 =	2.8
Sofia (Greece)	18.2	25.0	31.7	0	10.4 +	1.9 =	12.3
Thomas (Germany)	28.9	10.9	10.9	0	9.3 +	0 =	9.3
Victoria (Spain)	13.9	10.0	14.9	19.6	2.8 +	1.5 =	4.3

D. Total percentage values for the whole corpus of data:

Table 4. Total percentage values for the whole corpus of data

Incidence of C: by TOKENS	35.2
Incidence of C: by TYPES	39.0
Incidence of C: in bisyllables (TOKENS)	47.8
Classes of sounds with greatest concentration of C:	
Unvoiced dental stop /t/	28.3
Unvoiced alveolar-fricative /s/	19.6
Lateral liquid /l/	16.6

Brief consideration of the quantitative data suggests the following interpretive hypotheses:

1. notwithstanding the rise in the acquisitional curve of some learners (sometimes explained by specific extra-linguistic factors, e.g. for Maike, who had a high level of language proficiency and was firmly situated within an Italian-speaking context), progress with the long consonants is irregular in the interlanguage corpus. This confirms the idea that C: is a feature that is difficult to acquire and relatively unstable in individual diachrony, as it is in diachrony *tout court*;
2. the concentration of long consonants produced correctly in bisyllables (with C: post-tonic position) is consistent with the evidence of historical-evolutionary data of western proto-Romance. (cf. below 3.3);
3. the correlation between high-frequency words (see high incidence in the corpus of the morphological and lexical classes already found for the first three learners, with particular regard to modifiers and past part. and indicative verb forms) and C: reveals another meeting-point between the lexicalist hypothesis of sound change propagation (Bybee 2000a) and the spread of the categories in interlanguage;[17]
4. the concentration of C: in segmental classes (coronals) which are marked and particularly exposed to sound change and to

the greatest typological diffusion make it plausible that the acquisition of the feature started from these phonemes and continues to consider them a preferential target for correct production. A similar hypothesis has been put forward as an explanation of the sound change that triggered the explosion of the processes of assimilation in the late Latin period (see below).

3.3. Italian consonant length acquisitional data compared with the diachronic data

The feature of consonant length has been the subject of monographs and historical studies which have investigated its philological profile and the structural transformation in the Romance area.[18] For the developments in late Latin and its direct descent to the various central forms (still the synchronic base of Standard), the diachronic data can be found in Giannini and Marotta (1989), containing the lexicon of Latin gemination from the Classical period (labelled as Corpus I) to the more fragmentary phase of the post-Classical and proto-Romance period (Corpus II , cf. Giannini and Marotta 1989: 83 ff.). I will refer to this study for the analytic description of the internal structural aspects of Latin and proto-Romance gemination (in its links with the evolution of the syllabic and accentual structure) and of the sociolinguistic aspects (expressively and pragmatic markedness of the feature). The closing section of the publication summarises the retention of long consonants in western Romania and the accompanying explosion of assimilatory processes (of the type *octo* > *otto* of central-southern Italy), in contrast with the syllabic model with the 'weak' coda in all the rest of the Romance area (degemination and simplification of consonant clusters are sure symptoms of this and have been unanimously diagnosed, cf. Marotta 1993).

There follows an outline of the conclusions which are relevant here:

1. in the lexicon of Latin gemination, the disyllabic type predominates (55.8 percentage value);
2. the distribution of geminates in the classes of sounds reaches peaks of paradigm frequency in the liquids and the unvoiced dental stops (the whole range is included by the single natural class of the coronals);
3. Latin gemination does not affect the voiced consonants: the long obstruents in Latin are negatively indicated with respect to the feature of sonority, in contrast with the corresponding liquids and nasals (in this case again we refer to the natural class of sonorants).

The lack of voiced geminates, later partially inherited by Italian, is also justified on phonetic-articulatory grounds: the manner of articulation differs in the cases of stops and sonorants (the long variant of stops being produced with an increase in the duration of the closure that precedes the plosion, whilst the long sonorants are articulated continuously for a longer time without total obstruction).

The distribution of the feature by classes of sounds in Latin linguistic history also has a typological and universalistic motivation. On this level confirmation may be obtained from consideration of the following aspects, which are directly involved in the distribution of the length feature:

a. the intrinsic length of the segments: the unvoiced obstruents are intrinsically longer than their voiced correspondents, and are therefore more likely to exploit the length feature. From the articulatory viewpoint, gemination is actually a reinforcement process and, as such, will more naturally affect the natural classes which contain harder sounds, since the length produces an increase in glottal pressure;[19]
b. devoicing processes in relation to gemination: Cravens (1987) has discovered that in some dialects of Corsican degemination first affects the voiced consonants /b d g/, then the unvoiced obstruents /p t k / and lastly the sonorants /r m n/. The Corsican data are particularly interesting because they reveal that degemination

acts on phonological classes (degemination affected the Romance area along the same lines, starting with the unvoiced obstruents and so on until it affected liquids and nasals much later).

The second process that produces long consonants in the diachronic phonology of western Romance is the assimilation of consonantal clusters of the (Italian) type *octo* > It. *otto, septem* > It. *sette* and, following internal syllable syncopation, *speculum* > It. *specchio*. The foremost targets of this rule are the [+coronal] segments, a natural class which is unmarked in the structural and typological senses in terms both of maximum frequency and diffusion in the natural languages (the 317 languages that make up the UPSID corpus have at least some coronal consonants, except Hawaiian),[20] and of the configuration of articulatory properties (the coronals are under-specified at the articulation node point and this leaves it particularly exposed to the various types of phonological processes relating to weakening in articulation, such as assimilation, consonantal harmony and so on). Two essays by Marotta (1993, 1995) explain the genesis and nature of late-Latin assimilations and the special status of the coronals in the synchronic phonology of Italian, with typological and experimental evidence. Assimilation is seen as a weakening process when compared with substitution, but also as a partial reinforcement when compared with elimination; it is thus not surprising that the dentals are at the forefront of the obstruents involved in the change.[21]

4. Interpretation and conclusions

The manner of acquisition of the feature of consonant length offers the following possibilities of comparison with the principles of typological generalisation and the processes of diachronic evolution:

1. greatest incidence of C: in lexical and rhythmic-prosodic structures of a disyllabic type, coinciding with specific morphological classes;

2. greatest incidence of the length feature in classes of sound of the coronal type and in classes with the highest frequency for each type in world languages (unvoiced dental obstruent, unvoiced alveolar-dental fricative, lateral liquid);
3. leading role of the factor of frequency in the distribution of the feature in both lexical and sound classes;
4. relative independence of the facts noted in 1-3 from the first-language type.

General conclusions and interpretation of results:

1. from the analysis and comparison of the typological, acquisitional and diachronic data presented and discussed here, there appears to be a certain correspondence; the concept of mapping involving the historical and individual evolution of interlanguage is arguably grounded on empirical evidence (above all in relation to the phenomenon of concentration into lexical classes, point 1, and, at least in part, to the distribution of the feature of consonant length by classes of sounds, point 2);
2. equally evident is the partial correspondence and similar concept of mapping between acquisitional data and typological generalisations in distribution of the consonant length feature over the natural phonological classes (also in relation to the long consonant that derives from phonological processes such as assimilation, and which more readily affects same classes of sounds);
3. in identifying the elements that could have triggered the individual types of phonological process (the historical process of gemination, the cognitive process of acquisition and the typological distribution of the feature in the natural languages), the frequency factor has a leading role both in terms of absolute statistical incidence of the segment (consistent with the statistical and typological indications) and in terms of the high rate of textual incidence of the lexical items containing the specific segments (consistent with the Bybee's lexicalist

hypothesis to explain the criteria of progression of sound change).

Indirectly, the interpretation suggested here relegates the influence of L1 on the process of acquisition to a lower level: data are comparable and essentially homogeneous in a transverse direction in the different types of consonant lists belonging to the base languages (French, Brazilian Portuguese, Spanish, German and Modern Greek). Also absent is a hint of a link between the lesser or greater structural distance between L1 and L2, which may be laid out on a hypothetical scale of distance from Italian as follows: Spanish, French, Brazilian Portuguese, German, Modern Greek.

This allows, and indeed encourages, us to assign greater theoretical importance and empirical weight to conditioning by strategical principles of a general nature, confirmation of which is offered by the description of the dynamic typology and by historical-reconstructive linguistics.

Further study may lead to the determination of real constraints which alone will govern the rules of category transformation and change, of the restructuring and reprocessing of a foreign language, and of the spread of or limitations on the same categories in the languages of the world.

Notes

1. For Italian L2, consider the studies on the syntax of relative clauses and on verb categories, including tense (cf. Comrie 1998, Giacalone Ramat 2000).
2. Croft (1990): *unrestricted universals* are the universal characteristics of languages, such as the presence of V and C and the existence of N and V. Therefore, they establish the restriction on linguistic types on the basis of the relevant parameter (in the presence of a gap in the linguistic types that are logically possible: see, for instance, the distribution of vowels and nasals). *Implicational universals* are more interesting because they establish a relationship between two logically independent parameters.
3. The classificatory requirement of languages developed above all in morphology: ever since the 19th-century studies by the Schlegel brothers, Schleicher and Humboldt, the target was "a form of classification that subdivides lan-

guages on the basis of their belonging to a certain structural type" (Cristofaro and Ramat, 1999: 16).
4. There have also been strong methodological objections (cf. Croft 1990: 45ff.).
5. In the markedness theory, extending to all levels of grammar including the phonological, there are two prime criteria (Croft 1990: 72):
Behavioural:
   a. Inflectional: number of cross-cutting distinctions/phonemes the marked and unmarked values contain;
   b. Distributional: number of syntactic/phonological environments in which the marked and unmarked values occur;
   c. Cross-linguistic: number of language types in which the marked and unmarked values occur.
Frequency:
   a. Textual: number of occurrences of the marked and unmarked values in text;
   b. Cross-linguistic: number of languages in which the marked and the unmarked values are found.
6. Interlanguage phonology data warn against setting aside the diffusionist position: among the more recent studies, for different target languages, Giannini and Costamagna (1998: Italian L2), Gomez (1999); most recently, for an interesting study of the limitations imposed by the lexicon in the formation of interlanguage phonology cf. Gierut et al. (1999).
7. It is well known that the frequency factor was earlier suggested as a key to discovering the determining criteria, in the essential paper in which Jakobson proposed the first hypotheses on implicational hierarchies and the occurrence of phonemic series in the languages of the world (Jakobson 1944 = 1971: 58-59).
8. For the results of the first part of the research into consonant length in Italian L2, cf. Giannini and Costamagna (1998); see also Gierut et al. (1999).
9. The model therefore criticises and refutes the hypothesis of the critical period, and holds that the perceptive and productive capability relating to new phonological categories does not end at the age of 6. The learner will be able to produce the sounds of L2 more or less correctly depending above all on his/her ability to grasp the phonetic distance between a sound in L2 and the L1 sound closest and most similar to it.
10. The tendency to identify groups of the type /b#p/ as /#p/ or /p#p/ in Koster's data (1987) seem indirectly proportional to the level of linguistic competence acquired: an increase in the level of linguistic competence leads to decreasing dependence on the phonetic characteristics of the linguistic segments, in the sense that greater tolerance is developed towards incomplete or diminished specification of the phonemes.

11. Cfr. Paradis and Prunet (1991) for a general discussion on the special status of coronals and Marotta (1995), where such a special condition of coronal segments in coda position of Italian syllabic pattern has been convincingly demonstrated.
12. The detailed presentation of UPSID is contained in Maddieson (1984), in which there is also an analytic index of the segments that make up the sample. The language families considered are the following:

IE	21
Ural-Altaic	22
Niger-Congo	31
Nilo-Saharan	21
Afro-Asiatic	21
Austro-Asiatic	6
Australian	19
Austro-Tai	25
Sino-Tibetan	18
Indo-Pacific	27
Amerindian	89
Others (Drav.,Cauc., Esk. etc.)	18

13. These are the summarised generalisations that can be inferred from Maddieson (1984: 9 ff):
    a. average index of consonants: 22.8 (variation from 6 > 95)
    b. average index of vowels: 8.7 (from 3 to 46)
    c. average proportional value of the ratio between nr. of consonants and nr. of vowels: 0.402 = the number of vowels in the type language is less than half the number of consonants.

    Some possible predictions concerning the likelihood of individual segments being present:
    1. Wider inventories tend to have a greater proportion of consonants.
    2. A limited inventory has a higher probability of including a certain common segment than a wider inventory, and a wider inventory has a higher probability of including an unusual segment than a more limited one.
14. In this way it is possible to predict not only that the upper and lower limits tend to be very flexible, but also that areal/genetic deviations from the central tendency should be expected. Thus the persistence of larger than average inventories in the Caucasus and more limited ones in Polynesia is explained by the consideration that the fundamental contacts of the languages of these areas have been with languages which have the same tendency.
15. For a detailed presentation of the criteria for listening and determining forms with C:, of the doubtful cases (brought together in a class of their own, defined in terms of intermediate consonants and excluded from the quantitative calculation of the long consonants), I refer to Giannini and Costamagna 1998. I will limit myself to recalling that a control sample analysed with a spectro-

graph enabled us to determine an acoustic threshold above which we could assign the segment to the long-consonant category.
16. In Spanish the digraph *rr*, e.g. in *carro*, corresponds in pronunciation to an uvular fricative /R/; Greek has undergone a process of degemination: Ancient Gr. βαλλω ['ballo] > Modern Gr.['valo]. In French geminates can be occasionally employed in morphological oppositions of the verbal system (as *courait* vs. *courrait*, future tense and conditional mood, respectively).
17. The gemination lexicon of the individual learners is significantly marked by the existence of recurrent terms that are concentrated in certain lexical and morphological classes. Some examples (coinciding to a large degree with the data already published for the 3 informants mentioned above, cf. Giannini and Costamagna 1998): modifiers (such as *bello, tutto, quello, spesso*), the present indicative and past participle forms (such as *fanno, hanno, detto, fatto*), and prepositions (such as *della, nella, dalla*). The interlanguage lexicon is also formed predominantly from frequently-used lexical items, and in these one can distinguish the syllabic/prosodic specimen that might have facilitated the correct articulation of the long consonants.
18. Cf. Graur (1929) as the first monograph specifically dedicated to the topic in question, which has been followed by occasional contributions in the philological and linguistic fields.
19. Confirmation of this can also be found in Italian: for both simple and geminated consonants, the unvoiced are longer than the voiced. (cf. Carminati 1984).
20. The hierarchical frequency of the fricatives is /s/ > /ʃ/ > /f/; of the stops, /t/ > /k/ > /p/ (moreover, if a language has 4 points of articulation instead of the usual 3, two are coronal). The ideal inventory of 20 consonants constructed by Maddieson contains 10 coronals (cf. Maddieson 1984, Giannini and Marotta 1989, Marotta 1995).
21. The experimental data: even in the so-called slips of the tongue (for English see Stemberger 1991) the coronals, because they are unmarked and predictable, affect errors only minimally compared with the other points of articulation (dorsal, labial etc.), which are fully specified. Of any two given obstruents which share the same point of articulation, labials and velars are involved in an error (and in perceptive confusion) much more often than dentals, just as appears to happen in processes such as weakening, substitution, assimilation etc. The highest frequency in L1 is of all the segments with alveolar-type articulation, above all at the level of infantile babbling, and in linguistic pathology the coronals are much more affected (insertion, elimination etc.) than the other segments.

References

Barlow, Michael, and Suzanne Kemmer (eds.)
    2000   *Usage-Based Models of Language*. Stanford, CA: CSLI Publications.

Bybee, Joan L.
    2000a   The phonology of the lexicon: Evidence from lexical diffusion. In: Michael Barlow and Suzanne Kemmer (eds.), 65-85.

Bybee, Joan L.
    2000b   Lexicalization of sound change and alternating environments. In: Michael B. Broe and Janet B. Pierrehumbert (eds.), *Acquisition and the Lexicon, Papers in Laboratory Phonology*, 250-278. Cambridge, Cambridge University Press.

Carminati, Maria Nella
    1984   The voicing contrast in Italian medial single and geminate stops. *Cambridge Papers in Phonetics and Experimental Linguistics* 3:1-25.

Chomsky, Noam, and Morris Halle
    1968   *The Sound Pattern of English*. New York: Harper.

Cravens, Thomas D.
    1987   The syllable and phonological strength: Gradient loss of gemination in Corsican. In: Anna Giacalone Ramat, Onofrio Carruba and Giuliano Bernini (eds.), *Papers from the 7th International Conference on Historical Linguistics*, 163-178. Amsterdam: Benjamins.

Comrie, Bernard
    1984   Why linguists need language acquirers. In: William Rutheford (ed.), 14-29.

Cristofaro, Sonia, and Paolo Ramat (eds.)
    1999   *Introduzione alla tipologia linguistica*. Roma, Carocci.

Croft, William
    1990   *Typology and Universals*. Cambridge, Cambrige University Press.

Croft, William, Keith Denning, and Suzanne Kemmer
    1990   *Studies in Typology and Diachrony for Joseph Greenberg*. Amsterdam: Benjamins.

Eckman, Fred R.
    1984   Universals, typology and interlanguage. In William Rutheford (ed.), 79-105.

Ferguson, Charles
    1990   From esses to aitches: Identifying pathways of diachronic change. In: William Croft, Keith Denning and Suzanne Kemmer (eds.), 59-78.

Flege, James
    1997   The role of phonetic category formation in second-language speech learning. *New Sounds 97 – Proceedings of the Third International Symposium on the Acquisition of Second Language Speech*, University of Klagenfurt, 8-11 September 1997: 79-88.

Giacalone Ramat, Anna
    2000   Typological considerations on second language acquisition. *Studia Linguistica* 54: 123-135.

Giannini, Stefania, and Lidia Costamagna
    1998   Acquisizione di categorie fonologiche e diffusione lessicale del mutamento linguistico: affinità strutturali. *Archivio Glottologico Italiano* 83: 150-187.

Giannini, Stefania, and Giovanna Marotta
    1989   *Fra grammatica e pragmatica. La geminazione consonantica in latino*. Pisa: Giardini.

Gierut, Judith A., Michele L. Morrisette, and Annette H. Champion
    1999   Lexical constraints in phonological acquisition. *Journal of Child Language* 26: 261-294.

Gomez, C. Abreu
    1999   Directionality in linguistic change and acquisition. *Language Variation and Change* 11: 213-230.

Graur, Alexandru
    1929   *Les consonnes géminées en latin*. Paris: Champion.

Greenberg, Joseph
    1966   *Language universals, with special reference to feature hierarchies*. (Janua Linguarum, Series Minor, 59.) The Hague: Mouton.

Greenberg, Joseph H.
    1991   Two approaches to language universals. In L. Waugh and S.Rudy (eds.), *New Vistas in Grammar*, 417-435. Amsterdam: Benjamins.

Hajek, John
    1997   *Universals of sound change in nasalization*. Oxford (UK)/Boston (Mass): Publications of the Philological Society.

Hardcastle, William J., and John Lave (eds.)
    1999^2 *The handbook of phonetic sciences*. Oxford: Blackwell.

Jakobson, Roman
    1944   *Kindersprache, Aphasie und Allgemeine Lautgesetze* (in 1971, It. transl. *Il farsi e il disfarsi del linguaggio*, Torino, Einaudi: 9-104).

Jakobson, Roman, and Linda R. Waugh
    1979   *The sound shape of language* (It. transl. *La forma fonica della lingua*, Milano, Il Saggiatore, 1984).

Kay, Jonathan
    1989   *Phonology: A Cognitive View*. Hillsdale (NJ): Erlbaum.

Kiparsky, Paul
1995 The phonological basis of sound change. In: John A. Goldsmith, (ed.), *The Handbook of Phonological Theory*, 640-670. Cambridge (Mass.): Blackwell.

Koster, Cor J.
1987 *Word Recognition in Foreign and Native Language. Effects of Context and Assimilation*. Dordrecht: Foris.

Lass, Roger
1997 *Historical Linguistics and Language Change*. Cambridge: Cambridge University Press.

Maddieson, Jan
1984 *Patterns of Sound*. Cambridge: Cambridge University Press.

Maddieson, Jan
1999 Phonetic universals. In William J. Hardcastle and John Lave (eds.), 619-639.

Marotta, Giovanna
1993 Dental stops in Latin: A special class. *Rivista di Linguistica*, 5: 55-101.

Marotta, Giovanna
1995 Sindrome delle coronali e coda sillabica in italiano. *Quaderni del Dipartimento di Linguistica – Università di Firenze* 6: 15-34.

Mioni, Alberto
1993 Fonetica e fonologia. In: Alberto A. Sobrero (ed.) *Introduzione all'italiano contemporaneo. Le strutture*, 101-139. Bari: Laterza.

Paradis, Carole, and Jean-Francois Prunet
1991 *The Special Status of Coronals: Internal and External Evidence*. New York/London: Academic Press.

Rutheford, William E. (ed.)
1984 *Language Universals and Language Acquisition*. Amsterdam: Benjamins.

Stemberger, J.P.
1991 Radical underspecification in language production. *Phonology* 8: 73-112.

Index of subjects

Accomplishment, 11, 189, 199-200, 267-269, 274-278, 280, 283-284, 286-287
Achievement, 11, 189, 199-200, 267-272, 274-287
action-in-progress, 280-281, 285-286
actionality, 11, 199, 268
Activity, 4, 199, 268, 271-272, 274-278, 280-281, 283-287
adult language acquisition, 223, 225, 293, 359, 398
adverbial, 238, 271, 369-371, 387
    adverbial clauses (*see* adverbial constructions)
    adverbial constructions, 3, 182, 194-195, 201, 211, 214
    adverbial modifier, 186-187, 208-209
    adverbial subordination, 120, 182, 193-194, 208
    proadverbials, 370, 372-373, 396-397
    temporal adverbial, 63, 389
African languages, 334
Aktionsart, 238, 240, 268, 380
Arabic, 257, 333-334, 349, 395, 420
    Algerian Arabic, 368
    Arabic dialects, 334
    Moroccan Arabic, 213, 228-229, 234, 239, 247, 249-250
aspect, 91, 182, 193, 196, 240, 267-283, 366, 395
    acquisition of, 280-283
    aspectual classes, 267
    aspectual constructions, 188

aspectual marker, 242, 269, 282
aspectual system, 13, 390
    grammatical aspect, 268, 281, 368, 380-382
    inherent aspect, 11, 234, 267-269, 272-277, 282-283
    lexical aspect (*see* inherent aspect)
Australian Aboriginal languages, 26

Banda-Linda, 335
basic variety, 4-5, 84-85, 91, 101-102, 116, 118, 150, 196, 226, 228-229, 245, 249, 256, 349
bilingual acquisition, 40-41, 44, 48, 74
bilingual development (*see* bilingual acquisition)

Caddo, 343-345
Cantonese, 7, 39-41, 44-77, 87, 92-94, 118
Celtic languages, 333
centre of attention, 12, 330, 338, 356-357
Chinese, 12, 44-45, 50, 57, 72, 76, 116, 145, 149, 153, 174, 196, 291, 293-294, 297-298, 300, 302-303, 305, 321, 335-337, 341, 344-345, 349
    Chinese dialects/languages, 7, 43, 56, 76, 95, 113
    Mandarin Chinese, 39, 45, 56-57, 93-94, 118, 272, 295-297, 321

442 *Index of subjects*

Wú Chinese, 93, 113, 118, 213
Chinese-style topic, 336, 343
chunks of knowledge, 343
clause combining strategies, 5, 195, 202, 210
cleft structures, 5, 229, 232, 353
cognitive typology, 396
compounds, 128, 135-138, 143-144, 146-147, 157-158, 167, 169-170, 173-174
consonant length, 14, 407-408, 412-413, 418-419, 421-423, 425, 427, 432-433, 435
constituent recognition domain 43
construal of events, 365-399
construction,
   comparative, 113
   converbial, 183, 185-186, 190, 201-202, 209, 212, 214, 312
   correlative, 20
   double object, 45
   double subject, 338
   existential, 94, 134, 160, 222, 229-231, 350, 352, 358, 370-371, 373, 396
   genitive, 157-159, 161, 170, 172-173
   locative-possessive, 139, 161-162, 165, 167, 169
   noun-modifying, 25, 29, 33-34, 69, 72
   partitive, 133, 138, 140-141, 150
   passive, 5, 340-341
   possessive, 9, 125-174
   prepositional, 131, 135, 138-139, 147-148, 161-162, 166-167, 169-171, 174
   presentational, 231, 233, 245, 248-250, 352, 358, 373
contact, 20, 196, 406, 411, 415, 422, 436

creole, 10, 120, 221, 223-225, 233, 240, 255
   English-based Creoles, 225
   French-based Creoles, 10, 221-222, 241
   Haitian Creole, 242, 253-255
   Indian Ocean Creoles, 233, 240, 253, 258
   Lesser Antilles Creole, 243, 258
   Louisiana Creole, 252, 258
   Mauritian Creole, 241-242, 254
   Réunion Creole, 232, 254
   Seychelles Creole, 233
creolisation, 10, 221, 223-225, 257

definiteness, 9, 88, 94, 132-135, 143-145, 151, 153-155, 157-158, 167-169, 174, 373
detachment, 329, 335, 346-347
developmental asynchrony hypothesis, 42, 67-69
deverbal nouns, 131, 141, 164
differential acquisition, 22
direct object, 8, 21-24
dominance, 39, 41-42, 47, 50-51, 67-69, 75, 77
durative situation, 268-269
dynamic situation, 367, 389

egocentric reference, 357
English, 6-7, 9-11. 13-14, 25, 28, 30-32, 34, 39-77, 87, 90, 93-95, 119, 126, 129, 138, 145, 147, 149-150, 166, 168-169, 171-173, 186, 189, 192, 200, 214-215, 267-287, 291, 296-297, 300-307, 310, 314, 321-322, 336, 346, 349, 356, 365, 368-369, 371-372, 374-375, 377-

Index of subjects 443

379, 384, 386-387, 390, 392-393, 395-397, 413
American English, 34
Scottish English, 34
entry into state, 270-271, 279
European languages, 20, 35, 84, 120, 291, 297, 300, 303, 306, 321, 323

false start, 337
finiteness, 4, 10, 182, 196, 208, 221-258
first language acquisition, 13, 23, 120, 225, 359
foreigner talk, 111, 118, 223
French, 12, 221-258, 296-298, 300-306, 314, 316, 318, 321-323, 342, 346, 348-350, 352-353, 358, 360, 365, 368-369, 371, 413, 424-425, 433, 436
   French L2, 221-258, 303, 304, 307, 310, 311, 350
functional equivalent, 27
functional typology, 2, 13, 183

generic noun, 86-87, 94, 103, 116
German, 11-13, 93-94, 107, 138, 149, 166, 172-173, 207, 214, 297-298, 300-305, 311, 314, 316-318, 321-323, 365, 368-370, 372-375, 377-379, 389, 392, 395-397, 413, 433
Germanic languages, 5, 138, 214, 300-301, 332
gerunds, 9-10, 181-215
grammaticalisation, 127-128, 148-149, 169, 171-172, 183, 190, 209, 214, 222-224, 226-228, 233-234, 241-244, 256-257, 329, 337-338, 357, 403

acquisitional, 127, 150
diachronic-typological, 127-128, 171

habitual, 270-271, 284-285
habituality, 238
hanging topic, 330
hierarchy,
   implicational, 2, 4-5, 13-14, 83, 435
   noun phrase accessibility hierarchy, 2, 6-7, 21-24, 40, 59, 61, 305

Iaai, 334
iconicity, 3, 10, 221-258, 406
   diagrammatic, 226-227, 244
   motivational, 221
imperfective, 91, 189, 193, 195, 268, 278, 382, 392
implicational map, 9, 85, 88-90, 94-95, 108-113
implicational universals, 1, 83, 115, 405, 434
indefiniteness, 88, 109, 143, 154
   markers of, 94, 116, 118, 168
indefinites, 90, 94-98, 100-103, 105, 107-113, 116, 119
   free choice indefinites, 94
indirect object, 8, 21-22
Indo-European languages, 331-333
information organisation, 13-14, 214, 365-399
input, 12, 42, 45, 48, 55, 67, 91, 93, 103, 111, 119, 150, 170-172, 212, 223, 244, 256, 292, 301-303, 320, 322-323, 349, 358, 360
interlanguage phonology, 403-436
interpersonal relations, 139, 141
isomorphism, 40, 221, 226, 256

444 *Index of subjects*

Italian, 2, 4-5, 8-11, 14, 35, 83-120, 145-146, 168, 181-215, 283, 348, 353, 356, 365, 368-369, 371, 373, 403-436
Italian L2, 9, 14, 83, 85-87, 91-120, 181-215, 403-436

Japanese, 10-11, 29-33, 71, 267-287, 335-339, 341

Kannada, 342
Korean, 214, 336-337, 341

language types, 83, 85, 93, 335, 347, 360
learner variety, 1-2, 4-5, 10, 14, 83-86, 96, 98, 101, 108, 110, 111, 113-116, 196, 223, 226-229, 231-234, 240, 244, 250, 301-302, 304-305, 310, 314, 318, 321, 323, 354, 365, 368, 372-373, 375, 390, 393-394, 398 (*see also* basic variety, pre-basic varieties, post-basic varieties)
left dislocation, 12, 61, 327-361
leftmost sentence periphery/edge, 329-331, 334, 338, 345
levels of knowledge, 359
lexicalisation patterns, 10, 89-90, 95, 108
locative relations, 130

markedness, 2-4, 9-10, 115, 127, 192-194, 210-211, 404-405, 407-411, 420-421, 423, 425, 430, 434

markedness differential hypothesis, 3
matching, 22-24
Mean Length of Utterance (MLU), 41, 50, 77
Modern Hebrew, 24, 119, 138, 145, 215
monolingual acquisition, 42
motion events, 13, 368, 375-376, 378
moved element, 336
mutual knowledge, 357

natural order principles, 236-237, 240
negation, 4, 10, 86, 100-101, 103, 105, 107, 109, 117-119, 222, 229, 244, 256
    direct, 88, 90, 94, 98, 100, 109-110, 112-114, 118
    holophrastic, 101
    multiple, 109
    scope of, 109-110
non-standard variety, 25, 34-35, 114, 120
null-anaphor language, 30

oblique object, 21-22
ontological categories, 88
Optimality Theory, 24, 190
overexplicitation, 11
overgeneralisation, 9

part-whole relations, 331, 349
Pavia Project, 86, 91, 117
peripheral element, 331
perspective, 279, 312, 321-322, 365-399
    object-based perspective, 371-373
    perspective taking, 279-280, 365-399

protagonist-based perspective, 378, 387, 389-390, 398
spatial perspective, 370, 372, 374
pidgin, 223-225
pidginisation, 223-224
possessee, 125-126, 128-131, 138-147, 162-167, 174
possession, 125-174
    adnominal, 125-174
    body-part relations, 126, 128, 130, 136, 139, 141, 170
    disposal, 130, 136, 138, 141, 143-144
    kinship relations, 126, 128, 136, 140, 170-171
    legal ownership, 126, 128, 130, 136
    possessor-article complementarity, 145
    subset relations, 140, 164
possessor, 21-22, 125-174
post-basic varieties, 85, 91, 101, 109, 228, 234, 247
posture verbs, 271-272, 277, 279, 287
pragmatic inference, 31, 211
pragmatics, 25, 339, 354
pre-basic varieties, 91, 101-102, 108-109, 234, 240, 244-245
premature subjects, 343-344
prenominal modification, 7, 40, 63, 67, 69, 75
preverbal marker, 10, 242
principle of adjacency, 99, 108, 113-114
Principle of the Separation of Role and Reference, 347
processing, 40, 65, 73, 74, 256, 350, 411, 415, 422, 425
progressive, 10-11, 187-190, 193, 195, 199-201, 208, 214, 242-243, 268, 280-283, 384-386, 394
punctual event, 268, 286

quaestio, 358, 367, 370
qualified learner, 150
question words, 94, 116, 118

reanalysis, 209, 222, 224-228, 233, 241-244, 252, 255-256
referential movement, 327, 353, 355
relative clauses, 19-35, 39-77
    adjoined, 6, 25-29
    appositive, 26, 191
    classifier relatives, 44-45, 47, 54, 62
    discontinuous, 28
    embedded, 26, 64, 335
    functions of, 47-50
    head noun, 6, 8, 20-23, 29-31, 39, 43-44, 53-56, 70-75, 77
    in bilingual children, 39-77
    internally headed, 45
    non-reduction type, 20
    postnominal, 7, 39-40, 42-43, 51, 57-58, 60-62, 64-65, 68, 70, 73-74, 76
    prenominal, 4, 7, 39-44, 51-63, 67, 77
    pronoun-retention type, 20, 34-35
    relative-pronoun type, 20, 28
relativization, 19-35, 39-77
    gap strategy, 21, 24, 29, 63
    of direct object, 21-24
    of subject, 7-8, 21-24
    of time circumstantials, 8
resumptive pronoun, 7, 39-40, 51, 56, 58-65, 74-75, 232-233, 335
result-state, 279, 282-283
Romance languages, 5, 7, 35, 182-183, 189, 300, 332, 358, 371, 396, 408, 423, 429-431

scaffolding, 234, 237
scope relations, 84

semi-formal learner, 150
Sinitic languages (see Chinese dialects/languages)
Slavonic languages, 332
sloppy identity co-reference, 331
Spanish, 4, 138, 149, 166, 172-173, 192, 214-215, 349, 365, 368-369, 371-373, 421, 433, 436
spatial expressions, 148, 366, 369
state verbs, 269-272, 274-284
subjacency, 32
subject, 7-8, 21-24, 366, 369-371, 396
Subject-prominent languages, 293, 296-297, 303, 340
subordinate clause, 27-31, 35, 83, 112, 133, 182, 186, 190, 192-195, 201, 205, 211, 238
subordination, 3, 5, 27, 44-45, 91, 113, 120, 181-215, 312
Swedish, 9, 90, 125-174

Tamil, 188
-te i-(ru) [aspectual marker], 269, 278-282
temporality, 222, 234-242
temporal relations, 183-185, 382, 384-383, 389
Tigrinya, 87, 91, 93-95, 113, 196, 213
time,
 reference time, 380-381
 situation time, 380, 384, 389, 392
 topic time, 380-384, 387-392
 utterance time, 380-382
Tok Pisin, 28
topicalisation, 12, 298, 327-361
Topic-prominent languages, 293, 295, 297, 303, 340-344, 350, 358
trace, 140, 164
transfer, 3, 7, 11, 22, 39-42, 44-45, 54-56, 59-60, 66-69, 74-77, 107, 111, 113, 115, 119, 171, 224, 283, 301-302, 305, 349-350, 352-353, 356, 372, 393-394, 398
translation equivalents, 25-27, 276
Turkic languages, 30
Turkish, 5, 30, 215
typological distance, 93, 117

verbal morphology, 91, 226, 234, 239
verb-second constraint, 13, 368-369, 396
verb classes, 199, 278
viewpoint, 268, 381, 386

Warlpiri (Walbiri), 26-28
Welsh, 145, 333

Zarma, 334-335

Index of authors

Abbott B., 373
Agostinos-Tädlā, 118
Ahrenholz B., 291
Alleyne M., 254-255
Alsagoff L., 57
Altman H., 343
Andersen R.W., 4, 155, 169, 171-172, 210, 224, 226, 234, 267-270, 273, 280, 284
Andersson E., 131
Andorno C., 215
Ard J., 40, 60
Arends J., 224-225
Axelsson M., 154, 156

Baissac Ch., 233, 254
Baker P., 224-225, 233, 241-243, 254-255
Bardovi-Harlig K., 234, 267, 280
Battistella E.J., 194
Becker A., 84
Berman R., 119, 192, 214-215, 366, 368, 395
Bernabé J., 258
Bernini G., 111, 117-118, 215
Berretta M., 119
Berruto G., 118, 195, 201, 215
Bertinetto P.M., 189, 200, 214
Bickerton D., 119, 224-225
Bisang W., 188
Börjars K., 129, 132-133, 174
Braidi S., 3, 44, 181, 194
Brinton L.J., 386

Brown P., 28
Bruneau Ch., 243
Brunot F., 243
Bruyn A., 223
Bybee J., 14, 414, 429, 433

Carminati M.N., 437
Carroll M., 84, 294, 322, 367, 371-374, 376, 378-379, 397-398
Caruana S., 196, 201, 214-215
Ceglia L., 183, 185, 188, 215
Chafe W., 328, 336, 343-344, 346-348, 393
Chappell M., 76
Chaudenson R., 224-225, 232-233, 240-241, 253-254, 258
Chini M., 195, 201, 212-213, 215, 291
Chomsky N., 420
Clahsen H., 150
Claudi U., 222, 227
Cloarec-Heiss F., 335
Cole P., 24
Comrie B., 1-8, 19-21, 27, 30, 34, 40, 59, 61, 69, 71-72, 75, 83, 189, 287, 381, 403-404, 434
Cooper R., 174
Corne Ch., 224, 233, 241-242, 254
Costamagna L., 423-424, 434-436
Cravens T.D., 431
Cristofaro S., 5, 8, 85, 111, 114-116, 120, 215, 434
Croft W., 1, 3, 126-127, 175, 192-193, 221-222, 434

Danon-Boileau L., 222
DeGraff M., 222, 224, 233
De Groot C., 214
de Hoop H., 190
De Houwer A., 41
Delsing L.-O., 129, 174
De Mauro T., 187, 191, 194
Dietrich R., 84, 196, 210, 237
Dimroth Ch., 84
Dinale C., 183-184, 186, 214
Dittmar N., 127, 150, 227
Döpke S., 41-42, 50
Dotter F., 120
Dowty D.R., 270, 272-273
Dryer M., 43-44
Duff P., 229-230

Ebert K.H., 214
Eckman F.R., 2-3, 127, 192, 194, 405
Ellis R., 115

Fattier D., 242, 257
Ferguson C.A., 1, 4, 410
Ferraris S., 195, 215
Ferreri S., 186
Fiorentino G., 7, 35
Flege J., 14, 415
Francis W.N., 272
Fraurud K., 130, 174

Gass S., 2, 22, 40, 60
Gawlitzek-Maiwald I., 41
Genesee F., 41-42, 68
Giacalone Ramat A., 2, 4-5, 8, 83, 117-118, 120, 127, 189-190, 195, 199-201, 215, 227, 283, 406, 434
Giannini S., 423-424, 430, 434-437
Gierut J.A., 435

Gilbers D., 190
Giorgi A., 145
Gisborne N., 66
Givón T., 2, 5, 11, 222, 291, 306
Goodman M.F., 241, 252
Gomez C.A., 434
Gorsemann S., 149
Gougenheim G., 241, 243
Graumann C.F., 367
Graur A., 436
Greenberg J., 2, 127, 192, 334-335, 409-410, 421
Gumperz J.J., 366
Gundel J., 293
Gupta A.F., 56-57, 66

Haig J.H., 32
Haiman J., 2-3, 146, 194, 210-211
Hajek J., 411
Hale K., 25-27
Halle M., 420
Halm U., 395
Hammarberg B., 127, 149-150, 172
Haspelmath M., 8-10, 85-90, 94-95, 108-109, 112, 116, 118-119, 126, 131, 145-146, 169, 182, 188, 194, 212, 222, 224, 227
Hawkins J.A., 2, 39-40, 43, 61, 64, 75-76, 83, 130-131
Hazaël-Massieux G., 223, 240-243, 253-255, 258
Heine B., 126, 148, 190, 222, 227
Hellberg S., 131
Hendriks H., 192, 296, 299-300, 303, 305-306, 347, 349, 351-352, 354, 356, 358
Hickmann M., 291, 296, 299-300, 303, 305-306, 320
Hinds J., 336
Hirschbühler P., 343
Ho C.L., 57

Hoiting N., 368
Holmberg A., 174
Hopper P., 2, 227
Huang J., 77
Huang P.Y., 297-298
Hulk A., 41
Hünnemeyer F., 222, 227
Hyltenstam K., 6, 40, 60, 127

Ingham B., 333-334

Jaeggli O., 297
Jakobson R., 412, 435
Jennings W., 224, 240
Jin H.G., 293
Johnson M., 148
Jordens P., 222

Kageyama T., 269, 274, 279-280
Kahrel P., 119
Kauffman T., 224
Kay J., 419, 421
Keenan E.L., 2-3, 21, 27, 40, 45, 59, 61
Kellerman E., 398
Kempe V., 317-318
Kiparsky P., 413-414
Kleiber G., 222
Klein W., 2-5, 84, 116, 127, 150, 182, 196, 210, 222-223, 226, 228-229, 237, 244, 293-294, 350, 354, 359, 367, 370, 380-381
Kogan L.E., 118
König E., 10, 182-183, 202-204, 212
Koptjevskaja-Tamm M., 125-126, 145, 148, 182
Kortmann B., 120, 183, 185-186, 192, 214
Koster C.J., 415-418, 435
Koyama S., 280

Kucera H., 272
Kuno S., 269, 274
Kurono A., 280

Lado R., 1
Lakoff G., 148
Lambert M., 388, 397
Lambrecht K., 291, 303, 328, 346-348, 360
Langacker R., 130, 174
Lass R., 412
Lehmann Ch., 26-28, 127, 227
Levelt W.J.M., 365
Levinson S.C., 366, 368
Li C.N., 297, 329, 335-336, 340-341, 343-344, 378
Li P., 272, 280
Longobardi G., 145
Lonzi L., 183-185, 214
Lucy J.A., 368
Lyons Ch., 145

MacWhinney B., 317-318
Maddieson J., 410, 421, 435, 437
Marotta G., 430, 432, 435, 437
Matsumoto Y., 29-30, 34, 287
Matthews S., 44-45, 50-51, 59, 66-67, 118
Mayer M., 375
McDaniel D., 65
Mckee C., 65, 77
Meillet A., 226
Meisel J.M., 41, 150, 222, 226, 350
Milano E., 351
Miller J., 34, 333, 356
Mioni A., 423
Moignet G., 243
Moravcsik E., 192
Moretti B., 215
Mufwene S., 224-225

Index of authors

Mühlhäusler P., 224
Müller N., 41
Muñoz C., 291
Myhill J., 366

Naigles L.R., 368
Nedjalkov V., 183
Nespor M., 183
Neumann-Holzschuh I., 258
Newbrook M., 66
Newmeyer F.J., 221
Nicoladis E., 41
Nishi Y., 274, 287
Norde M., 129, 148
Noyau C., 196, 210, 237
Nuese R., 367

Ozanne Rivierre F., 334

Paradis C., 420, 435
Paradis J., 41-42, 68, 76
Parkvall M., 224
Pavesi M., 6
Pederson E., 368
Perdue C., 3-5, 84, 115-116, 127, 150, 196, 223, 226, 228-229, 244, 293-294, 349-351, 354, 358-359
Pérez-Leroux A., 40, 61
Perridon H.C.B., 174
Pfaff C.W., 127, 226-227, 234
Pienemann M., 150
Pitkänen A., 148, 174
Plank F., 126
Policarpi G., 186
Posner R., 225
Prudent L.-F., 251-252, 258
Prunet J.-F., 420, 435
Pusch L.F., 183, 191, 202

Pustejovsky J., 174

Radford A., 221
Ramat P., 85, 111, 114-116, 120, 434
Ramsey S.R., 118
Renzi L., 214
Roberts S.J., 225
Rohlfs G., 119, 186
Roland F., 303
Rombi M., 186
Ross J., 336
Roßdeutscher A., 380

Safir K., 297
Salvi G., 214
Sankoff G., 28, 223
Saunders G., 41
Schmid S., 215
Seiler H.-J., 126-127
Serianni L., 184-186
Serzisko F., 127
Sharwood Smith M., 398
Sheldon A., 23
Sheu S., 280
Shibata M., 280
Shirai Y., 267-270, 272-274, 280, 284-285, 287
Skiba R., 127
Slobin D.I., 226, 366, 368, 395
Smith C.S., 267-269, 277
Smoczyńska M., 119
Snedeker J., 65
Sohn H., 337-338
Solarino R., 183-186
Solnit D., 76
Sorace A., 191
Sornicola R., 329, 331, 349, 351, 354, 356-357
Speedy K., 252, 258
Sridhar S.N., 342

Starren M., 238
Stemberger J.P., 437
Stolz Th., 149
Syea A., 254

Tager-Flusberg H., 70
Talmy L., 277-279, 287, 395
Tarone E., 293
Tavakolian S., 74
Taylor J.R., 130, 144, 174
Teleman U., 131
Tenny C.L., 267
Tersis N., 335
Thomason S.J., 224
Thompson S., 297, 328, 335-336, 340-341, 343-344
Tracy R., 41
Traugott E.C., 227
Trévise A., 349-356, 358, 360-361

Ultan R., 126

Valdman A., 233, 241, 252, 258
Valli A., 226
van der Linden E., 41

Van Hout R., 238
Vendler Z., 11, 189, 267-268, 270, 272-273, 278, 283
Véronique D., 229, 232, 240, 244, 256, 294, 322
Viberg Å., 127
Villarini A., 214
von Stutterheim Ch., 294, 322, 367, 370, 388

Watkins T.A., 333
Weinert R., 333, 356
White L., 194, 293
Wierzbicka A., 395
Wijk-Andersson E., 156
Williams J., 294
Winford D., 225
Wirth J.R., 192

Yeung L., 44
Yip V., 44-45, 50-51, 59, 66-67, 118
Yuan B., 298

Zemskaja E.A., 332

List of contributors

Giuliano Bernini
Dip. di Linguistica e Letterature Comparate
Università di Bergamo
Piazza Vecchia, 8
I-24129, Bergamo, Italy
gbernini@unibg.it

Mary Carroll
Institut für Deutsch als Fremdsprachenphilologie
Plöck 55
D-69117, Heidelberg, Germany
carroll@mail.idf.uni-heidelberg.de

Bernard Comrie
Max Planck Institute for Evolutionary Anthropology
Inselstrasse 22
D-04103, Leipzig, Germany
comrie@eva.mpg.de

Anna Giacalone Ramat
Dip. di Linguistica
Università di Pavia
Strada Nuova 65
I-27100, Pavia, Italy
annaram@unipv.it

Stefania Giannini
Dip. di Scienze del Linguaggio
Università per Stranieri di Perugia
Piazza Fortebraccio, 4
I-06122, Perugia, Italy
giannini@unistrapg.it

Bjorn Hammarberg
Dept. of Linguistics
Stockholm University
SE-10691, Stockholm, Sweden
ham@ling.su.se

Henriëtte Hendriks
RCEAL
University of Cambridge
Keynes House
Trumpington Street
Cambridge, CB2 1QA
United Kingdom
hpjmh2@cam.ac.uk

Maria Koptjevskaja-Tamm
Dept. of Linguistics
Stockholm University
SE-10691, Stockholm, Sweden
tamm@ling.su.se

List of contributors

Stephen Matthews
Dept. of Linguistics
RM 125, Main Building
The University of Hong Kong
Pokfulam Road, Hong Kong
matthews@hkucc.hku.hk

Yumiko Nishi
Dept. of Linguistics
203 Morrill Hall
Cornell University
Ithaca, NY 14853-4701
yn25@cornell.edu

Yasuhiro Shirai
Department of Asian Studies
Cornell University
351 Rockefeller Hall
Ithaca, NY 14853
ys54@cornell.edu

Rosanna Sornicola
Dip. di Filologia Moderna
Università di Napoli (Federico II)
Via Porta di Massa 1
I-80133, Napoli, Italy
sornicol@unina.it

Daniel Véronique
UFR Didactique du français langue étrangère
Université Sorbonne Nouvelle
(Paris III)
46 rue Saint Jacques,
15230 Paris Cedex 05
daniel.veronique@paris3.sorbonne.fr

Christiane von Stutterheim
Institut für Deutsch als Fremdsprachenphilologie
Plöck 55
D-69117 Heidelberg, Germany
stutterheim@mail.idf.uni-heidelberg.de

Virginia Yip
Dept. of Modern Languages and Intercultural Studies
3/F., Fung King Hey Building
Main Campus
The Chinese University of Hong Kong,
Shatin, N. T., Hong Kong
vyip@humanum.arts.cuhk.edu.hk